BEHAVIOR
PRINCIPLES
IN
EVERYDAY
LIFE

Second Edition

BEHAVIOR PRINCIPLES IN EVERYDAY LIFE

John D. Baldwin

Janice I. Baldwin

University of California
Santa Barbara

Prentice-Hall   Englewood Cliffs, N.J. 07632

Library of Congress Cataloging in Publication Data

BALDWIN, JOHN D. (date)
    Behavior principles in everyday life.

    Bibliography: p.
    Includes indexes.
    1. Behaviorism (Psychology)   2. Psychology, Applied.
I. Baldwin, Janice I.   II. Title.
BF199.B28 1986   150.19′43   85-9534
ISBN 0-13-074238-4

Editorial/production supervision
    and interior design by Eva Jaunzems
Cover design by Ben Santora
Manufacturing buyer: Barbara Kelly Kittle

Printed in the United States of America

10 9 8 7 6 5 4 3 2 1

ISBN   0-13-074238-4   01

Prentice-Hall International (UK) Limited, *London*
Prentice-Hall of Australia Pty. Limited, *Sydney*
Prentice-Hall Canada Inc., *Toronto*
Prentice-Hall Hispanoamericana, S.A., *Mexico*
Prentice-Hall of India Private Limited, *New Delhi*
Prentice-Hall of Japan, Inc., *Tokyo*
Prentice-Hall of Southeast Asia Pte., Ltd., *Singapore*
Editora Prentice-Hall do Brasil, Ltda., *Rio de Janeiro*
Whitehall Books Limited, *Wellington, New Zealand*

*This book is dedicated to B. F. Skinner,
George Homans, Albert Bandura, J. F. Scott,
and the many others who have pioneered in
applying behavior principles to everyday life.*

Brief Contents

Detailed Contents

Preface

The first edition of *Behavior Principles in Everyday Life* was a preliminary attempt to present the basic principles of operant and Pavlovian conditioning, along with social learning theory and cognitive behaviorism, as they apply to everyday life. Four years later, we are fortunate to be given the opportunity to extend and refine the type of behavior analyses begun in the first edition. The new edition contains a larger number of behavior principles than the first edition, and it develops them more clearly and in more subtle detail. There is significantly increased attention to such important topics as the interaction of operant and Pavlovian conditioning, antecedents as predictive stimuli, compound schedules, behavioral contrast, concurrent schedules and choice, reasoning, emotions, intermittent reinforcement, cumulative records, the law of effect, behavior modification, self-control, habituation, recovery effects, vicarious emotions and vicarious conditioning, rehearsal and covert conditioning, internal motivation, learned helplessness, and many other topics. *All the principles are presented in italics to aid the reader in identifying the key material.*

In addition, we have shifted the style of the examples in order to deal with a broader range of everyday life events. The second edition contains a much larger number of short and succinct examples that illustrate the behavior principles quickly and lucidly. We have reduced the number of long examples, especially when their length may have obscured the main points. The shift to shorter examples has allowed us to cover a larger range of topics, which helps students learn more of the behavior principles and apply them to a greater variety of interesting events.

*   *   *   *

The extension of behavior science to everyday life has the potential to advance behavior science in the areas of training, research, therapy, and theory. *First, studying behavior principles in natural settings helps students learn how to apply the principles of behavior to a broad range of different behaviors and different contexts.* When students study behavior principles with examples from laboratory or clinical research, they sometimes fail to learn how the principles apply to all behavior. Although they have acquired a verbal repertoire for describing and analyzing laboratory or clinical examples, their skills may not be applicable to behavior outside the laboratory or clinical setting, and they may fail to understand the applicability of behavior science to all forms of behavior. Studying behavior principles in everyday life facilitates the generalization of analytic skills to a large number of different behaviors and different settings. It also helps students better understand the principles and appreciate their power, utility, and relevance.

Second, both laboratory and clinical research can be broadened and enriched by focusing increased attention on the complex behaviors and controlling variables seen in natural environments. Studying the behavior patterns seen in everyday life raises countless questions about behavior and its multiple controlling variables, which often suggest research topics that are valuable in laboratory and clinical studies. Once students of behavior learn to apply behavior principles to both natural environments and research environments, observations in each type of setting can expand their understanding of behavior in the other environment and stimulate more questions, more hypotheses, and more theories about behavior in general.

Third, the study of behavior principles in everyday life can increase the effectiveness of behavior therapy. A primary goal of therapy is to produce behavioral gains that persist in the client's natural environment. However, generalization is often inadequate—especially when therapists focus primarily on behavior change in the therapeutic setting and neglect differences between that setting and the client's natural environment. The generalization and maintenance of behavior change must be programmed—not left to chance.[1] In order to increase generalization, behavior therapists must be knowledgeable about behavioral variables in natural environments and design programs that bridge the gap between therapeutic and natural settings. For example, treatment gains that are produced with artificial reinforcement, contrived models, or unnatural rules are not likely to generalize to natural environments unless behavior is gradually shifted to more natural forms of reinforcement, models, and rules. This book will make it easier for counselors and therapists to identify behavior variables in natural contexts and design the steps needed to ensure generalization.

Fourth, continued efforts at making careful, objective, scientific observations of everyday behavior will provide naturalistic data that can expand both the theoretical and applied branches of behavior science. Data on the complicated events seen in the natural environment are valuable in understanding complex behavior patterns and solving the types of problems found outside the laboratory and clinic—for example, in family relations, education, business, industry, complex organizations, community and local government, politics, social welfare, juvenile delinquency, crime, and so forth. By expanding

---

[1]Birnbaum (1976); Goldstein and Kanfer (1979); Goetz et al. (1979, 1981); Costello (1983).

behavior science to deal with the complexities of natural environments, it should be possible to develop increasingly effective means of applying behavior principles to important problems at the individual and societal levels.[2]

Fifth, the careful extension of behavior principles to the natural environment can benefit all the academic disciplines that study human behavior—psychology, sociology, anthropology, political science, business, education, history, etc. For people in disciplines that deal with naturally occurring behavior, behavior science is more relevant, more easily learned, and more readily applied when presented with examples from everyday life than with examples from laboratory and clinical research.[3] In addition, the type of analysis presented in this book may help in developing an empirically grounded theory that can unify the work done in the different academic disciplines that deal with human behavior in natural environments. Each discipline has developed specialized theories for dealing with its own core subject matter; but few have produced theories with as much potential for unifying all the disciplines as has behavior science. The behavioral analysis of everyday life can facilitate the broader use of behavior science because it fuses experimental research and observations in natural environments. It deals equally well with both individual behavior and social behavior. It includes both overt actions and private events—thoughts, feelings, emotions. And it is well suited to explaining the interaction of behavior and societal-ecological factors, tracing changes in both behavior and environments as each component of the interactive system evolves and changes over time.[4]

*   *   *   *

Much of the inspiration for writing and improving the book has come from teaching bright and inquisitive students whose intellectual curiosity has stimulated our own thought and study. We thank all those students for their questions, suggestions, and enthusiasm. We also thank Professor Jay Alperson of Palomar College, Professor Thomas E. Billimek of San Antonio College, Professor David C. Meissner of Alfred University, and Professor Kenneth N. Wildman of Ohio Northern University for their careful reading of this text in manuscript and for their helpful comments and criticism. Finally, we would like to express our gratitude to Ed Stanford and John Isley for their willingness to publish a book that attempts to advance behavior science in a new direction.

J. D. B.
J. I. B.

[2]Mead (1934), Skinner (1953), Staats (1975) and other behaviorists have shown considerable interest in applying behavior science to both individual and societal problems.

[3]Psychodynamic theory has been applied to several fields, in part because it deals with human behavior and has been easily accessible to students and scholars in many disciplines.

[4]Staats (1975); Baldwin (in press).

1

Science and Human Behavior

● *In this chapter you will learn about behavior science: its main goals, its origins in laboratory research, and the benefits of extending behavior science to deal with everyday life.*

People have always been curious about their own behavior, their relationships with others, and the countless intricacies of everyday life. Given the enormous complexity of human behavior and social interactions, it can be very difficult to identify the basic principles that explain everyday behavior if one works only from the data of daily experience. The main premise of this book is that the basic behavior principles developed through the experimental analysis of behavior can be of great assistance in understanding and explaining human behavior in natural settings. Our goal here is to explain these principles in a way that is easy to grasp and useful in understanding much of everyday life.

The two main reasons for applying behavior principles to everyday life are increased understanding and practical benefits. First, the inquisitive individual finds life full of intriguing questions. "Why do I feel happy one day and sad the next?" "Why are some people creative or cheerful, whereas others are not?" "Why do some parents do so much better than others in raising their children?" There are countless other important issues that come up every day throughout life. Questions about human behavior have probably occupied people's attention more than questions about the sun, stars, weather, plants, or animals; but the answers have been slower in coming. Because the sciences of physics, chemistry, and biology developed before the behavior sciences, most people know more scientific information about the physical and biological world than they do about behavior. The behavior sciences have only begun to blossom in the present century, and most people still do not know the basic behavior principles that have been well documented in the past several decades. However, in recent years, things have been changing. Now that the behavior sciences have developed a body of well-established principles, they too are beginning to have an influence beyond the laboratory. Behavior principles are being used increasingly in therapy, education, child rearing, marital counseling, self-control, business, and government. Behavior science is coming of age. This book extends the range of behavioral applications to include everyday life. It will allow the inquisitive individual to use scientific guidelines to help answer the questions that have always been the most interesting: ''Why do we behave the way we do?''

Second, there are practical benefits for applying behavior principles to everyday life. As people gain information about their own behavior, they are in a better position to direct their own lives, change things they do not like, and accomplish things that otherwise might have been beyond their reach. In addition, an increased knowledge of behavior principles as they operate in social interactions can allow people to develop greater sensitivity to others, learn to improve the quality of their behavior in interactions, and create more rewarding relationships. The behavior principles discussed in this book can also help people become more playful and creative, convert aversive social interactions into positive ones, gain greater control over their own thoughts and actions, and much more. Behavior science is pushing back the shroud of mystery that has long surrounded much of human behavior, enabling ever more people to benefit from improving the quality of their own behavior and their social relations.

Human behavior is, for the most part, learned behavior. Most people learn only a small portion of the skills, talents, and sensitivities that they could learn. They develop only a fraction of their human potential. If they knew more about the basic principles of learning, they could develop considerably more of their capacities. The principles presented in this book explain how behavior is learned and modified. Knowledge about the behavior principles can help people learn new behavior faster, more easily, and in a more rewarding manner than is otherwise possible. For this reason alone, behavioral science is one of the most important of the sciences: It gives people the intellectual tools they need to make learning and developing their human potential a rewarding and fulfilling experience.

A GROWING SCIENCE

Behavior science is concerned with all of human behavior: talking, making love, eating submarine sandwiches on summer picnics, painting canvases, selling real estate, learning new things, forgetting old things. Everything that we do—even thinking and fantasizing—is behavior,[1] and behavior science provides powerful tools for explaining why we behave as we do.

---

[1]Mead (1934), Skinner (1969; 1974), Mahoney (1974), Meichenbaum (1977), and many other behaviorists include thinking as a behavior that must be analyzed in any comprehensive theory of human behavior. ''An adequate science of behavior must consider events taking place within the skin of the organism, not as physiological mediators of behavior, but as part of behavior itself'' (Skinner, 1969:228).

We are surrounded by and involved with behavior all the time; yet few people attain a good grasp of the fundamental principles that explain behavior. We are so close to behavior at all times that we often cannot see the forest for the trees. We know individuals and their idiosyncrasies so well that we often fail to see the broad patterns that underlie all behavior. To understand the universal principles of human behavior, it has been useful to draw upon laboratory research based on the experimental analysis of behavior.

Behavioral science emerged in the early 1900s as a reaction to the unscientific, introspective psychological theories of the times. *From the beginning, the main goal of behavior science has been to develop an empirical study of behavior based on objective observations of both behavior and its controlling variables.* Much of the early behavioral work was conducted in the laboratory where accurate, reliable experimental research could be done under controlled conditions. In order to locate the basic principles, simple behavior patterns were selected and studied under simplified environmental conditions. Over the decades, increasingly more complex laboratory experiments became possible and the original behavior principles were elaborated and extended to cover increasingly complex behavior patterns. As the behavior principles became better understood, it was possible to extend learning theory beyond the laboratory to clinical applications and to the natural environment. The *Journal of Applied Behavior Analysis* was established in 1968 to publish the results of applied research in natural settings, and its success is evidence of the utility of extending behavior analysis to everyday life. Ethology—the European school of animal behavior research—has also stimulated much interest in the study of behavior in natural contexts.

These multiple influences have expanded modern behavioral science beyond its original emphasis on laboratory research. The study of everyday life is one of the newer branches of the discipline. All behavior scientists share a deep commitment to conducting accurate, objective analyses of behavior. The major change resulting from the new emphasis on observing behavior in natural settings has been an increased attention to complex behavior patterns along with the process of behavioral development and socialization through which these patterns are learned.

The natural environment is considerably more complex than laboratory environments.[2] Multiple factors operate simultaneously and produce numerous interaction effects that are usually not created or studied in the laboratory. It is true that studying behavior in natural contexts forces the observer to relinquish the experimental control and simplified conditions that make laboratory studies so powerful. *However, the extension of behavioral science to the natural environment is essential for understanding how the behavior principles apply to everyday events and how they can be used most effectively to solve problems at both the individual and societal levels.* Skinner, Homans, Bandura, Scott, Wolf, Burgess, Kunkle, Baer, Mahoney, Meichenbaum, Akers, and many others provide models for extending behavior analyses to real world problems in government, education, therapy, aggression, crime, self-control, moral behavior, and so forth. If there is a loss of laboratory control, there is a compensating gain in relevance.

In one sense, the behavioral analysis of everyday life parallels astronomy, while

[2]To some, the problems of studying behavior in the natural environment appear so formidable that they would not attempt it themselves. However, both laboratory and field studies have their strong points, and each can complement the other nicely to provide a better overall understanding of behavior (Bandura and Walters, 1963:39f; Mason, 1968).

laboratory forms of behavioral science parallel laboratory physics.[3] Both astronomy and laboratory physics study the physical world and their theories dovetail nicely. But astronomy relies on careful observation of the remote skies and natural experiments rather than on experimental manipulation of carefully controlled variables in the laboratory. In spite of the absence of laboratory control, astronomy has flourished. It was the first of the modern sciences to blossom during the Renaissance, and careful observations of the stars continue to yield data that shape the development of theory in contemporary physics. The behavioral study of everyday life—based on careful observation and natural experiments—has the potential to yield valuable information on complex natural behavior patterns and to hasten the development of the behavioral sciences.

Louis Pasteur—the French scientist who applied his knowledge of chemistry and biology to many everyday problems—said, "In the fields of observation, chance favors only the mind that is prepared." The world around us provides a constant source of interesting examples of natural behavior. Yet most people are not prepared to "see" the intriguing principles that are operating constantly, right before their eyes. The behavior principles derived from laboratory research prepare us for making sensitive observations of everyday life.

This book is designed to make the basic principles of behavior science easy to understand and easy to apply to all types of daily events. Hundreds of examples have been selected from everyday life to illustrate the various principles. The book builds from the most basic of the behavior principles in early chapters to encompass ever more subtle considerations. Because the basic principles in the first several chapters provide the foundations on which all later principles are constructed, the reader will immediately see in the early chapters some of the most powerful of generalizations about behavior along with their applications to meaningful daily events. The later chapters develop the additional empirical generalizations needed to understand the full range of human experience. The final chapters provide information of special importance in making life more positive and giving people better control over their own thoughts and actions. To help the reader identify and master the key ideas, all the important principles are accentuated by the use of bold or italic print. We have attempted to make the book both sensitive and scientific, based on the belief that science can be one of the most useful and humanistic ways of understanding and dealing with the complexities of the world in which we live.[4]

[3]Comparing the behavioral study of everyday life with astronomy (because neither has access to laboratory controls) is not an excuse for not making careful, scientific observations. Astronomy has flourished *because of* its detailed observations, precision, and willingness to interface with laboratory data in multiple areas. When controls and natural experiments are available, astronomers are eager to use them; however, astronomers do not give up their work merely because they cannot obtain the control possible in the laboratory. The special data and insights available from the natural environment are worth the extra effort needed to make naturalistic observations, even when the controls of laboratory experiments are not possible.

[4]Bronowski (1965; 1977).

CONCLUSION

The purpose of this book is to present the principles of behavior in a manner that will facilitate their application to everyday life. Knowledge of the behavior principles as they operate in everyday life can help people understand more of their own lives and help them improve the quality of their behavior and social relationships. The behavioral analysis of everyday life is a natural outgrowth of a science that began with laboratory research, then was extended to clinical applications, and more recently has been expanded to applied behavioral research in natural settings. Continuing this line of development to include the behavioral analysis of everyday life can potentially advance behavior science and other academic disciplines dealing with human behavior.

2

Operant
Conditioning

● *In this chapter you will discover how voluntary behavior is learned and altered over time, depending on the types of effects it produces and the types of cues that precede it.*

Operant conditioning is one of the most basic forms of learning affecting virtually all forms of human behavior. Thorndike and Skinner were among the early leaders in developing the principles of operant conditioning. This chapter explains the basic features of operant conditioning—how behavior is modified by its consequences. Additional aspects of operant conditioning are discussed throughout the book.[1]

The earliest formulation of operant principles is known as the *law of effect*. This law is based on the observation that voluntary behavior is influenced by its effects. If an artist is experimenting with the use of pastels and creates some nice effects, the good effects increase the chances that the artist will use pastels more in the future. If the explorative use of pastels had led to bad effects on several consecutive canvases, the artist would be less likely to continue using them. *According to the law of effect, behavior that produces good effects tends to become more frequent; whereas behavior that produces bad effects tends to become less frequent.*

More recent formulations of operant principles have expanded on the law of effect. *Behavior is influenced not only by the effects that follow it, but also by the*

---

[1]For greater detail on operant conditioning see Nevin and Reynolds (1971), Honig and Staddon (1977), Favel (1977), Zeiler and Harzem (1979), Kalish (1981), the *Journal of the Experimental Analysis of Behavior*, and the *Journal of Applied Behavioral Analysis*. In several examples in this chapter many factors besides simple reinforcement or punishment are in operation (namely models, rules, prompts, or schedules). We are neglecting these factors in this chapter for the sake of simplicity. These additional factors are discussed in subsequent chapters.

situational cues that precede it. A behavior may have good effects in one situation but bad effects in another situation. Stepping on the accelerator has good effects when the traffic light is green and bad effects when it is red. As a result, people become sensitive to situational cues—to *antecedent* cues—that precede their behavior and help them discriminate whether a behavior is likely to produce good effects or bad effects in a certain situation. The green and red lights of a traffic signal help people discriminate whether stepping on the gas will produce good or bad effects.

Thus, behavior is influenced by both the *antecedent cues* that precede it and the effects—or *consequences*—that follow it. The principles of operant conditioning can be expressed in a simple A–B–C formulation, where A, B, and C stand for *antecedent cues, behavior, and consequences.* The relationship between these three elements is symbolized as follows:

$$\text{A: B} \rightarrow \text{C}$$

Antecedent cues come before behavior; the consequences of behavior occur after the behavior. The arrow between B and C indicates that the behavior *causes* the consequences. Skillful use of pastels produces pleasing consequences. Stepping on the gas at a red light causes accidents—and traffic tickets. The colon between A and B in the equation indicates that antecedent cues do not cause behavior; they merely *set the occasion* for behavior. Having a canvas on an easel does not cause an artist to create a picture; it merely sets the occasion for the artist to do any of a variety of things—sit and think, make a charcoal sketch in a note book, mix any of several colors on the pallet. Antecedent stimuli do not automatically elicit a response; they merely set the occasion for behavior. Operant behavior is usually produced through the voluntary nervous and muscular systems, and antecedent stimuli cue the appropriateness of possible voluntary behaviors (rather than triggering responses as in a stimulus-response reflex).

A basic feature of operant conditioning is that *the consequences of a behavior influence (1) the future frequencies of the behavior and (2) the ability of antecedent cues to occasion the behavior in the future.* This means that the third element in the A: B→C equation influences the future status of both of the preceding elements. Therefore, the starting point for analyzing the A: B→C relationship is with the consequences. The consequences (C) are the *prime movers* of operant conditioning: They cause the behavior (B) to become more or less frequent, and they cause the antecedent stimuli (A) relevant to each behavior to become cues which set the occasion for repeating or not repeating the behavior in the future. The future likelihood of any given operant behavior is increased or decreased by the type of consequences that follow the behavior. *Consequences that cause a behavior to become more frequent are called reinforcers. Consequences that cause a behavior to become less frequent are called punishers.* Stated in terms of the law of effect, reinforcers are *good effects* that increase the probability of a behavior, and punishers are *bad effects* that decrease the probability of behavior. When a coach tries several different strategies for improving team performance, those strategies that produce good effects—reinforcers—are likely to be retained and developed further; and those strategies that produce bad effects—punishers—are likely to be abandoned.

The antecedent stimuli that set the occasion for operant behavior can come from inside or outside the body—from our own thoughts, emotions, or body movements; from other people's words or actions; from any object or living thing. Feeling happy may set the occasion for phoning a friend or writing a poem. A sudden breeze may set the occasion for closing the window or putting on a sweater.

The consequences that reinforce or punish behavior are also *stimuli,* and they too can come from inside or outside the body. Thoughts, emotions, other people's behavior, objects, and living things can all function as reinforcers and punishers. Athletes often push their bodies to the limits because daily improvement is rewarded by thoughts that they might break a record or qualify for Olympic or professional competition. Whereas reinforc*ers* and punish*ers* are *stimuli,* the *process* by which these stimuli affect behavior is called reinforce*ment* and punish*ment*. Reinforc*ers* such as food provide reinforce*ment* for eating. Punish*ers* such as cuts provide punish*ment* for mishandling sharp knives.

This chapter describes the basic interrelationships among the three parts of the A: B→C equation. It shows how reinforcement and punishment affect both antecedent cues and behavior. Antecedent cues associated with behavior that is reinforced or punished become predictors of *when* and *where* the behavior may be reinforced or punished in the future. Chapter 5 presents additional information about the antecedent stimuli that precede operant behavior. The consequences that follow operant behavior are not unchangeable, and some consequences may serve as reinforcers at one time and as punishers at another. The factors that determine whether a consequence is a reinforcer or punisher (or neither) are discussed in Chapters 6 and 7.

THE OPERANT: INSTRUMENTAL BEHAVIOR

One way to understand operant behavior is to appreciate that it *operates* on the environment in ways that produce consequences. If a person is playing the piano, the person is operating on the environment—operating the keys on the keyboard—in such a way as to produce music. The quality of the music and comments from listeners are the consequences that condition the person's operant performance at the piano. Coordinated and sensitive playing produces good music and social approval that reinforce the skills needed for playing well. Poor playing sounds bad, is likely to be criticized, and hence is punished.

Operant conditioning is sometimes called instrumental conditioning because it is *instrumental* in changing the environment and producing consequences. Working late at the law firm may be instrumental in winning a complex case in court (a reinforcer). When you see a police car, slowing down to the speed limit is instrumental in avoiding a traffic ticket (a punisher).

An operant is usually defined by its ability to produce certain consequences (rather than by the physical appearance of the responses involved). For example, ''a successful forward pass'' is an operant. There are many possible behavior patterns that could result in a successful forward pass. No two quarterbacks pass quite the same, and there is even variation in the passes of any single quarterback. However, any one of these variations that results in the consequence of a completed forward pass belongs to the same category of behavior. Thus, an operant is a *response class* (see shaded area in Figure 2–1) that can

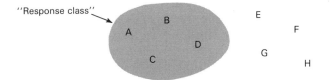

FIGURE 2–1   A response class consisting of four behavior patterns (A, B, C, and D).

contain many varied performances (A, B, C, D), though not all performances (E, F, G, H) are included. A few examples of operant response classes are: a funny joke, a friendly smile, a critical comment, a backward glance, singing beautifully, thinking logically. If a singer comes on stage and sings off key, the poor performance is likely to result in complaints, criticism, and declining attendance at future performances. There are millions of ways to sing poorly, and any of them will bring on punishing consequences. There are also many ways to sing beautifully, and these result in reinforcing consequences. *Any behavior patterns that produce the same consequences belong to the same response class.*

   Since reinforcers and punishers are the prime movers of operant conditioning, the remainder of the chapter is organized around the four fundamental ways in which consequences affect behavior: (1) reinforcement, (2) extinction (i.e., the discontinuation of reinforcement), (3) punishment, and (4) discontinuation of punishment.

REINFORCEMENT

Reinforcers that follow an operant increase the likelihood that the operant will occur in the future. A reinforcer is also called a reinforcing stimulus (S^R). The process by which the frequency of behavior is increased is called reinforcement.[2]

   The speed with which a person learns an operant behavior depends on the complexity of the behavior, the person's present level of skills, the reinforcers involved, and numerous other variables. The activities of a freshman during the first weeks on campus illustrate some of the effects of reinforcement on behavior. The freshman plans to major in journalism or communication studies and is hoping to get a position on the campus newspaper. Thus, many facets of the campus newspaper will function as reinforcers for the student. Let us consider how two behaviors—one easy and one more difficult—are learned due to the reinforcers associated with journalism and newspapers.

   The easy behavior is that of picking up and reading the campus newspaper. The first day on campus, the freshman notices that the paper is distributed free at the dorms, takes one, and reads it. These operants are rewarded by seeing the latest news, pictures, and cartoons. The instant reinforcement increases the chances that the student will pick up and read the paper in the future.

   Figure 2–2 presents a *cumulative record* of the student's responses over the first 42 days (6 weeks) at school. Cumulative records provide a convenient way of visualizing

---

[2]This is basically a descriptive statement and hence does not involve circular logic. See note 1 in Chapter 6.

patterns of behavior by showing the *total* number of responses that a person has made over a period of time. The lines in the cumulative record take one step upward each time a behavior is performed; they remain horizontal as long as the person does not do the behavior. The total number of responses performed is shown at the left of the cumulative record. The light line in Figure 2–2 shows the freshman's cumulative record for picking up the daily newspaper. On the first day on campus, the student picked up the paper and was rewarded by seeing the news, cartoons, and photos. The cumulative record shows that the student repeated the behavior each day for the first 5 days of the week. There are no responses on the next 2 days, since the school paper is not published on Saturday and Sunday. Each following week, there are five responses followed by the pause on Saturday and Sunday. Since picking up the paper is an easy response to perform and produces immediate reinforcement, the student learned it on the first day and never missed a single opportunity for obtaining this reinforcer during the entire 6 weeks shown on the cumulative record.

The second behavior, shown by the dark line in Figure 2–2, is that of working at the campus newspaper office. This behavior requires considerably more skill and effort than simply picking up a paper at the dorms, and the cumulative record shows that the student

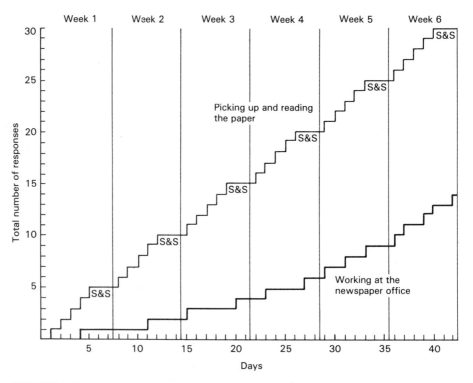

FIGURE 2–2 A cumulative record showing the total number of times a student performed two different operants over a 6-week period. Saturday and Sunday—the days on which one response could not be performed—are indicated by "S & S."

learned this activity more slowly. On the fourth day of class, the freshman visited the newspaper office for the first time to see if there was a chance of working on the newspaper, and the editor suggested that the freshman try writing a sample article. It was rewarding to talk with the editor and be offered a chance to write a trial article. The student went home and worked for several days on the sample piece, trying to polish something that would be acceptable for publication. Not until day 11 of class did the student return to the newspaper office with the sample article. The editor read the piece, gave the student encouraging feedback, made some useful changes, and suggested a new assignment for the coming weekend. The encouragement provided reinforcement for writing articles. Four days later, the student returned to the newspaper office with the next piece, which was accepted for publication with almost no changes. More rewards. As the student learned how to write better, the average time needed to prepare each article became shorter. During the next weeks, the student returned to the news office with increasing frequency, and each visit to the office was rewarded by positive feedback on the articles and increasingly friendly interactions with the editors, reporters, and staff. During the first weeks of class, there were sometimes 5- or 8-day pauses between visits to the office; but as the student gained the skills for writing good articles, the student came to work at the office more frequently, even on weekends.

The cumulative record shows that easy behaviors (such as picking up the paper) may be learned almost immediately and performed at the maximal level for long periods of time. More difficult behaviors (such as working for the newspaper) are usually learned more slowly. However, in the last week shown on the cumulative record, the student worked at the news office 5 days out of 7, making this behavior just as frequent as the easy behavior of picking up the newspaper 5 days each week. Once mastered, behaviors that require more skill may be performed as frequently as simpler activities, if they produce ample reinforcement.

Discriminative Stimuli

When a behavior (B) is followed by reinforcing stimuli (S^R's) in one context but not in other contexts, the antecedent context cues associated with reinforcement become discriminative stimuli (S^D's).

$$S^D: B \rightarrow S^R$$

These S^D's (pronounced *ess dees*) set the occasion for future responses. For example, if an American is in a foreign country where very few people speak English, signs reading "ENGLISH SPOKEN HERE" become S^D's that set the occasion for speaking English with the natives. When the signs are present, there is a good chance that speaking English will communicate and be reinforced by meaningful replies. When the signs are absent, the chances are that no one will understand, and that using English will not be reinforced.

The stimuli that best predict when and where behavior is likely to be reinforced are most likely to become S^D's. A sign reading "ENGLISH SPOKEN HERE" is obviously a good predictor that speaking English will produce rewarding results. Numerous other cues could become S^D's for using English. Since the well-dressed staff at international hotels and restaurants usually speak English, they may serve as S^D's for using English—if a person has had rewarding experiences speaking English with such people. Students at foreign universities often speak English, hence indicators that a person is a university student may become S^D's for speaking English—for those who have had reinforcing results in talking with students.

When a behavior is not *followed by reinforcement, the stimuli that best predict nonreinforcement become S^Δ's, discriminative stimuli for* not *responding.* These S^Δ's (pronounced *ess deltas*) are cues that signal that the behavior is not likely to be reinforced in this particular context (whereas S^D's signal that reinforcement is likely). In a foreign country, shops with signs reading "ENGLISH SPOKEN HERE" become S^D's for speaking English; and shops *without* such signs become S^Δ's for not using English, if English is rarely spoken there. Since natives who are poor and uneducated seldom speak English, cues that a person is poor or uneducated also may serve as S^Δ's for not speaking English.

In both of the last two paragraphs, it is clear that *several* cues can become S^D's and S^Δ's for the same behavior. There isn't just one S^D and one S^Δ for each behavior. S^D's for speaking English may include signs in English, styles of dress, and locations (such as international restaurants or hotels). In addition, each individual may learn to respond to different cues, depending on his or her unique past history of reinforcement. A student may be sensitive to certain cues as S^D's and S^Δ's, whereas a banker is sensitive to others.

The stimuli that are S^D's for one behavior may be S^Δ's for another behavior. When a foreigner who knows no English first visits the United States and confronts doors marked "PUSH" and "PULL," the person may not discriminate between these two cues, and randomly push or pull on doors until one of the two acts is rewarded. Gradually, "PUSH" signs will become S^D's for pushing and S^Δ's for pulling, since pushing is reinforced and pulling is not. Likewise, "PULL" signs will become S^D's for pulling and S^Δ's for pushing, since pulling is reinforced and pushing is not. Any stimulus—a person, place, or thing—can become an S^D for all the behaviors that have been reinforced in its presence and an S^Δ for all the behaviors that have not been reinforced in its presence. An international bank becomes an S^D for changing foreign currency into dollars and an S^Δ for all sorts of activities that are not rewarding to do in a bank. A post card provides S^D's for writing on it and S^Δ's for not chewing and eating it. As people learn to discriminate between the S^D's and S^Δ's for a given operant, they are more likely to perform this behavior in the presence of S^D's than in the presence of S^Δ's. However, the S^D's do not cause behavior. A foreign traveler may walk past several banks before entering one to change money, or buy ten post cards and only write six.

Sometimes people learn to discriminate between two rewarding experiences merely because one provides *more reinforcers* than the other. Antecedent cues that predict *more* reinforcement become S^D's; and cues that predict *less* reinforcement become S^Δ's. There may be two restaurants that both provide quite good food; but a person finds one somewhat better than the other. The better restaurant becomes an S^D for dining and the poorer one an S^Δ for not dining. *Thus antecedent cues can become S^Δ's (1) because they are associated with* no *reinforcement or (2) merely because they are associated with* less *reinforcement than is available elsewhere.*

Discriminations may be learned quickly or slowly. Often subtle discriminations between *more* and *less* reinforcement take longer to learn than easy discriminations between reinforcement and *no* reinforcement. When people move to a new town, they have to learn numerous new discriminations, such as the best places to eat, shop, and obtain medical care. If the new town has three chains of grocery stores—X, Y, and Z—a newcomer may learn to discriminate among the three types of stores at different rates. The first time the newcomer walks into store Z, it may be obvious that the low quality and limited choice of products would make shopping there unrewarding. Thus, store Z quickly becomes an S$^\Delta$ for not shopping, and the newcomer may walk out of the store without buying a thing.

However, the discrimination between stores X and Y may not be so easy. Several neighbors recommend store X, but other people recommend store Y. For several weeks the newcomer randomly and *indiscriminantly* switches back and forth between X and Y, not noticing much difference between the food in the two stores. Both stores provide good food, hence both are S^D's for shopping. The cumulative record presented in Figure 2–3 shows that for the first 10 weeks, the newcomer shopped five times at store X and five times at Y. However, during the next several weeks a few small incidents revealed that food at the two stores was not equal. On week 13, the meat at store Y was not very fresh.

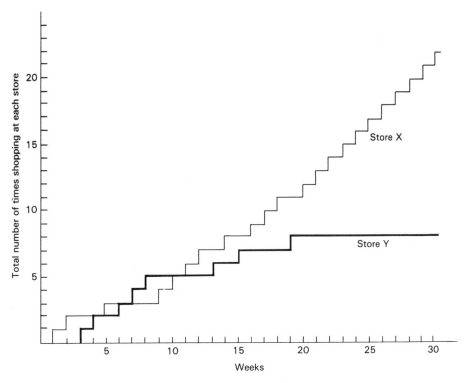

FIGURE 2–3 A cumulative record showing the total number of times a person shopped at two different stores, X and Y. Notice the similar frequency of responses in the first 10 weeks before the discrimination, then the very different pattern of responding in the last 10 weeks, after the discrimination was clear.

Although this alone would not be enough to make a person stop shopping at store Y, it suggests a possible difference in the quality of food at the two stores. On week 15, the lettuce at store Y was wilted and bruised. The newcomer had never noticed such problems at store X. On week 19, a quart of milk from store Y was sour. Gradually the newcomer discriminated that shopping at store Y was slightly less rewarding than shopping at store X. Between weeks 10 and 20, store Y ceased to be an S^D for shopping and became an S^Δ for not shopping. This S^Δ was not based on the total absence of rewards, because store Y had many fine products. However, *small but regular* differences in the quality of the reinforcers are enough to cause a person to learn to discriminate subtle differences. After week 19, store X was an S^D for shopping and store Y was an S^Δ for not shopping.

Figure 2–3 shows that as the person began to discriminate the differences in food quality between weeks 10 and 20, the person gradually stopped shopping at store Y. After week 19, the cumulative record shows no additional choices of store Y. Simultaneously, the record shows increased shopping at store X, since the person was shopping there every week instead of only half the time. People develop numerous subtle discriminations among situations that provide similar—but somewhat different—reinforcement: between good and outstanding restaurants, between so-so discos and great discos, between good medical service and exceptional medical service.

Positive and Negative Reinforcement

There are two kinds of reinforcement: positive and negative. To reinforce means to strengthen; and both positive and negative reinforcement strengthen behavior. They both increase the likelihood that people will repeat a behavior in the future. *The critical difference is that positive reinforcement occurs with the onset of a reinforcing stimulus and negative reinforcement occurs with the termination of an aversive stimulus.* In terms of the law of effect, positive reinforcement consists of the *onset of good effects;* and negative reinforcement consists of the *termination of bad effects.* The onset of pleasurable music provides positive reinforcement for turning on the stereo. The termination of an aversive sound provides negative reinforcement for turning off the alarm clock in the morning. Receiving an award for breaking a track record provides positive reinforcement for regular exercise and training. Getting rid of a sore throat provides negative reinforcement for taking throat lozenger. Increasing the number of smiles and laughs at a party provides positive reinforcement for telling jokes and funny stories. Decreasing the number of fights in a marriage provides negative reinforcement for going to a marriage counselor and following the counselor's advice.

The antecedent cues that precede any kind of reinforcement—positive or negative—become S^D's. Thus, the S^D's of increasing darkness in the evening set the occasion for turning on the lights, because this operant produces the positive reinforcement of being able to see things at night. The S^D's of yawns and sleepiness set the occasion for turning off the lights late at night, because this operant produces negative reinforcement by terminating the glaring lights that make it hard to sleep. The antecedent cues that precede behavior which produces neither positive nor negative reinforcement—or less reinforcement than available elsewhere—become S^Δ's.

Most behavior can be strengthened by both positive and negative reinforcement.

Consider politeness. If your being polite is followed by smiles and kind words from other people, the onset of good effects provides positive reinforcement for your politeness. If you are polite to someone who is grouchy and the person *stops* being grouchy, the cessation of bad events provides negative reinforcement for your politeness. Little children often receive both positive and negative reinforcement for running to their parents. If Mother is sitting in the living room and her child climbs onto her knee and asks to play "horsey," Mother may bounce the child on her knee. The *occurrence* of the game reinforces the child's response of approaching Mother and asking to play. Thus, bouncing the child provides positive reinforcement for coming to Mother. On the other hand, when a child gets a splinter in the finger, the child may run to Father for help in removing it. When Father removes the splinter, the *termination* of the aversive stimulation from the splinter reinforces the child's response of coming to Father. Thus, removing the splinter provides negative reinforcement for approaching the adult for help. Parents become S^D's for approach due to both positive and negative reinforcement.

Positive Reinforcement.   *People usually enjoy learning via positive reinforcement because it increases the good effects and pleasurable experiences in their lives.* Thus positive reinforcement is an ideal method for helping people learn things in ways that they will enjoy. The child who learns to help around the house via positive reinforcement—appreciative and loving comments from the parents—will enjoy helping the parents (rather than doing it out of duty or fear of reprimand). Parents who show sincere, loving attention to their child as positive reinforcement for politeness, friendliness, sharing, and consideration will have a child who takes pleasure in treating others well.

Positive reinforcement is an ideal method for enhancing creativity. People have the potential to be either creative or uncreative. The particular subset of this human potential that any given individual develops depends in part on the patterns of reinforcement, as one study on childhood creativity shows.[3] While children were playing with building blocks, they were given social reinforcers for either building novel, creative forms or repeating old forms. The children who received rewards only when they built interesting new structures learned to become quite creative and innovative in their block play. The other children, who received rewards for repeating old patterns, became less creative because their repetitive patterns were incompatible with novel, creative ones. Similar studies have shown that reinforcement will increase creativity in writing, easel painting, and other artistic endeavors.[4] Throughout life, all of us receive reinforcers for both creative and noncreative responses. The more often reinforcement follows creative rather than non-creative behavior, the more likely we are to develop the creative aspect of our human potential. Unfortunately, many people's daily lives are filled with tasks and duties that reinforce repetitive behavior rather than innovative behavior. One of the goals of the behavioral sciences is to help people increase the positive reinforcement for creative and innovative behavior.[5]

[3]Goetz and Baer (1973).
[4]Goetz and Salmonson (1972); Maloney and Hopkins (1973).
[5]Mahoney (1975).

Positive reinforcement can be given in either *natural* or *artificial* ways. We have all heard adults give children clearly artificial and contrived praise: "Maria, what a *nice* log house you have built." Unnatural praise and artificial rewards are sometimes not very effective in reinforcing behavior. Highly contrived, unnatural rewards can even *decrease* the frequency of an operant if they are used in a manipulative manner.[6] However, natural and sincere positive feedback is usually both pleasurable to receive and effective in reinforcing behavior. Natural positive reinforcement occurs quite spontaneously when people show enthusiastic and supportive responses to things that others have done: "Wow! You've got a powerful backhand, Sonia!" "It was so kind of you to drop by, Tom." Genuine smiles and appreciative comments on other people's behavior are the most common forms of natural positive reinforcement seen in everyday life—even though most people are not aware that they are giving or receiving positive reinforcement when these natural forms of positive feedback are exchanged.

Some people tend to give much more positive reinforcement than others. Instead of commenting mostly on the faults and inadequacies of others, the positive person tends to focus on the good and show genuine pleasure about it: "Gee, I really like those new photos you made." This style of social interaction provides others with positive reinforcers for good things they have done rather than criticisms for their failures. As you can imagine, it is a pleasure to know positive people since they are generous with positive feedback. As a consequence, positive people tend to be well-liked.[7]

Positive reinforcement is being used ever more commonly in business and industry to reward productive workers and create good rapport between employees and management. For example, "golden handcuffs" are used to keep highly valued employees— such as the engineers who design computer chips—from leaving a company. Since other companies try to lure skilled employees away with higher salaries, an employer has to make it rewarding for the employees to stay. The employer may offer a top employee golden handcuffs, such as a new Porsche with a low interest, 10-year loan *and* a promise that the company will take over all the payments after the employee stays with the company for 5 years. To reap the rewards of having the car fully paid off, the employee must stay with the company for the entire 5 years. Positive reinforcement helps the worker decide to stay and it creates good feelings about the company.

Since industrial productivity can be hurt significantly by worker absenteeism, there have been efforts to reduce tardiness by providing positive reinforcement for promptness. A company in Mexico devised a method of positive reinforcement to solve its problems with worker tardiness.[8] Every day that workers reported to work on time, they received slips of paper stating that their punctuality had earned 2 extra pesos for the day (an increase of 4 percent above normal wages). The workers could collect these slips and cash them in at the end of the week. Figure 2–4 shows how effective the rewards were in reinforcing punctuality. Before the start of the program, when there were no special rewards for punctuality (at A), only 80 to 90 percent of the workers arrived on time. During 8 weeks when positive reinforcers were given for being on time (B), punctuality

---

[6]Lepper and Greene (1975); Condry (1977).

[7]Thibaut and Kelley (1959); Homans (1974).

[8]Hermann et al. (1973).

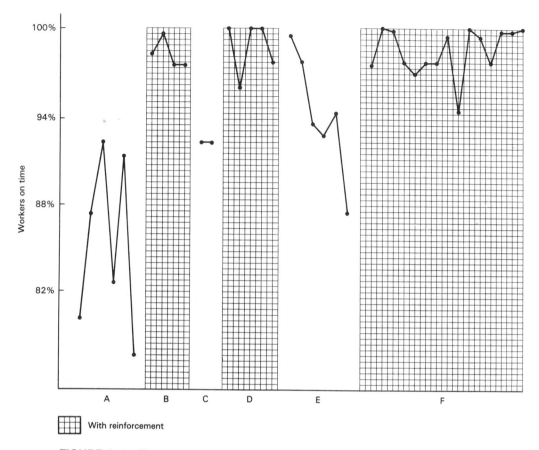

FIGURE 2–4 The percent of people being punctual under six reinforcement conditions.
Redrawn from Hermann et al. Copyright © 1973 by the Society for the Experimental Analysis of Behavior, Inc.

improved markedly, with 97 to 99 percent of the people being on time. Then there was a 4-week period in which no rewards for promptness were given (C), and the promptness scores decreased to 92 percent. When the rewards were reinstated for the next 9 weeks (D), the punctuality scores again increased, reaching 95 to 100 percent. During the next 12 weeks, reinforcement for punctuality was again removed (E), and the rates of punctuality decreased. For the final 32 weeks of the study (F), positive reinforcement for punctuality was reinstated, increasing the frequency of the response class significantly.

Positive reinforcement can come from nonsocial sources, as is seen in the following example of the reinforcement of *selective perception*. People pay attention to only a fraction of all the stimuli in their environment—neglecting many of the things that happen around them. One of the determinants of this selective perception is positive reinforcement. Perhaps you have had a "lucky find" and noticed the rapid change in visual attentiveness produced by this type of positive reinforcement.

For example, while walking down the street, Mike happens to notice some green paper near the edge of the sidewalk. Much to his surprise, it is a dollar bill. When he picks it up he sees a second bill just a few inches away. Both are dusty. No telling who had dropped them or when. So Mike puts them in his pocket and continues on his way. A few moments later, he notices a change in his own behavior. He is no longer looking at the trees or houses. Instead, his eyes keep scanning the ground, as if looking for another lucky find. The behavior of looking down had been followed by the positive reinforcement of finding money. This positive reinforcement strengthened the operants of glancing down and scanning the ground. After such a lucky find, people sometimes note that they watch the ground more than usual for several days. Since focusing attention on one thing or another takes little effort and is easy to learn, one positive reinforcement can have long lasting effects on patterns of selective attention.

Negative Reinforcement.   Whereas positive reinforcement brings good effects and pleasurable experiences into our lives, negative reinforcement occurs when we escape or avoid aversive experiences. Having a splinter removed is a pleasure; but it involves some pain in the first place. Avoiding a speeding ticket by being polite with the police officer is rewarding, but your palms may have been sweating before the officer let you know you were off the hook. Removing splinters and avoiding traffic tickets are rewarding; but the rewards of negative reinforcement are based on the termination of aversive situations rather than the onset of good effects and pleasurable experiences.

The two main classes of behavior produced by negative reinforcement are escape and avoidance.[9] *Escape* responses are those operants that allow a person to get away from aversive stimuli *after* the aversive stimuli are present. *Avoidance* responses are those operants that allow a person to prevent the occurrence of aversive stimuli *before* the aversive stimuli appear. Pesky flies are a pain in the neck. Behavior that terminates them and their bothersome buzzing is strengthened through negative reinforcement. We *escape* the pesky flies by swatting them when they are present. We *avoid* them when we put up screen doors or fly paper to prevent their presence. Critical people are sometimes like pesky flies: ''Why didn't you do it this way? Why can't you do that differently?'' There are many *escape* responses that might be reinforced: For example, it might suffice to say politely, ''I could get along without your comments.'' If this did not work, some people might say ''Buzz off,'' ''Shut up,'' or something even stronger. There are numerous responses people use to *avoid* criticism—such as avoiding interaction with critical people or avoiding doing those behaviors that are likely to be criticized. Some people attempt to polish their behavior beyond reproach to avoid criticism.

Escape involves *reacting* after an aversive event is present. Avoidance involves *proacting*—taking preventative steps—before an aversive event arises. People react to splinters by pulling them out; they proact by putting on gloves before handling rough cut wood. People react to hangovers by taking aspirin; they proact by not drinking so much that they would get a hangover.

Escape behaviors are usually learned before avoidance behaviors. This is es-

---

[9]Early theories of avoidance and negative reinforcement have often stressed the role of conditioned aversive stimuli (and sometimes the concomitant aversive conditioned emotional responses) in mediating avoidance behavior; however, there is reason not to include these putative mediating events in a general theory of negative reinforcement (Hineline, 1977).

pecially true in childhood. First, children learn to escape wet underpants by removing them. Later they learn to avoid having wet underpants by avoiding urinary accidents. First they learn to escape the class bully by running when they see him. Later, they learn to avoid places where the bully is. As people grow up and gain experience, they usually learn increasing skills for proacting and avoiding problems, and avoidance becomes more common than escape. However, when totally new and unexpected problems arise, even adults may return to the pattern of first learning how to escape, then how to avoid. During the first weeks after moving to a new city, a person may get caught in heavy traffic that takes an hour to escape. After living in the new city several months, the person may learn to avoid driving in congested parts of town at the bad hours for heavy traffic. It usually takes more time and experience to learn to proact and avoid than to react and escape. After moving to a new city, a person may have to get caught in heavy traffic several times before learning how bad the traffic can be. It may take even longer to learn when and where the traffic is worst. Eventually all the "when and where" cues of time and place become S^D's that allow the person to proact and avoid heavy traffic. However, before these cues become S^D's, the only cues available to the person are the S^D's for escape—namely, the S^D's of being caught in a traffic jam.

Some couples allow their marriages to deteriorate into fights and arguments; then they react by trying to escape the aversive situation through marital counseling, divorce, or having affairs. Other couples who see their friends having marital troubles may proact by working on improving their communication and resolving differences before problems arise, thereby avoiding at least some of the fights and arguments that might damage their marriage. Unfortunately, many people do not learn to proact soon enough to save their marriages.

National, state, and local governments often utilize negative reinforcement in the form of tax breaks. In some states, if homeowners insulate their homes, add solar heating, and install other energy-saving equipment, they qualify for tax breaks and avoid paying a portion of their taxes. Commuters may learn to form car pools if it results in their avoiding toll payments. In the San Francisco area, cars with three or more people are allowed to cross the Golden Gate Bridge and Oakland Bay Bridge toll-free during the busy hours of the day, whereas cars with only one or two people in them have to pay a toll. The use of car pools is negatively reinforced by the avoidance of two aversive events: (1) paying the regular toll, and (2) being delayed by the toll lines. Due to negative reinforcement, more people use car pools today than before programs such as this were initiated.

Backpackers frequently learn camping skills by negative reinforcement. The backpacker who pitches a tent at the base of a trail may be awakened in the middle of the night by water flowing into the tent. This distressing state of affairs can negatively reinforce any of a variety of responses for escaping the aversive condition. The tenter might try to move the tent, try to get invited into someone else's tent, or spend the night in a poncho under a tree. In addition, the negative reinforcement may condition the camper to look for high ground when selecting future tent sites. Aversive stimulation motivates people to explore a variety of responses that might terminate the aversive stimuli. Only successful means of avoiding aversive situations are actually negatively reinforced.

People who never camp out—who live protected from the elements in well-built houses—may not appreciate that the technology for building houses that stay dry in rains, warm in winter, and insect free in summer is largely a result of negative reinforcement.

Over the centuries, countless inventions have been made—then negatively reinforced—because they seal out rain, cold, insects, bears, and so forth. Much of technology consists of devices and practices that reduce unpleasant experiences and decrease aversive events. To the degree that a given technology does successfully reduce or terminate aversive experiences, there will be negative reinforcement for retaining—and further perfecting—that technology.

In everyday conversation, negative reinforcement conditions numerous skills for sensitively guiding the course of discussion. Because certain topics can lead to embarrassment and other topics trigger anger or hostility, conversation is a potentially risky business. When people blunder into touchy topics which insult, injure, embarrass, or anger others, friendly social interaction can turn into an aversive experience. Any responses that allow the people to escape or avoid the aversive situation will be negatively reinforced.

For example, religion can be a touchy topic in conversation between strangers. One person's chance derogatory comment about a certain religion may elicit anger in the listener and bring the conversation to a halt. On the brink of falling into an unwanted clash about religion, a third person may calmly let the topic slide, laugh good-naturedly, and return to an earlier, safer topic. "But as we were saying before, the important thing is to . . . ." If the other people follow suit, the three will have successfully avoided a potentially embarrassing or difficult situation. The skills of laughing and smoothly changing subjects are often negatively reinforced by the successful avoidance of an aversive experience.

People can learn a number of different skills for proacting in regard to touchy topics. Some may learn to ask fellow conversationalists what their beliefs are before mentioning some strong personal opinion. Others may learn to toss out a leading comment and see how the listeners respond—conservatively or liberally—before sharing their own opinions. If people see someone else treading dangerously close to a potentially embarrassing topic, they may avoid the aversive consequences by diverting the conversation. "Mary, weren't you telling us earlier about your . . . [safe topic]?" As people successfully defuse dangerous topics, the avoidance of embarrassing situations negatively reinforces the skills of diplomacy, courtesy, finesse, and sensitivity.

Naturally, some people never learn to be tactful. But some people never learn how to hit pesky flies or resolve marital conflicts. Later chapters demonstrate how shaping, models, prompts, rules, and schedules combine in complex patterns to help or hinder each individual in learning the skills for coping with the multiple facets of everyday life. For example, if a person is exposed to social models who are graceful and considerate in guiding conversations away from touchy topics, the models' behavior and advice (i.e., rules) will help the observer learn subtle skills more rapidly than if no models or rules were available.

EXTINCTION

Once an operant has been reinforced and become common in a given S^D context, there is no guarantee that the frequency of the response will remain the same in the future. Either *extinction* or *punishment* will cause a response to become less frequent. Hence both of these processes work in the opposite direction from reinforcement. *Extinction consists of the discontinuation of any reinforcement (either positive or negative) that had once maintained a given behavior. When reinforcement is withdrawn, the frequency of the response declines.* Whenever anything goes on the blink or stops working, we learn to stop using it. We stop using the old vacuum cleaner when it no longer picks up dirt from the floor. It has ceased to be instrumental in doing the job, hence no longer produces rewarding results. We stop putting quarters in the candy machine after losing several quarters in a row and getting no candy.

Extinction can take place because (1) there is no *reinforcement associated with a certain behavior or (2) there is* less *reinforcement associated with that behavior than with some superior alternative.* We stop shopping at grocery store Y when we find that it is less rewarding to shop there than in store X. We stop using the old route back and forth to home when a new expressway is completed that shortens the trip by 15 minutes. We stop voting for one politician when it is clear that another politician does a better job supporting the issues we value. Less rewarding behavior is extinguished when a superior alternative becomes available.

Antecedent stimuli that are regularly associated with nonreinforcement—or with less reinforcement than a superior alternative—become S^Δ's for not responding during extinction. Before the candy machine is broken, it is an S^D for inserting quarters; but after it is broken it becomes an S^Δ for not inserting quarters. Two grocery stores are S^D's for shopping if we like them equally; but one becomes an S^Δ after we learn that it is less rewarding to shop there than at the other store. (Shopping at store Y was put on extinction when we discriminated that its products were not as good as those at store X.) When Karen first went to college, she talked about all the things that she used to love talking about with her high school friends back in Hometown. Some of these topics went over nicely, but others were of no interest to her college friends. Talking about those topics which did not interest her new friends was extinguished (since no one showed positive responses), and Karen gradually stopped mentioning them while at college. Her college friends became S^Δ's for not talking about certain topics at college. (Karen's high school friends will remain S^D's for bringing up those topics if they continue to show interest when she talks with them.)

The rate at which response frequency declines during extinction depends on the individual's prior history of reinforcement. When extinction begins, people give up a behavior pattern much faster if the behavior had been *rewarded all the time* in the past, instead of having been *rewarded only part of the time* in the past. If your car has always started on the first try, you are likely to give up quickly and call a garage if it will not start one morning. However, if someone else is used to trying ten or twenty times before their car starts, they are less likely to give up quickly on a day when it is impossible to start the car. They have been rewarded *intermittently*—since the car usually started only one out of ten or twenty tries, and it is hard for them to discriminate that extinction has begun once the car finally will not start at all. *After a history of intermittent reinforcement, the frequency of behavior usually declines more slowly during extinction than does behavior that had been continuously reinforced.* (This will be explained more completely in Chapter 12.)

The following examples show common forms of extinction after the discontinuation of positive and negative reinforcement.

Extinction after Positive Reinforcement

When positive reinforcement for a given operant is terminated, the frequency of the previously reinforced response declines. If a person who had been earning $20,000 a year in a bank were told that the salary could no longer be paid (though the person could continue working if he or she wanted to), what would happen? Most people would stop coming to work (unless some other effective reinforcer were operating). Behavior maintained by positive reinforcement usually becomes less frequent when reinforcement is removed.

Some children learn to whine, pout, or throw tantrums because these behaviors bring them attention from others. Terry frequently whined.[10] His parents often reinforced his behavior by paying attention to him. If whining did not attract attention, Terry usually began shouting. The frequency of whining and shouting is shown in Figure 2–5 at A. The whining and shouting were so aversive that his parents usually paid attention to Terry just to quiet him. (The parents' paying attention was negatively reinforced because their attention terminated the aversive whining and shouting.) One day, Terry's parents switched their strategy and stopped paying attention to Terry when he whined or shouted. They ignored him. Because reinforcement had been terminated the response was on extinction. The frequency of whining and shouting fell abruptly to less than half the prior rate, and it continued to decline further over the next several days (B in the figure). Then, for three days, Terry's parents again paid attention to whining and shouting (period C), and the frequency of these activities rose. Convinced that it was better to put whining and shouting on extinction than to reinforce them, the parents again ignored these responses (period D). Once more, the undesirable responses became less frequent. Thus *reinforcement increases the frequency of behavior, and extinction decreases it.* During the reinforcement periods, the parents were S^D's for Terry's whining and shouting. During extinction, the parents became S^Δ's for whining and shouting, since they no longer reinforced the obnoxious behavior.

The coming and going of fads usually reflects a two-phase cycle: (1) a period of positive reinforcement followed by (2) a period of extinction. When a new style of clothing, novel slang word, or unusual toy comes on the scene, it brings novelty (which is usually a positive reinforcer); and people who try the fad often receive a great deal of social attention (which is also a positive reinforcer for most people). When hula-hoops were first invented, they were an instant success (phase 1). You saw them everywhere. But as the novelty wore off and reinforcement declined, the fad faded—due to extinction (phase 2). Fad diets come and go for similar reasons. When someone comes up with a novel diet that promises to help take off the pounds, the novelty of the method rewards people for talking about and trying the new diet. After the novelty fades—and little weight has been shed—people lose interest, and the fad diet fades into oblivion.

Several years ago a fad of light bulb eating spread across several college campuses. Most students were surprised, a bit skeptical, but clearly interested when they first ran into someone who said he or she was going to eat a light bulb tonight at 7:00. "It's better than dorm food." The humor, the audience interest, and the growing excitement for the 7:00 o'clock show all served as reinforcers for the incipient bulb eater. Sure enough, at 7:00

---

[10]Hall et al. (1972).

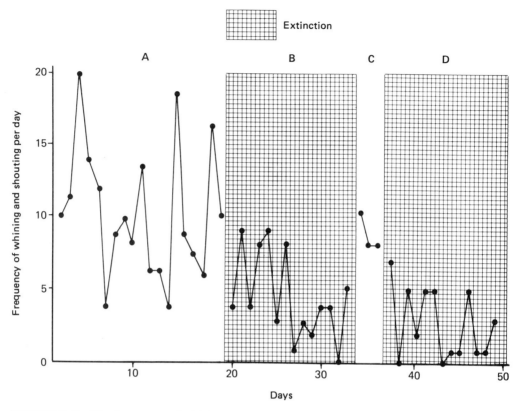

FIGURE 2-5 The frequency of whining and shouting.

Redrawn from Hall et al. Copyright © 1972 by the Society for the Experimental Analysis of Behavior, Inc.

several people were there to watch. The watchers' attendance was reinforced by the novelty of the show. As the bulb eater ingested a 75-watt bulb, social attention from the amazed audience provided the positive reinforcers which produced phase 1, the rise of a fad. On being coaxed to reveal the secret, the bulb muncher might have claimed: "As long as you chew it up very, very fine, it doesn't hurt much." Daredevils who imitated the feat also received the positive reinforcers of attention and novel experience. The fad spread.

As the novelty of bulb eating wore off, there was a *natural* shift from reinforcement to extinction (phase 2). After seeing ten or twenty bulbs go down the hatch, most observers ceased to be surprised by the trick. Interest waned and people no longer flocked to watch the bulb munchers. Thus, there was neither novelty nor social attention for bulb eating—and since the bulbs did not taste good in the first place, there was no other reinforcement for bulb eating. With the onset of extinction, bulb eating declined in frequency. (The importance of social exchange in reinforcing behavior can be seen clearly here. The bulb eater could no longer offer enough novelty reinforcers to bring an audience; thus the audience's attendance was on extinction. As the audience no longer provided social attention to reward the bulb eater, bulb eating was also put on extinction.)

Extinction after Negative Reinforcement

When an operant is established via negative reinforcement, the removal of the negative reinforcement (i.e., extinction) usually causes the frequency of the behavior to decline. The extinction of negatively reinforced behavior occurs as the second phase of a two-phase sequence: (1) a person has learned some response that helps escape or avoid an aversive stimulus, then (2) the stimulus ceases being aversive or is no longer present. During the second half of the sequence—the extinction phase—the behavior becomes less frequent. This two-phase cycle often corresponds to the coming and going of problems in life. After presenting several examples of this, we will look at a major exception to this pattern.

World War II brought widespread destruction to Europe. The loss of buildings, transportation lines, easy access to food supplies, and many of the basic amenities of life created great hardship. Faced with the unpleasant problems of surviving and rebuilding under adverse conditions, the people learned to be frugal, to conserve scarce resources, and to salvage things that would have been thrown away in more affluent times. This was the learning phase (phase 1) in which practices for escaping or minimizing aversive circumstances were acquired due to negative reinforcement. If people were wasteful of food and firewood, they were likely to be hungry and cold. On the other hand, if they avoided unnecessary waste and salvaged anything of use, their behavior was negatively reinforced by the escape from hunger, cold, and other inconveniences.

Within a decade of the end of World War II, a new prosperity began to emerge in Europe. The problems of scarcity became less severe, thus there were fewer reasons to be frugal. There was no longer strong negative reinforcement for conserving, salvaging, and scrimping. These changes marked the beginning of extinction (phase 2). Within ten years, many Europeans had abandoned much of their postwar frugality.

Other temporary hardships produce the same kind of two-phase cycle. Whenever a part of the country undergoes extreme drought, water becomes scarce and costly. Due to negative reinforcement, people learn to save and recycle water: Frugal practices help them avoid prohibitive water bills and fines for excess usage. When the rains come and the hardship is over, what happens to the frugal practices of saving and recycling water? These operants are now on extinction due to the lack of negative reinforcement, and water conserving activities quickly become less common.

Daily problems can produce cycles of negative reinforcement and extinction. If you happen to get in a bitter argument with a friend, the aversive experience creates negative reinforcement for avoiding your friend or for avoiding any potentially touchy topics in subsequent conversations. Extinction begins as soon as you and your friend succeed in squelching further conflicts. As extinction proceeds, you gradually feel less apprehensive and nervous while talking with your friend, and your cautious conversational responses decline in frequency. Eventually you are back to being your old, "natural" self around your friend—no longer having to carefully avoid potentially touchy topics.

The Exception: Avoidance Retards Extinction.   There is an important exception to the general statement that behavior learned via negative reinforcement declines in frequency after the onset of extinction: *People sometimes continue doing well-learned avoidance* *responses long after negative reinforcement has ended.* Some people learn strong avoidance responses that never decrease in frequency, even during extinction. Consider people's responses to a man who is unbearably boring and self-centered. People avoid him because any response that averts an interaction with him is negatively reinforced by their avoiding a painfully dull conversation. After the man confronts his problem and works for months to overcome it, people *still* continue to avoid him. Why? They have learned such strong avoidance responses that they never start a conversation with him, thus never discover that he is now a much more likeable person. *Avoidance of a once aversive situation can prevent people from learning that the situation has ceased being aversive, thus avoidance responses may continue even when there is no longer any negative reinforcement.*

If an elementary school child has some very bad experiences in gym class—because the teacher is strict and insensitive—the child may learn to make excuses to avoid class. Making excuses is negatively reinforced, since it helps the child avoid further aversive experiences in gym. When the child goes to junior high school, the new gym teacher may be kind and supportive, yet the child may have learned so many excuses for avoiding gym class that the total avoidance would prevent the child from learning that junior high gym could be fun. Strong avoidance responses deprive a person of the opportunity to learn that things that once were aversive are no longer aversive. Thus avoidance can produce long lasting effects on behavior. Bad experiences with gym classes in the early grades can produce such long lasting avoidance of sports and physical activity that a person may never explore physical activities and develop athletic skills, even though it might be rewarding to do so at later times.

PUNISHMENT

When an operant is followed by a stimulus that suppresses the frequency of the operant in the future, the stimulus is called a punisher. The process by which the frequency of a response class is suppressed is called punishment.[11] If a person receives a hefty fine after driving through a red light, the punishment is likely to suppress the behavior of running red lights in the future. When people disagree with you each time you mention a certain topic, their critical feedback is likely to suppress your bringing up that topic with them in the future. This response suppression takes place even when you are completely unaware that other's comments have caused you to stop mentioning the criticized topic.[12]

Any stimulus regularly correlated with the punishment of an operant may become an S^Δ—discriminative stimulus—that sets the occasion for not responding. After people receive reprimands or traffic fines for driving through red lights, red lights become S^Δ's for not advancing (whereas green lights are S^D's for driving ahead). People stop trying to pet snarling dogs after being bitten by them, and snarling dogs become S^Δ's for not petting. Employees with nice salaries stop contradicting the boss after the boss threatens

[11]Walters and Grusec (1977); Axelrod and Apsche (1983).
[12]Centers (1963).

to fire them if they cannot control their tongues; and the boss becomes an S^Δ for not making further contradictory comments.

Both punishment and extinction reduce the frequency of behavior; however, punishment usually does so more rapidly and more completely than extinction does.[13] For example, after a child has learned to pout or whine because these responses are reinforced by attention, the frequency of pouting or whining can be reduced by either extinction or punishment. If the parents cease paying attention whenever the child begins to pout or whine, they have opted for the extinction method. If they deduct 10 percent of the child's allowance each time the pouting or whining appears, they have opted to use punishment. Both methods work; however, punishment usually causes a much more rapid decline in responding than extinction does. Punishment is a process by which behavior is actively suppressed, whereas extinction is a process by which behavior becomes less frequent due to nonreinforcement.

Figure 2–6 shows the cumulative records for behaviors that were always reinforced before time X, then switched to either extinction or punishment (at time X). It is clear that punishment (lower graph) causes much faster cessation of responding than does extinction (upper graph). (An unbroken horizontal line in a cumulative record shows that no responses are being made.) In a house with a long dark hall, people are likely to turn on the hall light whenever they walk through the hall at night. The cumulative records in Figure 2–6 show typical patterns of light switch use during evening hours. Before time X, there is a rather steady rate of responding—as people use the light switch about six or eight times an evening. At time X, the switch goes bad and no one fixes it. If flicking the switch no longer turns on the light, the behavior is on extinction (since there are no rewarding results). For several days, people keep on flicking the switch—"out of habit"—every time they go through the hall at night. However, the frequency of responding gradually declines due to extinction, as is shown in the upper half of Figure 2–6. On the other hand, if the faulty light switch gave a moderate shock every time people touched it, the response of flicking the switch would be suppressed much sooner, as is shown in the bottom half of Figure 2–6. Punishment reduces response rates faster than does extinction.

Punishment produces the fastest suppression of behavior when it is strong, immediate, and not opposed by reinforcement. Extremely intense and immediate punishment can suppress behavior permanently.[14] After getting a serious shock from bare wiring while trying to fix a faulty light switch, most people learn not to handle bare wiring without first checking to see that the power is off. Weak and delayed punishment is usually less effective than strong and immediate punishment. When parents see their child taking another child's toy, they may say "No-no, don't do"; but a verbal reprimand alone is a weak punishment and may not be very effective in suppressing the behavior. The longer the delay between the behavior and the reprimand, the weaker the suppressive effect. Many parents learn to take immediate and strong action to stop a child from taking things from other children.

When punishment is opposed by reinforcement, behavior is influenced by the relative intensity and frequency of both punishment and reinforcement. The opposing effects

[13]Lovaas and Simmons (1969).
[14]Appel (1961); Storms et al. (1962).

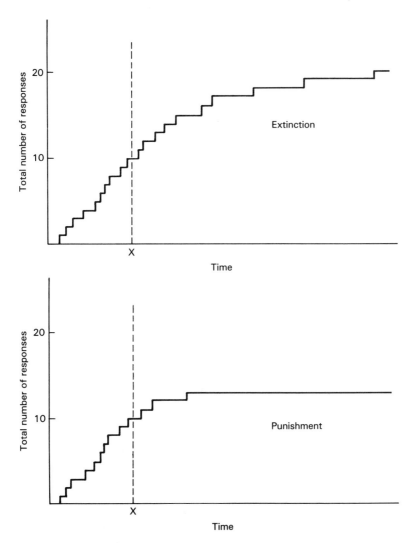

FIGURE 2-6   The cumulative record of responses that were reinforced before time X, then switched to either extinction (above) or punishment (below) at time X. Note that punishment produces a much faster cessation of responding than does extinction. (A horizontal line indicates no additional responses.)

of reinforcement and punishment are based, in part, on the *intensity* of each. If a light switch in the hall works (a reinforcer) but gives a weak shock (a mild punisher) when used, people may continue to use the switch at night because the reinforcement of light outweighs the discomfort of a weak shock. However, if the shock were more intense and painful, the punishment of shock might outweigh the reinforcement of light and suppress responding. The *cost/benefit ratio* of punishment to reinforcement helps predict how much response suppression will occur. When costs are high and benefits are low, there is more response suppression than when costs are low and benefits are high.

Also, the *frequency* of punishment and reinforcement affects the cost/benefit ratio. If a behavior is always rewarded, but punished only one time in ten, the intermittent punishment is less likely to suppress responding than would more frequent punishment. People who are criticized every time they mention their belief in ESP to strangers are more likely to stop talking about ESP with strangers than people who are only criticized one time in ten. If a boy criticizes his girlfriend every time she plays tennis with him, his criticisms are punishers that may suppress her playing. She may continue to play tennis with him if the frequency of rewards is greater than the frequency of punishment; but she is likely to quit playing if the criticisms are more frequent than the rewards.

Mild or infrequent punishment can totally suppress behavior if an alternative behavior is available—with a better cost/benefit ratio—to replace it. People may completely stop doing a mildly punished behavior if they have access to an alternative behavior that offers more reinforcement and/or less punishment. When parents use verbal reprimands—a weak punisher—to deal with a child who is taking toys from other children, the reprimands may have little effect on their child's behavior because the rewards of playing with toys outweigh the weak verbal punisher. However, if the parents give their child several interesting toys or spend more time playing with the child, the reprimands for stealing toys from other children—coupled with rewards for alternative behavior—may stop the unwanted behavior.

Positive and Negative Punishment

There are two kinds of punishment: positive and negative. The terms "positive" and "negative" indicate whether punishment occurs with the *onset* or *termination* of the stimulus that follows the operant: Positive indicates onset, and negative indicates termination. *Positive punishment occurs with the* onset *of an aversive stimulus that suppresses behavior.* If you spill hot coffee on your hand while going to a table in the cafeteria, the onset of an aversive stimulus punishes the clumsy act. This is positive punishment. *Negative punishment occurs when the* termination *of a rewarding stimulus suppresses behavior.* If a clumsy action results in your dropping and losing a ten-dollar bill on a windy day, the loss serves as punishment for the clumsy act. Thus, the loss of a positive reinforcer is a negative punishment.

When referring to either positive reinforcement or positive punishment, the term "positive" indicates that operant conditioning results from the *onset* of a stimulus. When referring to either negative reinforcement or negative punishment, the term "negative" indicates that operant conditioning results from the *termination* (through escape, avoidance, or loss) of a stimulus. This is easily understood in terms of the law of effect:

Positive reinforcement occurs with the onset of good effects.
Positive punishment occurs with the onset of bad effects.
Negative reinforcement occurs with the termination of bad effects.
Negative punishment occurs with the termination of good effects.

Positive Punishment.   Positive punishment occurs whenever an act leads to aversive experiences. The physical environment is often a source of positive punishment. Careless handling of fire, knives, bees, machines, and certain other objects leads to aversive consequences; hence careless responses are suppressed by naturally occurring positive punishment. Since these natural punishers continue to affect us all through life, careless responses remain suppressed all through life.

Little children sometimes fantasize that they can fly. Fairy tales entice them to dream of soaring above the house, off to a special world for kids only. With high levels of positive reinforcement awaiting the first successful flight, the child prepares a Superman or Wonderwoman cloak from a discarded sheet and climbs onto the garage roof. Ready for takeoff! The child arranges the magic cloak and steps to the edge. Looking down to the ground ten feet below already gives the illusion of flight. Just one more step to go. TAKEOFF! Free flight . . . THUMP! Due to the laws of gravity flying children receive positive punishment—an aversive experience—after each jump. How strong the punishment is depends on whether the flight ends in a haystack, in a soft garden plot, or on pavement. The haystack jumper may chalk up the failure of the first flight to technical error and jump several more times before the mild but consistent punishment finally suppresses the behavior. The child who hit the pavement may not fly again. One strong positive punishment may suffice to suppress the response once and for all. After childhood, jumping off buildings remains well suppressed throughout most people's lives.

There are numerous social forms of positive punishment. Some are intentional—such as spankings, reprimands, and hostile criticism. Others are quite unintentional—such as an insensitive comment that was made without anyone realizing how much it would hurt one of the listeners. Because each person has a unique history of past conditioning, social punishers often affect people differently; a cold stare or insolent answer could be very aversive to one person and hardly noticed by another.

Most people are, however, sensitive to many of the natural social punishers that punctuate social interactions. Imagine that you are talking with people you met last week whose names you should have already learned. If you accidentally call someone by the wrong name, the error may lead to an embarrassing situation. The positive punishment resulting from making an error may suppress your using other people's names until you are certain that you cannot be in error. After several punishments for sloppy name use, you might not say an individual's name unless you had just heard someone else use the individual's name beforehand, and hence were certain that the name was safe to use. (In addition to suppressing wrong responses, the aversiveness of social errors can cause a person to learn—via negative reinforcement—new skills for avoiding social blunders. For example, you might learn to listen closely when people are first introduced, and to rehearse the name several times to yourself so you will be sure to remember it. Thus, aversive situations can both (1) cause wrong responses to be suppressed, via positive punishment, and (2) cause other skills to be acquired and strengthened, via negative reinforcement.)

Negative Punishment.   Whereas positive punishment occurs when an operant is followed by an aversive stimulus, negative punishment occurs when an operant leads to the loss of a positive reinforcer. When people drop or lose things of value, the loss produces

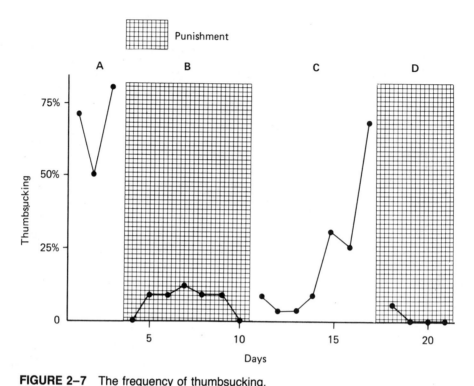

FIGURE 2-7 The frequency of thumbsucking.

Redrawn from Knight and McKenzie. Copyright © 1974 by the Society for the Experimental Analysis of Behavior, Inc.

negative punishment that often effectively suppresses further clumsy behavior. Have you ever lost your wallet full of money and identification cards? The loss negatively punishes the negligent behavior that led you to misplace it in the first place. Such negligent behavior is less likely to occur in the future. Clumsy, inconsiderate, or crude behavior in social interaction may result in a loss of friends or of possible social contacts. When a person pulls a boner at a cocktail party and several of the listeners soon turn to join other conversations, the loss of social reinforcers negatively punishes the behavior of saying dumb things in public. Loss of love—when a good relationship goes on the rocks—punishes and may well suppress some of the inconsiderate behavior that damaged the relationship. Loss of a driver's license punishes fast driving and often suffices to suppress speeding in the future.

Parents can use negative punishment as an effective means of helping children overcome problem behavior. For example, thumbsucking as a frequent and persistent response can cause problems for a child. The thumbsucker is often teased and treated as if somewhat immature. Severe dental problems can result from thumbsucking, too. A study at the University of Vermont using children as old as 6 to 8 years showed that thumbsucking could be totally eliminated by negative punishment.[15] All three children in the study

[15]Knight and McKenzie (1974).

had been persistent thumbsuckers since infancy. The parents used bedtime for 10 to 20 minutes of operant conditioning each day. At first the parents read favorite stories to their children with no regard for whether or not there was thumbsucking (see Figure 2–7, period A). This did not eliminate the undesired behavior. Then a period of negative punishment was initiated. The parent stopped reading when the thumb touched or entered the mouth and only resumed reading when the thumbsucking ceased. There was a *rapid* suppression of thumbsucking in all three girls, as can be seen in the data on 6-year-old Rosie (period B). When the negative punishment was temporarily discontinued and the parent read stories whether or not the child sucked on the thumb, the response reappeared (period C). Reestablishing negative punishment again suppressed the response (period D). Thumbsucking was eliminated in all three children.

DISCONTINUATION OF PUNISHMENT

Punishment does not cause behavior to be "unlearned" or "forgotten." It merely suppresses the frequency of responding. *Often the effects of punishment are only temporary; and when punishment no longer occurs, the rate of responding usually increases.* This phenomenon is called *recovery*. In many cases, previously suppressed behavior completely returns to the frequency it had before punishment began. After the police stop using radar speed checks on a certain stretch of highway, people who used to speed return to their old practices of speeding along that road.

    Recovery is fastest and most complete when the original punishment was mild or infrequent and there is reinforcement for doing the behavior. The milder the original punishment, the sooner a behavior is likely to recover after the end of punishment. For example, if you have a skiing accident that breaks both legs, this intense punishment may suppress skiing permanently, even after your legs are out of the casts. On the other hand, if you merely take a hard fall while skiing down a steep slope, this less intense punishment may keep you off the slope for the rest of the afternoon; but tomorrow you may be ready to try it again. In addition, reinforcement hastens recovery. The more reinforcement there is for a behavior, the sooner and faster the recovery will take place after the end of punishment. People who break both legs in skiing accidents are more likely to return to skiing if there are rewards for doing so: They really enjoy the sport, all their friends ski, they are close to winning in major competitions, or they earn their living skiing. If one person loves to take evening walks and a second person only goes out occasionally at night, who will be back on the streets sooner after a curfew is lifted?

    Jumping off the porch or garage roof in order to fly like a bird is a response that is usually well suppressed in childhood by the punishment of hard falls. Most people make no further attempts at free flight for the rest of their lives. However, there are special circumstances in which soaring like a bird is not followed by punishment—namely, when using a parachute or hang glider. As the parachutist steps to the airplane door for the first jump, there may be some hesitancy—seen as approach-avoidance responses when the novice alternates between approaching the jump point, then stepping back. However, after several successful jumps (without punishment), the parachutist jumps from the plane without any sign of hesitation or avoidance. Jumping from heights is no longer suppressed when the punishment is removed; hence there is a recovery of the response, even though it had been suppressed since childhood.

Mention of any topic that leads to social embarrassment, discomfort, or other aversive consequences will be suppressed by punishment. However, when the topic no longer leads to punishment, recovery effects are likely. For example, people who live or work together often develop joking relationships to help smooth daily interaction. Normally, jokes about people dying, "kicking the bucket," or "croaking" may be part of the acceptable patterns of joking. However, when someone close dies, jokes about death may suddenly be met with cold responses. "That's not funny now, Joe." For the period of time that the death is salient, joking about death is punished and remains suppressed. Eventually, the death recedes far enough into the past that the punishment ceases and there is a recovery in the frequency of joking about croaking.

Cigarette smokers often experience strongly aversive side effects from smoking when they have a serious chest cold or prolonged attack of emphysema. Smoking makes both chest colds and emphysema even more aversive, hence punishes acts of smoking as long as the smokers are sick. However, after the sickness, there are fewer aversive side effects to smoking; and all too often the frequency of smoking behavior returns to previous high levels. This recovery of smoking after temporary suppression is most likely for individuals whose smoking has been followed by high levels of positive reinforcement.

TIMING AND CONTINGENCY OF CONSEQUENCES

Generally, operant conditioning is most likely to occur when reinforcers and punishers follow immediately after an operant.[16] The longer the delay between behavior X and its consequences, the less effect the consequences have on behavior X. In addition, any other responses Y and Z that may have occurred between behavior X and the consequences may be modified instead of behavior X.

There are two qualifications to the above generalization. First, close timing between behavior and reinforcers or punishers does not always produce operant conditioning. Humans and other advanced species are sensitive to the difference between reinforcement and punishment that are the *consequences* of their behavior and those that are not consequences. *Reinforcers and punishers that are not a consequence of a behavior have little ability to produce operant conditioning, even if they follow immediately after the behavior.*[17] If you make a joke about the rainy weather and two things happen—your friend laughs at the joke and a sudden loud thunder clap startles you—one event is a consequence of your joking, and the other is not. Because your friend's laughter is a consequence of your joking, it will reinforce that behavior. However, the timing of the loud thunder clap is purely coincidental (not a consequence of your joking); and it will not suppress your joking, even though equally loud noises serve as punishers when they are consequences of behavior. The noise may startle you, but it does not produce operant

---

[16]Grice (1948a,b); White and Schlosberg (1952).
[17]Killeen (1978); Hammond (1980).

conditioning. In fact, you might keep on joking with your friend: "By Jove, I think someone up there heard us complaining about the weather." *Operant behavior is modified by its consequences; reinforcers and punishers that are not consequences of behavior usually produce little operant conditioning, even if they occur immediately after a behavior.*

When reinforcers and punishers are consequences of a behavior, they are called *contingent* reinforcers and punishers. Contingent reinforcement strengthens behavior. Contingent punishment suppresses behavior. Reinforcers and punishers that are not consequences of behavior are called *noncontingent* reinforcers and punishers. Noncontingent reinforcers and punishers have little ability to produce operant conditioning.

If a salesperson greets a customer in a friendly manner and the customer smiles in return, the customer's smile provides contingent reinforcement for the salesperson's friendly greeting—because it is a consequence of the salesperson's behavior. If the salesperson gives a friendly greeting to a second customer then slips and sprains an ankle, the painful sprain is not likely to suppress the response of making friendly greetings (even though it occurred immediately after it), because the sprained ankle is not a consequence of giving a friendly greeting.

Although the painful sprain does not affect behaviors that did not cause it, it can punish and suppress those behaviors that *did* produce it, such as stepping on round or slick objects lying on the floor. Each behavior is modified by its own consequences—but not by consequences of other behaviors (or by other noncontingent reinforcers and punishers). Thus, close timing of a behavior and a reinforcer or punisher does not assure operant conditioning if the reinforcer or punisher is not a consequence of the behavior in question.

There is a second qualification to the generalization that operant conditioning is most likely to occur when reinforcers and punishers follow immediately after an operant. *Contingent reinforcement and punishment need not be immediate to modify operant behavior: Delayed consequences can cause operant conditioning if a contingent, causal relationship between a behavior and its consequences is detected.* If a salesperson greets a customer in a cheerful manner before starting the regular sales routine, the customer may be more likely to make a purchase 15 minutes later. Even though the delay between the cheerful greetings and increased sales is relatively long, the causal relationship between the behavior and its consequences increases the likelihood that the delayed consequences will reinforce cheerful greetings.

More than any other species, humans are capable of detecting causal relationships between behavior and delayed consequences. Much of this ability to respond to delayed consequences involves complex cognitive mediation. As we reflect back over the events of the past hours, days, or weeks, we often notice the connections between behavior and delayed consequences. *The more frequently and vividly we recall a behavior and its delayed consequences, the more likely the behavior is to be modified.*[18] Reflecting on the numerous good things that happened after taking an impromptu 3-day trip may reinforce making similar short trips at a later time. Thinking about the problems that arose after inviting some people to visit for summer vacation may suppress the response of inviting

---

[18]Mahoney (1974); Bandura (1977); Meichenbaum (1977); Rosenthal and Zimmerman (1978); Schwartz (1984:450*f*).

people for such long stays in the future. Even though there may be a long delay between the original behavior and its contingent consequences, thinking about the behavior and its consequences at about the same time allows us to rehearse the chain of events with little delay between memories of the behavior and memories of its consequences. Thus cognitive rehearsal allows behavior to be associated with immediate and contingent reinforcement or punishment. As people discover causal relationships between behavior and its delayed consequences, they may also make verbal rules—"I ought to take little 3-day vacations several times a year"—and these rules further enhance the effect of delayed consequences (see Chapter 11).

Although the earliest formulations of operant principles stated that operant conditioning is based on *immediate* reinforcement and punishment, there is more to the story. *First,* reinforcers and punishers must be contingent on behavior—that is, be consequences of behavior—to produce much effect. *Second,* if a contingent relationship is detected between behavior and delayed reinforcers and punishers, even delayed consequences can modify operant behavior.

CONCLUSION

Operant behavior is behavior that operates on the environment and is instrumental in producing consequences. The frequency of operant behavior can be modified by (1) reinforcement, (2) discontinuation of reinforcement (extinction), (3) punishment, and (4) discontinuation of punishment. Reinforcers and punishers are the prime movers of operant conditioning. Reinforcement increases the likelihood of a behavior, and punishment decreases the likelihood of a behavior. When a given pattern of reinforcement or punishment is discontinued, the frequency of the operant usually returns to the level it had prior to the beginning of this reinforcement or punishment.

The antecedent cues that best predict that a behavior may produce either positive or negative reinforcement become S^D's—discriminative stimuli for responding. The antecedent cues that best predict that a behavior may produce nonreinforcement or punishment become S^Δ's—discriminative stimuli for *not* responding. Although reinforcers and punishers are more effective when they occur immediately after a behavior rather than after a delay, they are most effective if they are consequences of the behavior—that is, if they are contingent on the behavior. Even delayed consequences can produce operant conditioning if they are contingent and this causal connection is detected.

3

Pavlovian Conditioning

• *In this chapter you will learn how biologically established reflexes—such as sexual responses, emotional responses, and psychosomatic symptoms—function in everyday life, and how they are conditioned during each individual's unique history of life experiences.*

Ivan Petrovich Pavlov (1849–1936) studied biologically established reflexes and the processes by which new stimuli become associated with these reflexes. The type of learning that Pavlov discovered is commonly called *Pavlovian conditioning;* but it is also known as *classical conditioning* and *respondent conditioning.*[1] Pavlovian conditioning affects almost all[2] reflexes—including salivation, eye blinks, the sexual response, emotional responses, and psychosomatic symptoms. *Stated simply, Pavlovian conditioning occurs when a neutral stimulus is paired with a reflex and eventually becomes capable of eliciting reflexive responses.*[3]

RAPID CONDITIONING

For simplicity, we will first consider a type of Pavlovian conditioning that can occur after one pairing of a neutral stimulus and a reflex (even though most Pavlovian

[1]Choice of terminology varies among the various schools of behavioral science. We use the term *Pavlovian conditioning* because this label causes the least confusion for students.

[2]Several reflexes—such as the knee jerk, biceps reflex, Achilles reflex—do not condition (Bijou and Baer, 1965:36).

[3]The research on Pavlovian conditioning is presented in greater detail by Rescorla (1967, 1969, 1980), Rescorla and Wagner (1972), Terrace (1971), Fantino and Logan (1979).

conditioning requires multiple pairings). Various types of rich, diseased, or poisoned food can make a person sick at the stomach and trigger the reflexive responses of nausea and vomiting. It may take only one pairing of a certain type of food with the sickness reflex to condition a strong negative response to that particular food. Such rapid conditioning reflects considerable *biological preparedness* for the conditioning of the sickness reflex.[4] Since avoiding bad food is important for survival, this biological preparedness is easily traced to evolutionary causes: Those who are prepared to learn quickly to avoid bad food have the best chances of surviving.

The rapid conditioning of negative responses to certain foods is common in everyday life. For example, if a friend invites you to a nice restaurant and coaxes you to try the seafood, you may innocently select something too rich for your stomach. When the scallops wrapped in bacon arrive, they look and smell delicious. Fried in bacon fat and smothered with sour cream sauce, they are sweet and succulent. Much to your surprise, one or two hours later your stomach starts complaining. The rich, heavy food was too much for you, and you feel weakness and nausea coming on. After another half hour, you are burping up potent odors, and shortly thereafter everything comes up. Terrible taste! And your stomach does not calm down for another hour.

The rich food triggered a basic reflex that is a part of a biological safeguard system which rejects bad food from the body. Pavlovian conditioning builds from this basic reflex. Each time the sickness reflex is elicited by bad food, the type of food you ate before you got sick becomes associated with the feelings of sickness. The taste, the odor, and even the thought of scallops wrapped in bacon cease to be appetizing stimuli. In fact, the next time you notice scallops on a menu or sit next to someone who orders scallops, you may feel weak in the stomach, perhaps a bit nauseous. Due to Pavlovian conditioning, a new stimulus—scallops—has become associated with the biologically established sickness reflex. The learning experience has established a *conditioned food aversion*—in this case, a dislike for scallops.

Pavlovian conditioning allows each individual to learn the particular foods in his or her environment that trigger the sickness reflex. Someone in California may eat a rich abalone dinner that triggers an intense stomach sickness. For that person, abalone becomes the conditioned stimulus that later causes queasy feelings, whereas scallops cause no aversive feelings. A native in an Amazonian rainforest might become sick after trying a newly discovered red berry, and thus learn a taste aversion associated with that food. We all begin life with the same biologically established reflexes. But Pavlovian conditioning gives us the flexibility to go beyond the biologically determined responses. Each individual's unique life experiences create patterns of conditioning that reflect the person's past history of learning.

Learning allows us to benefit from experience. If you get sick once from a certain food, the conditioned nausea you feel when exposed to that food in the future will help prevent your making the same mistake twice.[5] In some cases—as with poisonous foods—this can make a life-or-death difference. In a study of 517 undergraduates, 65 percent of

---

[4]Breland and Breland (1966); Skinner (1969); Seligman and Hager (1972); Logue et al. (1981).

[5]In this example—and in others in this chapter—there is an interaction between operant and Pavlovian conditioning: The future avoidance of bad food results from operant conditioning. This interplay is common because, in everyday life, operant and Pavlovian conditioning are frequently intertwined (see Chapter 4).

the students had at least one food aversion.[6] Most of these developed several hours after eating a food that caused sickness. The taste of the food was more likely to become the *conditioned stimulus* (CS) for the conditioned aversion than were the appearance or odor of the food. Unfamiliar foods were more likely than common foods to become the CS's for food aversions.

TWO TYPES OF REFLEXES

A reflex consists of a stimulus-response sequence in which the stimulus (S) elicits a response (R).

$$S \rightarrow R$$

A tap on the kneecap elicits a knee jerk. Bad food in the stomach elicits stomach contractions and vomiting. Touch to the genitals elicits the sexual response.

The most basic type of reflex is the biologically established or innate reflex, which is called an *unconditioned reflex* to indicate that no conditioning is involved. In all unconditioned reflexes, only a certain biologically determined stimulus can elicit the reflexive response. This stimulus is called an *unconditioned stimulus* (US) to indicate that no conditioning is needed for this stimulus to elicit the reflexive response. The response that is elicited by the US is called an *unconditioned response* (UR) to indicate that no conditioning is necessary for the production of this response. The unconditioned reflex is the US→UR sequence in the top line of the following figure. A sting or cut on the hand is a US that elicits the UR of rapidly pulling back the hand.

	Before conditioning	Onset of conditioning	During conditioning	After conditioning
1. Innate	US ⟶ UR	US ⟶ UR	US ⟶ UR	
2. Learned		NS	CS ⟶ CR	CS ⟶ CR

The second type of reflex, the *conditioned reflex,* is created through Pavlovian conditioning. All Pavlovian conditioning builds from innate, unconditioned reflexes. Before conditioning, only a US is capable of eliciting a reflexive response (the extreme left panel in the above figure). At the onset of conditioning, a *neutral stimulus* (NS) is paired with the US one or more times (the dotted vertical line in the figure). During conditioning, the neutral stimulus becomes a *conditioned stimulus* (CS) that elicits a *conditioned response* (CR). The conditioned reflex is the CS→CR sequence in the bottom line of the figure. After a conditioned reflex is established, the learned CS→CR sequence can operate even in the absence of the unconditioned reflex (the extreme right panel in the figure).

Pavlovian conditioning occurs when a neutral stimulus is paired with a reflex and

[6]Louge et al. (1981).

becomes a CS capable of eliciting a CR. Before a person develops a conditioned food aversion, only the US of bad food in the stomach can elicit the sickness reflex. After a person eats rich food and becomes sick, the taste of the particular food becomes a CS with the power to elicit reflexive responses of bad feelings in the stomach and nausea. After conditioning, the CS can elicit nausea and bad feelings *before* a person makes the mistake of getting rich food in the stomach (the US) a second time. Thus, CS's contain important information: In the case of food aversions, they serve as warning stimuli that signal danger by eliciting nausea before a person eats a food that has caused sickness in the past.

Although a CS is capable of eliciting a reflexive response, the conditioned response (CR) is not the same as the unconditioned response (UR). Although the CR is often similar to the UR, it sometimes is quite different.[7] *Usually the CR is less intense and slower to appear than the UR, though other differences are possible.* After a person learns a conditioned food aversion, the taste of the food is a CS that elicits the CR of nausea and aversive feelings. This CR is noticeably different from the UR of strong stomach contractions and vomiting. When parents spank a child for running into the street, the painful spanking is a US that elicits tears and crying. Stimuli associated with the spankings— being in the street and seeing father approaching in anger—become CS's that elicit the CR of tears and crying. However, the tears and crying elicited by the CS's are not as intense as those elicited by a painful spanking (the US).

Predictive Stimuli

Which stimuli are most likely to become conditioned stimuli? When a person is in a restaurant eating rich food that will soon trigger the sickness reflex, countless stimuli are present that might become associated with the reflex. Among these are the sounds of background music, sight of the waiter and other people, topics of conversation, and the taste of rich food. Which of these stimuli is most likely to become associated with the sickness reflex? *The stimuli that are most strongly correlated with a US are most likely to become CS's.*

All advanced species are sensitive to correlations between reflexes and the cues that precede them. The antecedent cues that are best correlated with a reflex are most likely to become CS's. In most people's lives, being sick at the stomach is relatively unusual. Eating some novel, rich food—such as scallops wrapped in bacon—stands out as un-usual, too. It is more easily associated with sickness than all the other restaurant stimuli that are not unusual—such as background music, people, and topics of conversation. Stimuli that were commonly present when food did not cause sickness are not likely to become associated with the unusual event of nausea and sickness.

The more highly correlated a CS is with a US, the more information it conveys about the US. This information makes it a *predictive stimulus* that signals that a certain US and unconditioned reflex are about to appear. The taste of rich food is a good predictor that we may get sick if we swallow the food. The background music, people in the restaurant, and topics of conversation are not predictors of possible sickness. A person could go to the same restaurant where a food aversion developed, listen to the same music, and talk about the same topics without getting sick *if* the person simply ordered a

---

[7]Bitterman and Woodard (1976); Holland (1977).

different kind of food. Only the unusual rich food stands out as highly correlated with and predictive of sickness; it is most likely to become the CS for sickness.

Cancer patients who receive chemotherapy often experience nausea and vomiting as a side effect of the strong chemicals used in such therapy. Chemotherapy is the US that elicits unconditioned sickness. After having chemotherapy, some patients begin to experience conditioned nausea and vomiting *before* they come to therapy. Seeing that it is time to go to therapy is a predictive cue that is correlated with chemotherapy (the US), hence the calendar and clock provide the CS's that elicit conditioned illness before therapy begins.[8]

Although people are sensitive to correlations between predictive cues and reflexes, they do not always make the correct associations. For example, cancer patients who receive chemotherapy sometimes develop conditioned aversions to foods that they have eaten before going to therapy. Patients who eat ice cream before their chemotherapy may develop an aversion to ice cream, and they learn to avoid eating ice cream after just one pairing with sickness.[9] Although food is sometimes correlated with sickness, in this case the association is incorrect. The calendar and clock provide better predictive stimuli. Even though wrong stimuli sometimes become CS's for reflexive responses, totally erroneous associations are not too common.

NORMAL CONDITIONING

Most Pavlovian conditioning does not take place as rapidly as the learning of food aversions. *In most cases, a neutral stimulus must be paired with a US on several occasions before it becomes a CS capable of eliciting a noticeable response.*

The sexual response is a reflex that usually conditions at a rate that is typical of most other reflexes.[10] The sexual responses of males and females are biologically established reflexes mediated by the lower spine,[11] and Pavlovian conditioning of these reflexes usually requires several conditioning experiences. Tactile stimulation to the genitals is the unconditioned stimulus that elicits the unconditioned responses of penile erection, vaginal lubrication, and, with sufficient stimulation, orgasm. Thoughts, words, visual images, odors, and a multitude of other stimuli can become sexual CS's that elicit sexual responses (CR's) if those CS's have been paired with the unconditioned sexual reflex (US→UR). However, sexual conditioning—like most other Pavlovian conditioning—usually requires multiple pairings to establish the conditioned reflex.

Most boys learn to masturbate in their early teens.[12] During masturbation, tactile stimulation to the genitals serves as the US that elicits unconditioned sexual responses of

---

[8]The conditioned nausea and vomiting before therapy are not relieved by drugs. However, Pavlovian counterconditioning has proven effective in minimizing the conditioned nausea (Morrow and Morrell, 1982).

[9]Bernstein et al. (1982).

[10]Of all the reflexive responses considered in this chapter, sexual responses and emotional responses are the two types of reflexes that play the most important role in everyday life and social interaction. Because sexual and emotional reflexes are so important in daily life, they will appear in numerous examples throughout the chapter.

[11]Katchadourian and Lunde (1980:87–90).

[12]Kinsey et al. (1948); Hunt (1974); Annon (1975).

penile erection and pleasurable sensations. Pavlovian conditioning enters the picture if other stimuli happen to become paired with the sexual reflex. For example, one afternoon a boy may see a magazine picture of an attractive woman. That night, if the boy masturbates, his thoughts may turn to the visual image of the woman. Because the visual image is being paired with the sexual reflex, it begins to become a conditioned stimulus. After only one pairing, the boy will not notice any marked change when looking at pictures of women in magazines. However, the teenage male will probably use visual images of female bodies on numerous occasions while masturbating, hence there will be multiple pairings of female images and the sexual reflex. As a result of Pavlovian conditioning, the images become CS's that are capable of eliciting a variety of sexual responses—including erection of the penis and pleasurable emotional responses—even in the absence of the US, direct sexual stimulation.[13]

Each individual can learn a unique set of sexual CS's, depending on the person's unique history of Pavlovian conditioning. One woman may have had very positive sexual interactions with a gentle lover; and for her, various images, sounds, and other stimuli present when making love with this man may become sexual CS's. Even thinking about these cues may elicit sexual arousal. A second woman who had come from a background that punished sexual interest or expression might find that she had very few sexual CS's, because she had few chances for the conditioning process to create these CS's. Variations in conditioning are perfectly ''natural'' in the sense that each person will have a unique set of CS's due to the unique conditioning each individual experiences.

Some women use vibrators because the gentle vibrating stimulation is quite effective in eliciting sexual responses, from early excitement all the way to orgasm. Gentle stimulation to the genitals is the US that elicits the unconditioned sexual response (UR). Because the mechanical hum of the vibrator is always paired with the use of the vibrator, it is a predictive stimulus for pleasurable sensations and can become a CS after repeated pairings with the US. After numerous pairings, some women have reported that the vibrator's sound acquires exciting and positive associations for them, as the following case illustrates. Mrs. X had been using a vibrator for several months. One afternoon she happened to be at Mrs. Y's house for a neighborly chat. During the visit, Mrs. Y's daughter came home from school, dropped her books, turned on the electric organ and went out to the kitchen for a soft drink before coming back to play some music. When the organ's electric motor was switched on, Mrs. X noticed its humming sound right away; it sounded familiar and pleasant. As she continued to chat with her neighbor, she began to realize that she was becoming sexually aroused. As the humming sound continued, her sexual excitement built to higher levels. The hum of the organ was similar to the hum of Mrs. X's vibrator, hence the sound was a CS that elicited a conditioned sexual response (CR).

A large number of stimuli can be conditioned to be sexual CS's: sounds, odors, words, thoughts, stimulation to the earlobes, caressing of the neck, and so forth can become conditioned erotic stimuli. For the conditioning to occur, an individual must usually have had repeated experiences in which a stimulus is paired with the unconditioned reflex.

---

[13]Marks et al. (1965); Mees (1966); Marks and Gelder (1967); Tollison and Adams (1979).

People with unusual histories of sexual conditioning are likely to have their sexual response conditioned to unusual CS's. Beyond a certain point, a person's unusual conditioning may strike others as "odd" or "abnormal," but the conditioning process that produces uncommon sexual CS's is the same Pavlovian conditioning that produces "normal" CS's. A history from the clinical literature demonstrates how unusual sexual CS's can be conditioned in the natural environment.[14] Mr. A. came to a therapist because he was afraid that his habit—tying himself up tightly in black shiny rubber and masturbating—was getting out of control. Because he had difficulty in releasing himself recently, he had become afraid that he might die someday if he could not escape his bonds.

When Mr. A. was 17, a group of boys tied a rubber groundsheet over his head and masturbated him. Although the experience was somewhat frightening, it was erotically exciting. Afterward, he often tied himself in black rubber objects while masturbating. As a consequence, being bound with black rubber became a CS with the ability to elicit sexual responses.

During the years that followed, Mr. A. had not made many friends and had not established a sexual relationship. He was often alone, and his masturbatory activities were among the more pleasurable things in his life. The frequent pairing of black rubber objects with the sexual reflex eventually produced conditioning so strong that Mr. A. felt powerless to restrain himself from using black rubber objects.

The therapist attempted to reverse the man's conditioning by pairing black rubber objects with aversive experiences rather than the emotionally positive sexual reflex. This effort to counteract the past positive conditioning is a process called *aversive counterconditioning* (see p. 57). During therapy Mr. A. tied himself with rubber groundsheets and was given a drug that induced nausea. After only a few sessions, Mr. A. lost interest in and discarded his collection of rubber objects. For the first time in years, he began to go out to dances and other social events where he might meet women.

SEVEN DETERMINANTS OF STRONG CONDITIONING

Several variables determine the speed with which Pavlovian conditioning takes place and the strength of a conditioned reflex after conditioning.

First, as the number of pairings of a CS with a US increases, the CS acquires increasing ability to elicit a CR. Except in cases of strong biological preparedness, one pairing of a neutral stimulus with a reflex produces only a small effect. Each additional pairing increases the power of the CS to elicit a CR. After ten pairings with a US, a CS has a stronger effect than after one pairing. The more often a person pairs a certain sexual fantasy with the US's of the sexual reflex, the more power the fantasy will take on (as a CS) to elicit sexual responses. The CS acquires greater power to elicit the CR each time the CS is paired with the US, until maximal conditioning has been reached.

Second, when a CS is always associated with a given US, the CS takes on a greater ability to elicit the CR than if pairing is only intermittent. If a stimulus precedes a US 100 percent of the time, it is much more likely to become a CS than if it preceded the US only

[14]Oswald (1962).

20 or 50 percent of the time. If a woman always wears a certain perfume before making love, and never wears it at other times, the perfume is likely to become a CS that will elicit sexual arousal for her and her husband. If she also wore the perfume while jogging, feeding the dog, and doing other nonsexual activities, the weaker correlation between the perfume and sex would limit its ability to become a CS for sexual feelings.

When multiple *stimuli precede a US, the stimulus that is most highly correlated with the US is most likely to become a strong CS.* The most highly correlated stimulus stands out as most conspicuously associated with the reflex, which facilitates conditioning. If gentle loving words always precede making love but perfumes are only associated with sexual interaction part of the time, the loving words are more likely than perfume to become CS's for erotic feelings. The highly correlated cues are better predictors of sexual pleasures; and they tend to overshadow the less predictive stimuli to become the strongest CS's.

Third, stimuli that are the focus of attention are more likely to become CS's than inconspicuous or unnoticed stimuli. Actions that focus a person's attention on relevant predictive stimuli and minimize the number of distracting or irrelevant cues facilitate the rapid conditioning of effective CS's. When a father sees his child run into a busy street in pursuit of a bouncing ball, the father may rush over and give the child a spanking. The spanking is a US that elicits UR's of crying and painful feelings. Running into the street is one of the stimuli that may become a CS that elicits conditioned fear responses (CR). Without knowing the Pavlovian principles, the father may attempt to maximize the conditioning of the child's fear of running into the street by reducing the distracting and irrelevant stimuli while spanking the child. He may take the ball out of the child's hands, turn the child toward the traffic, and spank the child while saying "You could get killed by those cars." By focusing the child's attention on the traffic in the street (the intended CS) while delivering a painful spanking (the US), the father will help the child learn to fear getting close to the traffic in the street.

Fourth, strong US's produce stronger conditioned reflexes than weak US's do. If a parent gives a child a strong spanking (US), it will produce more conditioned fears than a mild spanking will.

Fifth, a stimulus must occur before—not after—a US for conditioning occurs. If a neutral stimulus occurs *after* the US has appeared, Pavlovian conditioning rarely occurs.[15] Attempts to create "backward conditioning"—in which a neutral stimulus follows a US—almost always fail. It makes sense that we would not have evolved a tendency to associate things in backward causal order.[16] If a person became sick from eating bad food and *afterward* drank some warm broth to soothe the stomach, it is obvious that the broth did not cause the sickness; and it would be maladaptive to associate the soothing broth with the causes of sickness. In Pavlovian conditioning, stimuli that are present shortly *before* a US appears are most likely to become effective CS's.

Sixth, short time lags between the onset of a CS and the onset of a US facilitate Pavlovian conditioning. In the laboratory, intervals of 0 to 5 seconds between the CS and US produce stronger conditioning than do longer intervals. The optimal interval between

---

[15]See Kimble (1961:156f) for a review of the literature on backward conditioning.
[16]Baldwin and Baldwin (1981:86).

the CS and US is often reported to be approximately 0.5 seconds.[17] If a person fantasizes while sexually stimulated, the close temporal pairing of fantasy and sexual stimulation (the US) facilitates the conditioning of the fantasies as CS's that elicit sexual arousal. As the time lag between a predictive stimulus and a US increases, Pavlovian conditioning becomes slower and less effective at producing CS's.

Cognitive processes sometimes allow people to associate a predictive stimulus and US that are normally separated by long time periods.[18] As a person reflects on a series of earlier events, predictive cues and US's that were originally separated by a long time gap may be brought into close temporal and causal association in memory. Repeatedly recalling predictive stimuli and related US's causes the predictive stimuli to become CS's. This type of Pavlovian conditioning is called *covert conditioning,* since the cognitive rehearsal allows conditioning to take place without any overt stimuli or physical actions. Imagine the cognitive experiences of people who were badly burned one night when their house burned to the ground: They had accidentally left the stove on before going to bed, and it had started the fire. As these people repeatedly recall going to bed without checking the stove and the horror of being seriously burned (the US), thoughts of not checking the stove become CS's for anxiety. Even though there was a long time lag between the original act of not checking the stove and the US of being badly burned in the fire, the cognitive rehearsal of the events brings them into close association, and is effective in producing Pavlovian conditioning.[19] After such an accident, people sometimes develop a strong fear of going to bed or leaving the house without checking the stove several times, since not checking the stove is the CS for fears of fire.

Seventh, there are special cases where biological preparedness allows some conditioning to proceed rapidly, with few pairings and with long delays between the CS and US. People's ability to learn food aversions after one bad experience which may involve an hour or more time lag reflects considerable biological preparedness.

COMMON CONDITIONED RESPONSES

Numerous reflexes can be conditioned through Pavlovian conditioning. Table 3–1 lists some of the more common ones. Most of these reflexes are mediated by the autonomic nervous system to maintain internal biological functioning. Conditioned reflexes are created when neutral stimuli are paired with the US's of these unconditioned reflexes.

Several reflexes have to do with *digestion*—such as the salivation reflex studied by Pavlov in the laboratory. The unconditioned salivation reflex is elicited in humans by the presence of food in the mouth. Through Pavlovian conditioning, we learn to salivate when exposed to cues that are regularly paired with food. Seeing a juicy steak put on the table can literally make a hungry person's mouth water. Other digestive reflexes include the sickness reflex discussed earlier, "butterflies in stomach" experienced with tension or

[17]Kimble (1961:156f); Terrace (1971).

[18]Mahoney (1974); Meichenbaum (1977); Bandura (1977); Rosenthal and Zimmerman (1978).

[19]This type of covert conditioning is also called *covert sensitization* (Cautela, 1967; Barlow et al., 1972; Bellack and Hersen, 1977).

TABLE 3–1   A Partial List of Unconditioned Reflexes

US	UR
Digestive system	
food	salivation
bad food	sickness, nausea, vomiting
object in esophagus	vomiting
Reproductive system	
genital stimulation	vaginal lubrication
	penile erection
	orgasm
nipple stimulation	milk release (in lactating women)
Circulatory system	
high temperature	sweating, flushing
sudden loud noise	blanching, pounding heart
Respiratory system	
irritation in nose	sneeze
throat clogged	cough
allergens	asthma attack
Muscular system	
low temperature	shivering
blows, shock, burns	withdrawal
tap on patelar tendon	knee jerk
light to eye	pupil constriction
novel stimulation	reflexive orienting
Infant reflexes	
stroking the cheek	head turning
object touches lips	sucking
food in mouth	swallowing
object in the hand	grasping
held vertically, feet touching ground	stepping

fear, and the loss of control over urination or defecation occurring during extreme fright or anxiety.

There are a number of reflexes in the *reproductive* system. The reflexes of sexual arousal, from early excitement through orgasm, can become conditioned to various stimuli. Mothers who breast-feed their infants sometimes find that the milk letdown reflex (which releases the milk from the ducts to the nipple) is triggered before the baby begins to nurse. Merely seeing the baby reaching for the breast—or thinking about breastfeeding—can become a CS for the mother because it regularly precedes the US of the infant's sucking on the nipple.

The *circulatory* system is involved in numerous responses of the digestive, reproductive, and other systems. For example, exertion increases heart rate and blood flow to the entire body, and sexual stimulation causes vasocongestion in the genital areas.

Circulatory system reflexes can be conditioned independently of other response systems. A strong, pounding heartbeat can result from US's such as startle or sudden pain; and strong heartbeats can be conditioned to numerous CS's during a person's life. The person who has associated precarious heights with painful falls may experience a pounding heart by merely looking down from a high place into a canyon or street. Blushing is a cardiovascular reflex in which blood vessels in the outer layers of the skin open and allow blood to flow to the surface. In times of fright, people with fair complexions turn "white as a ghost." This is blanching, the opposite cardiovascular response from blushing: The capillaries in the outer layers of the skin close, forcing the blood deeper inside, depriving the skin of the ruddy color created by blood near the surface. Both blushing and blanching can become conditioned to a variety of CS's that are paired with the unconditioned reflexes.

Reflexes of the *respiratory* system include coughing, sneezing, hiccups, and asthma attacks. Some psychosomatic illnesses result from Pavlovian conditioning. Conditioned asthmatic responses have been found to be elicited by a broad range of CS's, including perfume, the sight of dust, the national anthem, radio speeches by politicians, elevators, horses, police vans, caged birds, goldfish, waterfalls, and children's choirs.[20] If Senator X happened to give several speeches during hay fever season while Mr. B. was suffering from a series of asthma attacks, the good senator's voice might accidentally become a CS for Mr. B.'s asthmatic response.

Reflexive responses of the *muscular* system include jerking away from sources of pain, jolting to higher muscle tension when startled, and relaxing after taking certain drugs. People who use alcohol to relax after a tense day's work sometimes find that merely pouring their first drink of the evening elicits the sensations of relaxation. (Pouring the drink is a CS because it has been paired with the US's of a drug that elicits relaxation.)

Babies are born with a variety of muscular reflexes which help insure their early survival. For example, the newborn reflexively sucks when objects touch the lips; and this is adaptive because it produces milk from the nipple. After several weeks, this response can be elicited by CS's—such as being moved into a nursing position or held in certain ways—that regularly precede nursing. After two months, the sounds, odors, and patterns of touch that have been associated with nursing become capable of eliciting the sucking responses.[21]

Emotional Responses

Most unconditioned reflexes have an emotional component that is either pleasurable or aversive. The US's that elicit the overt aspects of the sexual response also elicit pleasurable sensations. If a child falls while running down the driveway, the hard blow is a US that elicits tears, crying, and aversive sensations.

When CS's are created via Pavlovian conditioning, they can also elicit emotions if they have been paired with a US that elicits emotions. Fantasies that have been paired with masturbation or sexual relations become CS's that elicit pleasurable feelings. If a child has

[20]See Dekker and Groen (1956).
[21]Brackbill (1960).

had several painful falls while climbing trees or standing on high places, the view from heights becomes a CS that elicits a variety of conditioned responses: such as a pounding heart, fear, and anxiety. As the child steps closer to the edge of a cliff, the number of predictive stimuli associated with painful falls increases, and the child feels even more frightened. The emotional response elicited by a CS is called a *conditioned emotional response* (CER), and it is a subset of the overall conditioned response (CR). Like all conditioned responses, CER's do not directly parallel the unconditioned emotions. Falling to the ground produces pain (the unconditioned emotional response); whereas the view from heights, after being paired with falls, elicits fear and anxiety (the conditioned emotional responses). A couple may regularly light candles in their bedroom before making love. After several pairings, the candlelight may become a CS that not only elicits sexual excitement but also elicits positive CER's, even before any direct physical sexual stimulation occurs. But the conditioned emotional response (CER) to candlelight is clearly different from the unconditioned feelings of making love.

Because CS's are predictive stimuli, CS's associated with US's that have emotional components can elicit pleasant or unpleasant emotions *before* a US appears. For example, a sexy nightgown is a CS that elicits sexual feelings before any other hint of sex arises, if such apparel is a good predictor that sexual pleasures lie ahead. The threat of a spanking is a CS that can make a child cry before anyone even touches the child, if such threats are good predictors that the parents are very likely to give a painful spanking.

Due to Pavlovian conditioning, many of the stimuli that surround us become CS's for either pleasurable or aversive CER's. Seeing a smiling face in the crowd provides a CS that elicits pleasurable feelings. Hearing someone say something crass provides a CS that elicits bad feelings. People may have similar or different emotional responses to any given stimulus, depending on whether their past Pavlovian conditioning with the stimulus has been similar or different. Since many people have had similar experiences with painful falls, many people respond to views from high places as CS's for fear or anxiety. However, people who have learned the skills for mountain climbing or working on tall buildings usually feel little fear when looking down from high places (unless they perceive predictive cues associated with a real risk of falling). The more similar two people's past Pavlovian conditioning in a given situation, the more similar their emotional responses will be to the stimuli in that situation. Two people who have both climbed extensively in the Alps can describe their experiences climbing various peaks and have similar emotional responses, since they had similar histories of Pavlovian conditioning. Since no two people have had exactly the same past learning experiences, no two people have exactly the same conditioned emotional responses to daily events.

New CS's with emotional impact are continually being created by Pavlovian conditioning. For example, when a mother first begins breast-feeding her new baby, the infant's sucking on the nipple is a US that elicits the milk-release reflex and pleasurable sensations for the mother. Through Pavlovian conditioning, the predictive stimuli that precede breast-feeding become CS's that also elicit pleasurable feelings for the mother. Eventually, just seeing the baby tugging at her blouse and trying to reach the nipple is a CS capable of eliciting the milk-release reflex and pleasurable feelings (even before actual breast-feeding begins). Mothers love their infants for a variety of reasons; but those mothers who breast-feed report that the pleasures of breast-feeding enhance their positive feelings toward their babies.

Aversive experiences also give rise to new CS's. When people make embarrassing blunders in social interactions, a variety of situational cues—such as the individuals or touchy topics present at the time—can become CS's that will elicit uncomfortable emotional responses in the future. For example, the next time a student sees the professor who heard the verbal blunder that embarrassed several people in the class, the professor may be a CS that elicits feelings of discomfort and sweaty palms or blushing. Even when talking with a complete stranger, the student may experience discomfort when the touchy topic comes up that caused embarrassment in the past, since the topic is now a CS for aversive feelings. Since people usually avoid CS's associated with negative CER's, it is not uncommon to see individuals steer clear of topics—or people—that have been associated with embarrassment in the past. The people and topics are predictive stimuli that embarrassment could arise again.

Even cognitive stimuli can serve as CS's that elicit CER's. When a mother thinks about breast-feeding, she may experience warm and pleasant feelings. Just thinking about the embarrassment of saying something very inconsiderate or stupid in front of the whole class may elicit uncomfortable feelings.[22]

As people examine the causes for their emotions, they often learn to trace those feelings back to the stimuli—either US's or CS's—that elicited them. It is clear that certain people and touchy topics are CS's for embarrassment and discomfort, whereas smiles and attractive faces are CS's for pleasurable feelings. The eliciting stimuli can come from outside or inside the body. Even thoughts, fantasies, and dreams can be CS's that elicit emotional responses.

The more skillful people become in locating the causal stimuli, the better people can understand their feelings and emotions. Sometimes people search back in their memories trying to discover how they got in a certain mood. Was it the topic of conversation? The mention of an old romance that ended painfully? A pleasant talk with an attractive person of the other sex? As people locate which stimuli elicit which emotions, they often learn to produce desired emotions by selecting US's and CS's that elicit those emotions. When Sonia wants to get into a more positive mood, she may put on a tape of her favorite cheerful music rather than listening to a radio station whose music makes her sad. (For many people, cheerful music is a CS that elicits good feelings.) When people discover that certain thoughts usually make them feel unhappy, they may decide to stop thinking about those things, perhaps turning to activities that can distract their attention from the thoughts that are CS's for unpleasant emotions.

However, it is not always easy to identify and label emotional responses.[23] A

---

[22]For data on the Pavlovian conditioning of thoughts and the ability of thoughts to produce future conditioning, see Staats (1968, 1975) and Mahoney (1970, 1974).

[23]The discrimination and labeling of emotional feelings are learned through operant conditioning from models, rules, prompts, and differential reinforcement (see Chapters 8, 9, 10, and 11). The verbal community usually has difficulty in teaching the individual to label these internal states accurately (Bem, 1970; Skinner, 1974:22f; Baldwin, 1985). Parents cannot see inside their child's skin and determine whether the child is correct or incorrect in discriminating between and labeling various emotional responses; hence they cannot give accurate

person may feel a pounding heart and a lump in the throat but not be able to discriminate whether the feeling is excitement or fear. For example, at a Halloween masquerade party in the hotel ballroom, everyone is playing tricks and joking. Suddenly the fire alarm goes off and the lights go out. Everyone is laughing, and you are too. You notice your heart pounding; but you are not certain if you are frightened or merely excited by the latest surprises of the party. Your decision to label the emotional response as fear or excitement will depend largely on environmental conditions, including the responses of other people. If everyone else laughs and responds to the alarm as a fun prank, you will probably conclude that your emotional response is one of excitement. If several other people show clear signs of fear or panic, you may conclude that your pounding heart is a fear response. People are often influenced by the responses of others when labeling their own emotional responses.[24] Naturally, any evidence that there is or is not a fire in the building will influence your labeling, too.

EXTINCTION

Extinction occurs whenever a CS is present but is not paired with a US. After a person learns skills for climbing mountains without having any painful falls, the person will have many exposures to the CS of views from high places without the US of falls; and this will reduce the power of the CS of views from heights to elicit feelings of anxiety. *When a CS is no longer paired with a US, it gradually loses its ability to elicit conditioned responses; and the conditioned reflex (CS→CR) becomes weaker.* The more often a CS is present without a US, the weaker the conditioned reflex becomes. Eventually the stimulus ceases to elicit a conditioned response.

Extinction occurs naturally at all periods of life. The following examples illustrate the two-phase cycle of conditioning followed by extinction. Figure 3–1 shows the typical development and decline of a conditioned reflex seen during conditioning and extinction. The CS takes on increasing ability to elicit a CR during conditioning, then loses that power during extinction.

Numerous childhood fears that were once very strong disappear due to extinction. Children often learn to be afraid of strangers, hypodermic needles, big dogs, playing in the street, and so forth. If riding into the street on a tricycle is paired with several spankings, being in the street will probably become a CS that elicits fear or anxiety. However, as the years pass and the child gains the skill, coordination, and strength to bikeride safely in the street, the original sources of aversive conditioning are removed.

---

feedback when the child describes internal feelings, and this handicaps the child in learning to describe them accurately. Because socializing agents are handicapped in teaching discriminations and labels about internal feelings, the individual will find it harder to understand things inside his or her body than things outside the body (Skinner, 1969:229f). Note that society relies heavily on external cues in teaching a person to understand his or her emotions. If a child is clearly unhappy, the parents may select either the word "sad" or "jealous" to prompt the child's use of emotional labels, depending on whether the child lost a toy or saw a playmate receive a nicer toy. As a result, the child comes to rely on external cues to understand the otherwise difficult to understand internal feelings. Three hundred years ago, Spinoza realized that the emotions were best understood in terms of external cues (Elwes, 1955:128f); his analysis of emotions is one of the best in the philosophical literature (Wienpahl, 1979:121–127).

[24]White et al. (1981); Baldwin (1985).

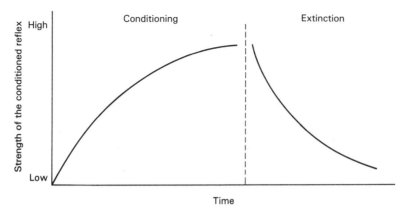

FIGURE 3-1   The typical development and decline of a conditioned reflex seen during conditioning and extinction.

The parents stop reprimanding if their child follows other children into the street, and the child now has the skill to avoid close calls with traffic. The childhood fears extinguish because the CS of bikeriding in the street is no longer paired with aversive experiences. The same extinction usually occurs with fears of other stimuli, such as fires, thunderstorms, being in the dark, or being alone. Thus, it is the process of extinction that allows us to ''outgrow'' childhood fears.

Extinction is not limited to fears and other negative emotional responses. Positive conditioned reflexes and nonemotional conditioned reflexes extinguish, too, if no longer paired with their original US's. When babies breast-feed, the breasts become CS's that elicit pleasurable feelings for the baby due to pairing with the US's of food and physical contact. Merely seeing the breasts before nursing can elicit a smile and positive CER's from a child who is being nursed. When mother ceases breast-feeding, the extinction process begins. At first the child may still look to mother's breasts and pull her blouse to reach them, indicating that the breasts are still CS's for pleasure. However, after breast-feeding has ended, the breasts are no longer associated with the US's of nursing and they gradually cease to elicit pleasurable CER's.

Similar cycles of conditioning and extinction occur at other times in life. When a couple's home is destroyed by a fire which was started by their accidentally leaving the stove on, they become conditioned to fear making mistakes that can cause fire. Leaving the house or going to bed without checking the stove are CS's that elicit fear. After this conditioning, they may be very careful with the stove and other appliances for months or years. However, as time passes and they have no more accidents with fires, the extinction process begins to reduce the strength of the CS's for fearing fire because these CS's are no longer paired with accidents. Gradually, the CS's lose their ability to elicit fear, and the couple becomes less worried about fire than they were in the months immediately after their house burned. (However, occasional memories of the fire produce enough *intermittent reconditioning* to prevent the fear of fire from totally disappearing. Intermittent reconditioning helps explain why some conditioned reflexes never completely disappear after the onset of extinction.)

Many Americans have eaten fattening foods since childhood. Through years of Pavlovian conditioning, the sight, odor, and thought of spare-ribs, bacon, sausage, and other fattening foods become CS's capable of eliciting salivation and pleasurable anticipation when sitting down to eat. After the doctor tells an overweight patient to switch to a low-fat diet and the person makes this change, the conditioned responses to high-calorie foods are put on extinction. When a person sees friends eating fattening foods at a restaurant, the sight, odor, and thought of these foods is no longer paired with the pleasures of eating them; and the CS's provided by these foods gradually lose their power to elicit conditioned responses. Several years later, a once-fat person may find it hard to believe that these foods were so appetizing that merely thinking about them would elicit pleasurable anticipation.

Spontaneous Recovery

Although extinction weakens conditioned reflexes, conditioned reflexes regain some of their strength during periods between extinction experiences, due to a process that Pavlov called "spontaneous recovery."[25] Whereas conditioning takes place when a CS is paired with a US and extinction takes place when a CS appears without its US, spontaneous recovery occurs during periods after extinction—when the CS is not present at all. If a person is afraid of heights, a 2-week vacation spent hiking in the mountains provides extinction experiences that help diminish those fears. However, during the months between this year's vacation and next year's vacation, spontaneous recovery will occur. When the person returns to the mountains 12 months later, there will be a *partial* recovery of the fears—a spontaneous recovery that requires no additional conditioning. The person will feel more fear on the first day of the second year's hiking than at the end of the first year's hiking, showing a partial recovery of fears. However, the person will feel less fear than at the beginning of the first year, because spontaneous recovery does not return a conditioned reflex to the full pre-extinction level.

Spontaneous recovery occurs with positive emotional reflexes and nonemotional reflexes, too. When a mother ceases breast-feeding, she causes the child's positive conditioned responses to the breast to be extinguished. Each time the child reaches for the breasts and is not allowed to nurse, the positive conditioned responses become weaker. If there is a pause of several days in which the child cannot reach for the breasts—because the mother is away or is too busy to spend much time with the child—there will be spontaneous recovery of the positive conditioned responses, and the child will show a stronger positive response to the breasts after the pause than before.

Avoidance Retards Extinction

Extinction occurs whenever a CS is present but is not paired with a US. *If a person avoids contact with a CS, extinction cannot take place.* What happens if one person with a fear of skiing due to past falls hires a good ski instructor but another person with the same fear totally avoids skiing? The person who receives instruction and learns to ski without falling finds that the fears of skiing extinguish but the person who avoids skiing does not.

---

[25]Pavlov (1927:58f).

Good instruction hastens extinction by pairing the CS's that elicit fears of skiing with the neutral stimuli of "no falls," "no pain," and "no problems." Of course, the person feels frightened the first few times the instructor requires practice on skis, because being on skis provides the CS's that elicit the CER's of fear and trembling legs. But good instruction helps the person learn to ski without falling, and this assures that the CS's of skiing are no longer paired with the US's of painful falls. This causes the conditioned fears to extinguish, and eventually being on skis will not elicit fear.

On the other hand, the person who avoids ski instruction is avoiding the opportunity to have the CS's associated with skiing to occur in the absence of falls. Thus, extinction cannot take place. Because avoidance prevents extinction, the CS's will retain their power to elicit fear. The avoidance response may prevent this second person from ever getting on skis again; whereas the first person may eventually learn to ski well and enjoy it.

Some people go to great lengths to avoid CS's that elicit fear, and their avoidance patterns can persist for years since they never have the extinction experience needed to neutralize the CS's. For example, people who fear flying in airplanes often suffer considerable inconvenience as they resort to trains, buses, or cars for long trips that would have been much easier by air. Children sometimes learn conditioned fears of authority figures (the CS) if authority figures—the principal, the police, and the minister—are distant, powerful, and frightening sources of punishment or threat. Those children who avoid interacting with authority figures as they grow up often retain their fears of such people well into adulthood. Twenty-five years later when they must contact the principal because their own 8-year-old is having trouble in the third grade, they may experience emotional discomfort because their old childhood fear has never had a chance to extinguish. Only after they are forced to interact with the feared authority figure can extinction begin to neutralize their lingering childhood conditioning. (It is surprising how many people carry childhood fears well into adulthood—if not all through life—even though those fears are irrational in light of their adult skills and experience.)

Conditioned fears and anxieties are less likely to extinguish naturally than are conditioned pleasures. The reason is simple: CS's that elicit fear motivate the avoidance responses that retard extinction; whereas this is not true of CS's that elicit pleasure. The person with a conditioned fear of speaking up in groups is likely to avoid the feared behavior, which prevents the fear from extinguishing. Because CS's for pleasurable emotions are not avoided, extinction can occur once these CS's cease to be paired with pleasurable experiences. The baby who has been breast-fed for months responds to the breasts as CS's for pleasurable feelings. Once the mother decides to stop breast-feeding, extinction begins as soon as the infant tries to nurse. Since nursing is pleasurable, the child does not avoid nursing. Instead, the child attempts to nurse, which ensures that extinction will begin, because the CS's of seeing and touching the breasts are no longer paired with the US's of nursing. Thus, the extinction of pleasurable associations is not retarded by avoidance responses.

Therapeutic Extinction. Some people have persistent fears that bother them for years because strong avoidance responses prevent extinction. One form of behavior therapy designed to reduce such fears involves extinction. *Therapeutic extinction takes place when a person confronts fear-inducing CS's in a safe environment that is free of other* *types of aversive stimuli.* As the person experiences the feared CS's in the absence of other aversive stimuli, the CS's lose their power to elicit fear. Consider the case of a man who had developed a fear of opening and walking through doors after a series of traumatic conditioning experiences during World War II.[26] While behind enemy lines, he had received a tip that in a nearby house a group of German soldiers wanted to surrender. He suspected a trap. As he approached the doorway—which was deep in shadow under a balcony—his apprehension rose. Finally, he burst through the door to be startled by the sight of twelve enemy soldiers waking from a night's sleep. He captured them and stood guard over them for 10 stressful hours, until he could take them in after dark. He was forced to kill one of the prisoners who was goading the others to attack him, and the man he shot "died horribly in the no-man's land between us." This experience and several other battle traumas caused the man a great deal of anxiety and guilt associated with bursting into dangerous situations. The fright and guilt were so intense that he became fearful of opening doors. Soon he learned to avoid doors—the fear-inducing CS's— although this severely restricted his activities. Therapy consisted of repeated extinction experiences in which the man stopped avoiding the fear-inducing CS's of opening doors: As he practiced his most feared behavior—bursting through a closed doorway—in the safe therapeutic environment, the conditioned fear began to extinguish. After each session he felt less fear and guilt about opening doors, and at the end of five sessions the extinction was complete. His irrational fears did not reappear.

Many childhood or irrational fears can be overcome by repeatedly confronting the feared CS in a context that is basically neutral or nonthreatening, so that extinction can take place.

HIGHER ORDER CONDITIONING

After a stimulus is paired with a US and conditioned into a CS, this first CS can condition other stimuli into conditioned stimuli, in the absence of the original US. The process of using one CS to create another CS (without reintroducing the US) is called higher order conditioning.

In the first three sections of Figure 3–2, a stimulus (S_1) is paired with a US (dotted vertical lines) and becomes a conditioned stimulus (CS_1). The last two frames show secondary (or higher order) conditioning, as a second stimulus (S_2) becomes the CS_2 by being paired with the CS_1 alone. The US is not present in higher order conditioning, the last two frames. After the second conditioned reflex ($CS_2 \rightarrow CR_2$) is established, it can be used to condition a third stimulus (S_3) into a conditioned stimulus (CS_3). This is third order conditioning. Laboratory data indicate that fourth order conditioning is either unlikely or rare. The US→UR is the basic biological reflex from which all Pavlovian conditioning is built. The CS_1 is never as strong as the US in eliciting a response. The CS_2 produces a weaker response than the CS_1, and the CS_3 is still weaker in producing a response.

[26]Little and James (1964).

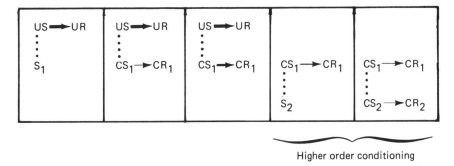

Higher order conditioning

FIGURE 3-2 In higher order conditioning, the CS_2 is created by being paired with a CS_1 (without the US being present).

The reasons that higher order conditioning is not as strong as first order conditioning are simple. First, the US from which all Pavlovian conditioning takes its strength is not present in higher order conditioning. Second, the higher order CS's are being conditioned from other CS's *which are on extinction* because they are not being paired with their original conditioning stimuli.

Higher order conditioning might be involved in a young child's learning to respond to the cues that are predictive stimuli—or warning signals—associated with spankings. If a parent is about to spank a child for running into the street or pulling dishes off the table, there is a good chance that a raised hand or scolding finger precedes the actual spanking. The spanking provides the US that elicits pain, and the raised hand or scolding finger becomes a CS_1 for fear and crying because of its direct pairing with the US. Many young children immediately desist from obstreperous behavior as soon as they see the hand or finger gestures which are closely associated with and predictive of spankings.

Next, a second stimulus can be paired with the CS_1 via second order conditioning. While presenting the CS_1 of a raised hand, the parent may say "No, Freddie," in a tone of voice that differs from normal conversation. Even before the child can understand the language, "No, Freddie" can become a CS_2 via second order conditioning. As Freddie reaches to pull a coffee cup off the end table, "No, Freddie" elicits fear and suppresses the response to some degree. If Freddie turns to look at his father, the father may well be wagging his finger (the CS_1), which elicits a stronger fear response and strengthens the second order conditioning of the CS_2 ("No, Freddie"). Note that the US of spanking was not present.

Third order conditioning is possible if yet another stimulus is brought into use. Some parents use very subtle cues to warn their children of impending discipline: a firm squeeze on the shoulder, clearing the throat, or giving a steady stare. If any of these is paired regularly with the CS_2 ("No, Freddie"), the new cue can become a CS_3 via third order conditioning. If the parents are consistent in using the cue, the steady stare or cleared throat can suppress the undesired behavior and elicit fear.

Higher order conditioning is not limited to reflexes with aversive emotional components. Both positive and nonemotional reflexes can become conditioned to higher order stimuli. The nursing mother who gets pleasure from seeing the baby reaching for the nipple (CS_1) might develop a CS_2 of talking about breast-feeding with friends, if talking is paired with the CS_1 of the infant's trying to reach the breast.

Multiple Order Conditioning

In everyday life, conditioning rarely occurs in the neat 1, 2, 3 order of pure higher order conditioning (although this neat order can be attained in the laboratory). Instead, neutral stimuli may become CS's due to a few direct pairings with a US, then several associations with a CS_2, and perhaps some coincidental pairings with CS_1's and CS_3's. These multiple conditioning experiences strengthen the CS, although they are not pure cases of first order, second order, or third order conditioning. A person's fear of heights may result from some childhood falls (US's), verbal warnings about falling (CS's), and numerous other CS's that elicit fears associated with broken bones, emergency rooms, big hypodermic needles, and so forth. We will call this *multiple order conditioning* to indicate that first, second, and third order processes can be mixed together in any combination.

Multiple order conditioning is quite common in everyday life. For example, people often rely on multiple order conditioning when trying to persuade others that a given activity or cause is good or bad. In trying to convince someone that jogging is a great activity, the jogger may list all sorts of positive things associated with running: It is invigorating, it makes you healthy, it helps you lose weight, it makes you feel stronger and more independent, and on and on. Many of these words are CS's that elicit positive feelings in the listener; but it would be unlikely that all were pure CS_1's or pure CS_2's. In almost all cases, words such as "good health" and "invigorating" have become CS's for positive emotions due to a multitude of different conditioning experiences with many US's and CS's. The ability of the words "good health" or "invigorating" to elicit positive feelings in the listener depends less on whether they are pure CS_1's or pure CS_2's than on the fact that they have had multiple pairings with all sorts of US's and CS's that elicit positive feelings. The more successful the jogger is in using words that elicit positive feelings in the listener, the more likely the listener is to be persuaded that jogging is good. The listener's new positive feelings about jogging result from multiple order conditioning.

Pamphlets for people who are trying to stop smoking describe numerous aversive conditions associated with smoking: the black and damaged lungs, the discomfort of being out of breath, the dangers of being out of shape, the suffering of the emphysema victim, the agony of lung cancer, the lonely children left without a parent, and so forth. Most of these words are CS's based on multiple order conditioning from many different types of US's and CS's. The multiple and redundant conditioning of these words as CS's for uncomfortable feelings increases the chances that they may persuade the reader that the dangers of cigarette smoking outweigh the pleasures.

Often the CS's produced by multiple order conditioning are quite strong and generalized because they have gained strength from many sources in a variety of different contexts. For example, the words "youth" and "vigor" almost always carry positive connotations because they are usually CS's for pleasurable feelings. This positive effect can be traced to multiple order conditioning from many different kinds of pleasant experiences associated with youth and vigor. (This important effect will be discussed further in Chapter 7 on generalized conditioned reinforcers.)

COUNTERCONDITIONING

Once a CS has been conditioned to elicit a certain response, this CS can be paired with a US or CS that elicits a different and incompatible response. This is *counterconditioning*. The second conditioning counteracts the effects of the first conditioning by combining (1) *extinction* (since the original CS is no longer paired with the stimuli from which it was originally conditioned) and (2) *new conditioning* (in which the CS is paired with the new US's or CS's that elicit responses incompatible with the old ones). Counterconditioning occurs in everyday experience and is also a central procedure in behavior therapy.

In everyday life, people's responses are often conditioned one way at one age, then conditioned another way at a later time. The small child may be knocked down several times by a big dog and learn to fear dogs. Dogs become fear-eliciting CS's due to association with painful falls. What happens if the child makes a new friend who loves dogs, has two affectionate beagles, and often has the dogs around while the children are playing together? The child who once feared dogs may find the fears disappearing.[27] Playing with the friend elicits positive emotions that counteract the fears the child originally had in the presence of dogs. At first the child may be apprehensive when the two dogs are nearby; but slowly the fear-eliciting CS's are counterconditioned by (1) the absence of aversive stimuli and (2) the presence of positive stimuli arising from social play. After playing several times in the presence of the dogs, the child's earlier fears will disappear. If the child has additional positive experiences around the dogs, the conditioning can continue even further, such that dogs become CS's for pleasurable emotions. Perhaps the children take the dogs along on a picnic, and have fun throwing sticks for the dogs to retrieve. Because fun and games are paired with the presence of the dogs, the dogs eventually become CS's that elicit warm, positive feelings; and the child may ask to have a dog for a pet.

Counterconditioning can work in the other direction, too. Some men are socialized to respond to powerful cars and fast driving as CS's for thrills and excitement. Just seeing an ad for a sleek, fast sports car and thinking about racing it at high speed can provide enough CS's to elicit a surge of excitement. These positive associations with speed can be counterconditioned if speed is paired with sufficiently aversive events. After a man's first nearly fatal accident while driving fast, the CS's of speed may be counterconditioned to the point that the man no longer enjoys fast driving; and after a second major accident several months later, speeding may be completely counterconditioned to a CS that elicits uncomfortable feelings. The rate of counterconditioning is influenced by the number of positive and negative stimuli present during counterconditioning. A professional driver—with fame, publicity, prize money, and a very rewarding lifestyle all centered around racing—might experience so much positive conditioning from these multiple sources that two accidents could not tip the balance toward the negative side. A teenager whose peer group lived and breathed cars, speed, racing, and thrills might also have so many positive social experiences paired with racing that two near misses with death would not tip the balance. However, many people would become quite apprehensive about fast driving after

[27]Bandura et al. (1967).

one serious accident and, after the second accident, would experience considerable anxiety when the speedometer pushed toward the high numbers.

Therapeutic Counterconditioning

In behavior therapy, counterconditioning is commonly used to change people's conditioning to CS's that elicit unwanted emotional responses. *Systematic desensitization* is the procedure used to countercondition CS's that elicit troublesome fears and anxieties; and *aversive counterconditioning* is the procedure for reconditioning CS's that elicit problematic positive emotions. In both cases, the CS is paired with stimuli that elicit opposite and incompatible emotions.

Systematic Desensitization. *People can overcome fears and anxieties by first pairing those CS's that elicit mild anxiety with stimuli that elicit relaxation and other pleasurable feelings, then gradually repeating this with CS's that elicit higher and higher levels of fear and anxiety when they feel comfortable doing so.* This process is called *systematic desensitization.* Although this process is usually done by imagining the fear-inducing CS's while relaxed, real-life exposure to the feared CS's in safe contexts tends to produce more effective counterconditioning.[28]

A common fear is that of speaking up in a group of strangers—such as in a classroom, a PTA meeting, or a public gathering. People with this fear have opinions or questions; but every time they are about to raise their hand, their heart begins to pound, a lump comes to their throat, they fear being criticized, and they cannot bring themselves to venture a single word. There are many possible causes for the fear of speaking in groups of strangers: having been criticized when asking questions in earlier school years, experiencing embarrassing failures when speaking to groups in the past, and so forth. Aversive experiences can make speaking up in a group a CS that elicits anxiety.

There are a variety of ways therapists can help countercondition this fear of public speaking. First, the client is taught relaxation skills, because relaxation is incompatible with fear and nervousness; then counterconditioning can begin, by pairing mildly fear-inducing stimuli with the incompatible responses of relaxation. The client may be given a series of exercises to carry out: At first the client practices relaxing and speaking in small groups of friends, then in larger groups of friends. Eventually the client is ready to relax and talk in small groups of strangers and finally in even larger groups of strangers. The exercises are done in a series of gradual steps—the client may take weeks or months to overcome the fears of one experience before going on to the next step. After getting used to small groups of strangers, the client may be encouraged to volunteer for a job that involves talking with strangers in public. A person could volunteer to be the receptionist at a local clinic, to do door-to-door canvassing, or anything else that (1) involves contact with strangers, and (2) is fairly easy, safe, and rewarding. The client's fears are counterconditioned by relaxation and eventually by the positive rewards of successful interaction. This process systematically desensitizes the person to prior fears. Speaking up in front of

---

[28]Goldstein and Kanfer (1979).

strangers—a CS that once elicited fear—may eventually become a CS that elicits pleasure.

Aversive Counterconditioning. *When CS's that elicit problematic positive emotions are paired with aversive stimuli, they gradually lose their attractiveness and become either neutral or aversive.* This process is called *aversive counterconditioning.* This type of behavior therapy is used with people who have strong attractions to activities that are self-defeating, dangerous, or socially unacceptable, such as drug abuse, incest, pedophilia, and compulsive behavior. For example, compulsive gamblers have a history of positive associations with gambling, which causes many facets of the gambling experience to become CS's that elicit pleasurable feelings. As a result, some gamblers cannot stop gambling even if they are losing and deeply in debt. This compulsive behavior can destroy their marriages, endanger their jobs, and sometimes lead to stealing as a way of raising money. Aversive counterconditioning can be used to remove the strong positive associations with gambling and make it either neutral or unattractive to the person. For example, compulsive gambling has been treated by pairing electric shock with the objects and behaviors that are commonly involved in gambling. One man who lost each week's paycheck to the one-armed bandits was given shocks during all phases of playing—from inserting the coin to seeing the outcome—until all aspects of playing the slots became CS's that elicited uncomfortable feelings.[29] Another man who gambled compulsively on the horses received shock while fantasizing about gambling, selecting his horse from the daily paper, watching the horse races on TV, and so forth. The counterconditioning ended successfully when the gambler ceased to find gambling positive.[30]

Generally, aversive counterconditioning is considered only a stopgap method that must be coupled with other therapy to have lasting success.[31] Once an inveterate alcoholic is "cured" by pairing alcohol with aversive experiences, what is to prevent the person from becoming reconditioned such that alcohol is once again a CS for pleasurable feelings, as it was before treatment? When alcoholics leave therapy and return to their everyday lives, they may begin to drink a second time due to conditioning experiences like those that produced the original alcohol problem. An unhappy marriage, a depressing job, a group of buddies who like to haunt the local bars, or a multitude of other factors can create situations that recondition alcohol to be a CS with pleasurable associations as effectively as the therapist had counterconditioned it.[32] To help the ex-alcoholic avoid becoming reconditioned to love alcohol, the therapy must go beyond aversive counterconditioning. Marriage counseling may be needed to solve family problems so the client can begin to enjoy coming home at night without having to get drunk first. Helping the ex-alcoholic find a more gratifying occupation could solve problems resulting from an underpaid or monotonous job. Getting the person into an athletic group, community

[29]Barker and Miller (1966).

[30]Goorney (1968).

[31]Bandura (1969:509).

[32]People faced with aversive situations—e.g., an unhappy marriage, a high pressure job—may discover that alcohol can bring relaxation and decrease aversive sensations. The reduction of aversive stimulation reinforces their further use of alcohol and conditions alcohol into a CS with pleasurable associations.

activity, service club, or engrossing hobby may help fill the hours that used to spiral downhill from boredom to booze to stupor.

CONCLUSION

Pavlovian conditioning builds from unconditioned reflexes in which an unconditioned stimulus (US) elicits an unconditioned response (UR). When a neutral stimulus precedes the US and is well correlated with the appearance of the US, this predictive stimulus becomes a conditioned stimulus (CS) that elicits a conditioned response (CR). Seven determinants of strong conditioning are presented. In everyday life, some of the most conspicuous examples of reflexes and Pavlovian conditioning involve sexual responses, psychosomatic responses, feelings, and emotions. Conditioned responses are weakened during extinction, in which a CS is present without the stimuli from which it gained its strength. However, extinction may not take place if a person avoids the CS, which occurs commonly with feared CS's. Higher order conditioning occurs when a CS is created after being paired with another CS (rather than with a US). Counterconditioning reverses the conditioning of a CS by pairing the CS with stimuli that elicit different and incompatible effects. Extinction and counterconditioning appear naturally in everyday life and are used extensively in behavior therapy.

The next chapter demonstrates how operant and Pavlovian conditioning intertwine. Subsequent chapters show how social learning experience—from models, rules, and prompts—adds further complexity to human behavior.

4

Operant and Pavlovian Conditioning Together

● *In this chapter you will learn how operant and Pavlovian conditioning are intertwined throughout much of everyday life.*

In everyday life, operant and Pavlovian conditioning frequently occur together and interact, as we will illustrate later in this chapter. But first, let us contrast the two forms of conditioning.

DIFFERENCES BETWEEN OPERANT AND PAVLOVIAN CONDITIONING

The two types of conditioning have similarities as well as differences. In order to minimize confusion in distinguishing the two, we will briefly examine several major differences between operant and Pavlovian conditioning.[1]

1. The Role of Reflexes. *Pavlovian conditioning builds from reflexes, whereas operant conditioning need not.*[2] In Pavlovian conditioning, a conditioned reflex can be established only if there is a prior reflex (conditioned or unconditioned) from

[1]For a discussion of the differences and similarities between the two, see Terrace (1971), Millenson and Leslie (1979), Schwartz (1984).

[2]Although operant conditioning *need not* build from reflexes, it has been shown that reflexes can be modified by operant conditioning (Miller, 1969, 1978; DiCara, 1970).

which to build. Ultimately, all conditioned reflexes (CS→CR) depend on biologically wired-in unconditioned reflexes (US→UR) for their strength; and, during extinction, all conditioned reflexes cease to appear if isolated long enough from unconditioned reflexes.

Operant behavior is not dependent on reflexes. Operant behavior is much more modifiable than reflexive behavior. It can be shaped into varied forms, whereas reflexes, even conditioned reflexes, are relatively constrained by the biological makeup of the species. There are countless variations on the operants of sexual foreplay; but the reflexive responses of the penis and the vagina are relatively invariant, no matter whether elicited by US's or CS's.[3] The operant activities of cooking and dining can be performed in innumerable ways, but salivation and other digestive reflexes are relatively invariable.

An important difference between reflexive and operant behavior is that reflexes are *elicited* and operants are *emitted*. Both US's and CS's have the power to elicit reflexive responses: When an eliciting stimulus is present, it triggers a reflexive response. However, S^D's do not elicit operant behavior: They merely set the occasion for the operant— which may or may not be emitted, depending on prior patterns of reinforcement and other variables.

2. The Internal-External Continuum.[4] *Reflexive responses usually function in maintaining the smooth operation of internal bodily processes, whereas operant behavior is usually instrumental in affecting the external environment.* There is actually a continuum from internal to external, and the boundaries of operant and Pavlovian conditioning overlap in the gray areas between the extreme types; but the majority of reflexive and operant responses differ in their internal or external orientations.

For the most part, reflexive responses facilitate the functioning of internal bodily processes. Bad food is vomited out and, through conditioning, the food becomes a CS that elicits enough nauseous feelings to keep people from eating the food in the future. Reflexive responses are usually mediated through the involuntary (autonomic) nervous system and the smooth muscles. It is true that a person can gain voluntary control over bodily functions via special operant biofeedback training; but most people cannot voluntarily induce vomiting, sexual arousal, heart rate changes, blushing, or other reflexive responses (except by exposing themselves to an appropriate US or CS).

On the other hand, operant behavior is generally oriented to the outside environment (rather than to maintaining the body's internal economy). Operant behavior is usually instrumental in coping with external events. Operants are typically under voluntary control, involving the skeletal muscles (rather than the smooth muscles). Thus, it is easy for a person to control the operant facial gestures of smiling or lifting the eyebrows, but more difficult to control the involuntary muscles in the blood vessel walls which cause blushing or blanching.

3. The Role of Reinforcers. *Although reinforcement is necessary for operant conditioning, it is not needed for Pavlovian conditioning.* This is seen in the following diagrams of Pavlovian and operant conditioning.

---

[3]Masters and Johnson (1966).
[4]Skinner (1938:112; 1953:113–115); Terrace (1971).

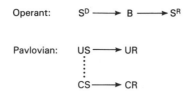

Reinforcing stimuli (S^R) are essential for the acquisition and maintenance of operant behavior (on line 1 of the diagram). Reinforcing stimuli strengthen behavior and cause antecedent stimuli to become S^D's. In contrast, the reflexes that are involved in Pavlovian conditioning operate without reinforcement (lines 2 and 3). The unconditioned reflex (line 2) is biologically wired in and does not need reinforcement to function. Pavlovian conditioning occurs when a predictive stimulus is paired with the US and becomes a CS (line 3). Reinforcement is not necessary for producing Pavlovian conditioning or for the functioning of the conditioned reflex. Therefore, reinforcers (S^R) do not appear in either line of the diagrams of Pavlovian conditioning.

The sexual reflex can be triggered by stimulation to the genitals (the US)—without the need of any reinforcement. If fantasies are paired with the sexual reflex, the fantasies can become CS's that elicit sexual feelings, again without any reinforcement needed. However, reinforcement is essential for acquiring the operant skills related to sexual behavior: Sexual activities that produce pleasurable experiences and positive feedback from a partner are more likely to be repeated than are behaviors that produce unrewarding effects.

4. The New Thing Which Is Learned. *In Pavlovian conditioning, a person learns to respond to a new stimulus as a CS that elicits a reflexive response.* Over the years, a person may become sick from eating unusual foods on several occasions. Each time this happens, a new food becomes a CS for nausea and a food aversion. While the conditioned response of nausea is not new, each new food that becomes a CS capable of eliciting the conditioned response is new.

In operant conditioning, people learn new behavior patterns. Reinforcement and punishment modify the form and frequency of behavior patterns. This is markedly different from Pavlovian conditioning, in which the reflexive response patterns are relatively fixed. Both the form and the frequency of all operant behaviors needed for preparing food can change in countless ways over the years; but the reflexes elicited by food (for example, salivation and digestion) remain relatively unchanged all through life.

OPERANT AND PAVLOVIAN CONDITIONING INTERTWINED

Although it is possible to distinguish analytically between the two forms of conditioning (as we have just done), in everyday life operant and Pavlovian conditioning are frequently intertwined.[5] Let us examine several ways in which the two forms can occur together.

---

[5]There has been a growing awareness of the importance of studying the interactions between operant and Pavlovian conditioning (Teitelbaum, 1977; Schwartz and Gamzu, 1977; Schwartz, 1984).

1. Pavlovian Conditioning as a By-Product of Operant Conditioning. *Operant conditioning often produces some Pavlovian conditioning as a side effect.*[6] (Pavlovian conditioning can occur, of course, without operant conditioning.) The Pavlovian conditioning of emotional responses is generally the most visible of these side effects of operant conditioning.[7] During operant conditioning, the reinforcers and punishers can function as stimuli that elicit emotional responses. After these emotions have been elicited several times by the reinforcers or punishers, stimuli that are regularly associated with the reinforcers or punishers will become CS's that can elicit emotional responses due to Pavlovian conditioning. Thus, both the S^D and *behavior* that precede reinforcers or punishers can become CS's for emotional responses. In the future, merely noticing the S^D or doing the behavior provides the CS's that elicit emotions.

When a child is about to stick a knife into an electric toaster to fish out a crumbling piece of raisin bread, a parent may shout "NO!" and threaten to punish the child. The parent is actually trying to use verbal punishment to suppress the operant behavior of sticking metal objects into the toaster, and this may succeed if verbal threats have been followed by stronger forms of punishment in the past. In addition, there is a Pavlovian side effect: The stimulus of "knife-in-toaster" becomes a CS that elicits anxiety due to pairing with the threat of punishment. In the future, the CS of "knife-in-toaster" may elicit emotions of fear or apprehension even if the parent is not present to threaten punishment.

If a person receives generous positive social reinforcement for a behavior, not only does the frequency of the operant behavior increase, the activity becomes a CS that elicits pleasurable feelings, due to Pavlovian conditioning. After repeated learning experiences, merely engaging in the behavior (even in the absence of social reinforcers) generates the CS's that elicit pleasant emotional responses. Some people write poetry, play music, or play basketball "for the sheer joy of it." The behavior seems to arise from internal motivation, because merely doing the behavior produces pleasure. One aspect of the pleasure that provides internal motivation can be traced to Pavlovian conditioning: The behavior became a CS that elicits pleasure because it has been paired with positive reinforcement and pleasurable experiences in the past.[8]

Although Pavlovian conditioning regularly occurs as a side effect of operant conditioning, the opposite need not be true. Pavlovian conditioning can take place without operant conditioning occurring as a side effect. When a person watches a play, movie, or TV program, Pavlovian conditioning occurs if the stimuli elicit emotional responses. By the second scene of a play, various features of each performer have become CS's, depending on the emotions aroused in the observer during the first scene. Thus, the viewer may come to "love" or "hate" certain characters in the play, yet the experience *may* have no effect on operant behavior.

2. CS's that Elicit Emotions Can Reinforce or Punish Operant Behavior. *Any stimulus that becomes a CS through Pavlovian conditioning can function as a reinforcer*

---

[6]Staats (1975:87).

[7]The Pavlovian side effects are not restricted to CER's. Other CR's—such as penile and vaginal changes, sweating, laughter, crying—may be involved.

[8]Chapter 6 shows that sensory stimulation is a second major cause of internal motivation.

or punisher if that CS elicits pleasurable or aversive emotional responses.[9] If your favorite radio station was playing certain popular tunes the summer you fell in love, many of those songs may become CS's that elicit tender and loving feelings. When you hear one of these songs a couple of months later, you may notice that it has a special ability to elicit pleasurable emotions. You may comment, "Hey, they're playing our song," when you notice the record eliciting feelings with special emotional significance. In addition, the song may provide enough pleasurable CS's to reinforce operants such as buying your own copy of the record and playing it numerous times—since listening to the music is reinforced by the CS's that elicit wonderful feelings. Conversely, CS's that elicit aversive feelings can serve as punishers or negative reinforcers. If you have ever been sharply criticized for voicing your views on a topic about which you know very little, voicing these views becomes a CS that elicits embarrassment or uneasy feelings. In the future, these CS's punish and hence suppress the tendency to mention similar views. These CS's may also serve as negative reinforcers that increase the likelihood of your tactfully skirting the topic or learning better arguments.

The mass media demonstrate how Pavlovian conditioning can cause subsequent changes in operant behavior. The media present carefully selected stimuli—pictures, words, sounds—that often function as CS's designed to have specific effects on the observer-listener. People exposed to newspapers, magazines, television, or radio are barraged with countless CS's, many of which elicit pleasant or unpleasant emotional responses, depending on past conditioning. In essence, the media provide stimuli that massage the emotions of the observer and condition new emotional responses according to Pavlovian principles. After the Pavlovian massage creates new CS's, these may reinforce or punish the operant behavior of buying product X, voting for candidate Y, or speaking out in favor of issue Z.

Before an advertisement for a cigarette company is placed in a national magazine, it is subjected to weeks or months of testing. Photographs are made from many different angles in an effort to select the one with the most favorable effect. Skin blemishes or unbecoming shadows are airbrushed out. Dozens of people mull over the pictures and text, deciding which poses or wordings they find most appealing. Whether they are intentionally applying Pavlovian principles or not, the ad designers are sifting out (or airbrushing out) the stimuli that are likely to be CS's that elicit unpleasant feelings in the viewing audience. They are also trying to maximize the number of stimuli that elicit pleasurable emotions. Naturally, each viewer will have unique prior conditioning to each stimulus, hence have different responses to each one; but some stimuli—such as beautiful people, quaint places, magnificent landscapes—tend to be CS's that elicit positive feelings for most people. Therefore, a common advertising strategy is to place a picture of the product being sold in the midst of a scene that contains numerous pleasing images—all of which are CS's for pleasurable feelings. According to the principles of Pavlovian conditioning, the advertised product acquires some positive associations by being paired with the numerous CS's that elicit pleasant feelings. Some ads do not even have words: They merely present a collage of pleasure-eliciting CS's, such as a handsome cowboy sitting nonchalantly on his beautiful horse in an idyllic mountain meadow, smoking a Brand X

---

[9]See Chapter 7 on conditioned reinforcers and punishers.

cigarette. Flipping through the magazine, many viewers (even nonsmokers) may pause over the attractive mountain scene because the CS's for pleasurable emotions act as reinforcers that strengthen the operant of prolonged viewing—which in turn increases the likelihood of longer exposure to the Pavlovian conditioning that associates Brand X with CS's for pleasant feelings. After viewers have seen repeated positive ads for Brand X, the experiences will tend to condition Brand X into CS's with positive associations, hence a reinforcer (except for those people with strong negative conditioning about smoking). If the local store does not have a cigarette smoker's favorite brand, the smoker is likely to select Brand X rather than a less well-advertised brand.

Does this subtle type of conditioning work? A multimillion dollar advertising industry exists because it does. For every dozen people who will never switch brands (or never smoke), there are a few people who just might switch if exposed to repeated subtle conditioning experiences.[10]

Not all media influence is based on the presentation of CS's that elicit pleasurable emotions. Drama, fiction, advertising, and news often utilize CS's that elicit fear, anxiety, sadness, compassion, hatred, or other emotional responses; and these CS's may, in turn, suppress certain operants or negatively reinforce others. For example, advertisements and posters that have been designed to suppress behavior often use CS's that elicit anxiety. Smokey the Bear is shown standing in a burned forest, surrounded by forlorn and homeless animals, all of which are CS's that elicit unpleasant feelings. Ads exhorting us not to drive while drunk show a smashed car with a dead body being taken away on a stretcher, along with other fear-eliciting stimuli associated with death. The Pavlovian conditioning produced by such media messages increases the chances that people will respond to forest fires and auto accidents as CS's for anxiety or unpleasant feelings, and these aversive CS's help suppress the operants which might cause fires or accidents.

Media often present CS's associated with anxiety to negatively reinforce escape or avoidance responses. Most people have been conditioned to be sensitive and alert to CS's that elicit unpleasant emotions. Stimuli that signal impending trouble often catch our attention and thus help us prepare for or prevent aversive consequences. We are negatively reinforced for being alert to these CS's because our preparation aids us in avoiding the aversive events associated with the CS's. Advertisers capitalize on this. A picture of a burning house and a bereft family looking on helplessly provides visual CS's that give emotional impact to the ad's caption, "Is your home insurance adequate?" This scene may make the homeowner slightly anxious. The reader may seek to allay the anxiety elicited by the verbal and pictorial CS's by recalling the fact that he or she already has a good insurance policy; but if the current policy is inadequate, the person may read further in the ad for information which could diminish the fear of loss.[11] If the brand of insurance being advertised promises generous coverage, it will become a CS associated with security and escape from anxiety, merely because it is paired with a solution to the problem. For the worried reader, this positive CS reinforces careful reading of the ad and increases the probability of phoning the insurance company.

[10]Bem (1970:70f); Broad (1980).

[11]Some people learn to avoid looking at media communications that portray aversive CS's (Leventhal, 1970).

Thus, CS's that elicit pleasant or unpleasant emotions can be employed to increase the frequency of operant behavior because they can serve as positive and negative reinforcers. Millions of people spend several hours a day viewing media stimuli, mesmerized by the emotional massage that is conditioning new CS's for positive or negative emotions, thereby creating new stimuli that will serve as reinforcers or punishers.

3. Response Disruption. *Operant behavior can be disrupted by reflexive responses and vice versa.* People who are learning new operant behavior often find that emotional responses and other reflexive responses can disrupt their underlearned operant performances. For example, while you are practicing a new piece on the piano or learning lines in a play, someone may walk into the room. If you have been conditioned to fear criticism or making mistakes in public, the presence of the other person will be a CS that elicits uncomfortable emotional responses. In turn, these emotional responses may distract you from your underlearned operant activity and disrupt your performance. Being criticized repeatedly for one's poor playing of a certain passage of music can make that passage a CS that elicits anxiety. After this happens, you begin to feel anxious as you play a piece of music and approach the problematic passage. This anxiety may cause you to make increasing numbers of errors, which only adds to your anxiety until eventually you fear the prospect of starting the piece. Such emotional conditioning causes people to have what is called a "psychological block" that prevents them from playing a piece and makes them fearful of practicing that piece in the future. (If people have overlearned a specific piece of music, it takes a much more intense emotional response to disrupt their operant performance. Professional pianists have overlearned their performances so well that they are not prone to experience disruption even though they feel "butterflies" or other emotional responses during a concert.)

Emotions need not be aversive to disrupt operant performances. You and a friend may be engrossed in a precision task—such as fixing a delicate object—when one of you cracks a joke. If this leads to a funny story, more jokes, and other buffoonery, the numerous witty words serve as verbal CS's that may elicit enough laughter to disrupt your precision activities. You may try to keep working while chuckling at each other's jovialities; but as you keep dropping the tiny parts you are forced to say, "Hey, we have to cut the clowning if we're going to get this thing fixed."

Reflexive responses can sometimes be suppressed or interrupted by operant activities. A person may have learned to find certain kinds of off-color stories funny: The stories provide verbal CS's that elicit laughter. Yet the person may have learned that it is improper to laugh at such stories in more refined company. What happens when the person hears a witty off-color story in a social setting where laughter would be inappropriate? Most people learn that laughter can be suppressed by tensing the stomach and diaphragm muscles. The verbal CS may elicit definite jerks and spasms—incipient laughter responses—in the diaphragm; but the operant tensing of these muscles prevents the full-blown laughter response. Thus, the person can hide conditioned responses to off-color stories.

The game of "flinch" shows how a reflexive response to an aversive CS can be interrupted or suppressed by operant activities. In this game, one person hits at, but does not quite touch, the arm of the second person. The rules of the game are simple: If the second person flinches, the first person gets to make a real hit of any strength. During childhood most people have numerous learning experiences that condition the stimulus of "object moving rapidly toward the arm" into a CS associated with pain. The stimulus of "object moving rapidly toward the arm" is frequently followed by the painful experience of being hit by the object. Being hit is a US that causes pain and a reflexive flinch response. After repeated pairings, the stimulus of "object moving rapidly toward the arm" becomes a CS that can elicit the flinch and anxious feelings. Thus, the naive person who is accosted by an enthusiastic flinch player is usually a sitting duck, strongly conditioned to give a flinch response when first subjected to a fake blow. After losing several times in a row and developing a sore arm, an initiate to the game may learn certain operant skills for suppressing the flinch response or may learn to avoid getting involved in the game. The flinch can be suppressed somewhat by tightening one's muscles or by focusing one's attention away from the fake blow; and these operants are negatively reinforced by the avoidance of aversive consequences.

4. Reflexes Modified by Operant Conditioning.   At first psychologists thought that reflexes could not be changed by operant conditioning. *More recent data show that the frequency and form of many reflexes can be modified by reinforcement and punishment.*[12] For example, blushing is a reflexive response that appears during embarrassment, guilt, and a variety of other aversive experiences. If a teenager has often become very embarrassed while talking about sex with adults, this type of conversation will become a CS that can elicit blushing (due to Pavlovian conditioning). Once the blush has been elicited, subsequent reinforcement or punishment can alter the person's tendency to blush in the future. If a person receives sympathy when others detect that the person is blushing, the sympathy and loving concern can reinforce the blushing response and make the person more prone to blush easily in the future. On the other hand, if blushing is usually punished—perhaps by a curt comment, "You act like a baby, Fred"—the blushing will be suppressed. As a result of operant conditioning, some people are less likely than others to blush. Each individual's propensity to blush is influenced by his or her unique history of reinforcement and punishment for this reflexive response.

There are numerous universal emotional responses—such as smiles, laughter, frowns, blushes, and tears—seen in people all over the world. These reflexive emotional responses are most invariant in early childhood, before they are modified by social learning experience. Over the years, the form and frequency of all these reflexes can be modified by operant conditioning, such that some people smile and laugh much more than others, some cry more easily than others.[13] For example, smiles and laughter are reflexive responses elicited by moderately surprising or novel events and certain other positive stimuli. The novelty and surprises of the rides at the amusement park elicit smiles and laughter in most young people. Due to Pavlovian conditioning, various facets of amusement parks become CS's that elicit smiles and laughter. Reinforcement and punishment can then modify the probability that these responses will occur in the future. Some people's smiles and laughter may be reinforced by frequent positive feedback from

[12]Miller (1969, 1978); DiCara (1970).
[13]Ekman et al. (1980).

friends. Other people's smiles and laughter may be punished more than reinforced, such as when peers say that it is childish to get excited by the rides. After years of operant conditioning in numerous circumstances, some people will frequently show signs of enjoying themselves while others seldom crack a smile.

CONCLUSION

In everyday life, operant and Pavlovian conditioning are frequently entwined in complex patterns. The first part of this chapter presents four characteristics of operant and Pavlovian conditioning that allow us to distinguish between them and isolate their different effects on behavior. Then the chapter describes four ways in which the two processes interact.

Chapter 5 reveals still other ways that operant and reflexive responses are interwoven. Both operant and reflexive responses become conditioned to appear when certain antecedent stimuli (either S^D's or CS's) are present. The complex and ever changing collage of multiple stimuli in everyday life produces a rich interplay of operant and reflexive responses.

5

The Stimulus Collage

● *In this chapter you will learn how multitudes of antecedent stimuli from both outside the body and inside the body affect our behavior.*

In the chapter on Pavlovian conditioning, we saw that US's and CS's are the stimuli that appear before reflexive responses and elicit them:

$$US \rightarrow UR$$

$$CS \rightarrow CR$$

As stated in the chapter on operant conditioning, the stimuli that appear before an operant when it is reinforced are called S^D's (discriminative stimuli). S^D's set the occasion for responding:

$$S^D: B \rightarrow S^R$$

When operants are extinguished or punished, the discriminative stimuli that correlate with extinction or punishment are labeled S^Δ's. These stimuli set the occasion for *not* responding. All of these stimuli—US's, CS's, S^D's, and S^Δ's—are antecedent stimuli; that is, they precede behavior and control the future appearance of the behavior. In everyday life, people are constantly surrounded by multitudes of stimmuli, many of which function as US's, CS's, S^D's, or S^Δ's. This chapter describes the effects of these multiple antecedent stimuli on behavior.[1]

MULTIPLE ANTECEDENT STIMULI

Up to this point we have discussed antecedent stimuli in a simple manner, as if each response were under the control of one predominant or overpowering antecedent stimulus. However, the situation is usually more complex. Vast numbers of stimuli from the environment and from within our bodies affect our responses. The world we perceive is like a collage of stimuli: an intertwined patchwork of images, scenes, figures and backgrounds that form one overall picture. The stimulus collage of life differs from an artist's collage by engaging all of our senses. Whereas the artist's collage is created only to be looked at, the stimulus collage of everyday life is a rich intermingling of sights, sounds, odors, tastes, touches, and feelings.[2] Some of the stimuli capture our attention, whereas others lie in the background or are not consciously perceived; some have strong effects on our behavior while others have weak effects. The study of behavior requires that we become sensitive to the stimulus collage and how it influences behavior.

Each stimulus in the stimulus collage can function as (1) a US or CS for reflexes, (2) an S^D or S^Δ for operants, (3) both of the above, or (4) a neutral stimulus. Neutral stimuli have no particular influence on behavior, but they can become conditioned into CS's, S^D's, or S^Δ's. The following example illustrates how stimuli can have multiple functions. When a person looks at a beautiful painting, the stimuli of the art work can function as both CS's and S^D's. The CS's of the painting may elicit positive emotional responses and reinforce pausing to admire the work. The stimuli also function as S^D's for thoughts, comments to fellow viewers, and perhaps a step forward to see a small detail painted in a dark corner of the canvas.

The ability of any stimulus in the stimulus collage to influence behavior depends on (1) an individual's past conditioning (or lack of conditioning) with the stimulus or similar stimuli, (2) the salience (i.e., conspicuousness) of the stimulus in the present stimulus collage, and (3) the presence of other stimuli that produce facilitative or competing responses.[3] These points are illustrated in the following three paragraphs.

First, *past conditioning* can cause any stimulus (even relatively small or faint ones) to have significant influence over behavior. A mother who hears the faint cry of her sick baby in the next room may find that her thoughts and attention are instantly drawn to the child in spite of the fact that she is in the midst of an interesting conversation. The baby's crying functions as a CS that elicits emotional responses in the mother and an S^D for the

---

[1]For a more extensive discussion of the topic, see Nevin (1971a); Rilling (1977); Mackintosh (1977); Rodewald (1979).

[2]Although laboratory research on US's, CS's, S^D,'s and S^Δ's often focuses on simple situations in which only a small number of stimuli are studied at a given time, natural settings are more complex; hence it is imperative to consider an entire collage of stimuli when studying behavior in natural environments.

[3]In addition to these three factors, the effectiveness of US's depends on (a) the degree to which we are biologically prepared to respond to them, and (b) in the case of US's that function as unconditioned reinforcers, the individual's current state of deprivation or satiation.

mother to go to the aid of the sick child. Crying became an emotion-eliciting CS during past conditioning in which crying correlated with danger to the infant and problems for the mother. Crying became an S^D for helping the infant because helping was negatively reinforced by termination of the stressful situation.

Second, if the infant had been in the same room with the mother, early signs of distress would have been more *salient*—more noticeable—to the mother. She would have noticed the infant's restlessness and early whimpers (which were not salient when the child was in the next room), and she would have helped the infant before the child began to cry. Thus, the proximity, conspicuousness, and salience of stimuli increase the likelihood that the stimuli will affect behavior.[4]

Third, the ability of any given stimulus to control behavior can be increased or decreased by *facilitative or competing responses* produced by other stimuli in the stimulus collage. If the mother of a crying infant had been talking to a neighbor about her efforts to be a good mother when she first heard the baby cry, the S^D's of the conversation would have facilitated her operants of taking care of the child. On the other hand, if the mother had been engaged in a bitter quarrel with her husband about his neglecting the child, the S^D's of the quarrel might have set the occasion for competing responses. She might have said: "There she is crying again. Why don't *you* go see what's the matter this time? How come I'm always the one?" This turn of events makes it unlikely that she would be quick to respond to the baby's crying. Distracting stimuli—such as a ringing phone, someone at the door, something burning in the kitchen—can also decrease the ability of a given stimulus to influence behavior.

Stimulus Control

Those stimuli in the collage that are effective in producing responses are said to have stimulus control over the responses. The cries of a sick baby usually have control over a mother's responses. However, stimulus control is relative and dependent on the relationship among the numerous elements of the stimulus collage. The ability of the baby's cry to control the mother's responses depends on the other stimuli in the stimulus collage.

Everyday conversations contain multiple stimuli—both verbal and nonverbal—that can control a large number of different responses. Sometimes the stimuli keep the conversation on a single, logical track. However, during the course of the interaction, various stimuli often arise that control seemingly extraneous thoughts and words, sometimes causing the whole conversation to be sidetracked. Imagine yourself having a conversation with two or three friends, trying to decide what to do over the weekend. Judy is enthusiastically pushing the idea that you should all go backpacking and spend Saturday night at her favorite camping area. Her conversation provides numerous S^D's that control thoughts and "free associations"[5] about hiking and camping: the backcountry trips you took last

---

[4]During operant and Pavlovian conditioning, a salient stimulus can overshadow less salient (but more valid) stimuli and gain an undue amount of stimulus control over the responses being conditioned (Kamin, 1969; Rescorla and Wagner, 1972; Mackintosh, 1975, 1977). Even after a valid S^D or CS has gained control over an operant or reflexive response, a more salient stimulus can mask the S^D or CS control of the valid stimulus.

[5]Free associations are not free in the sense of being uncaused. They are evoked by S^D's such as the thoughts, words, or other events in the current stimulus collage. They are described as free associations only

year, the time you got poison oak all over your arms and face, and so forth. The stimulus collage also provides CS's that elicit emotional responses: Judy's enthusiasm, smiles, and vivid descriptions are powerful CS's that elicit positive emotional responses which make the idea of backpacking sound appealing, but the thoughts of the poison oak are CS's that elicit bad feelings that partially counteract your positive feelings.

Judy's words and your thoughts all serve as S^D's for your telling the poison oak story and asking Judy whether there is any poison oak at her camp site. But just before you open your mouth, Fred interjects, in response to the S^D's of *his* stimulus collage: "I heard the campground was closed, and anyway there is a carnival opening at the fairgrounds that *everybody* is going to." Suddenly the stimulus collage has been radically altered by the new topics; and a whole new set of ideas and free associations occur to you. You are torn: Should you go back and mention the poison oak experience, or blurt out the funny story about what happened last year at the carnival. After Fred tells his story, he looks at you and asks, "What do you think about the carnival idea?" This is just one more S^D for the carnival story, and out it comes. Everyone laughs. Then Judy has another story about the carnival. The original conversation about camping has been lost; the conversation has been sidetracked. As the earlier S^D's disappear, so do the thoughts about camping and poison oak that had been so prominent a few minutes before.

Sidetracked conversations occur when one person's comments serve as S^D's for thinking and talking about a different topic. This digression provides new S^D's for other verbal responses which may keep a conversation moving away from the original topic.

Stimuli from sources outside the conversation can also affect the total impact of the stimulus collage on the participants. If someone turns on some loud music, the conversation will tend to become louder as the participants raise their voices to escape the aversive consequences of not being able to hear what other people are saying. Blaring music and loud talk are S^D's for laughing, acting a bit sillier than normal, or moving to the beat of the music. The S^D's of quiet music could have had different effects, for example, setting the occasion for quieter, perhaps more serious conversation.

Clocks, record jackets, ashtrays, or other background objects in the room also enrich the stimulus collage. At times they have such noticeable effects on behavior that they emerge from the background. Without realizing what he is doing, Fred casually begins twirling an ashtray on the coffee table. The ashtray is an S^D for the twirling response, even though Fred does not notice because his attention is focused more intently on the conversation. For Judy, the twirling ashtray may be an S^D for saying, "That makes me nervous, Fred. Could you please stop?" While glancing around the room, your eyes happen to focus on the clock, a previously inconspicuous S^D in the background. "Gads! It's four o'clock and I promised to be downtown at three-thirty." This comment again sidetracks the conversation and heads it in a new direction.

The stimulus collage contains multiple antecedent stimuli that affect our thoughts, words, and other behavior. Sometimes the flow of stimuli controls smooth chains of thought and action, but complex and jumbled stimulus inputs can easily control complicated and disjointed response patterns.

---

because they are unexpected and surprising—that is, they are not the most logical or predictable responses to the S^D's (see Chapter 14).

EXTERNAL AND INTERNAL STIMULI

The antecedent stimuli that influence behavior can be located either inside or outside the body.[6] The stimuli that lie *outside* the body are detected through the five senses. Seeing or hearing a friend coming in the front door alters your stimulus collage, adding external stimuli that can be CS's for conditioned reflexive responses such as pleasant feelings and a smile, and S[D]'s for operant behaviors such as greetings and friendly banter. Your friend's responses then serve as the antecedent stimuli for your next set of thoughts, feelings, and responses.

Stimuli from *inside* the body also contribute to the total stimulus collage. A toothache is an internal US that elicits the emotional response of pain. It is also an internal S[D] for such operants as calling the dentist or taking a pain reliever. If your heart begins to beat rapidly, the internal sensations may function as CS's, especially if you have been conditioned to worry about tachycardia or the possibility of heart attacks.[7] Likewise, feeling excess rumbling or growling in the digestive tract can function as a CS that elicits anxiety in a person sensitized to the possibility of getting ulcers. Again, these internal stimuli may also function as S[D]'s that lead a person to diet, exercise, or go to the doctor. Internal stimuli can elicit pleasurable feelings, too. When people are in good physical condition, the bodily sensations of deep breathing and smooth muscle movements while jogging or climbing in the mountains are likely to be CS's of internal origin that elicit pleasurable emotional responses. The internal stimuli may also serve as S[D]'s for thoughts about how good it feels to be healthy and strong.

A person's behavior can be influenced simultaneously by both external and internal stimuli. The external CS's of hearing your employer criticize your latest work may bring a lump to your throat, a quiver to your voice, strong heartbeats, and other emotional responses. These responses then serve as internal S[D]'s for thoughts such as "I hope she doesn't think I'm nervous about this. She might think I'm not in control of the situation." Your thoughts that your nervousness might be visible to your employer may add to the internal CS's that elicit further emotional responses—such as sweating—and these responses might be S[D]'s for additional worried thoughts. Sometimes people's anxiety escalates to ever higher levels as each new worry leads to strong emotional responses that only cause more worry. (Actually, studies show that other people are much less aware of our emotional responses than we are. Most of our emotional responses are inside our bodies, and these internal responses are less salient to others than they are to us.[8] This is important to know, because it helps people avoid the spiral of increasing anxiety that results from fearing that others can see how worried or nervous we are in difficult situations.)

People may learn to respond to either external stimuli, internal stimuli, or both as the cues for a given behavior. Eating, for example, can be controlled by numerous

[6]Although stimuli from inside the body can gain stimulus control over operants or reflexive responses much the same as can stimuli from outside the body, it is harder for society to help the individual learn to correctly identify internal stimuli than external ones (Skinner, 1974:21ff; Baldwin, 1985).

[7]Valins and Ray (1967).

[8]McEwan and Devins (1983).

external stimuli (such as the clock hands pointing to noon, being in the kitchen, smelling delicious food, seeing other people eating, being told to eat), and internal stimuli (such as stomach sensations that indicate hunger). Fat people sometimes respond to different S^D's for eating than lean people do.[9] Lean people tend to respond primarily to the internal S^D's of an empty stomach as the primary cue to eat something, and they do not eat when they are not hungry. On the other hand, fat people are likely to eat whenever they encounter any of numerous external S^D's related to food. Thus, just walking through the kitchen can add 200 calories to a fat person and have no effect on a lean person. All the S^D's of the kitchen entice the fat person to try a piece of candy, peek into the refrigerator, and finish off the leftovers. These external S^D's have little effect on the lean person unless an empty stomach signals the lean person that it is time to eat.

People's own behavior can influence the type of stimuli—from both external and internal sources—that control their own behavior. For several days Linda has been intending to see her professor about a test question she thought was unfair. As she stands in front of the professor's door, ready to knock, she feels her heart pounding in her chest. Linda has had some embarrassing experiences after going in to talk with professors during office hours: On two occasions, they have asked her questions she could not answer and then been critical of her lack of understanding. Hence, approaching a professor's office and knocking serve as external CS's that elicit anxiety and a pounding heart. The closer Linda gets to knocking on the professor's door, the more external CS's there are that elicit emotional responses, and the harder her heart pounds. She walks away from the professor's door—pretending to read something on a nearby bulletin board—and her heart ceases pounding so hard. She returns to the professor's door, again exposing herself to the external CS's that cause her heart to start pounding. As Linda wonders what she should do, her thoughts serve as internal CS's that also elicit emotional responses and affect her heartbeat. First a fear-eliciting CS: "What if Professor Adams thinks I'm stupid for asking her this simple question?" Her heart pounds more strongly. Then Linda has a thought that is a CS for relaxation and comfort: "But she told us to come in and chat, and she seems so friendly." The pounding of her heart decreases a little. "Teachers are human after all." Another decrease in the pounding. "But what if I can't think of anything to say? She'll think I'm stupid." The pounding becomes more noticeable. Whenever Linda focuses attention on aversive thoughts, the pounding increases; but focusing on relaxing thoughts has the opposite effect.

It is possible for the internal and external stimuli of the total stimulus collage to control *competing responses,* in which case one response may interfere with the expression of a second response. It has been shown that many people cannot enjoy sexual relations because their basic sexual reflexes are disrupted by competing responses.[10] Sexual interaction provides numerous external US's that normally elicit pleasurable sexual responses. However, negative thoughts about sex can function as CS's that elicit anxiety and guilty feelings which are emotional responses that interfere with normal sexual functioning. Anxiety alone can stifle sexual arousal, causing a man to lose his erection, a woman to cease vaginal lubrication, and both to fall short of orgasm. During

---

[9]Schachter (1967).
[10]Masters and Johnson (1970); Tollison and Adams (1979).

childhood some people are taught that sex is dirty or that sex for pleasure (as opposed to sex for having children) is sinful. This socialization can cause thoughts of sex to become CS's that elicit guilt and anxiety. Even after the person is married, the guilt-eliciting CS's often remain strong and interfere with sexual responses. Sexual responses can be elicited by the US's of genital stimulation and many related CS's; but for these people, the thoughts of doing something as "dirty" and "animal-like" as sex are CS's that elicit the anxiety that interferes with the natural sexual reflex.

Although we cannot easily observe the internal stimuli that other people experience, we can perceive and study our own internal US's, CS's, S^D's, and S^Δ's. Also, by understanding that each individual's stimulus collage includes both external and internal inputs, we will be aware that other people are responding to stimuli we cannot detect.

GENERALIZATION (OPERANT)

When an operant has been reinforced in the presence of certain stimuli and comes under S^D control of those stimuli, there is a tendency for similar stimuli to control the response, too. This is generalization.[11] New stimuli can control a response to the degree that they resemble the original S^D's associated with reinforcement. For example, on first hearing the music of Bach, a person may learn to identify two or three pieces as Bach's work. Thus, the music becomes an S^D for saying, "That's Bach's 'Toccata and Fugue.'" Generalization enters the picture when the person hears a new piece of music and responds, "That's Bach." Some features of the new music are sufficiently similar to those of the earlier pieces that they control the verbal response. The person's generalized response may be right or wrong. The new piece may in fact be by Bach, or it may be by Vivaldi or Corelli; however, the response to stimuli that are similar to the original S^D reflects generalization whether it is correct or incorrect.

Generalization occurs all the time, as old responses appear in new situations. *The more similar the new setting is to the setting in which a behavior was learned, the more likely that behavior is to occur.* If someone asks directions while on the street, one efficient response is to give verbal instructions and to point in the direction the person should go. When talking to people with reasonable vision, pointing is generally reinforced by the following consequences: Pointing facilitates the transfer of information, decreases the problems arising from misunderstanding, and hastens the onset of thanks for being of help. Thus, pointing is reinforced in the S^D context of "stranger asking for directions on the street." The response of pointing while giving directions usually generalizes to other similar stimulus settings such as S_1 and S_2 in Figure 5–1. When a blind person stops a passerby on the street and asks directions, it is not unusual to see the passerby pointing toward the blind person's destination while giving instructions. Obviously, the pointing is unnecessary and not likely to be reinforced; yet the stimuli of this situation (S_1) are so similar to those of a sighted person's asking directions (the S^D) that generalization is likely (unless the passerby had prior experience helping the blind). If we consider another

---

[11]Honig and Urcuioli (1981). Generalization is seen with S^Δ's, too: once a person has learned not to respond in the presence of a certain S^Δ, similar stimuli will also control not responding. In order to minimize confusion in the text, the effect of S^Δ's is not introduced until we reach the topic of discrimination.

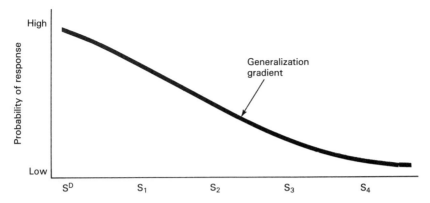

FIGURE 5–1   The probability of pointing in various stimulus contexts.

stimulus collage (S_2) that differs still more from the original learning context (S^D), the response is even less likely. Inside a large building with no windows for seeing the outside environment (S_2), a person is unlikely to point when asked for directions. When a speaker cannot see the other person, such as while giving directions by phone (S_3), pointing is even more unlikely. When giving directions in a letter (S_4), it is extremely unlikely that anyone would point while writing the directions.

The probability of responding to each of the stimuli (S^D, S_1, S_2, S_3, S_4) produces a curve called a *generalization gradient* (see Figure 5-1). The shape of the curve—that is, the amount of generalization to new stimuli—depends on the nature and salience of the stimuli in each collage, along with a person's past history of conditioning.

Whenever a behavior comes under the control of specific S^D's, there is a certain amount of generalization to other similar situations. The degree of generalization depends on the strength of S^D control of all the S^D's in the stimulus collage. Many of the salient and predictive stimuli in the contexts where a behavior is reinforced take on partial S^D control over that behavior.[12] In the original learning context—the S^D context—where several of these predictive stimuli are present, the probability of responding is high. As a person moves into situations that are increasingly different from the original S^D context in which the response is reinforced, there are fewer and fewer stimuli that resemble the original S^D's. *As the stimulus collage becomes increasingly different from the original one and the number of controlling S^D's for the response decline, the probability of the response declines.* This is seen in Figure 5–1: The probability of the response declines as the stimulus context changes from S^D to S_4. In addition, the generalized response—when it does appear in unreinforced contexts (S_1, S_2, S_3, and S_4)—is usually performed less quickly, less intensely, and less rapidly than the response in the original S^D context.[13]

---

[12]In the laboratory, the single best predictive stimulus becomes the dominant S^D that controls the response. Because the natural environment is often much more complex and variable than in the laboratory, some predictors may be present during some reinforcement periods but absent in others. Thus, multiple predictive stimuli may become S^D's for a response. The more S^D's that are present for a given behavior, the more likely the behavior will be emitted (Miller and Ackley, 1970; Weiss, 1972).

[13]More technically, they have a longer latency, lower amplitude, and slower rate than the similar responses in the original S^D context (Nevin, 1971a:117f).

Advantages of Generalization.   Given the constant changes that occur during life, we are never exposed to exactly the same stimulus collages in which our responses were learned in the past. As the Greek philosopher Heraclitus observed some 2500 years ago, "You could not step twice in the same river, for other waters are ever flowing on to you." The world is always changing. We never experience exactly the same stimulus patterns twice. Yet our world is similar enough from day to day that we can respond to our ever changing environment with many of the same operants that worked for us yesterday.

As we gain skills, our ability to apply them to new situations (due to generalization) is often adaptive. If we learn to be intellectually critical of the promises of politicians, our new skills may generalize such that we also become critical of the promises of other authority figures. The tendency for responses that were reinforced in the presence of certain stimuli to occur in the presence of similar stimuli (via generalization) is often efficient. Otherwise we would have to learn these responses from scratch in each separate situation.

Extent of Generalization.   The amount of generalization that occurs can vary. If you learn to be intellectually critical in response to certain S^D's, the tendency to apply your critical skills may generalize extensively, moderately, or only to a small degree, depending on numerous variables. Figure 5–2 shows these three generalization gradients. When there is extensive generalization, many new situations (S_1, S_2, S_3, and to some degree S_4) will set the occasion for being intellectually critical. When there is limited generalization, a person may be intellectually critical in situations that are quite similar to the original learning environment (the S^D context), but never show this response in situations that differ much from the original S^D context (such as situations S_2, S_3, and S_4).

If generalization is broader than would be desired and causes a person to emit a response in inappropriate circumstances, the response is said to be *overgeneralized*. If parents tell a young child to always do what the teacher says, the child may overgeneralize and uncritically obey a teacher even when the teacher is requesting unusual behavior, such as in the case of child sexual abuse in preschools. Sometimes overgeneralization occurs when a person learns a new fact and begins to "explain" everything in terms of this one

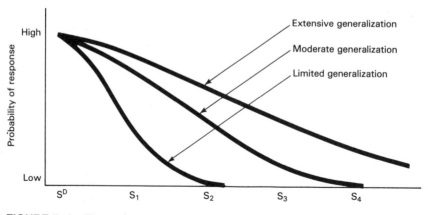

FIGURE 5–2   Three generalization gradients.

new fact. When first learning about sunspots and their effects on climate, a child may try to "explain" daily weather, the parents' moods, bad test grades, and much more in terms of sunspots. After learning that diet can affect health, vitality, and mood, some people overgeneralize and begin to "explain" all types of ailments and psychological conditions in terms of diet. This type of overgeneralization is nicely summarized in the old saying, "Give a small boy a hammer, and he will find that everything needs hammering." Once in possession of the new tool, the child not only hammers nails (the appropriate behavior), but hammers tables, chairs, rocks, pets, and many other things (the inappropriate and overgeneralized behaviors). Intellectual tools can be used in an overgeneralized manner, too.

Sometimes generalization is not as broad as is desired. This is called *under-generalization.* Students may learn a theory in the classroom or from a book and may be able to express their knowledge on a test; but often the new intellectual skills do not generalize to help them understand events in their own lives that were not included in the textbook examples. Their learning has not generalized far enough. Undergeneralization can be a problem in psychological therapies.[14] People may overcome shyness, alcoholism, or problems controlling temper flareups in a therapeutic environment, but the new skills sometimes fail to generalize to their everyday environments. Often special steps must be included in therapy to overcome the problems of undergeneralization. Some therapists make the therapeutic environment as similar as possible to people's everyday environments—or they carry out the therapy in natural settings—to improve generalization. Sometimes friends and family will be involved in the therapy so they can become part of the S^D collage that sets the occasion for the newly acquired behavior. Another valuable method for avoiding undergeneralization is to assure that there will be *additional reinforcement* when the person utilizes skills gained during therapy in other situations (see next topic). To do this, behavior therapists attempt to train and reinforce behavior patterns that will work—that is, produce reinforcing results—when the person uses them in everyday settings. In addition, a person's friends or family may be taught how to provide additional reinforcement for the newly acquired behavior when it occurs in their presence.

Additional Reinforcement.   *If a generalized response is reinforced in new contexts, the reinforcement can further increase the probability of the response in these new contexts.* A college student who learned to be intellectually critical of politicians (S^D) may show generalized intellectual criticism of authority figures (S_1), adults in general (S_2), parents (S_3), and friends (S_4). This original generalization gradient shows a decrease in response probability as the stimulus collage becomes progressively different from the original S^D collage (see Figure 5–3). If, however, the student receives reinforcers for being intellectually critical in all the situations from S_1 through S_4, the probability of critical responses will be increased in all four situations (the solid line in Figure 5–4). (The stimuli in the figure are now labeled S^D's because the operant has been reinforced in the presence of each stimulus.) A person may easily earn the respect and admiration of others for not being a "push-over" or for "using one's brains" and thus receive reinforcement for critical thinking in a large number of contexts.

[14]Birnbrauer (1976); Goldstein and Kanfer (1979); Goetz et al. (1979, 1981); Guess et al. (1978); Costello (1983); Schwartz (1984).

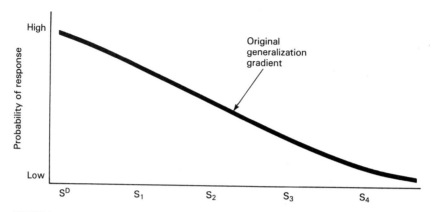

FIGURE 5–3   The original generalization of critical skills.

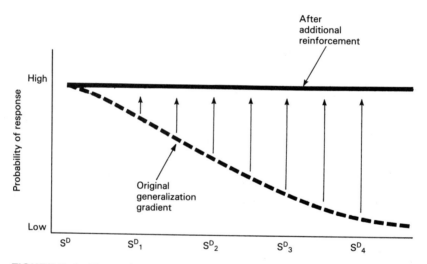

FIGURE 5–4   The probability of critical responses after reinforcement in various stimulus contexts.

Generalization is a mechanism by which old operants are emitted in new situations. If the old response works well in the new context, it will be reinforced. At first the generalized response may appear tentative, weak, or incomplete in the new context; but after being reinforced, it may become a high probability response to the new S^D's.

DISCRIMINATION (OPERANT)

When people learn to respond differently to different stimuli, they have learned discriminations. Whereas generalization involves performing the same response in various situations, discrimination involves making different responses to different stimuli.

Discrimination occurs when people learn that a response that was reinforced in certain contexts is either punished or not reinforced in other contexts.

When first asked for directions by a blind person, you might answer and give the generalized response of pointing, since the current stimulus collage is so similar to all prior contexts in which pointing has been reinforced. However, pointing is not instrumental in communicating with blind people. It is wasted effort, hence not reinforced. In fact, it may be punished. Your pointing and saying "Go that way," may be followed by a comment, "I'm blind. I can't see." This comment may serve as a punisher for pointing when giving directions to blind people. It may also elicit negative emotional responses and make you feel stupid or insensitive. Due to punishment, the special glasses or white cane used by the blind person become discriminative stimuli (S^Δ's) for not pointing.

The primary cause of discrimination learning is differential reinforcement, that is, different patterns of reinforcement or punishment in the presence of different stimuli. Those antecedent stimuli that precede reinforced responses and are good predictors of reinforcement become S^D's for responding; whereas those antecedent stimuli that precede and predict punishment or nonreinforcement become S^Δ's for not responding. If there is differential reinforcement for pointing—i.e., reinforcement for pointing with sighted people, and punishment or nonreinforcement for pointing with blind people—the different consequences cause predictive stimuli associated with sighted people to become S^D's and predictive stimuli associated with blind people to become S^Δ's. Eye contact from another person is a predictive cue that the person is sighted, and special glasses or canes are predictive cues that the person is blind.

Differential reinforcement affects the original generalization gradient as is shown in Figure 5–5. Punishment or nonreinforcement from the blind person decreases the probability of pointing in this S^Δ context. The effects of punishment or nonreinforcement generalize to some degree, so the new response gradient (solid line in the figure) is depressed not only in the S^Δ context but also in similar contexts. If a person receives further punishment or nonreinforcement for pointing in future interactions with blind people, the response curve would be suppressed even further.

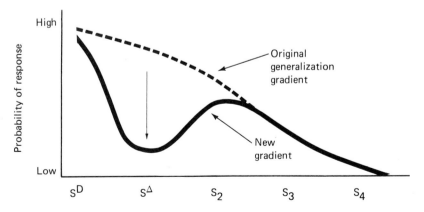

FIGURE 5–5 The probability of pointing after differential reinforcement.

Social Sensitivity.   Some people learn to discriminate subtle differences in wines, cheeses, French cooking, and other tastes. Other people do not. Some people learn to discriminate subtle differences in facial expressions, body postures, and numerous social expressions. Others remain insensitive to all but the most obvious social cues. The learning of the subtle discriminations required for social sensitivity is based largely on differential reinforcement.[15]

Facial expressions would not be important to us if they did not correlate with different patterns of reinforcement and punishment. If people wore identical masks that hid all facial cues, the masks would be useless in discriminating one person from the next or discriminating between friendly and hostile moods. However, the human face changes in ways that often correlate with a person's inclination to respond in a positive or negative manner to our behavior.[16] For example, when you begin joking with someone who is smiling, there is a better chance that the person will reciprocate in a positive way than if smiles were absent. Thus smiles are predictive stimuli which become S^D's that set the occasion for friendly joking (along with other responses that have been reinforced in this S^D context).

Note that the very same facial expression that functions as an S^D for joking can function as an S^Δ for other responses. If you try to start a serious philosophical discussion while a friend is smiling, your friend may punish your serious response: "Cut the super serious stuff and have fun for once." If serious talk is usually squelched, disrupted, or mocked, whereas joking is reinforced, the smiles of others are predictive stimuli that become S^Δ's for not engaging in serious talk and S^D's for joking. The cues in the stimulus collage are the same in both cases; but the discriminating person brings a history of learning experience to the collage that makes the smiling *function* as an S^D for one response and *function* as an S^Δ for another response, depending on the patterns of reinforcement or punishment associated with each behavior.

Our sensitivity to other people's feelings and emotions is also based largely on differential reinforcement for *noticing* cues about their emotional responses and *accurately describing*—to ourselves or out loud—the relevant emotions. People often comment about each other's moods. "You look sad today, Julie." Julie may reply in a way that provides positive or negative feedback: "Yeah, I really feel blue today," or "No, I'm just a little tired." This type of positive and negative feedback for making social discriminations provides several types of differential reinforcement: (1) Merely being correct is a reinforcer for many people (and being incorrect is a punisher); (2) Correctly identifying another person's emotional responses often helps coordinate social interaction, hence is reinforcing (whereas errors are less helpful in producing social coordination and reinforcement); (3) People who have learned to value sensitivity automatically experience more reinforcement when they have succeeded in being sensitive than when they have been insensitive. Repeated differential reinforcement is essential for learning and refining subtle discriminations. When the social feedback is positive, it reinforces sensitive obser-

---

[15]Models and rules can provide useful information that facilitates the *acquisition* of discriminations and sensitivity; but differential reinforcement is essential for assuring that these discriminations will be *utilized* and *refined* to subtle levels (see Chapters 9 and 11).

[16]Ekman (1972, 1980).

vation and description of other people's emotional cues; and those cues become S^D's for making similar sensitive responses in the future. When the feedback is negative, it punishes the incorrect identification of social cues and the cues become S^Δ's for not making incorrect responses in the future. Some people may fail to identify expressions much more often than they succeed, and eventually the high ratio of failure may suppress such comments altogether. Gradually, these people learn to stay on safer, more reinforcing topics, such as the weather or the latest news. Other people may succeed so often at judging moods that they receive high levels of reinforcement for continuing the practice; and this in turn gives them the chance to learn even more advanced, subtle discriminations.

This does not mean that the sensitive person can tell you exactly *which* stimuli are serving as the S^D's for correct discriminations about the feelings of others. Since language does not provide good words for describing complex patterns of facial expressions, it is difficult to learn to talk about (or learn verbal awareness of) the subtle cues that control advanced discriminations. In addition, there are few reinforcers for explaining *how* we made accurate discriminations; hence people are not likely to learn this skill even if they have learned to be very sensitive. Thus, a person can be sensitive and not be able to explain verbally to others which social cues serve as S^D's or S^Δ's for the sensitive responses.[17]

Generalization Versus Discrimination.   Generalization and discrimination are often described as opposite kinds of effects—two poles of a continuum.[18] *Generalization refers to the process by which we respond in the same way to different stimuli. Discrimination refers to the process by which we respond differently to different stimuli.* After learning to identify several paintings by Picasso, a person may be able to look at new pictures, recognize the similarities, and say, "That's a Picasso!" Generalization *increases* the number of stimuli which will control a response. Differential reinforcement conditions us to discriminate certain differences in stimuli. When looking at an early Picasso, a person may receive positive feedback for saying, "That's from the blue period," but negative feedback for saying, "That's from the rose period." The differential reinforcement makes the picture an S^D for saying "blue period" and an S^Δ for not saying "rose period." Discrimination *reduces* the number of stimuli that will control a response.

GENERALIZATION (PAVLOVIAN)

When a predictive stimulus precedes a reflex and becomes a CS that elicits a reflexive response, stimuli that are similar to the CS will elicit the response, too. This is generalization. New stimuli can elicit a conditioned response to the degree that they resemble the original CS to which the response was conditioned.

---

[17]People often learn to make a discrimination or perform a behavior without having verbal explanations for how they do the given act. Thus, "we can know more than we can tell" (Polanyi, 1966). It takes special learning experiences for people to acquire the self-descriptive skills needed for them to become "aware" of the nature of their own actions (Skinner, 1969:244; 1974:153). See Chapters 11 and 14.

[18]Rilling (1977:433).

After a child has been knocked down a few times by the neighbor's big dog, Rover, the dog becomes a CS that elicits crying and other negative emotional responses when the child sees the dog approach. This fear can generalize to other dogs. Figure 5–6 shows the generalization gradient for the child's fear of various types of dogs. Because other big dogs have certain similarities to Rover—large size, loud bark, and perhaps color—they can also elicit fear in the child, though not as much fear as Rover does since these dogs do not look exactly like Rover. Medium sized dogs resemble Rover to a lesser degree, hence have even less ability to elicit the fear responses. Small dogs would be expected to elicit the least fear.

If a child is raised in a home with a very authoritarian father who frequently uses punishment for transgressions, a stern look and serious interrogation from the father can become CS's for fear since they often precede and predict punishment. This fear response may generalize to other "authority figures." At the age of sixteen, Charlie experiences aversive conditioned emotional responses in the presence of various men in authority roles, especially those who carry themselves in a somber, stern, and unfriendly manner— similar to his father's demeanor. For example, the seriousness of police officers, ministers, and judges might elicit moderately strong aversive emotional responses, as is shown in Figure 5–7. Charlie's boss might be slightly less similar to the stimuli of the punitive, authoritarian father. The appearance of a friendly businessman might be sufficiently different that little fear is elicited in his presence.

Additional Conditioning.   *When a reflexive response generalizes to new contexts, it may become even stronger in these contexts if it undergoes additional Pavlovian conditioning in these contexts.* Charlie's original generalization is based on prior conditioning with a stern, punitive father. As Charlie gains additional experience with other adults, the original generalization gradient may be modified. On the very first day of his new job,

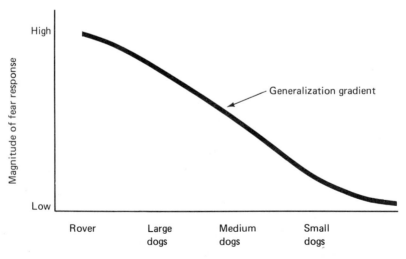

FIGURE 5–6   The amount of fear elicited by various stimuli.

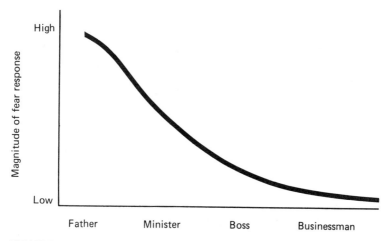

FIGURE 5–7   The generalization of fear of "authority figures."

Charlie may experience little fear in the presence of his boss. However, the boss may turn out to be a real villain. He may harass workers who do not do perfect work. He may make people work late with no extra pay to correct errors that only a perfectionist could find. After several days on the new job, Charlie will acquire new conditioned fears of authority figures. This conditioning may modify the original generalization gradient, as is shown in Figure 5–8. There is a definite increase in the negative conditioned emotional responses elicited by the boss, as his unique mannerisms become new fear-eliciting CS's associated with authority figures. Also, this new conditioning generalizes such that businessmen and ministers may take on additional generalized ability to elicit negative emotional responses.

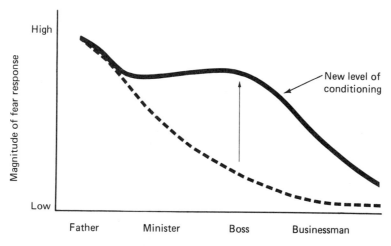

FIGURE 5–8   The generalization gradient after additional conditioning.

DISCRIMINATION (PAVLOVIAN)

If two stimuli originally elicit the same reflexive response, then one of these stimuli is paired with a different reflex (or with neutral stimuli), a person will learn to respond differently to the two stimuli. This is discrimination learning in Pavlovian conditioning. Due to this type of Pavlovian conditioning, two stimuli that once elicited similar responses come to elicit different responses.

As the son of a stern, authoritarian father, Charlie may have several psychological problems for which he eventually seeks counseling. Because he has no other place to turn, Charlie may go to the local minister for help. When he first visits the minister's office, he may feel anxious: The minister is an authority figure who elicits relatively strong generalized fears. Much to Charlie's surprise, the minister is warm and friendly. He gently discusses Charlie's past and shows compassion for Charlie's problems. The minister's kind and gentle behavior elicits no fear. Rather it elicits comfortable feelings of relaxation and counterconditions Charlie's original fears, as is shown in Figure 5–9. After several visits to the minister's study, Charlie finds that he no longer experiences fear as he interacts with this man. The new conditioning experience has produced a discrimination: Although certain authority figures elicit fear, others do not. The minister's face is heavily lined and stern, like Charlie's father's; but his voice is quiet and gentle. The characteristics unique to the minister become crucial parts of the total stimulus collage because they elicit discriminated conditioned responses to otherwise stern-looking people.

Discriminations are learned when there are different patterns of conditioning associated with the stimuli that had once appeared to be similar. While some stimuli continue to be paired with the original fear response, others are not. The differential conditioning produces discrimination.

As we proceed through life, each of us has a vast number of conditioning experiences with authority figures—and all other types of people. These different experiences condition a multitude of fine discriminations that no diagram can easily convey. One

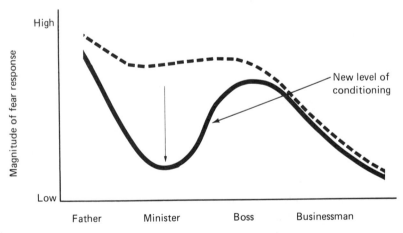

FIGURE 5–9 The generalization gradient after discrimination conditioning.

minister may be very friendly; another, cold and aloof. One boss may be a tyrant; and the next, generous and fair. The unique conditioning associated with each individual creates a complex interaction of generalized and discriminated responses. Because we all have unique histories of Pavlovian conditioning, we all have unique conditioned responses to the stimulus collages in life.

THE ROLE OF WORDS IN THE STIMULUS COLLAGE

Words can appear in either the external or internal parts of the stimulus collage. In the written or spoken form, external words often play an important role in the control of behavior. Even when alone and quiet, people tend to carry on internal verbal dialogues, silent conversations with themselves. These external and internal words can function as S^D's, S^Δ's, or CS's. Words such as "What time is it?" are S^D's that usually have obvious effects; but subtle effects can be important, too. For example, one's choice of words can steer a conversation in one direction or another, or even sidetrack a whole train of thought. Each person's words serve as S^D's for pursuing certain topics and S^Δ's for not introducing other topics. The countless words that you are exposed to each day have a cumulative effect on how you vote, what career you select, or the toothpaste you use. The role of words as CS's is often most visible in young children.[19] A simple ghost story contains so many words which function as fear-eliciting CS's for children that it can frighten a young child. On the other hand, because happy fairy tales contain CS's associated with pleasant emotions, they can elicit smiles and laughter from children.

Even adults can talk or think themselves into the depths of depression if their words are CS's that elicit negative emotional responses. Conversely, by focusing on words that function as CS's for pleasant emotions, people can talk or think themselves into a cheerful mood.

Complex or Ambiguous Situations

When a situation is complex or ambiguous and people do not know how to respond to it, words can often have a powerful influence in controlling behavior. When several thirsty hikers come upon a pool of water in an otherwise dry stream bed, they may find themselves in an ambiguous situation. The water functions as an S^D for drinking; but the slightly stagnant condition of the water serves as an S^Δ for not drinking. As they vacillate between drinking and not drinking, a local person approaches them and says, "That water's bad." The verbal label adds crucial discriminative stimuli—verbal S^Δ's—to the total stimulus collage and brings an end to the hikers' vacillation. The verbal S^Δ's tip the balance in favor of not drinking. The verbal label also functions as a CS. Prior to hearing the verbal label, the hikers were influenced by both the US of water (which is attractive when people are thirsty) and the CS of a slightly stagnant odor (which is unattractive if people have had aversive conditioning with such odors). At first, the thirsty hikers were torn between the attractive and unattractive stimuli. However, the words, "That water's

---

[19]Dysinger and Ruckmick (1933).

bad,'' tipped the balance in favor of not drinking because they were CS's that elicit additional aversive feelings.

Much of life is ambiguous and complex, and the verbal labels that happen to be used can influence behavior significantly.

Operant Behavior.   Verbal labels can serve as S^D's that often have surprising strength in ambiguous situations. Imagine that you have just met Francine. She is clearly *different*. She enjoys making cynical jokes, but always in a friendly way with a big smile. At times her conversation seems unconnected and difficult to follow. Even the comprehensible things that she says seem a little weird. Francine writes poetry; but to you, her ten-line gems sound like ten randomly selected sentences. When you talk with Francine, she often breaks into laughter at the oddest times, in places that did not seem funny to you. And as you stand there looking puzzled, wondering what she found so humorous, she launches into an enthusiastic digression that catches you at a loss for words. Is Francine crazy? Or is she a genius? Maybe she sees things you are missing, writes poetry that is above your head, and finds your conversation humorous for its simplicity. Or maybe she is zany? The stimuli are ambiguous, and you are not certain how to respond to her behavior.

One day a close and respected friend mentions that Francine is truly brilliant, a person of remarkable insight. You may express your uncertainty; but the labels, such as ''brilliant,'' ''insightful,'' ''creative,'' ''gifted,'' and ''stimulating,'' are likely to have a strong effect. If a second person agrees with your friend's judgment that Francine is a genius; you are especially likely to be swayed. If you express some lingering doubts— ''But what about that insane poetry she writes?''—your friends may explain that Francine has already had her work published in literary magazines. The new verbal labels are S^D's that control different thoughts about Francine and may alter your future interactions with her. The next time you meet Francine much of the ambiguity will be gone and you will tend to respond to Francine as a genius.

When clear labels are added to the stimulus collage by a trusted friend, or several other people simultaneously, the labels act as strong, unambiguous S^D's for responses appropriate to the labels. The labels that are attached to people can have a powerful and long lasting influence on their lives and social interactions. A person who is labeled ''gifted'' or ''genius'' may be treated quite differently than if labeled ''crazy'' or ''schizophrenic.'' A complimentary label often affects others as an S$^\Delta$ for not criticizing the person. It serves as an S^D for thinking and saying positive things about behavior that might not have seemed so creative if displayed by a person who had been labeled as ''average.'' Labels that mark off criminals, weirdos, and people with mental problems can have the opposite effect. They are S^D's that alert people to expect trouble, to watch for any signs of deviance, and to shun the stigmatized person. Uncomplimentary labels are also S$^\Delta$'s for not showing acceptance, tolerance, friendliness, and so forth.

Once a person has acquired a label—either complimentary or stigmatizing—it is often difficult for other people to respond to the person's behavior without being con- trolled by the label.[20] For example, there have been studies in which totally normal people

---

[20]Although the social labels attached to a person can have an important influence on the person's future (Becker, 1963, 1964; Schur, 1965), labels are only one of many influences on social interaction (Akers, 1973; Kunkel, 1975).

have had themselves committed to mental hospitals in order to study the effects of labels.[21] Once labeled as schizophrenic, they blended in so well with the other inmates that neither the doctors nor staff noticed that these people were completely normal. Even though they displayed no abnormal behavior, the stigmatizing label prevented the doctors and staff from responding to them as normal.

Reflexive Responses. Labels play an important role in determining people's emotional responses in ambiguous situations. When a person who is not used to flying takes an airplane trip, the vibrations, noises, and sudden jolts due to air turbulence are US's and CS's that elicit mild anxiety. On the other hand, some of the stimuli in the plane are CS's that elicit relaxation and a sense of calmness: The flight attendants are friendly, and fellow passengers seem calm and comfortable. Thus, the US's and CS's of the stimulus collage—with no words yet spoken—elicit mixed emotional responses that vacillate between mild anxiety and relaxation. If the passenger now begins to listen to the person in the next seat, the words add new elements to the stimulus collage. "The last time I took this flight, several passengers got sick; and it feels bumpier today. And those noises. It makes you wonder if the engines will stay on! You remember that tragic accident where almost 300 people were killed when an engine broke off the plane. They went out of control and crashed. Makes you really worry about flying." These negative verbal labels function as CS's that elicit anxiety in the listener who had already been vacillating between anxiety and relaxation. As the person listens to the creaks of the airframe and thinks about what the fellow passenger had said, the negative thoughts are verbal CS's that elicit further anxiety.

The opposite could have happened. When air turbulence first elicited mild anxiety, the unseasoned flier might have mentioned it to the person in the next seat and received an optimistic reply. "Oh, I don't think we need to worry. I've read that airplanes are 99.999 percent safe, which is much safer than cars. They build them to withstand much more violent conditions than the strongest storm possible. If you want to worry, do it on the ground when you are riding in a car. Whenever I fly, I just sit back and relax. I never let the sounds bother me at all." Positive labels such as these are verbal CS's that can alter the stimulus collage so that the creaks and noises no longer elicit anxiety.

In both of the above cases, a person's internal stream of thoughts tends to prolong the effects of the verbal labels long after the fellow passenger speaks them. The noises and turbulence serve as S^D's for recalling the other passenger's words about the danger or safety of flying, and these words function as internal verbal CS's that elicit either fear or relaxation. Many seasoned travelers have learned to calm themselves on bumpy flights by using verbal labels that are CS's for relaxation.[22] They may have a lengthy internal dialogue on the safety of modern airplanes, and thus generate a long series of verbal CS's that elicit relaxation and counteract the potentially fear-eliciting stimuli.

Note that it is much more difficult for verbal labels to alter a person's emotional response when the stimulus collage is not ambiguous. If one is faced with a truly frightening situation—such as a harrowing automobile accident in which both other passengers

---

[21]Rosenhan (1973).
[22]Götestam et al. (1983).

died—thousands of positive and reassuring words will have little effect in modifying the emotions elicited by the unambiguously terrifying experience. At the other extreme, when an individual is enjoying one of the most positive experiences of life—such as falling in love—even a cynic may not be able to find enough negative words to destroy the beauty of the experience.

IDENTIFYING STIMULUS CONTROL

One of the best ways to identify stimulus control of either operant or reflexive behavior is to look for the stimuli that precede and best predict the given behavior. First, select a common behavior pattern, and then ask which stimuli usually occur just prior to and are highly correlated with the behavior. These are the major candidates for control stimuli of that behavior.

People often find it useful to identify the stimuli that control behavior that they want to perform more frequently or less frequently. The following example shows how identifying stimulus control can help a person gain better self-control. Nick has a problem that bothers both him and his friends: Every once in a while his temper flares up and he says things out of anger that he later regrets. To better understand and control the behavior, he might try to locate the antecedent stimuli that trigger his anger and harsh words. A good strategy would be for him to keep records of all the situations in which he has temper flare-ups. The "who, what, when, and where" questions are useful in identifying the antecedent stimuli that control behavior.[23] When Nick has a temper outburst—or even feels close to having one—he may ask himself about the antecedent events. "Who was present just before I started to feel angry? What was happening? What were we doing and saying? What was I thinking? When and where did the events occur?" Usually it is best to write down all the clues revealed by these questions. Since there could be multiple possible stimuli that trigger his anger, it might take several days before Nick has enough self-observations to identify the correct CS's and S^D's that trigger anger and harsh words.

For several days, Nick wrote down a brief description of the context cues—who, what, when, and where—that were present just before he had a temper flare-up. Nick discovered that he was most likely to get angry with people he knew well. When he was in public or with strangers, he could remain polite and poised even in difficult situations; but with his close friends—especially his fiancée—he tended to blow up quite easily. (Actually, this pattern is all too common: People usually control their tempers and harsh words much better when they are in the presence of strangers than when they are with friends and family.[24])

After making this observation, Nick asked himself "Why can't I be in better control with my friends and fiancée? After all, I care more about them than I do about the strangers I treat more politely!" Nick had all the skills needed for controlling his temper and being considerate with people. His self-observations revealed that strangers were the S^D's for these behaviors but that there were too few S^D's to evoke these behaviors when

[23]Watson and Tharp (1981:106f).
[24]Ryder (1968); Winter et al. (1973); Birchler et al. (1975).

he was with his friends. To increase the number of S^D's for controlling his temper with his friends, Nick made a resolution to verbally remind himself to control his anger whenever he was with friends. When noticing that he was beginning to get angry, he would break the response chain by reminding himself: "My friends deserve more considerate treatment." These thoughts were internal verbal S^D's that altered his stimulus collage in a way that increased the likelihood of his being considerate.

After using these self-reminders on several occasions, Nick noted that several potential temper outbursts were averted. It was rewarding for Nick to see his own progress; and these rewards strengthened his resolve to continue reminding himself to be considerate with close friends. There was a second source of reinforcement to help bring considerate behavior under S^D control of interactions with close friends: His friends and fiancée commented on the nice changes they had noticed in his behavior. His fiancée told him that she enjoyed being with him more now that he did not fly into a rage so easily. She felt better about their relationship and wanted to spend more time with him. Both forms of reinforcement—seeing his own progress and getting positive feedback from his friends—further reinforced the use of considerate behavior in the S^D context of being with close friends. After several months, Nick did not even have to remind himself to be considerate: The behavior had come under such strong S^D control of being with friends that it appeared "naturally," without self-reminders.

Knowing how to identify stimulus control can lead to a better understanding of many everyday events. For example, some people love going to horror movies and getting frightened by the suspense, blood, and gore. Many horror movie buffs have asked themselves the question: "If some friends have seen a movie before I see it, should I let them tell me about it or not? Will their description of the horror scenes make the movie less exciting when I see it?" It turns out that letting another person tell you about the frightening scenes in horror movies *increases* the emotional impact of the movies.[25] An analysis of stimulus control helps explain why. Movie producers and directors design horror films to contain numerous fear-eliciting CS's: rainy nights, dark passageways, eerie noises, and gruesome murders. If you let someone else tell you about a specific movie—the ax murder, the little boy's head flying off his body, and blood spurting out of his neck—his words are CS's that elicit emotions both when you hear them and later when you see the film. As you sit through the movie, your memory of your friend's words adds predictive stimuli that elicit emotional responses *before* the little boy ever gets cornered by the ax murderer. As you wait for the horrible scene, you will be thinking the words that your friend told you and already experiencing the fear-eliciting CS's before the ax begins to swing. As a result, you are getting an extra dose of fear-eliciting CS's because you entered the movie theater with verbal descriptions of the gore. Thus, in most cases, having someone tell you about the horrible details beforehand only increases the total number of fear-eliciting CS's in your stimulus collage. It is much the same as riding in an airplane during a bad storm and listening to a fellow passenger tell you about the horrors of airplane accidents: The other person's words add to the number of CS's that elicit fear. If you want your next horror movie to be more frightening, let someone tell you about it in advance.

[25]Cantor et al. (1984).

The skills for identifying stimulus control can pay off in countless ways. For example, some people's moods swing up and down without their knowing why. When their feelings are obviously related to the stimuli of the moment—as in a horror movie—people have no trouble tracing their emotions to antecedent stimuli. But most of everyday life is far more subtle than a horror movie, and people's moods may gradually swing up and down without their noticing the relevant antecedent stimuli. Many of the CS's of our daily stimulus collage have only weak control over our emotions; hence their effect on our mood is likely to be unnoticed unless people have learned to look for antecedent cues related to their emotional responses. Nevertheless, the large number of weak CS's in the stimulus collage can have significant cumulative effects on emotions. If you wake up in a neutral mood (neither happy nor sad), a lucky combination of CS's with weak control over positive emotions might put you in a good mood and make the day brighter, without your being able to point to any single event that was responsible. Too many CS's for aversive emotions can have the opposite effect; you can have a bad day even though you cannot locate any single cause. Naturally, the more closely that people study the relationship of antecedent stimuli and emotional responses, the more alert they become to the events that affect their moods. For example, they may begin to see how important a series of pleasant morning experiences can be for setting the tone of the whole day. If you hear some cheerful music on the radio when you wake up, think about some optimistic topics during breakfast, then have a phone call from a happy friend, you may start the day with an upbeat train of thoughts and feelings that help you focus on positive events all day.

All people are aware of *some* of the stimuli that affect their moods, and they often use this knowledge to avoid CS's that produce unwanted emotions and to locate CS's that elicit enjoyable emotional responses. You are doing this type of mood control when you put on a favorite record that makes you feel good or when you avoid reading newspaper articles on depressing topics. The more that people learn to identify the stimuli that affect their mood, the more skillful they can be at selecting CS's for the moods they want. After observing correlations between their moods and antecedent stimuli, some people learn to minimize arguments and sharp words (which elicit unpleasant emotions) and to increase the use of kind comments, humor, and friendliness (all of which elicit pleasing emotions). As a result they keep their own—and other people's—stimulus collages filled with stimuli that generate good feelings. Of course, this leads to rewarding results that reinforce the skills for observing, identifying, and controlling the emotion-eliciting stimuli in their lives.

CONCLUSION

In this chapter we have described the ways in which behavior is influenced by antecedent stimuli—US's, CS's, S^D's, and S$^\Delta$'s. In everyday life behavior is affected by a multitude of stimuli from inside and outside the body. The numerous stimuli of the stimulus collage often control a variety of operant and reflexive responses. When a behavior is under stimulus control of one set of S^D's or CS's, it may also appear in the presence of similar stimuli. This is generalization. In contrast, discrimination is learned when two sets of stimuli that had originally controlled the same response come to control two different responses, because the stimuli predict different patterns of conditioning. Words and verbal thoughts are elements of the stimulus collage that often have a great deal of influence over behavior, especially in complex or ambiguous situations where the other stimuli of the collage do not control any single predominant response pattern. It is possible to identify the stimuli that control a behavior by looking for the stimuli that both precede and predict that behavior, and doing so is useful for gaining knowledge of and control over one's own behavior.

Whereas this chapter focused on antecedent stimuli, the next two chapters are devoted to *consequences* that appear after operant behavior. Elements of the stimulus collage become S^D's or S$^\Delta$'s only because they are associated with specific consequences—either reinforcement, nonreinforcement, or punishment. In addition, various stimuli of the collage become CS's for pleasurable or anxious feelings due to pairing with reinforcers or punishers. Chapter 6 describes the biologically established reinforcers and punishers that are the prime movers of conditioning. Chapter 7 explains how additional stimuli can become conditioned reinforcers or conditioned punishers by being paired with the biologically established reinforcers or punishers.

6

Unconditioned Reinforcers and Unconditioned Punishers

● *In this chapter you will learn about the biologically established reinforcers and punishers—how they vary over time and how they are modified by learning.*

Reinforcers and punishers are the prime movers of operant conditioning. It is part of our biological nature to respond to certain stimuli as reinforcers and punishers without the need for any prior learning. These stimuli are called *unconditioned reinforcers* and *unconditioned punishers*. (They are also called *primary* reinforcers and *primary* punishers.) Other stimuli can become conditioned reinforcers and conditioned punishers if they are paired with the biologically established reinforcers and punishers.

This chapter describes several of the major unconditioned reinforcers and punishers and the ways in which they sometimes vary in power from moment to moment, day to day, and year to year. This analysis helps make clear the relationship between unconditioned reinforcers and punishers and several other topics, such as motivation, individual differences in people's responses to reinforcers or punishers, and changes in responsiveness to reinforcers and punishers over the life cycle. Most people are not very aware of the importance of unconditioned reinforcers and punishers in daily life. It is easy to take them for granted without realizing their numerous direct and indirect influences on behavior. Yet they affect behavior so profoundly that we should be more knowledgeable about them. People who are unaware often misuse them, making their own lives and the lives of others less rewarding and more aversive than need be. Knowing about the unconditioned reinforcers and punishers can help people avoid these unfortunate consequences.

THE RELATIVITY OF REINFORCERS AND PUNISHERS

Reinforcers and punishers are most easily defined according to their effects on operant behavior.[1] As we learned in Chapter 2 on operant conditioning, if a stimulus that follows an operant causes an increase in the future frequency of the operant, the stimulus is a reinforcer. If a stimulus that follows an operant causes a decrease in the future frequency of the operant, the stimulus is a punisher.

Having determined that a stimulus is a reinforcer or a punisher in one context does not mean that the stimulus will have the same function at other times or in other contexts. *Reinforcers and punishers are relative. They are not unchangeable things.* Food is a reinforcer when we are hungry, but it ceases to be a reinforcer after we have just eaten a big meal. A dark, quiet room is a reinforcer when we are tired and sleepy; but it is boring and aversive when we are awake and well-rested.

The ability to reinforce or punish behavior is not an intrinsic quality of a stimulus. Stimuli that can function as reinforcers or punishers are not transituational, that is, they need not have the same effects in all situations. A given stimulus can function as a reinforcer, neutral stimulus, or punisher in different situations. During childhood a person may consistently avoid eating brussels sprouts; yet in adulthood, the person may love eating them. Thus, brussels sprouts functioned as a punisher in childhood and a reinforcer in adulthood. Some women enjoy sexual relations for years; but after a traumatic rape any behavior that might lead to a sexual interaction becomes suppressed. For these women, sex was a reinforcer until they were raped, then it became a punisher. Grade school children often hold on to their parents while being hugged and kissed at home with the family; yet they may pull away if a parent hugs or kisses them in front of their friends. That is, the children respond to hugs as reinforcers at home by maintaining contact, yet respond to hugs in public as punishers by avoiding them.

Reinforcers and punishers can be placed on a continuum (see Figure 6–1), with powerful reinforcers (at one end) having the ability to raise the probability of behavior, and powerful punishers (at the other end) having the ability to suppress behavior.[2] In the middle of the continuum, the stimuli are called neutral because it is difficult to determine whether they have reinforcing or punishing properties. Adjacent to the neutral stimuli, the reinforcers and punishers are weaker than at the ends of the continuum. A given stimulus—such as food or sex—can take various positions on the continuum at different times or in different situations.[3] Thus, one cannot make a fixed classification of a given stimulus as either a reinforcer or a punisher—strong or weak—based on the intrinsic physical properties of the stimulus.

---

[1]This simplest definition of reinforcers and punishers involves circular logic. The best defense of circular definitions is usefulness (Kaplan, 1964). One can escape the problem of circularity (as we do in this chapter) by turning to either of two independent, noncircular definitions of reinforcers and punishers—the Pavlovian hypothesis (that reinforcers and punishers are US's or CS's) and the Premack principle. These two approaches are explained in greater detail by Dunham (1977). (Also see Meehl, 1950; and Burgess and Akers, 1966.) Interestingly, the simple definition of evolutionary fitness and survival is also circular (Lewontin, 1978:222); yet the theory of natural selection has become the central organizing principle of biology (Mayr, 1978:47). There are several other important parallels between natural selection and reinforcement that may help produce balanced biosocial theories of behavior, interaction, creativity, and social change (Baldwin and Baldwin, 1981).

[2]See Catania (1971) for further details.

[3]Morse and Kelleher (1970, 1977); Barrett and Glowa (1977).

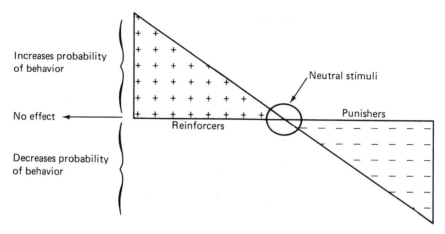

FIGURE 6–1   The continuum of consequences.

The relativity of reinforcers and punishers does not mean that these stimuli are completely arbitrary. The ability of reinforcers and punishers to modify behavior is rooted in our biological makeup. Our capacity to respond to food and water as reinforcers—and to cuts and burns as punishers—is crucial for survival; hence these biological predispositions have been established through evolutionary processes. As B. F. Skinner observed: "The capacity to be reinforced . . . must be traced to natural selection."[4] Individuals who are biologically predisposed to respond to food, water, or sex as reinforcing stimuli after periods of deprivation are less likely to starve, dehydrate, or leave no offspring than are individuals without these predispositions. People who are biologically predisposed to respond to stress, cuts, burns, and other hazards as punishers are more likely to avoid bodily harm and risk of death than individuals without these predispositions.

Thus, the predisposition to be reinforced or punished by stimuli such as food, water, cuts, and burns can be traced to evolutionary processes. These biologically important stimuli are called *un*conditioned reinforcers and *un*conditioned punishers to indicate that no conditioning is needed to make them effective. (They are also called *primary* reinforcers and *primary* punishers to indicate that they are the most basic of reinforcers and punishers.)

UNCONDITIONED STIMULI

Unconditioned stimuli (US's) have two separate functions: (1) they elicit unconditioned responses, and (2) most function as unconditioned reinforcers or unconditioned punishers.[5] When we are hungry, food is an effective US that (1) elicits salivation and

[4]Skinner (1969:206).

[5]Not all US's are reinforcers or punishers. Some lie in the neutral zone on the continuum shown in Figure 6–1. For example, changes in light intensity between low and moderate levels elicit reflexive changes in pupil size without being either reinforcers or punishers (Staats, 1963:53; 1975:36; Terrace, 1971:77). Only at higher intensities does light both elicit reflexive pupillary restriction and serve as a punisher.

TABLE 6–1 A Partial List of Unconditioned Reinforcers

Food
Water
Normal body temperature
Optimal levels of sensory stimulation*
Rest after exertion
Sleep
Caresses, rubbing, itching, scratching
Genital stimulation
Nipple and breast stimulation (especially during lactation)
Nicotine, alcohol, and various other drugs

*Optimal sensory stimulation is one of the least noticed of the uncondi-
tioned reinforcers, yet it is one of the most important unconditioned reinforcers
in everyday life, as is explained below.

positive emotional responses, and (2) reinforces operants which precede it. Scalding hot water is a US that (1) elicits a withdrawal reflex and negative emotional responses, and (2) punishes operants which precede it.

Unconditioned Reinforcers

Table 6–1 lists some of the unconditioned reinforcers that commonly influence behavior in everyday life. At any moment in time only a few of these stimuli may be capable of functioning as reinforcers, depending on an individual's level of *satiation* or *deprivation* for each stimulus.[6] *Generally, the more satiated a person is with any unconditioned reinforcer the less power that US will have to reinforce behavior. The longer a person has been deprived of a given unconditioned reinforcer, the more power that US will have to reinforce behavior.* When a person is satiated with food, food does not function as a reinforcer. However, when a person is deprived of food for many hours, food becomes increasingly reinforcing.

Satiation. Satiation occurs when a person has had so much of a certain US that the stimulus loses its ability to function as a reinforcer. Being itched, scratched, or rubbed for several minutes is pleasurable and rewarding; but itching and rubbing cease to be reinforcers after a given part of the body has been stimulated for an extended period of time. The fifth Hershey bar you eat in a row will not taste as good as the first one. After working hard on a hot day, a swallow of cool spring water is a refreshing experience; but the water ceases to function as a reinforcer after you have drunk several glasses. Sexual stimulation loses its positive reinforcement qualities when partners engage in prolonged sexual stimulation without pauses. Inserting pauses between the Hershey bars—or other positive reinforcers—retards the process of satiation.

[6]Several decades ago it was common to describe motivation in terms of "drives" or "needs." Because drives and needs could only be inferred from behavior and were not directly measurable, many behaviorists ceased using the terms and now describe motivation in terms of hours of deprivation from reinforcers or exposure to aversive stimuli (see Skinner, 1953:141f).

Deprivation.   Deprivation is the opposite of satiation: The longer a person is deprived of a reinforcer, the more powerful the reinforcer becomes. In everyday life, deprivation can result from a variety of causes: natural, deliberate, and compulsory.

1. Natural Deprivation.   While engaging in long chains of activities that are reinforced by one type of reinforcer, people often do not notice that they are being deprived of other reinforcers. But when the long sequence of behavior terminates, they suddenly respond to the other states of deprivation. While playing basketball all afternoon, the players may not detect the increasing food deprivation. During an exciting afternoon at the stock exchange, the broker may forget to eat and not notice any signs of hunger. But when the players finish their game and the broker leaves the office, they may be surprised how hungry they have become and how strongly their attention is directed to food. Because active and busy people are usually very intent on the activities of the moment, they often do not notice levels of deprivation that others might consider to be aversive.[7]

2. Deliberate Deprivation.   People often deliberately abstain from eating before the big Thanksgiving meal because it makes the food seem tastier and allows them to eat more. People sometimes deliberately stay up until they are very tired before going to bed, because the deprivation makes them sleep more deeply, and they find this more pleasurable than light, fitful sleep after minimal deprivation.

3. Compulsory Deprivation.   Sometimes husbands and wives have to live in different cities because of the location of their schools or jobs. When they do get a chance to see each other, they often find that the days of deprivation have enhanced the degree to which touching, caressing, and making love are positive experiences. Poor people in underdeveloped countries may experience compulsory deprivation from which there is little relief. Many people in overpopulated areas of Africa and Asia are almost always in a state of food deprivation. Whereas most Americans eat the equivalent of 3.6 quality meals a day, the people of India average 0.7 quality meals a day.[8]

Extreme deprivation can cause people to do extreme behaviors. During the great famine of 1943 in China, people stripped the bark off trees in order to have something to put in their stomachs (even though bark is of minimal nutritive value).[9] There were reports that children were sometimes killed and eaten, in spite of the cultural and moral sanctions against such behavior. In the winter of 1846, a group of American pioneers—the Donner Party—was trapped in the mountains while heading west. Thirty-four people

---

[7]Having observed that reinforcers are only effective after a period of deprivation and that extreme deprivation is aversive, some scholars have concluded that reward is possible only after a prior aversive situation. This creates a bleak view of life, in which all behavior is motivated by the escape from or avoidance of aversive conditions. The examples given for natural deprivation in the text should make it clear that deprivation may go unnoticed by those who are active and busy. People with a large repertoire of interesting activities that fill their days are unlikely to notice deprivation states as much as people with little to do. In addition, some stimuli—such as optimal warmth and optimal levels of sensory stimulation—do not require deprivation to function as positive reinforcers (pages 104–122).

[8]Pritchett (1978).

[9]White (1978).

TABLE 6–2 A Partial List of Unconditioned Punishers

Extreme cold and extreme heat
Cuts, strong blows, sharp scratches
Shock, stings, burns
Sore skin
Overly full stomach or bladder
Effortful or strenuous work
Certain odors and tastes
Loud noise
Extinction
Lack of air
Water in the lungs
Poisons or diseases that cause nausea or sickness

died of cold and hunger. Many of the forty-five survivors kept from starving by eating the dead.[10] In October 1972, an airplane with forty-five people crashed in the snow-covered Andes at nearly 12,000 feet altitude.[11] Thirty-two of the forty-five passengers survived the crash; rather than die of starvation, the survivors decided after weeks had passed to cut the bodies of their dead companions into small pieces and eat them. Sixteen people survived the seventy-three days of cold and hardship until rescue came. Under extreme food deprivation, people are often motivated to act in ways they never would in other circumstances.

Unconditioned Punishers

Table 6–2 lists some of the unconditioned punishers that are common in everyday life. *Unconditioned punishers are not influenced by deprivation, nor does a person cease to find them aversive due to satiation.* After being cut several times in a half hour while learning to operate a new machine, people do not "satiate" on cuts and cease to find them aversive. The seventh cut hurts about as much as the first. After going 6 months without getting burned, there is no deprivation effect that increases the aversiveness of the next burn.

The fact that punishers are not influenced by deprivation and satiation can be understood in terms of biological adaptation. It is adaptive for individuals to cease finding food, sex, or water reinforcing when they have had enough of them. However, it is adaptive to find the unconditioned punishers to be aversive at all times, because they always pose a threat to health or survival whenever they appear.

Usually there is a threshold effect with punishers. Effort must exceed some threshold before we find it aversive. Sharp scratches must surpass a certain limit before they are aversive. Once above the threshold, increasing the intensity of the US increases the strength of the punishment effect. If the neighbor's cat gives you a superficial scratch every once in a while, this mild punisher may slightly suppress the frequency of your

[10]Rhodes (1973).
[11]Read (1974).

picking up the cat. However, if the cat regularly gave you quite painful scratches, the intense punishment might completely suppress your touching the cat.

There are two properties of unconditioned punishers that make it easy for people to learn to use physical punishment as a means of child rearing, coping with marital problems, and so forth. First, there are *immediate rewards* for the person who uses punishment on others. If one person wants to stop another from doing a given behavior, strong punishment usually produces immediate effects. Threats of punishment can also create instant motivation for behavior needed to avoid punishment: "If you don't clean up your room right this minute, I'll give you a spanking you'll never forget." If such threats have been backed up with strong punishment in the past, they can produce immediate results—due to negative reinforcement. The instant effectiveness of both punishment and negative reinforcement provides immediate rewards for the person who uses aversive control. Second, the unconditioned punishers are *always effective:* They do not lose their power to punish or negatively reinforce behavior after repeated use. In contrast, unconditioned reinforcers lose their effectiveness after a person reaches satiation: Food ceases to be a reinforcer after a person is full. Punishment never ceases to be aversive; thus, some people come to rely on aversive control because strong punishment almost always produces effects.

People who have not learned many cooperative means of dealing with others—based on positive reinforcement—are most likely to be drawn into heavy reliance on punishment. When their limited positive skills fail, they can always fall back on threats or punishers, with their immediate effects and persistent power.

Physical punishment is used far more commonly in everyday life than many people realize. For example, there are at least 2 million cases of child abuse per year in the United States (and there are probably many more).[12] Because small children cannot escape or fight back, parents meet little resistance in using corporal punishment in child rearing, and some escalate the intensity of punishment to dangerous, bone-breaking levels. Although small, dependent children cannot escape the parent who punishes so hard that bones are broken, older children frequently run away from home when staying is too aversive. Several million children run away from home each year.[13]

Violence begets violence: Children from violent homes often learn to use violence on others. They may not strike back at their parents for fear of getting a physical blow in return; but on the playground they fight and bully other children, imitating the use of unconditioned punishers they see at home.[14] Once they reach adulthood, the people from violent homes are more likely to be child abusers than people from nonviolent homes.[15] They are also more likely to expect and use physical violence in interactions with their spouse:[16] The husband strikes his wife when she refuses to comply with some wish; and she may accept this as "normal," if that is the way she saw her father treat her mother.

---

[12]Gil (1974:205).
[13]Chapman (1976).
[14]Bandura and Walters (1959, 1963); Hoffman (1960).
[15]Silver et al. (1969); Spinetta and Rigler (1972).
[16]Martin (1976).

Each year in the United States, at least 2 or 3 million wives—and perhaps twice that number—are severely beaten by their husbands.[17] The use of unconditioned punishers is not restricted to the home. Throughout history, people have used flogging, beatings, torture, lynching, inquisitions, witch-hunts, concentration camps, and war in the attempt to control others by inflicting pain.

In the long run, aversive techniques produce numerous problems. Punishment can condition a variety of responses ranging from fear, anxiety and avoidance, to hatred, violence, and revolution. All of these responses undermine stable, cooperative, and constructive social relationships. Modern behavioral science has demonstrated that most behavior can be learned—or prevented—through positive reinforcement without the bad side effects produced by aversive learning (Chapter 13). In addition, positive reinforcement makes learning much more pleasant than learning via punishment or negative reinforcement. One of the greatest challenges to modern society is to phase out the heavy reliance on punishment that has been so common in the past and to help people learn the power and pleasure of using positive reinforcement.[18]

MODIFYING UNCONDITIONED REINFORCERS
AND PUNISHERS

Because unconditioned reinforcers and punishers play important biological roles in survival and reproduction it might seem logical to assume that they would be biologically fixed and resistant to change (except for the short-term fluctuations due to deprivation and satiation). One might expect that food would always be a reinforcer for a hungry person, whereas being beaten would always be a punisher. But this is not the case. *Any US that serves as an unconditioned reinforcer or punisher can be modified to a different location on the continuum from strong reinforcers to strong punishers.* Some people learn to find food or sex to be more powerful reinforcers than is normally the case. Other people find so little pleasure in food that they have to remind themselves to eat. There are people who assiduously avoid sex, indicating that it functions as a punisher for them. Some people learn to find unconditioned punishers less painful than others, and a minority respond to them as positive reinforcers. Some children engage in hours of head banging and self-mutilation each day; and some adults are drawn to masochistic sexual practices that others would find aversive.

Any US that is an unconditioned reinforcer or punisher can be shifted to a new location on the continuum from strong reinforcers to strong punishers (Figure 6–2). This modification occurs through Pavlovian conditioning when the US is frequently followed by other reinforcers or punishers.[19] Pavlov's original experiments on dogs illustrate the phenomenon clearly.[20] For a moderately hungry animal, food is normally a US that elicits

---

[17]Strauss et al. (1980); O'Reilly (1983).

[18]Skinner (1971).

[19]Schedule effects (Chapter 12) provide a second, compatible explanation for the modification of unconditioned reinforcers and punishers (Morse and Kelleher, 1970, 1977).

[20]Pavlov (1927).

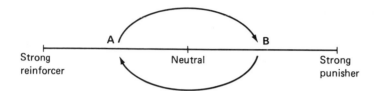

FIGURE 6–2   The modification of unconditioned reinforcers and punishers.

salivation and reinforces relevant operants. However, if food is regularly presented before a powerful punisher, such as strong shock, food also becomes a CS that elicits aversive emotional responses. After repeated presentations of food before strong shock, the dog will show signs of fear when food is presented. It may whine and yelp, cower, and pull its tail between its legs. Food can become so powerful a punisher that it suppresses eating. Food has been shifted from position A to position B in Figure 6–2.

The opposite modification can occur, too. A dog is made hungry by food deprivation. If shock precedes the presentation of food, shock can be conditioned into a positive reinforcer. After repeated pairings, the shock becomes a CS that elicits smacking of the lips and salivation, and also functions as a positive reinforcer. As long as the shocks reliably signal that the food is forthcoming, they will serve as positive reinforcers. Shock has been shifted from position B to position A in Figure 6–2.

The Modification of Reinforcers

In everyday life there are numerous examples showing how unconditioned reinforcers and punishers are modified by experience. Due to conditioning, some people have little interest in food, whereas others are overly responsive to food as a reinforcer. The same is true of sex and other unconditioned reinforcers. A variety of conditioning events can be responsible for decreasing or increasing a person's responsiveness to unconditioned reinforcers.

When an unconditioned reinforcer regularly precedes aversive stimuli, the unconditioned reinforcer becomes a weaker reinforcer, and may even become a punisher. Some children grow up in families where fights occur frequently at the dinner table. Dinner is commonly paired with nasty arguments and ugly criticisms, all of which elicit negative emotional responses. Eventually, food becomes a CS that elicits aversive responses and makes eating less reinforcing. Some people are constantly afraid of gaining weight or getting fat. Food is associated with the feared fat, which causes it to become a CS for aversive feelings and decreases the total positive reinforcement effect of food. As food loses its strength as a reinforcer, people eat less and lose weight. Sometimes people can become dangerously thin and close to death by starvation—as in extreme cases of anorexia.[21]

The research of Kinsey, Masters and Johnson, and others indicates that in our

---

[21]Walen et al. (1977). Anorexia can also result from positive reinforcement for not eating.

society it is common to find people for whom sex is not a positive reinforcer.[22] Case histories collected by these researchers show that when sex is continually paired with aversive circumstances, it ceases being a positive reinforcer and becomes aversive—a source of anxiety, worry, guilt, doubt, or fear. There are many kinds of experiences that can cause sex to become a punisher.

In some homes, the parents repeatedly stress that sex is dirty or sinful. Some parents punish masturbation with fear-eliciting threats about impending mental illness, acne, or damnation. When children ask questions about sex out of innocent curiosity, they may be chastised for thinking such "filthy thoughts." When a heavy dose of punishment and fear-eliciting threats is paired with sex, the aversive experiences can be stronger than the biologically reinforcing aspects of sex and can modify sex to be a punisher. While children are growing up they may not know that they are being conditioned to find sex aversive. A boy may realize that he does not like to talk about sex even though his friends do; but his prior conditioning would make it aversive for him to indulge in such "dirty, base, and animalistic thoughts." A girl may be aware that she does not like to be kissed and that she avoids it, but she may feel proud that she has a good reputation. By their late teens, the boy and girl know that they are not engaging in petting even though some of their peers do; but again they find that their abstinence shows higher values. Perhaps it is not until they are married and free to have sexual relations that they discover how anxious they actually feel when confronted with sex. Even after marriage, some of these people cannot bring themselves to do something that has been treated as "dirty" for so many years. Others engage in intercourse but find it aversive. After years of marriage some men and women admit that they have never enjoyed sex and that their rare love making was done to satisfy their partner's desires or to have children.

People can develop conditioned anxieties about sex in a very short time. After a man fails to have a full sexual response with his wife on several consecutive occasions, he may begin to fear that he is impotent. This fear can interfere with further sexual functioning and increase the chances of additional sexual failures. Each time sex is paired with failure, the aversive conditioning modifies sex toward the punishment end of the continuum of reinforcers and punishers (Figure 6–2). Now the invitation to make love presents a threat of failure and elicits performance anxiety. Sex has now become a punisher that functions as a negative reinforcer for avoiding situations that could lead to sexual interaction.

Sex need not remain a punisher forever. With the appropriate counterconditioning, sex can be modified to again be a positive reinforcer. Masters and Johnson's program of two weeks of intensive positive conditioning is very effective in establishing a normal and pleasurable sexual response even in people who have had years of sex-related anxieties or who never have had any sexual success.

When an unconditioned reinforcer regularly precedes other reinforcers, the unconditioned reinforcer gains even greater reinforcement value. For example, when food is paired with numerous other reinforcers—or the avoidance of aversive events—it can become an unusually powerful positive reinforcer, making it hard for people to stop eating

---

[22]Kinsey et al. (1948, 1953) and Masters and Johnson (1966, 1970) have shown that there is an enormous variation in people's sexual behavior. Much of this can be traced to people's history of conditioning.

even when they should. Some social settings regularly pair food with other positive reinforcers. The process can begin in infancy or later in life. Many well-intentioned mothers think that pudgy children are healthy children. When the youngster stops eating, the mother coaxes the child to have another helping of food. When dinner is over, mother scoops out a big helping of the child's favorite dessert. If the child is not seduced by the sweetness and flavor, the mother may encourage the child to eat by acting hurt—"Here I made it especially for you and now you won't eat it." When the child eats the extra food, the mother responds with warmth and affection. These multiple conditioning influences make food a more positive reinforcer than is biologically adaptive.

All through life, people are exposed to numerous types of social conditioning that increase the reinforcement value of food. When college students eat together in cafeterias or restaurants, food is often paired with rewarding social interactions, jokes, laughter, fun—and the avoidance of studying. These positive experiences help condition food further toward the left end of the continuum of reinforcers (Figure 6–2). All through adulthood, people frequently have food available while socializing, which continually pairs food with social reinforcers. In addition, people can become excessively attracted to food when eating is regularly paired with an escape from anxiety, boredom, or other aversive experiences. People who are bored look for something to do. Eating is something to do. Escaping the boredom is a reinforcer. Eating soon becomes an unusually powerful reinforcer due to the pairing with the escape from boredom. The round bellies that become increasingly prevalent as Americans enter their thirties and forties reflect, in part, the increasing power of food as a positive reinforcer.

The Modification of Punishers

Unconditioned punishers can lose some of their aversiveness—and even become reinforcing—if they are paired with numerous reinforcers.[23] Athletes often become conditioned to find the rigors of their sport less aversive than the ordinary person would. During the entire socialization of the football player, giving and receiving painful blows is paired with positive reinforcers: praise, team support, the excitement of the game, promotions to first string, comradeship with the "really hot players," social status, and so forth. After having violent blows paired with these positive reinforcers for years, the football player can not only tolerate higher levels of painful stimuli, but can actually find these stimuli less punishing. When unathletic people take up jogging for the first time, they often find the physical exertion sheer torture. They find it difficult to believe the experienced runner who says that the aversiveness will go away after a while. Many joggers quit before they find out. However, the joggers who receive enough reinforcement to keep running begin to discover that it is an exhilarating experience. If there are enough rewards for running, the sensations from the straining legs and pounding heart are no longer experienced as punishers.

Certain aspects of masochism can be traced to experiences in which unconditioned punishers were paired with numerous positive reinforcers. For example, a person who enjoys masochistic sexual practices usually has a history of conditioning that began when

[23]Green (1972).

mild punishers were paired with enjoyable sexual interactions. At first the incipient masochist might have an especially enjoyable sexual experience the time he or she was loosely tied to the bed and swatted gently on the derrière. The novelty of the experience, the laughter and fun, and sexual excitement all help to countercondition fears of being tied loosely and swatted gently. The next time, the fearless player has the ropes tied tighter and reexperiences the titillation of the "dangerous" game. With time, being tied tightly is progressively conditioned into a reinforcer by the positive stimuli of sex, fun, and games. Eventually the masochist enjoys stimuli that would be experienced as painful or frightening by most people.

THE PREMACK PRINCIPLE

Because all reinforcers and punishers can be modified by conditioning, not even the unconditioned reinforcers and punishers are fixed and unchanging. Knowledge about a person's past conditioning helps explain how any given unconditioned reinforcer or punisher may have been modified by experience. However, we do not always have access to the information we would need to determine a person's past history of conditioning. Is there any other way to determine whether a given stimulus is a reinforcer or punisher? Is there any way to determine where it lies on the continuum from strong reinforcers to strong punishers (Figure 6–2)?

The Premack principle[24] provides a useful method for answering this question.[25] In simplified form the Premack principle states: *Access to any high probability behavior (HPB) will serve as a reinforcer for any low probability behavior (LPB). On the other hand, doing an LPB will serve as a punisher for an HPB.* Note that the Premack principle focuses on behavior rather than on stimuli. For example, it directs attention to the behavior of eating, rather than to the stimulus of food. However, it is usually easy to infer which reinforcing or punishing stimuli are associated with any given behavior.

Parents frequently apply the Premack principle without knowing it. When a parent sees the children spending hours playing in the sandbox, the parent may use sandbox play (the HPB) to reinforce some low probability behavior (LPB), such as taking out the garbage. "You can play in the sandbox if you take out the garbage first." The HPB is used to reinforce the LPB. If cleaning up after the dog is an LPB in a child's daily activities, the parents may use the LPB to punish undesired HPB's, such as coming home late from school. "If you get home late one more time, you'll have to clean up after the dog for the next five nights."

The Premack principle can be used to understand all types of behavior in people of any age. If we observe that a woman spends a great deal of time talking about her

---

[24]Premack (1965, 1971). There is considerable empirical evidence to support the Premack principle. The strengths and weaknesses of the Premack principle are reviewed by Eisenberger et al. (1967), Danaher (1974), Dunham (1977), and others.

[25]This approach to the definition of reinforcers and punishers is not circular because one does not have to wait until *after* a consequence modifies an operant to decide whether the consequence is a reinforcer or punisher. Hence, the Premack principle helps solve the problem of circularity by providing an independent source of information about abilities to reinforce or punish (see note 1, this chapter).

children, it is clear that talking about the children is an HPB. The chance to talk about children should function as a reinforcer for any behavior that allows a conversation to turn to children. If the woman is listening to a conversation about real estate and only by chance interjects, "Do you have any children?" her chance question (which is an LPB) may sidetrack the conversation from real estate to children (her HPB). The opportunity to engage in her HPB will reinforce her asking the sidetracking question. In the future, she will be more likely to insert the question about children into her conversation. If a man never misses the "big game" on TV every weekend, watching the game is clearly an HPB. If the TV goes on the blink on Wednesday night, the man may either procrastinate about getting it fixed or promptly take it in for repairs. Because procrastinating may make him miss a game, this behavior will be punished by the loss of access to the HPB. Getting the TV fixed will be reinforced by the HPB of watching the game. Not surprisingly, most TV addicts learn some behaviors—buying a new set, going to a friend's house, getting the old set fixed—because these behaviors are reinforced by the HPB of watching their favorite programs.

Cutting oneself with sharp objects is an LPB for most people, hence it is identified as a punisher by the Premack principle. Any activity that causes people to cut themselves should be suppressed by the LPB. Thus, the LPB suppresses careless handling of knives and razor blades, and it negatively reinforces caution and other behavior that avoids the LPB. If we notice that one of the new lawyers in a firm never goes in to talk with the senior partner—even though most of the other lawyers do—it would appear that talking with the senior partner is an LPB for the new lawyer, hence a punisher. This LPB should function to suppress any behavior that would cause the new lawyer to have to talk with the senior partner. For example, making serious mistakes in a legal document would cause the senior partner to call a lawyer in for consultation. We would expect the new lawyer to be very cautious about such mistakes: The frequency of such mistakes would be suppressed by the consequences of having to do the LPB of talking with the senior partner.

The Premack principle sidesteps the problem of determining whether a given reinforcer or punisher is an unconditioned consequence or a conditioned consequence. The Premack principle works equally well in dealing with any combination of biologically established or conditioned reinforcers or punishers.

SENSORY STIMULATION

Sensory stimulation might well be called "the unknown reinforcer." Of all the unconditioned reinforcers, sensory stimulation is the one that people understand the least. Yet sensory stimulation is one of the most important reinforcers in everyday life.[26] It influences our behavior 24 hours a day, whether we are asleep or awake, alone or with others.

---

[26]Schultz (1965), Ellis (1973), and Zuckerman (1974, 1984) present some of the best integrated analyses of the reinforcement properties of sensory stimulation. Prior to this, many researchers had demonstrated that sensory input was reinforcing (Butler, 1958, 1965; Mason, 1965; Kish, 1966; Campbell, 1972). Baldwin and Baldwin (1977, 1978b, 1981) present a summary of the literature on sensory stimulation reinforcement in nonhuman primates and humans.

The remainder of this chapter describes the basic properties of "the unknown reinforcer," sensory stimulation.

Quantity and Quality

Sensory stimulation comes from all parts of the stimulus collage: both from outside the body and from inside the body. We continually receive stimuli from the external world via the five senses—seeing, hearing, smelling, tasting, and feeling. The more things happening in our environment, the more sensory stimulation enters the five senses. There are also internal sense organs that detect sensations from all parts of the body, including the brain. These sensors allow us to feel many internal responses, such as butterflies in the stomach, flutters of the heart, and the contractions in our muscles when we move arms, legs, or other body parts. We can also sense when our brain is alive with activity or dropping into an inactive state. Thought, fantasy, and daydreams can provide so much interesting sensory stimulation that people may neglect external sensory stimulation for the pleasure of mental stimulation. All the sense modalities can bring pleasure when they are stimulated by optimal *quantities* and *qualities* of sensory inputs.

Quantity. Sensory stimulation can be either a reinforcer or punisher, depending on the total quantity of stimulation entering the sensory systems. The total amount of sensory inputs from the entire stimulus collage—from outside and inside the body—can range anywhere from very low, to medium, to very high. *Under normal waking conditions, both low and high levels of sensory inputs function as unconditioned punishers. Between the extremes, there is an optimal, intermediate level of sensory stimulation that functions as an unconditioned reinforcer.* When we receive too little stimulation from external and internal sources, we experience the aversive feelings of boredom. Too much sensory stimulation, on the other hand, causes the aversive feelings of nervousness, anxiety, or hypertension. Between "too little" and "too much"—between boredom and anxiety[27]—there is an *optimal zone* where the sensory input is pleasurable. Optimal levels of sensory stimulation function as an unconditioned positive reinforcer.

If you were home alone one afternoon with nothing to do, you might become bored. Having nothing to do leaves you with low levels of sensory input, which cause boredom. Turning on the stereo might help relieve the boredom since the music provides increased amounts of sensory stimulation. Turning on the stereo is reinforced by the escape from boredom and the onset of pleasant sensory stimulation. If you have a powerful stereo system, you might turn it up full blast just to feel the full power of the 200 watt amplifier; but the volume would probably come down to a more comfortable level after a few minutes. Overly loud sensory inputs are aversive, hence provide negative reinforcement for turning down the volume. However, you won't turn down the volume to the point where you can hardly hear the music. Between the extremes of "too little" and "too much" sensory stimulation is the optimal zone, where the volume brings pleasure. People play their stereos at intermediate volume levels most of the time. Adjusting the volume to intermediate levels is reinforced by optimal levels of sensory stimulation. Note that the

[27]Csikszentmihalyi (1975).

optimal zone is fairly broad: There is a range of volume settings that people find reward-ing, depending on the type of music, time of day, and activities of the moment.

Most motorcyclists would get bored quickly if they always had to drive at 5 or 10 miles an hour. There is simply not much sensory stimulation produced by riding so slowly. However, at 40 to 60 miles an hour, both the rush of the wind and the rapidly changing visual inputs provide an optimal level of sensory stimulation that is exhilarating and rewarding to experience. If allowed to test a fast motorcycle at a race track, most motorcyclists would find some speed—perhaps 70, 90, or 120 miles an hour—at which the stimulus input from all the senses was too high. After experiencing the thrill of high speed for a few minutes, they would be ready to drop back to intermediate speeds. Driving at intermediate speeds is reinforced by optimal levels of sensory stimulation; and driving at extremely slow or fast speeds is punished by understimulation or overstimulation. Again, the optimal zone is broad, and it varies for different people on different occasions. Some people would find 40 to 60 miles per hour the optimal speed for motorcycling; whereas others would prefer 60 to 80 miles per hour—if the law would allow that pleasure.

People frequently adjust the quantity of sensory input to keep it inside the optimal zone, for example by adjusting the volume on the stereo. When we squint on a bright day, we are reducing the amount of light entering the eyes to a more pleasant level. When we turn on the lights at night, we are increasing the light to the optimal level. If our heads are so busy with thoughts that we cannot go to sleep at night, a sleeping pill helps turn off the excessive mental stimulation. If we have nothing to think about and feel bored, we may pick up the newspaper or turn on the TV to get inputs that stimulate our senses. When some people want more stimulation, they use stimulant drugs—such as coffee, amphetamines, or nicotine—which produce a quick "high" by increasing internal senso-ry inputs. Other people learn that exciting events and invigorating physical activities produce a "natural high." All these behaviors are done because they avoid the aversive states of under- or overstimulation (negative reinforcement) and because they produce the reinforcers of optimal sensory input (positive reinforcement).

Qualities.   At least three qualities of stimuli affect their ability to provide sensory stimulation: *Variety, Intensity, and Meaningfulness.*[28] These are easily remembered as *VIM*. Every stimulus has all three VIM properties, but the amount of variety, intensity, and meaningfulness found in different stimuli can vary greatly. One stimulus may be high in all three, while a second stimulus may be high in only one or two of these qualities.

Variety.   Variety is the spice of life! Some stimuli provide more varied experience than others. Going to Mardi Gras or a costume ball provides more variety than going to work for the thousandth time. All stimuli lie somewhere on a continuum from low variety to high variety. Familiar, monotonous, or simple stimuli provide low variety, and they are

---

[28]By breaking sensory input into the three components of variety, intensity, and meaningfulness, Fiske and Maddi (1961) provide a set of discriminations useful in identifying sensory stimulation phenomena in everyday life. It should be noted that their classification is not the only one possible. For example, the trichotomy of mental, physical, and emotional can be useful in many analyses of sensory input (Blum et al., 1967).

most likely to produce boredom. Novel, variable, complex, or surprising stimuli provide greater variety. The more novel and varied a stimulus input is, the more it adds to the total sensory stimulation a person experiences from the stimulus collage.

Intensity.   Each stimulus lies somewhere on a continuum from low intensity to high intensity: dark to bright, quiet to loud, gentle to powerful, soft to coarse. The more intense the stimulus is, the more it adds to the total sensory stimulation that a person experiences. Too much stimulus intensity is usually aversive—such as when the lights are too bright or the noise is too loud. But people become bored when the intensity of all the sensory inputs is reduced to very low levels—as in sensory deprivation experiments that isolate people from all intense stimuli.

Meaningfulness.   Each stimulus lies on a continuum from low meaningfulness to high meaningfulness. A stimulus is defined as meaningful to a person if a person responds to the stimulus. For example, the word "Danger" has meaning to people who speak or read English, and they respond to it. But it is meaningless to people who have not learned English. Neutral stimuli have low meaningfulness because they produce little or no response. US's and CS's are meaningful because they elicit reflexive responses. S^D's and S^Δ's are meaningful because they set the occasion for doing or not doing certain operants. The more meaningful a stimulus is, the more internal and external responses it produces, and the more it adds to the total sensory stimulation that a person experiences.

The total sensory stimulation that a person receives from a given stimulus collage depends on all three qualities of the stimuli. For example, for a nature lover, a quiet walk through the woods may provide low variety, low stimulus intensity, and high meaningfulness. The veteran laborer who operates an air hammer on a street repair crew experiences high intensity stimulus input, but limited novelty or meaningfulness. Entertainment usually is designed to bring variety into life. Some entertainment involves low intensity stimuli (e.g., a quiet classical guitar concert); other provides high intensity stimuli (a roller coaster ride). Some entertainment offers low meaningfulness (mindless entertainment); and other, high meaningfulness (a movie that triggers days of thoughtful reflection).

Relativity

All unconditioned reinforcers and punishers are relative: Sensory stimulation is no exception. The ability of sensory inputs to serve as reinforcers or punishers depends on several factors.

First, the ability of one source of stimuli to function as a reinforcer or a punisher is influenced by the other stimuli present in the stimulus collage. Doing daily exercises can be boring since it is so repetitive; but exercising to music—or with friends—can be fun, because exercising is now part of a more stimulating total sensory experience. A noisy, action-packed TV show may provide optimal levels of sensory input and reinforce our full attention if there is nothing else going on in the house. However, if the kids are screaming, the washing machine is overflowing, the toaster is belching billows of black smoke, and the phone has been ringing every couple of minutes, we may find the blaring TV nerve racking. It pushes the total amount of sensory stimulation so high that it is aversive, which provides negative reinforcement for turning the TV off—or shouting for someone else to turn it off.

Second, the ability of stimuli to provide novel and varied experience declines with repeated exposure.[29] A stimulus is most novel the first time a person experiences it. Repeated experience with the stimulus causes it to lose its novelty. This phenomenon is called *habituation.* The first time a teenager drives a car, the experience is novel, stimulating, and exciting. With repeated experience, the novelty "wears off," due to habituation. The first time we do anything, the behavior seems especially exciting, because it is novel. Since novelty is an important source of variety (the *V* in *VIM*), novelty is a crucial component of sensory stimulation.

Figure 6–3 shows how habituation reduces the total sensory stimulation of a stimulus as the novelty wears off. When you buy a new record, the music is most novel during the first several times you listen to it. Novelty adds to the total sensory stimulation obtained from playing the record, producing the optimal levels of sensory input that reinforce playing the record several times during the first week. After hearing the record 10 or 15 times, you notice that the novelty is already "wearing off." As the novelty declines, there are fewer sensory reinforcers for playing the record, and you play the record less frequently each week. Eventually, there is so little novelty that the record fails to produce optimal levels of sensory input, and soon you stop playing it (due to extinction).

A new house going up in the neighborhood provides more novelty than older houses (since the old ones have already lost their novelty). There is more sensory stimulation to reinforce looking at the new house than looking at the old ones when driving past. Over the months and years, the newest house will also lose its novelty, and looking at it will provide no more sensory rewards than looking at the other houses. It eventually "blends in," even though it "stood out" when it was new. New changes in the neighborhood may "stick out like a sore thumb" at first, because they are more novel than the rest of the stimuli. After enough time, habituation reduces the novelty of "sore thumbs," and they cease to provide reinforcement for looking at them more than other stimuli.

The speed of the habituation process can vary. Some stimuli lose their novelty quickly; others, slowly. *Habituation is usually slowest when a stimulus is complex, variable, and quite different from stimuli that are already familiar.* Some fast-paced movies with complex special effects provide so much novel stimulation that people go back several times before getting bored. Other movies, with less novel and complex content may get boring before we sit through the first viewing, and we would never pay to see them a second time. When a child receives several toys as birthday presents, the simple ones—and the ones most similar to old familiar toys—will lose their novelty faster than complex and totally new toys. The sooner a toy loses its novelty, the sooner the child stops playing with it (due to the lack of reinforcement).

Naturally, novelty is only one source of reinforcement; therefore a person may continue doing a behavior long after the novelty is gone, if the behavior is maintained by other reinforcers. A child may prefer an old familiar doll to new ones and play with it for

---

[29]Welker (1961, 1971).

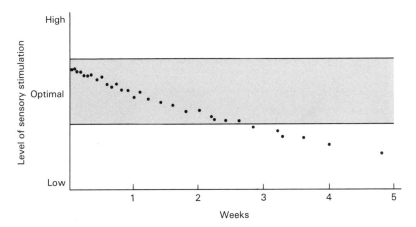

FIGURE 6–3   A phonograph record loses its novelty and ability to provide optimal sensory stimulation after repeated playing.
Each dot in the figure represents one playing of a phonograph record. As the novelty declines, the time between playing increases.

years if the old doll has become especially attractive because it is associated with many positive reinforcers—such as pleasant fantasies or security at night.

Third, after a person ceases to find a stimulus novel (due to habituation), the stimulus can regain a fraction of its novelty if there is a period of time in which a person does not encounter the stimulus.[30] The process by which a stimulus regains novelty is called *recovery.* Figure 6–4 shows the original habituation to a stimulus (from A to B), followed by a period of no contact (from B to C), then the recovery of interest (at C). If you are flipping through your record collection and see an album that you have not played for a long time, you may get it out and listen to it. Because it has been several months since you listened to the album last, the stimuli will have regained some of their novelty (at C). The album will not sound as novel as it did when you first played it (at A), but it will seem fresher and more interesting than the last time you listened to it (at B). Because the record has recovered enough novelty to again provide optimal levels of sensory stimulation, there are sensory reinforcers for playing it several times. During each replay, habituation again robs the record of its novelty. The decline of interest (from C to D) tends to be faster than the original habituation (from A to B). After the novelty has worn off this second time, the record again fails to provide enough sensory stimulation to reinforce playing it.

Some children saw *E.T.* several times when it first appeared. After seeing the movie five times, a child might eventually lose interest, since habituation has removed the novelty that reinforced viewing. Several years later, the child might watch *E.T.* on TV and show renewed interest in it, since the film seemed novel again due to recovery effects. It might only take one or two viewings before the novelty wore off the second time.

Behavior that is reinforced by novelty sometimes appears in repeated cycles of

[30]Welker (1961).

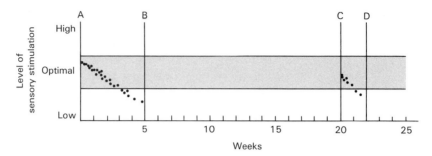

FIGURE 6-4   The first habituation period is between A and B. Recovery of novelty is seen at time C, after a period of no contact with the stimulus. Each dot in the figure represents one playing of the phonograph record.

habituation and recovery. Every June when a family goes to the lake for summer vacation, the novelty and excitement are especially strong during the first week, since there has been a whole year for the boating, water skiing, and picknicking to regain their novelty. However, the lake activities lose their novelty as the vacation progresses, and the family is ready to leave the lake after a couple of weeks. One year later, the cycle of recovery and habituation will occur again. People may go through periods of visiting Chinese restaurants several nights a week (until the novelty wears off), then go for months without eating Chinese food. During the pause, recovery effects make Chinese food novel again. The cycle of dining at Chinese restaurants may be repeated two or three times each year.

When parents buy roller skates for their child, they may initiate cycles of habituation and recovery. First, the child goes skating every day for several weeks, since there is abundant novelty to reinforce frequent skating. Gradually, the novelty wears off, the sensory reinforcers decline, and the child stops skating as frequently. Eventually, the skates end up in the back of the child's closet. The parents ask, "How come we never see you on your skates any more?" "Aw, skating is boring," the child responds. Once the novelty is gone, there are few sensory reinforcers for skating. After the child goes for months without skating, there is a partial recovery of novelty for skating. The child may rediscover skating one day and return to skating for two or three days before the novelty—and sensory reinforcers—again decline. This cycle of skating and not skating may repeat several times.

Fourth, there are individual differences in people's preferred levels of stimulus variety, intensity, and meaningfulness (VIM). All combinations of different levels of VIM are possible. One person may love high levels of V and I, but moderate M; whereas another prefers low levels of V and I, but high M. Such personal preferences can usually be traced to an individual's past learning experience.[31]

Some children grow up in active homes where the parents talk a lot, participate in

---

[31]Zuckerman (1974, 1984) postulates a genetic basis for individual differences in preferred stimulation levels. However, learning may be more important than Zuckerman's biological theory suggests (Baldwin, 1984).

several sports or clubs, have frequent house guests, entertain often, and encourage their children to have their friends over at any time. If there is generous positive reinforcement for participating in this high level of social activity, the children will grow up loving constant social activity. Solitude may be boring for them, since it is below their preferred level of frequent social interaction. Other people grow up in homes that are much quieter. A child may find that the happiest hours are spent daydreaming or playing quietly with favorite toys. Perhaps the parents read in the evening instead of having people over, and the child learns to enjoy reading because the parents show sincere interest in the things the child is reading and thinking about. In this type of home, a person may grow up loving quiet surroundings with the minimum of intrusive, high intensity sensory inputs. An outsider's first impression might be that the quiet person loves low levels of sensory stimulation. More careful observation would reveal that the person is actually enjoying high levels of novel ideas and meaningfulness, and only stimulus intensity is preferred at low levels.

People's personal preferences for different combinations of stimulus variety, intensity, and meaningfulness often influence their social interactions.[32] Two people who have learned to be highly social—talking and joking all day long with dozens of different people—are likely to get along well with each other; but neither will find it very exciting to interact for long periods with a quiet, reflective person who prefers serious, in depth conversation. On the other hand, two very quiet and serious people may get along perfectly with each other, even though neither finds much pleasure in interacting with highly talkative and socially active people.

Sensory stimulation preferences can be situation specific. A professor may love to teach in a very active manner—moving around and writing on the board all the time—because this helps the students get excited about the subject. Yet the professor may prefer very quiet and gentle forms of face-to-face interaction, since this is conducive to serious and meaningful conversation.

Fifth, there are individual differences in people's "taste" for different types of sensory stimulation. For example, most people enjoy listening to music because it can provide optimal levels of sensory stimulation. However, people have quite different "tastes" in music. Some people love rock, and others hate rock. Some love Baroque music, and others find it too mechanical. Taste preferences are learned. Teenagers receive social reinforcers from peers for liking rock music. Concert goers exchange social reinforcers for listening to and appreciating classical music. People usually develop a "taste" for types of music that are closely associated with pleasurable, meaningful, and reinforcing events.

People develop different tastes in art, literature, humor, conversational topics, and many other forms of sensory stimulation. Books provide sensory stimulation that is high in meaningfulness; but people have different tastes in meaningfulness. Some like biographies; others like mysteries; yet others prefer love stories. There is meaningfulness in all the books, but each individual's unique history of learning causes him or her to respond to different sensory inputs as meaningful.

Sixth, daily cycles of sleep and wakefulness alter the height of the optimal stimula-

---

[32]Maddi (1980).

tion zone.[33] When we are sleepy, the low levels of sensory stimulation of a dark, quiet room are optimally stimulating, pleasant, and rewarding; but when we are awake, such low levels of sensory stimulation are understimulating, boring, and aversive. When we are sleepy the sensory stimulation of bright and noisy areas is aversive; but this level of sensory input may be optimally stimulating and rewarding when we are awake.

There are biological regulatory systems that automatically adjust the optimal zone up and down to produce the daily wake-sleep cycle. Figure 6–5 shows the typical daily cycle of stimulus preferences, from noon one day to noon the next. During the afternoon and evening, people find intermediate levels of sensory stimulation to be optimal and reinforcing. Thus, being active and busy are reinforced by optimal stimulation and passivity is punished by boredom. However, as bedtime approaches, the optimal zone begins to descend, making it rewarding to seek out dark, quiet surroundings—which are, of course, most suited to sleep. All during the night, the low levels of sensory input most conducive to sleep are rewarding. If we are awakened by strange noises in the house that trigger a long chain of thoughts, the cognitive activity may provide so much internal sensory stimulation that we cannot go back to sleep. Cognitive activity that lies above the low optimal zone for sleep prevents us from sleeping and is aversive. We may try to stop it by counting sheep (a monotonous, low stimulation activity) or taking a sleeping pill.

When children are put to bed before they are tired, their optimal zones are still high (at A in Figure 6–5) and the bed is boringly understimulating (at B). Thus, children who are put to bed early often discover ways of boosting their sensory inputs above the boredom zone until sleep overtakes them. They fantasize in bed. They smuggle toys or books into the bed. They talk with their brother or sister or make a few trips to the bathroom. When their optimal zone is finally lowered by tiredness (at C in Figure 6–5), they find low sensory stimulation rewarding, snuggle in quietly, and go to sleep.

After a night's sleep, the optimal zone rises to the daytime levels (D in Figure 6–5). At this time, the low levels of sensory stimulation that are optimal for sleep become boring, and people need higher levels of sensory input for optimally rewarding experience. People open the curtains, let the light flood into the bedroom, and head out for a day of stimulating activity.

Some people wake up and reach their full daytime activity level faster than others. Their optimal zone shoots up to the full daytime level immediately upon awakening. In contrast, slow risers may need several hours—and perhaps several cups of coffee—before their eyes are completely open and they are ready for the day. These differences can be traced to a person's past conditioning. If there are highly rewarding activities that occur when a person gets up each morning, these reinforce the response of waking up quickly. On the other hand, if the morning is associated with few reinforcers or with aversive experiences, a person learns to wake up slowly.

Sensory stimulation is one of the most important reinforcers in everyday life because it influences behavior 24 hours a day, whether we are awake or asleep. Even though people prefer different levels of sensory stimulation at different times of day, stimuli are always impinging on the sense organs and there is always an optimal level of sensory input that is a reinforcer.

Seventh, the zone of optimal sensory stimulation is depressed by sickness and

---

[33]Kleitman (1949); Maddi (1980).

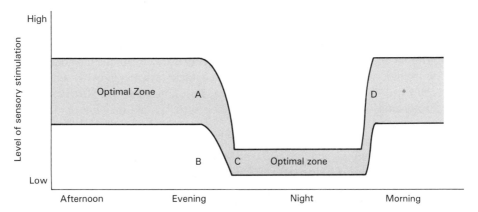

FIGURE 6–5   A typical wake-sleep cycle, showing how the optimal zone is lowered during sleep.

fatigue. When people are sick or exhausted, the body's regulatory systems automatically adjust the optimal zone such that lower levels of sensory stimulation are reinforcers. This makes it rewarding to seek out quiet, dark places. The bright sunshine of a clear summer day is painful to the eyes of a sick person. The aversiveness of bright daylight provides negative reinforcement for putting on sunglasses or going inside. Socializing at a noisy party also provides too much sensory input for the person who is sick or exhausted. Illness and fatigue cause a person to avoid stimulating activities that would be optimal for a healthy person and to seek out low levels of sensory input. Snuggling into a soft bed in a dark room is reinforced by the pleasures of low sensory input. The avoidance of activity is, of course, a biologically adaptive response to illness or exhaustion, since quiet and relaxation are conducive to rest and recuperation.

Staying Optimal

Since optimal levels of sensory stimulation are rewarding and both under- and overstimulation are aversive, there are both positive and negative reinforcers for seeking optimal levels of sensory stimulation. However, *most people cannot stay optimally stimulated all the time.* Few people lead lives that are totally free of boredom, and many people go through periods in which high levels of sensory input cause them to become nervous, tense, and anxious.

Children tend to experience the extremes of under- and overstimulation more often than adults. These extreme experiences occur because children have less power and skill than adults to control their surroundings and the activities of others. It usually takes years to gain the skill and control needed to avoid the situations that induce under- and overstimulation. The following examples show the different kinds of problems that children and adults face in staying optimally stimulated.

Childhood Problems.   Children are often caught in situations that cause under- or overstimulation. Being trapped in the house on a rainy day can cause boredom if a child has not learned a good repertoire of activities for self-entertainment. A child may turn on the TV set and be rewarded by a barrage of sensory stimulation. After a couple of hours, watching TV becomes boring. The child has habituated to the types of sensory stimulation it presents. The child gets up and begins wandering around the house, looking out the windows, opening all the closet doors, and looking through dresser drawers. Nothing novel in any of those places. The child wanders listlessly around the house, then goes up to the attic. Looking at the old clothes and antique toys may provide some novelty if the child has not been in the attic for a couple of months (due to recovery); however, habituation soon robs these stimuli of their novelty, and the child is back to boredom again.

Fidgeting is a common childhood behavior that is learned as a partial escape from boredom. Many a child has had to sit and listen while parents, relatives, or other adults linger at the dinner table to talk of abstract topics—the stock market, the local fund drive, the boss's duodenal ulcer—using words that are frequently incomprehensible to children. Clearly, there is rewarding sensory stimulation for the adults who enthusiastically talk and talk and talk, but the child has not had the learning experience needed to make the topics meaningful. The unlucky child trapped in this environment fidgets, rocks back and forth in the chair, shakes or kicks both legs, and looks around the room. All of these operants produce some sensory input, and hence are reinforced by the partial escape from boredom. For example, leg-kicking produces reinforcing sensory input from the movement of the muscles, from the leg hitting against the furniture, and from the wobbling of the chair. These may not seem like the most exciting types of sensory input possible, but they do provide some variety and stimulus intensity. The child's self-generated sensory stimulation may fall short of optimal stimulation, but it is better than nothing.

Children are sometimes thrown into situations that are totally novel for them. Being bombarded with high levels of sensory stimulation can overstimulate them to the point of panic and hysteria. Consider 2-year-old Billy's plight when taken for his first haircut. If Billy has never been inside a barbershop, he will be deluged with novel stimuli the first time that he is taken for a haircut. He is surrounded by bleak white walls with big mirrors reflecting in all directions. He hears the whirr of high-pitched motors and watches oddly dressed men in white uniforms doing weird things to the heads and faces of strangers who are sitting in unusual looking white chairs. Billy has never seen anything as bizarre as this place. He stands next to his mother, holds her leg, and looks around. Suddenly, a white-clad stranger picks him up and carries him to the chair. He is positioned, then wrapped in strange smelling, stiff, and rough cloth. If Billy has not started to cry by now, just wait until the cold steel tools are laid against his tender skin or the weird electric shears with ozone odor begin to cut and pull at his hitherto unshorn locks. The child is being exposed to a very high level of novel stimuli all jammed together into one small room and in one short period of time. He cries and screams with fear and anxiety. These emergency responses are based on inborn reflexes that can be elicited by a variety of aversive situations, including overstimulation. If Billy cries loudly enough, mother may come to comfort him. If she picks him up, hugs him gently, and says soothing things to him, she may help him escape overstimulation; but many young children are not easily calmed in such frightening situations.

As a child grows older and becomes familiar with a large number of different environments, novel situations are less likely to produce extreme overstimulation. When Billy is four years old and first goes to preschool, he is again exposed to a new set of environmental stimuli; but he will probably be less severely affected than he was in the barbershop two years before. By four years of age, he has become habituated to a large number of different types of buildings, places, playgrounds, adults, and children. The first time he goes to school and is surrounded with twenty new classmates, Billy will be exposed to a level of novelty and strange stimuli that exceeds his normal daily experience; but with four years of learning behind him, the situation will not be totally strange. On the first day of preschool, he may feel a little anxious and somewhat afraid to approach the unknown children for play. He is likely to avoid the strangest stimuli (the sources of greatest overstimulation) by staying near more familiar stimuli. If he knows a neighbor child, he may stay near this child on the first day. If his mother does not leave, there will be a tendency for him to remain near her. Thus, mild overstimulation does not produce crying or severe disruption of behavior; but it is aversive, and it negatively reinforces those activities which escape or avoid the overstimulation.

Adult Problems.   By adulthood, many people have learned to avoid both under- and overstimulation fairly well. However, not all adults are so lucky. Some are trapped in boring jobs and tedious daily routines that make boredom hard to avoid. People are most likely to experience boredom if they have routine lives coupled with few social contacts, few friends, few interests in life, or few hobbies. The problems of boredom can increase with advancing years, especially when people lose their spouse and close friends die or move out of the neighborhood. If people do not keep expanding their range of friends and activities, the loss of old companions and earlier interests can leave them with too few things to do.

Overstimulation usually becomes less of a problem as people get older. As the years pass and people habituate to most normal everyday events, there are fewer and fewer things that are novel enough to induce sufficient overstimulation to cause panic and hysteria. Nevertheless, highly unusual situations—such as being caught in a falling airplane, sinking ship, or war-torn city—can swamp even an adult's senses with so much novel, intense, and frighteningly meaningful stimuli that the person is overstimulated to the point of panic and hysteria.[34]

Milder forms of overstimulation are, of course, more common. Many adults feel some degree of nervousness and anxiety about moving to new environments, taking new jobs, or joining new groups. When people from small towns visit New York City or any other large city for the first time, they are barraged with much more sensory stimulation than they are used to: The high density of cars, people, signs, and fast business transactions generate a level of overstimulation that can be nerve racking. After several days in the big city, some find that the overstimulation has made them nervous, anxious, snappy with their family, and eager to leave for a more quiet vacation spot. (After living in a big city for a while, people usually habituate to much of the sensory stimulation, learn lifestyles that minimize overstimulation, and enjoy the varied opportunities that a big city offers.[35])

Some workaholics and upwardly aspiring people work all the time, loading them-

[34]Hebb (1972:199).
[35]Fischer (1981a,b).

selves down with ever increasing numbers of responsibilities until they are swamped with work. The constant high level of sensory stimulation often leads to tension and nervousness. People in stressful jobs can also suffer from stimulus overload. *Overstimulation can be wearing on the body, especially if the overstimulation persists for prolonged periods.*[36] Traffic controllers in the control towers of large airports are constantly inundated by sensory input as they handle the complex, ever changing patterns of planes on the ground and in the air; and they have an unusually high rate of heart disease and ulcers. Executives with heavy responsibilities and many pressing concerns also tend to have unusually high rates of physical breakdowns.

Reacting and Proacting.   Young children tend to *react* to under- and overstimulation, responding *after* the onset of these aversive events. Aversive sensations are the S^D's for reacting. As children gain skills, they gradually learn to *proact* in increasing numbers of situations. The cues indicating that over- or understimulation is about to arise become S^D's which allow people to act in advance to avoid aversive stimulation levels. By adulthood, some people are able to arrange their lives in ways that prevent most cases of under- and overstimulation.

Figure 6–6 shows the differences between reacting and proacting. Typical patterns of reacting are shown in the top half of the figure. For example, on a grey Saturday morning a young child might wander around the house aimlessly until totally bored (at A) before taking any action that would make the day exciting. If the child went outside and joined several children in play, their active games would create sensory inputs needed for optimal stimulation (at B). If several older children joined the games, their rough play might produce overstimulation for the younger children (at C). After being overstimulated, a young child might run inside where a parent's soothing words and physical contact would help reduce the child's sensory input levels into the optimal zone (at D). The child reacted to aversive levels of stimulation at A and C, after already being out of the optimal zone.

An older child might have proacted by going out to play *before* getting bored and by leaving play *before* it got too rough. Typical patterns of proacting are shown in the bottom half of Figure 6–6. When a person senses that current activities are not quite stimulating enough, the person switches to more stimulating activities before boredom begins (at X). If the person senses that subsequent activities are becoming too stimulating and taxing, the person switches to a quieter, more relaxing activity before becoming aversively overstimulated (at Y).

It is possible to proact in numerous situations. If all your roommates have said that they are going to leave town for the weekend, their statements can function as S^D's for proacting if you have been reinforced for proacting in similar situations in the past. You might plan a variety of stimulating activities for the weekend to assure that you would not be bored. Successfully avoiding boredom and having a stimulating weekend reinforces the proacting skills. If you have been given a demanding job that could easily produce

---

[36]Cobb and Rose (1973) report that hypertension in airport traffic controllers is four times higher than in pilots. Selye (1956) and Martindale (1977) have related ulcers, insomnia, nightmares, headaches, hypertension, and other diseased conditions to chronic overstimulation.

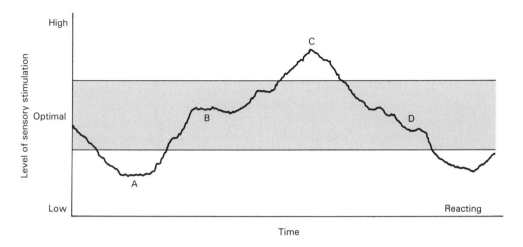

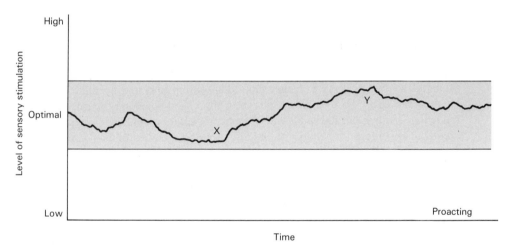

FIGURE 6–6   Typical patterns of reacting (above) and proacting (below).

overstimulation—such as editing the campus newspaper—the descriptions of your job responsibilities could be S^D's for proacting to minimize hectic events that could produce overstimulation. Early in the job, you could delegate responsibilities to other people, give them deadlines, ask everyone to give early warnings when difficulties arise, and help them solve their problems before they get out of hand.

Naturally, not everyone becomes equally skillful at proacting; nor does the ability to proact in some situations guarantee the ability to proact in others. However, as people gain skill at proacting, they can stay optimally stimulated more hours each day. A good understanding of sensory reinforcers is useful in helping people learn to proact and successfully regulate their sensory inputs. Hopefully, this chapter will help you understand sensory reinforcers more completely and become more skillful at staying optimally stimulated.

Social Reinforcers

Merely interacting with others provides numerous social reinforcers for most people. *Sensory stimulation produced by social interaction is one of the primary reasons why social activity is rewarding.* There are two main types of social reinforcers.

Stimulating interactions often provide social reinforcers by bringing optimal levels of sensory input. When a person needs stimulation, it is possible to obtain sensory inputs from a game of solitaire or a TV program; but many people prefer social interaction as a source of stimulating input. Getting on the phone and talking with a friend is often more rewarding than playing solitaire or watching TV. People who work at dull jobs frequently spice up their boring hours with friendly banter, jokes, and other interaction.[37]

People tend to evaluate others along a continuum from being "boring" to being "hyper." The boring person brings too little sensory stimulation to social interaction. The hyper person may talk so fast and skip from topic to topic so often that the interaction is too hectic. Between the extremes of boring and hyper, there are intermediate levels of stimulating interaction that are rewarding. There are times when it is fun to interact with someone who is "full of life," "bubbling with excitement," or otherwise very stimulating to talk with. But even a more moderate level of stimulation—just talking about people and the things they have been doing—is rewarding.

Stimulus-reducing interactions provide social reinforcers when a person is overstimulated. When anxious, nervous, or panicked by overstimulation, people need a source of gentle, soothing stimuli to reduce their total sensory load to a tolerable level. Because children can easily be overstimulated, they often need someone to turn to for stimulus reduction. Mother and father provide stimulus reduction by holding, caressing, hugging, and talking gently to the child. These soft, soothing, gentle stimuli—along with shelter from whatever highly stimulating inputs caused the overstimulation—help lower the child's stimulation levels into the optimal zone. Part of a child's love for the parents is based on the parents' ability to provide calm, comforting social contact in times of overstimulation.[38] (Teddybears and security blankets can also provide stimulus-reduction, though not nearly as much as loving parents can.)

People never outgrow their need for stimulus-reducing experiences—especially when they are overstimulated and stressed. Any hectic experience or major life transition can produce overstimulation and motivate the search for gentle, soothing contact for stimulus reduction and comfort. When a student first leaves Hometown and goes off to college in a strange city, there are so many novel stimuli to deal with during the first weeks that overstimulation is not uncommon. A student may seek out old acquaintances from Hometown or make new friends in order to have reassuring interactions with supportive friends. Telephone calls to family or close friends back in Hometown may help bring comfort, too. Although there are nonsocial sources of stimulus reduction—meditation, relaxation exercises, tranquilizers, alcohol—most people prefer to have comforting social contact when they are overly stimulated.

[37]Roy (1959–60).
[38]Korner (1974); Stern (1977); Ainsworth et al. (1978).

Internal Motivation

Sensory reinforcers help explain behavior that is often described as resulting from internal motivation.[39] For example, the creative work of artists who paint merely for the joy of painting—never even trying to show or sell a single piece of their work—is usually attributed to internal motivation. There does not appear to be any external source of reinforcement for their creative behavior, so it is easy to infer internal motivation.

Knowledge of sensory reinforcers helps clarify that there are both *external* and *internal* sources of sensory rewards for creativity. The artist who is working on a new canvas watches the visual effect of each new brush stroke on the ever changing painting. Each change on the canvas provides visual sensory stimulation that reinforces attention to detail, careful brush strokes, and tasteful selection of colors. There is also internal sensory stimulation from mental activity as the artist plans the piece, evaluates each step of progress, and decides what to do next. At times the artist may step back, gaze at the work, and take pleasure from the total sensory effect. However, there are more sensory reinforcers for painting than pausing: Working on an ever changing picture provides more sensory stimulation than does viewing a static picture. In addition, sensory stimulation is the natural reinforcer for developing increasing skills for creativity. The more creative the artist's work is, the more sensory reinforcers it produces in the form of novel and meaningful stimulation.

Creative behavior is rewarded by the sensory stimulation it produces, even if it never leads to social recognition, fame, monetary profit, or other conspicuous external rewards.[40] By definition, creativity is the production of new things. The creative scientist develops new theories. The creative sales manager develops new ways of marketing products. Creative behavior always produces novelty, hence it is always followed by the sensory reinforcers based on novelty. Sensory stimulation is the *natural reinforcer* for creativity, and it operates even if there are no social rewards—such as praise, fame, or money—for the creative act.

Exploration and play are two other behaviors (besides creativity) that are frequently attributed to internal motivation. They too are reinforced by optimal sensory stimulation. Exploration is sometimes described as being motivated by curiosity or inquisitiveness, two internal motivations. Yet exploration is actually oriented to and reinforced by novel sensory stimulation. The inquisitive child opens all the drawers in the house, because this explorative behavior is reinforced by seeing new things in each drawer. The explorer-adventurer travels to distant lands in search of new experiences. Explorative behavior is reinforced every time it produces optimal levels of novel experience. A sudden, novel, and surprising sensory event—if in the optimal zone—produces a sudden rush of pleasurable emotions—such as joy, excitement, or enthusiasm. When the inquisitive scientist discovers a new chemical reaction, the novelty provides instant sensory reinforcers and the rush of excitement that produces the "Eureka" experience.

---

[39]Conditioned reinforcers provide a second major source of the reinforcers for "internally motivated behavior" (Chapter 7).

[40]Baldwin and Baldwin (1981:209f, 230f).

Because children's play looks so spontaneous, it is often attributed to internal motivation. Nevertheless, it too is reinforced by optimal levels of sensory stimulation. This is most conspicuous when play is very active. When the children run around the yard, chasing each other and tumbling in the grass, their play is producing continuous sensory stimulation from external and internal sources, and it is obviously pleasurable for the children. Their physical movements, shouting, and laughter produce ever changing sights, sounds, tactile feelings, and meaningful communications. There is internal stimulation, too, from mental activity and muscular movement.

Playing a game of chess is also reinforced by sensory reinforcers; but both the behavior and the reinforcers are less conspicuous than in active childhood play. The chess player may sit quietly, scanning the chess board, thinking of strategies, rehearsing dozens of possible offenses and defenses. Each new game creates continuous novel mental stimulation for the person who knows the game and has opponents who play at a similar level. The sensory stimulation of internal mental activities provides sensory reinforcers for play.

Many people love to "play with ideas," and this form of play is also reinforced by mental stimulation. Many people enjoy the mental play of fantasies and daydreams. Business managers may play with ideas for changing their companies, developing new products, promoting old ones. Scientists and mathematicians play with hypotheses and theories, deriving much internal sensory stimulation and sensory reinforcement from the process. Einstein once commented: "When I have no special problem to occupy my mind, I love to reconstruct proofs of mathematical and physical theorems that have long been known to me. There is no *goal* in this, merely an opportunity to indulge in the pleasant occupation of thinking."[41]

Although exploration, play, and creativity are often attributed to internal motivation, all three are learned and maintained by the reinforcers of external and internal sensory stimulation.[42] Sensory stimulation is the natural reinforcer for all behavior that provides optimal levels of novelty, intensity, and meaningfulness. This is why people like variety, activity, and meaningful experience and do not settle into passive lifestyles as long as optimally stimulating alternatives are available.

On Growing Old

Unfortunately, optimally stimulating activities are not always available. Some people find that life becomes increasingly monotonous and boring as the years pass. Fewer and fewer things elicit feelings of excitement and enthusiasm for life. Some may notice this by the age of 30 or 40, others later; but it can become an especially serious problem in the later years of life.

There are several reasons why life loses its novelty. As people get older, they often settle into routines, and the deeper they get into ruts, the more they deprive themselves of variety—the spice of life. Also, most everyday experiences gradually lose their novelty due to habituation. The longer a person has lived, the fewer stimuli there are that still

[41]Dukas and Hoffmann (1979).
[42]Baldwin and Baldwin (1981).

provide novel and stimulating inputs. It is very easy for children to find fresh, novel experience in life. After all, everywhere they look, children find new stimuli. Playing with a bar of soap in the bathtub is novel for a child, but not for adults. As the years pass and fewer stimuli seem novel, people sometimes find it harder to stay optimally stimulated. They find that many things no longer seem as interesting and exciting as they were earlier in life.

Fortunately, there is no reason for life to become less stimulating and exciting as the years pass. Some people—for example, Eleanor Roosevelt, Pablo Picasso, Margaret Mead, George Burns—have remained alive, inquisitive, and creative well into their advanced years. Many other people who are less well-known have also led dynamic and stimulating lives well into old age.[43] *What can people do to keep their lives full of novel, stimulating experience, rather than settling into unstimulating ruts?*

First, it is wise to avoid tedious routines and repetitious behavior. Monotonous activities are boring. The more hours of the day that are devoted to repetitious behavior, the duller life becomes. After 8 hours at a tedious and repetitious job, the tired worker may not be able to think of anything but going home and sinking into a chair in front of the TV. In addition, monotonous tasks are *competing responses* that prevent people from doing more novel and stimulating alternatives. Each hour of routine, repetitious behavior represents one less hour available for more exciting possibilities. By minimizing repetitious routines, people can reduce boredom and open up time for more challenging and stimulating activities.

Second, people need to expand their range of interests and activities to counteract the effects of habituation. People who are not growing—people with unchanging interests and activities—find that the novelty eventually disappears from their lives, due to habituation. To stay ahead of habituation, people need to keep expanding their interests and activities—perhaps learning a new sport or hobby, joining a new group, volunteering for a good cause. New activities infuse life with the excitement derived from novel experience. Sometimes old activities can continue to provide novelty if a person explores numerous new variations on the old activity. For example, music can provide endless novel experiences for the musician who continually explores new types of music, plays with different people to learn new styles and techniques, or experiments with music from different cultures or historical periods. As habituation robs the old variations of their novelty, the new variations provide fresh sources of novelty.

Third, people need to develop mental and physical skills to continue to find novel experiences as the years pass. Young children—who have only limited skills—can find novelty almost anywhere they turn. Since so many things are new for them, even simple behavior such as opening all the kitchen cupboards can bring novel sights and sounds. However, after several decades of experience, people cease to find novelty in the simple things that interest young children. As habituation robs simple things of their novelty, increasing skill is needed to continue to discover new and stimulating experience. It takes physical skills to obtain the multiple sensory experiences of skiing, scuba diving, or playing a fast game of tennis. It takes mental skills to unlock the stimulating worlds of literature, computing, science, or chess. It takes artistic skills to enjoy the challenge and

---

[43]Comfort (1976); Montagu (1981).

stimulation of creating art and music. The more skills that people have, the less likely they are to run out of novel and stimulating experiences. Actually, the world contains a superabundance of sensory stimulation for those with the skills to locate it. People with few skills are limited to such a small range of experience that they may become bored with life; but people with many skills find an inexhaustible supply of sensory stimulation, more than any individual could experience in one lifetime.

Fourth, it is wise to choose friends and companions who value and display stimulating behavior. People who lead stimulating lives serve as models (Chapter 9) and sources of information (Chapter 11) that help others learn skills for attaining stimulating experience. People with a large repertoire of stimulating activities often provide opportunities for others to join them, share in exciting activities, and learn from them.

Fifth, it is wise to interact with people who provide reinforcement—not punishment—for seeking stimulating experience. Supportive friends and people who lead stimulating lives can be a wonderful source of social reinforcers—in the form of spontaneous enthusiasm, sincere encouragement, and useful positive feedback—for learning stimulating behavior. In contrast, people who belittle or criticize efforts to learn stimulating activities are punishing those behaviors. The higher the ratio of reinforcement to punishment, the easier it is to maintain a stimulating life and expand ones, range of activities and skills.

Sixth, health and physical fitness are important for many forms of stimulating behavior. People who remain healthy and fit are able to lead active lives well into the advanced years. Although people can be mentally active, alert, and alive long after they lose physical health and vigor, they lose access to many forms of sensory stimulation that require physical activity. People who learn good health practices increase the chances that they can lead active and stimulating lives well into the advanced years.

More than any other species, humans have the mental and physical potential for locating and creating novel experience even during the older years. The world contains an inexhaustible supply of sensory stimulation for those with the time, skill, and health to locate it. The earlier in life that a person learns the skills and good health practices for leading a physically and mentally stimulating life, the better prepared the person will be for continuing that lifestyle well into old age.

CONCLUSION

This chapter provides an introduction to reinforcers and punishers, with special attention to unconditioned reinforcers and punishers. Reinforcers and punishers are relative—not fixed. Unconditioned reinforcers gain or lose power to control behavior due to an individual's level of deprivation from or satiation with the reinforcer. In addition, Pavlovian conditioning can cause unconditioned reinforcers and punishers to become more reinforcing or more punishing due to pairing with other reinforcers or punishers. The Premack principle provides an efficient manner for evaluating reinforcers and punishers without need for knowledge about prior deprivation, satiation, or conditioning.

Sensory stimulation is one of the more important reinforcers in everyday life. Since people are always in one of the three levels of sensory stimulation—under-, over-, or optimal stimulation—the reinforcers and punishers of sensory stimulation affect behavior at all times. Every stimulus has three qualities—variety, intensity, and meaningfulness—and people learn different preferences for these. As are all reinforcers and punishers, sensory reinforcers are relative: Seven factors that cause sensory reinforcers to vary are described. People who learn skills for proacting can avoid the extremes of under- and overstimulation and stay optimally stimulated much of the time. Sensory stimulation is a key component of social reinforcers. It is also an important cause of activities—such as exploration, play, and creativity—that appear to reflect internal motivation. Although some adults cease finding their lives novel and stimulating as the years pass, there are six things that help people continue to enjoy optimally stimulating experience all through life.

7

Conditioned Reinforcers and Conditioned Punishers

● *In this chapter you will learn that all kinds of stimuli can become reinforcers or punishers. These conditioned stimuli are especially important when behavior is not followed immediately by unconditioned reinforcers or punishers.*

In the previous chapter, we learned that some stimuli function as reinforcers and punishers without any conditioning. Now we turn to those reinforcers and punishers that gain the ability to reinforce or punish through conditioning. These conditioned reinforcers and conditioned punishers are involved in the production of most everyday behavior. They are especially important in the performance of long chains of complex operants in which there are no immediate unconditioned reinforcers or punishers to maintain behavior. Conditioned reinforcers and punishers are also called *secondary* reinforcers and punishers to indicate that they are acquired through learning, rather than being biologically established, as are the *primary* reinforcers and punishers discussed in the previous chapter.

THE CONDITIONING PROCESS

When neutral stimuli repeatedly precede and predict reinforcers, they become conditioned reinforcers. When neutral stimuli repeatedly precede and predict punishers, they become conditioned punishers.[1] Stimuli can be conditioned to lie any-

[1]For further information on conditioned reinforcers and punishers, see Nevin (1971b); Gollub (1977); Fantino (1977); Millenson and Leslie (1979); Schwartz (1984).

where along a continuum from strong conditioned reinforcers to strong conditioned punishers. Because each individual has a unique history of conditioning, different individuals may respond to the same stimulus as reinforcing, neutral, or punishing. One person may find sarcastic humor very reinforcing and learn a range of skills for weaving such humor into conversations. Another person may find sarcasm aversive and avoid people who use it. A third person may be quite indifferent to it.

Conditioned reinforcers and conditioned punishers can be very powerful in their effects on behavior. A fifty-dollar bill is merely a piece of paper, and small children will respond to it no differently than they do to other colorful printed paper. However, after having money paired with a broad range of other reinforcers—food, drink, entertainment, clothes, shelter, travel, possessions—most people learn to respond to money as a strong conditioned reinforcer. Social attention, smiles, approval, sincere praise, and signs of affection are conditioned social reinforcers for most people. Criticism, scorn, frowns, insults, and signs of dislike are conditioned social punishers for most people. Conditioned reinforcers and punishers are very important in molding human behavior because (1) most people respond to a multitude of stimuli as conditioned reinforcers or punishers, and (2) many of these stimuli are major determinants of behavior. There are cases in which conditioned reinforcers and punishers can be stronger (i.e., more effective in changing behavior) than unconditioned reinforcers and punishers.[2] For some people, having a small waist and lean figure is more reinforcing than eating delicious food when hungry. Other people find "losing face" more aversive than taking their own lives, and will commit suicide rather than be disgraced in public. Having a lean figure and "losing face" are culturally conditioned reinforcers and punishers. In the examples above, the culturally conditioned reinforcers and punishers can override the effects of unconditioned reinforcers (food) and punishers (mortal pain) in controlling behavior.

PREDICTIVE STIMULI

Conditioned reinforcers and conditioned punishers are stimuli that were once neutral stimuli, but have acquired reinforcing or punishing properties because they *precede* and *predict* other reinforcers and punishers.[3] Typically, the stimuli that are most likely to become conditioned reinforcers or punishers are those that are the best predictors that reinforcement or punishment is forthcoming. The sight of your bowling ball rolling down the alley toward a perfect strike is a good predictor of a rewarding experience, hence it provides conditioned reinforcement for skillful bowling before the ball actually hits the pins. The sight of an angry dog approaching is a conditioned punisher because it is a predictor that there is a danger of being bitten. The sight of the dog punishes and suppresses approach to the dog and negatively reinforces avoidance or self-protection.

---

[2]Hursh (1977).

[3]These "other" reinforcers and punishers can be either *unconditioned* reinforcers and punishers or *conditioned* reinforcers and punishers.

Three Functions

Conditioned reinforcers and punishers are predictive stimuli that usually have the properties of both CS's and S^D's;[4] and as such they can have three separate functions. Two functions are based on the properties of CS's and one is based on the properties of S^D's. CS's can function as (1) *consequences* that modify operant behavior, and (2) *elicitors* of reflexive responses with emotional components. S^D's (3) *set the occasion* for operant behavior.[5] Both conditioned reinforcers and punishers have all three functions.

Conditioned Reinforcers.   As a person gains experience with predictive stimuli that precede reinforcement, those stimuli become conditioned reinforcers with the properties of both CS's and S^D's. As such, they can (1) *reinforce* behavior,[6] (2) *elicit* pleasurable emotional responses, and (3) *set the occasion* for operants. When a 4-year-old girl sees a gift-wrapped box with her name on it, the box is a predictive stimulus that something nice will happen if she opens the box. By 4 years of age, she has received enough presents to have learned that gift-wrapped boxes usually contain new clothes, a toy, or a doll, all of which are reinforcers. Thus, nicely wrapped boxes become conditioned reinforcers because they are predictive stimuli that regularly precede reinforcement. As a conditioned reinforcer, a gift-wrapped box provides CS's that *reinforce* the child's looking at the box and *elicit* pleasurable emotional responses. Since conditioned reinforcers also serve as S^D's, they *set the occasion* for operants such as opening the box. (If the box contains a new toy, the operant will be followed by the unconditioned reinforcers of novel sensory stimulation.)

Gift boxes are
$$\left\{ \begin{array}{l} \text{CS's that (1) reinforce looking at the box} \\ \text{CS's that (2) elicit pleasurable emotional responses} \\ \text{S}^D\text{'s that (3) set the occasion for opening the box} \end{array} \right.$$

Conditioned Punishers.   As a person gains experience with predictive stimuli that precede punishment, those stimuli become conditioned punishers with the properties of both CS's and S^D's. As such, they can (1) *punish* behavior, (2) *elicit* unpleasant emotional responses, and (3) *set the occasion* for operants that help avoid punishment. If you have had prior experience with wasps, the sight of several wasps trapped and flying around wildly in your kitchen provides predictive stimuli that you could get stung if you are not careful. The predictive stimuli are conditioned punishers, with the properties of both CS's and S^D's. As CS's, they can *punish* and suppress responses of moving too close to the

---

[4]Staats (1975:37f). They can also be S^Δ's that set the occasion for not performing an operant. For simplicity, only S^D's are described in the text.

[5]Although conditioned reinforcers and punishers often have this third function—serving as S^D's and S^Δ's—they need not (Stein, 1958). Nevertheless, in everyday life, it is common for both conditioned *and* unconditioned reinforcers and punishers to function as S^D's and S^Δ's.

[6]Generally, an individual must be deprived of an unconditioned reinforcer before conditioned reinforcers based on that US will begin to function to reinforce behavior. However, there are cases in which deprivation from one US will cause conditioned reinforcers based on other US's to become effective (Nevin, 1971b).

insects and *elicit* uneasy feelings or fear. As S^D's, they *set the occasion* for operants, such as leaving the room or opening a window so the wasps can leave.[7]

Wasps are $\begin{cases} \text{CS's that (1) punish moving too close} \\ \text{CS's that (2) elicit unpleasant emotional responses} \\ S^D\text{'s that (3) set the occasion for opening the window} \end{cases}$

Information

Information is a key determinant of the power of conditioned reinforcers and punishers.[8] Once people gain enough experience with stimuli that precede and predict reinforcement or punishment, the predictive stimuli are informative. Seeing a gift box with your name on it is informative: It is a conditioned reinforcer because the information predicts forthcoming reinforcement. Seeing wasps in the house is informative: It is a conditioned punisher because the information predicts a risk of being stung.

The amount of information that a person obtains from a stimulus depends on two things: (1) how well the stimulus predicts reinforcement or punishment and (2) how well the person has learned to respond to the stimulus as predictive of reinforcement or punishment. First, if a stimulus *always* precedes reinforcement or punishment in a regular manner, it is a much better predictor than stimuli that are only partially correlated with reinforcement or punishment. The better the correlation between a stimulus and subsequent events, the more informative it can be. However, the potential information available from a highly predictive stimulus is useless to people who have little or no experience with that stimulus and the reinforcement or punishment it predicts. Thus, learning is the second determinant of the amount of information a stimulus has for a person: A person must have had adequate experience with predictive stimuli and related consequences to learn to find them informative as conditioned reinforcers and punishers. Once again we see that the ability of stimuli to serve as conditioned reinforcers and punishers is based on learning. The young child who has no experience with wasps does not respond to the sight of them as predictive and informative stimuli the way that more experienced children do. Thus, the sight of wasps does not provide information about danger—nor serve as a conditioned punisher—until the child has adequate experience with them.

The more informative that a predictive stimulus is, the more power it can have as a conditioned reinforcer and punisher. As people gain experience with them, highly informative stimuli become much more powerful conditioned reinforcers or punishers than do stimuli with little predictive information.

Conditioned reinforcers are most powerful when they are highly informative of subsequent reinforcement and a person has learned to respond to the predictive information. People do not always respond to gift-wrapped boxes as conditioned reinforcers. A nicely wrapped box will not be a conditioned reinforcer for you if it is not your birthday and someone else's name is on the box. However, if it is your birthday and your name is

---

[7]They are also S^Δ's for not doing things that are likely to lead to stings—such as approaching or swatting at the insects.

[8]Egger and Miller (1962, 1963); Seligman (1966).

on the box, the very same box might be a strong conditioned reinforcer for you. Various elements in the stimulus collage—the box, name tag, day of year, and context cues—contribute to the predictive information that determines how strong a conditioned reinforcer can be.

In essence, conditioned reinforcers convey information that is "good news" (for those with relevant experience). A gift-wrapped box conveys the good news that a nice present is inside. The more good news information that is present, the more rewarding the box is. For most people, a super large gift box that is wrapped in very fancy paper conveys more good news than does a simply wrapped package the size and shape of a handkerchief box.

Conditioned punishers are most powerful when they are highly informative of subsequent punishment and a person has learned to respond to the predictive information. If you are driving ten miles an hour above the speed limit, the sight of a police car sitting in a side street just ahead might be a predictive stimulus that there is a danger of receiving a speeding ticket. However, the strength of the conditioned punisher depends on total information related to the situation. If you live in a city where it is common knowledge that the police arrest every violator they see, the sight of the police car is an excellent predictor that speeding will be punished. Hence it is a conditioned punisher that punishes speeding, elicits noticeable emotional responses, and sets the occasion for reducing speed. However, if the police in your town only stop out-of-state cars and rarely bother local people, the sight of the police car signals quite different information, and the car is less likely to serve as a conditioned punisher.

The information conveyed by conditioned punishers serves as "bad news" (for those with relevant experience). Seeing that a police car has pulled out and started to follow your car is "bad news"; you may have a noticeable emotional response and slow down even if the police car does not stop you. However, if the police car's flashing lights go on, the extra information is extra bad news. The more information there is that serious punishment could follow, the worse the bad news is, and the greater impact it has on your behavior and emotional responses.

Observing Responses.   Since conditioned reinforcers and punishers are informative, it is not surprising that people learn to pay attention to these stimuli. After all, the information is useless if the predictive cues go unobserved. The operant response class that is reinforced by information is sometimes called *observing responses*.[9] When we get in the car on a cold winter morning, we listen to hear if the engine will start. Hearing the electric starter crank and crank without any effect is bad news. Hearing the engine finally come to life is good news. We listen for both kinds of news, though the good news is much more pleasing to hear. Observing responses can be made through any sense modality: listening, looking, feeling, smelling, tasting, and attending to internal bodily sensations. The informative cues that are detected serve as CS's and S^D's that reinforce or punish behavior, elicit emotional responses, and set the occasion for subsequent actions. Hearing the engine start is good news that reinforces our having had the engine tuned recently, elicits good feelings about our reliable car, and sets the occasion for backing out of the driveway.

[9]Wyckoff (1969); Hendry (1969); Green and Rachlin (1977); Fantino (1977); Fantino and Moore (1980).

Observing responses are most likely to be performed in times of uncertainty. This is because information is most valuable—that is, most reinforcing—when people are not certain how to behave. Consider three alternative situations. If a behavior is *always* reinforced whenever it is emitted, there is no uncertainty about the chances of reinforcement, and there is no need to look for cues that predict that reinforcement is forthcoming. If a behavior is *never* reinforced, again there is no uncertainty and no need for observing responses. However, if a behavior is *sometimes* reinforced and *sometimes* punished on an unpredictable schedule, there is uncertainty about when to perform the behavior and when not. In these cases of uncertainty, any cues that predict reinforcement or punishment can be most informative and valuable. Informative cues can serve as S^D's for doing the behavior when it will be reinforced and S^Δ's for not doing it when it will be punished. This information helps a person attain reinforcement and avoid punishment in times of uncertainty, which makes the information valuable. Therefore, observing responses are common in situations where the consequences of behavior are unpredictable: Predictive information decreases uncertainty and increases the chances of attaining reinforcement and avoiding punishment.

The green and red lights of a traffic signal are conditioned reinforcers and punishers for driving through the intersection. Green predicts that one can drive through safely; red predicts risk or danger for driving into the intersection. The information provided by both red and green lights reinforces observing responses, and people usually glance at the lights often enough to keep track of current traffic conditions. When the traffic lights go out at a busy city intersection (and there is no traffic officer to give hand signals), it increases the uncertainty about who should drive through next and who should wait—which often leads to accidents or traffic jams. When the traffic lights begin working again, they provide the information that decreases uncertainty and reduces accidents.

We direct observing responses to many types of conditioned reinforcers and punishers. We observe the names on letters and gifts because the information tells us whether it is OK to open them or not. It is rewarding to open things with our name on them, but embarrassing to open things intended for others. The information on envelopes and name tags is a reinforcer because it reduces uncertainty and helps us attain reinforcement or avoid punishment. When people play tennis, baseball, or other sports, they frequently glance at teammates and opponents for information that is predictive of subsequent actions. Fast games are filled with uncertainty about the next possible turn of events, and good players learn to observe each other for relevant predictive information. When a left fielder sees the batter slug a hard one to deep left field, it is a conditioned punisher for not having played deeper and it reduces the uncertainty about how to play this batter in subsequent innings. When the batter sees a fielder miss the ball, it is a conditioned reinforcer for a well-placed hit, it elicits good feelings, and it reduces any uncertainty about running for an extra base.

While walking across campus, we glance quickly at the people walking toward us, to see if they will nod, say "Hi," or walk past without recognizing us. If we are uncertain when and where we might meet a friend, observing responses reduce the uncertainty. Informative cues help minimize punishment and increase the chances of reinforcement: They help us avoid the embarrassment of not saying "Hi" to someone who recognizes and greets us; and they increase the chances of starting a rewarding interaction with friends. In conversations, we glance at people's faces to see if they are smiling, frowning, or giving off any other emotional cues. Signs of pleasure are usually good news, and signs of unhappiness are usually bad news. These social cues are especially valuable when people are uncertain how an interaction is progressing. Studies show that when people interact with a stranger, they spend more time looking at the other person than when they interact with a friend.[10] There is more uncertainty when interacting with a stranger, thus more reinforcement for watching any informative cues.

Observing responses can be reinforced by either positive or negative reinforcement, depending on whether they bring information that helps in attaining reinforcement or avoiding punishment. It is easy to understand why people like to observe conditioned reinforcers: These stimuli provide positive reinforcement for being attentive, and they elicit pleasurable emotional responses. It is good news to receive a letter that reads: "Open this envelope for your free prize." Everyone is happy to hear the professor announce before handing back the tests that all the tests were well done and everyone will get an "A." It is good news to hear your tennis partner say that she has developed her serve considerably since you last played doubles together. When playing checkers, it is good news to see your opponent move a piece onto a square that will allow you to jump three of his pieces at one time.

Although people enjoy observing informative stimuli that predict reinforcement, usually they are not so happy to observe stimuli that predict punishment. Because conditioned punishers can elicit unpleasant emotions and punish observing responses, people sometimes avoid observing conditioned punishers. However, conditioned punishers can also provide negative reinforcement for making observing responses. What determines whether people observe conditioned punishers or not? It is frightening to hear strange noises in the house at night, especially if you walk out into the hall and see a burglar pointing a gun at you. Seeing the burglar is a conditioned punisher that elicits fear and punishes negligent acts (such as leaving the front door unlocked). Will the aversive sight also punish and suppress your observing the armed intruder? Or will it negatively reinforce your watching to see what he does? What determines whether you will observe or not? If the burglar raises his gun, cocks the hammer, and prepares to shoot, you may look away. However, if the burglar is young, nervous, and somewhat inattentive, you might watch him for informative cues about possible opportunities for escape.

Whether or not people observe conditioned punishers depends largely on whether or not escape or avoidance is possible.[11] If there is no way to escape or avoid an aversive situation, watching for extra information has no positive value—that is, it is not reinforcing. In fact, the information is aversive. Information is most valuable in times of uncertainty; and in cases of no escape, there is no uncertainty about punishment. If a burglar points his gun at your head and cocks the hammer, there may be nothing you can do to avoid being shot. The situation is ugly and the predictive stimuli elicit emotions of

[10]Rutter and Stephenson (1979).

[11]Whether a person will attempt to escape depends on several factors: How difficult it is to escape the current situation; how many skills the person has for escaping the situation; and the person's prior history of reinforcement for attempting to escape difficult situations. People who have often failed to escape in the past may develop learned helplessness and not attempt escape in situations where escape is possible (Seligman, 1975).

extreme fear and anxiety. The predictive stimuli are conditioned punishers that punish and suppress looking. You turn away in horror. However, things would be different if escape were possible. If the burglar was not pointing the gun at you and there was a possibility of escape or avoidance, you might watch the man closely, searching for informative cues that might help you escape. You might watch the burglar for a chance to knock the gun out of his hand or for a good moment to dash for the door. Cues that indicate the possibility of escape would be S^D's for observing closely if your observing responses had been negatively reinforced by the successful escape from difficult situations in the past. Since there is uncertainty about the best way to cope with the situation, the information is quite valuable—that is, an important reinforcer.

Observing conditioned punishers can be aversive; but there is negative reinforcement for paying attention to them if they convey information that can help in avoiding additional punishment. Amy cringes when she sees an "F" on her test, but she adds the points and reads the comments written next to each answer. The information may help her escape or avoid an aversive situation. If the information indicates that she was graded unfairly, she may ask for a regrade and perhaps get a better score. If the information makes her aware that the course is far over her head, she may decide to drop the class and avoid an "F" on her transcript. When two lovers have a quarrel, they may attend closely to each other's words. Hearing the other person's complaints can be painful, but it may provide useful information for avoiding problems in the future. When a person is fired for incompetence, it hurts the person to hear the employer list ten reasons for dismissal; but listening to the information may be useful in overcoming shortcomings or in demonstrating to the employer that the ten charges are actually unfounded.

Extinction of Conditioned Reinforcers and Punishers

When conditioned reinforcers and punishers cease being informative—that is, no longer precede and predict other reinforcers and punishers—extinction takes place, and the conditioned stimuli lose their power. If you have a new roommate who invites you to go sailing this weekend, the invitation is good news—a conditioned reinforcer—if similar invitations have often been followed by rewarding experiences in the past. However, when the weekend comes, your roommate is too busy to go sailing. Similar things happen over the next several weeks. After six out of six invitations end in cancellations, invitations from your roommate will cease being good news. Since the invitations are not followed by rewarding experiences, they lose their power as conditioned reinforcers. (However, invitations from more reliable friends will retain their power as conditioned reinforcers if those invitations are followed by rewarding experiences.)

Conditioned punishers also lose their power during extinction. If you move into a new apartment and a cranky neighbor threatens to call the police every time you play your stereo, the threats are bad news. Since they are conditioned punishers, they elicit aversive emotional responses and may stop your playing the stereo for a while. However, if you turn on the stereo later that week, hear more threats, and the threats are not followed by any stronger forms of punishment, the threats will begin to lose their power as conditioned punishers. After hearing vacuous threats for 2 months, the threats cease eliciting aversive feelings and cease suppressing your behavior.

Extinction of conditioned reinforcers and punishers is slower if those conditioned stimuli have previously been maintained by intermittent conditioning rather than by continuous conditioning.[12] Intermittent conditioning occurs when a conditioned reinforcer or punisher is followed by reinforcement or punishment only part of the time—for example, only one time out of ten or twenty. Continuous conditioning occurs when the conditioned stimulus is always followed by reinforcement or punishment. If seeing a present with your name on it is always followed by a rewarding experience, the sight of gifts is being maintained as a conditioned reinforcer via *continuous reinforcement*. If purchasing a lottery ticket is followed by winning cash roughly once in 500 times, the conditioned reinforcer is maintained by *intermittent reinforcement*. Conditioned punishers can also be maintained by continuous or intermittent conditioning. In everyday life, many conditioned reinforcers and punishers are based on intermittent conditioning. Research shows that intermittent conditioning retards extinction: Stimuli often continue to function as conditioned reinforcers or punishers long after the onset of extinction if they had been maintained by intermittent conditioning before extinction (see pages 227–230).

If all through your high school years, friends invited you to do things and *always* followed through, invitations would be conditioned reinforcers based on continuous reinforcement. If your first roommate in college *never* followed through after invitations, it would be easy for you to discriminate that invitations from your college roommate were quite different from the invitations you had been used to in high school. The sharp contrast between *always reinforcing* and *never reinforcing* makes it easy to discriminate that your college roommate's invitations are not predictive of reinforcement; the invitations quickly lose their power as conditioned reinforcers when you discriminate that they are not followed by reinforcement. Extinction is usually rapid when a person experiences a sharp contrast between continuous reinforcement and no reinforcement (that is, extinction). However, if you had gone to high school with friends who invited you to do things, but only followed through intermittently—maybe one time in ten or twenty—things would be different: You would be used to having invitations fall through a large percentage of the time, and invitations would be conditioned reinforcers that predicted *occasional* reinforcement. When you encountered a college roommate who *never* followed through after invitations, it might take you a long time to discriminate between *intermittent* reinforcement and *no* reinforcement. Subtle differences are hard to discriminate, and this would slow your learning that the college roommate's invitations are predictive of no rewards. You might continue to respond to your roommate's invitations as predictive of occasional reinforcement, even though they were actually predictive of no reinforcement. Thus, extinction takes place more slowly after intermittent reinforcement.

The effect of intermittent conditioning on conditioned punishers is similar. If in the past people had *always* called the police whenever they threatened to, you would be very wary of such threats. When you discovered that a cranky neighbor often threatened to call the police but *never* did so, it would be easy to discriminate that this person's threats were meaningless. It is easy to discriminate between threats that *always* predict punishment and threats that *never* predict punishment, and the meaningless threats cease to function as conditioned punishers as soon as you discriminate that they are not predictive of punish-

[12]Zimmerman (1957, 1959); Nevin (1971b).

ment. In contrast, if in the past you were used to hearing threats that were only *occasionally* followed by punishment, you would find it harder to discriminate between these threats that predicted *intermittent* punishment and the cranky neighbor's threats that predicted *no* punishment.

When conditioned reinforcers or punishers cease to predict other reinforcement or punishment, extinction takes place and the conditioned stimuli lose their power. Typically, extinction is slower if predictive stimuli have been maintained in the past by *intermittent* reinforcement or punishment than by *continuous* reinforcement or punishment. The subtle differences between intermittent conditioning and no conditioning (that is, extinction) make it hard to notice the onset of extinction after intermittent conditioning—that is, harder to learn that stimuli which once were conditioned reinforcers or punishers are no longer predictive of reinforcement or punishment.

SOCIAL REINFORCERS AND PUNISHERS

Most of us find that smiles, attention, compliments, affection, and merely being with other people are reinforcers; whereas frowns, criticisms, and insults are punishers. Infants, however, do not. The fact that most infants[13] are born into and raised in a complex social network guarantees that they will learn to respond to many social stimuli as conditioned reinforcers or punishers.

During the early years of life, the infant is highly dependent on the social environment for access to positive reinforcers and escape from punishers. Mother, father, or other caretakers bring food, fluids, warmth, sensory stimulation, and so forth; and they remove dirty diapers, open diaper pins, and other sources of irritation. If the child becomes frightened by overly novel stimuli, the familiarity of the caretakers and their gentle, soothing behavior help the child to escape aversive overstimulation. All these rewarding childhood experiences are preceded and predicted by the caretakers' approaching and directing attention to the child. Thus, receiving *social attention* becomes a powerful conditioned reinforcer because it frequently predicts the onset of important reinforcers or the termination of punishers. Conditioned social reinforcers tend to be quite effective across a large number of motivational conditions because these conditioned reinforcers have been established in a large number of motivational states (resulting from deprivation of various reinforcers and exposure to various punishers).[14]

Since social attention is a powerful conditioned reinforcer, it is not surprising that many children learn behaviors in the response class known as "attention-getting behavior." If a child says, "Look, Daddy, I can ride no hands," the attention-getting response is likely to attract attention and hence reinforce the child's behavior. There are many obvious forms of attention-getting behavior. "Look at me." "Look what I did." Fighting, acting out, throwing a tantrum, getting in trouble, jumping up and down, fidgeting,

---

[13]Feral children and children raised in closets provide striking examples of the ineffectiveness of many social stimuli which are powerful conditioned reinforcers or punishers for normal children of their own age (Davis, 1940, 1947; Curtiss, 1977).

[14]Skinner (1953:77).

and being a nuisance are all activities that tend to attract attention. Many children learn one or more of these attention-getting activities.

Parents and teachers often fail to understand that social attention is a reinforcer that maintains some of the problematic behavior they find most undesirable. After Diane has been squirming in her seat at school, talking to herself, and banging furniture around for ten minutes, the teacher may say, "Diane, sit down or else!" All of Diane's friends turn to look. The social attention may reinforce the undesirable behavior so much that the mild threat is ineffective.[15] Some teachers report that whenever they say "Sit down," the children jump up. Social attention is reinforcing the behavior that is causing the problems.

Naturally, obnoxious behavior is not the only attention-getting activity that children learn. Creative, considerate, and friendly behaviors often attract attention from parents, teachers, and other people. Children who draw well or are very kind often attract the teacher's attention and are likely to receive extra social reinforcers due to the special skills. These lucky children thus have desirable behavior further reinforced. The child who has no especially attractive skills that bring attention from adults is more likely to learn an unruly behavior as the only activity that brings attention in a class of twenty or thirty other children. Thus, while Sally is receiving reinforcers for her artistic behavior and Dick for his kindness to others, Diane is learning to be a nuisance because this behavior attracts attention to her. Behavioral research is helping teachers learn to treat the Dianes in their classrooms differently.[16] If the teacher (1) ignores Diane's undesirable attention-getting behavior and (2) gives attention to *any* of the more appropriate things that she does, Diane will learn better ways to get attention. It is a rare child who does not have *some* acceptable aspects of behavior for the teacher to reinforce with attention; but many teachers have not learned to give attention to these rather than to the more salient nuisance behavior.

Differential Conditioning

Due to differential conditioning, people learn to discriminate that one type of stimulus can be a conditioned reinforcer in one situation and a conditioned punisher in another. In spite of the fact that social contact and attention are usually associated with positive conditioning in childhood, children also receive punishers from parents and others. Because people can be a source of both reinforcement and punishment, the child learns to discriminate between the stimuli that precede and predict reinforcers and those that precede and predict punishers. Smiles, nods, signs of interest, gentle tones of voice, compliments, and praise are often followed by hugs, caresses, play, and other reinforcers; hence these stimuli may become conditioned reinforcers. Frowns, pursed lips, wagging fingers, harsh tones of voice, and criticism are often followed by punishment; hence these stimuli may become conditioned punishers. The young infant may not seem to "understand" when Mommy or Daddy is angry, because almost all social contact is a conditioned reinforcer for the infant. Yet as differential conditioning proceeds, the child will become more discriminating. As Daddy's smile turns into a penetrating stare, the child will cease playing with the food on the coffee table. These indications that the child has

[15]Serbin and O'Leary (1975).
[16]O'Leary et al. (1970); Hall et al. (1972); Sulzer and Mayer (1972); Axelrod (1977).

"understood" the nonverbal signals demonstrate that the child now discriminates between them, responding to one as a conditioned reinforcer and the other as a conditioned punisher.

Naturally as the years go by, each of us learns to be sensitive to countless social stimuli as conditioned reinforcers or punishers. Because we all have unique histories of conditioning, we do not all respond to the same social signals as positive or negative stimuli. Some people find obscene language very aversive, due to its close association with punishment in their past experience. Other people respond to obscenities as conditioned reinforcers because "four letter words" have always been a part of relaxed conversations in which people were laughing, joking, and having fun.

Some social signals—such as compliments and attention—can function as social reinforcers or social punishers, depending on the degree to which they predict reinforcement or punishment. For example, compliments can be sincere or they can be manipulative, and people usually learn to discriminate the differences as they grow up. Children often respond to compliments as powerful conditioned reinforcers since such praise from adults is often predictive of various other rewards. Yet as the years go by, most of us have experiences in which other people manipulate us with insincere compliments and praise, causing us to do something which turns out to be aversive. We have all been exposed to manipulative compliments, such as: "Gee, Jim, you're so good with the kids, why don't you take care of them for the afternoon." After people hear such compliments, they may get stuck doing extra work. Eventually, as people learn to discriminate the differences between sincere and manipulative compliments, manipulative compliments and overly generous praise become conditioned punishers. When someone tries to manipulate Jim with insincere compliments in the future, the manipulative compliments may now suppress the behavior rather than make it more likely.

In a similar manner, differential conditioning causes people to learn that not all forms of social attention are rewarding. Although social attention is often a reinforcer, being watched carefully is not. Surveillance often functions as a conditioned punisher. When people are engaged in enjoyable activities—such as playing games that produce reinforcing levels of sensory stimulation—no one has to watch to make sure that they continue playing. However, when people have to do aversive tasks, it is often necessary to have some type of surveillance to make certain that they do not stop or slow down. Thus the parents check to see that the children have mowed the lawn and taken out the trash; the boss checks to see that the workers finished enough quality work; the IRS checks to see that the income tax forms are filled out correctly. Because being under surveillance is often a good predictor that an activity is aversive, signs indicating that one's behavior is being monitored often become conditioned punishers. This is one reason people prefer jobs where there is no surveillance—and they can "be their own boss"—even though they might work equally hard at either job. Experiments have shown that when adults begin to watch children's play as if monitoring an aversive task, the surveillance alone suppresses the frequency of the children's play.[17] Being watched makes many people

---

[17]Although Lepper and Greene (1975) used attribution theory to interpret these results, the data clearly indicate that surveillance functioned as a social punisher. See Bandura (1977:107f) for a criticism of the use of attribution theory in cases such as this.

nervous and makes them feel uncomfortable, indicating that surveillance is a CS that elicits negative emotional responses. Being under surveillance often serves as an S^Δ for not playing around or wasting time, and an S^D for operants such as saying, "Stop watching me; it makes me nervous."

TOKENS AS REINFORCERS AND PUNISHERS

People often use objects as conditioned reinforcers or conditioned punishers. These objects are tokens that stand for other kinds of reinforcement or punishment. Money is a conditioned reinforcer for most people, but not all. Some societies utilize shells, arrowheads, necklaces, and other items. People from these societies might look at a twenty-dollar bill and be surprised that it could have much value, as we might be surprised at the great value they place on their exchange objects. However, any token can become a conditioned reinforcer when a group of people uses the token in exchange for other reinforcers.

High grades, diplomas, prizes, plaques, medals, and other honors are tokens given to those who excel. Many people have learned to find these tokens so rewarding that they will work long and hard to earn them. The conditioning begins early in life when parents shower attention on their children for earning good grades. Because high grades and diplomas often open doors to better colleges, more stimulating jobs, faster promotions, and other rewards, they can acquire additional reinforcement power. Of course, the person who always earned low grades (and was deprived of the reinforcers given to the A student) will learn to find the whole grading system to be aversive! Grades are paired with surveillance, failure, criticism, and lost opportunities.

The golfer who has an entire wall covered with medals and trophies may find these prizes more valuable than others realize. Each prize is associated with a victory. Each prize adds to the size of the total collection. The larger the collection, the more amazed and impressed are guests who exclaim, "Leslie, I'm impressed. I didn't know you were such an outstanding golfer." Whether it is a military medal, a Pulitzer Prize, or a bouquet of roses, tokens of esteem are associated with other reinforcers and hence become conditioned reinforcers for those who have had the chance to earn them.

Some tokens function as conditioned punishers. Traffic tickets, bills, statements of payments overdue, and other such tokens are stimuli that precede the loss of reinforcers. A ticket under the windshield wiper is an informative stimulus: Bad news! As a CS associated with aversive experiences, a parking ticket makes most people feel bad as soon as they see it, and it can also punish and suppress illegal parking. In addition, it functions as an S^D for paying the specified fine, since paying is negatively reinforced by escaping the more severe punishment given to those who fail to pay their traffic tickets.

As immortalized in the novel *The Scarlet Letter,* the letter "A" was a punitive token worn by adultresses in Puritan New England.[18] Other tokens of disapproval include handcuffs, chains, tattoos, and brands given to slaves, prisoners, outcasts, and deviants in some societies. Since people are not as eager to display tokens of disapproval as they are

---

[18]Hawthorne (1850).

tokens of success, these tokens often have to be physically affixed to the person or to the person's belongings to prevent the person from discarding the aversive token. Otherwise, society must monitor the recipient of the negative token and either reinforce displaying the token or punish not displaying the token. For example, the Jews in Hitler's Germany were liable for arrest if they did not wear the Jewish Star that identified them and stigmatized them in Nazi society. Few took the risk of not wearing it.[19] In years past when a child was punished by having to wear a dunce cap, the teacher had to watch the child to insure that the child did not take off the negative token.

GENERALIZED REINFORCERS AND PUNISHERS

When people learn that certain stimuli are predictive of a variety of different kinds of reinforcement in a broad range of circumstances, these stimuli become generalized reinforcers. Money is a clear example of a generalized reinforcer. Because money can be used to obtain many positive reinforcers or avoid many punishers in countless different situations, most people learn to respond to money as a generalized reinforcer. If you are hungry, money can bring food. If you are bored, money can buy entertainment. If you like the latest fashions, money can buy new clothes. If you get a traffic ticket, money can help you avoid the heavier penalties you would face if you did not pay. Most of us learn to respond to money as a conditioned reinforcer in many contexts and many deprivation states. Thus, money becomes a generalized reinforcer.

In spite of the broad generalization of monetary reinforcers, differential conditioning usually causes us to learn discriminations that prevent money from being a reinforcer in *all* circumstances. For example, possession of stolen money and counterfeit money can get a person into trouble. Hence, any information that money is stolen or counterfeit will generally suffice to turn the money into a conditioned punisher, which elicits aversive feelings and motivates avoidance. In addition, most people learn to discriminate that certain situations should not be associated with money. When you help someone because you love them, receiving money in payment can make it look like your behavior was mercenary, rather than an act of love. Others may then criticize: "You didn't help your grandmother because you loved her. You were just doing it for the money." This kind of social conditioning makes most people discriminate that they should not take money in situations where the positive value of love, friendship, patriotism, or higher goals would be blemished by the "crass materialism" of money. Thus, reinforcers need not be effective in *all* contexts in order to be labeled as generalized reinforcers.

Social attention, talking with others, and gregariousness are to some degree generalized reinforcers.[20] For some people merely being in the company of others reinforces walking up to strangers and striking up a conversation. Although some people sit alone in restaurants, bars, theaters, and parks, most prefer to sit and talk with others. Although they could walk along the beach alone, people usually cluster in groups of two or three. The extra reinforcers they obtain from being together facilitate the formation of groups.

[19]Hilberg (1961:121–122).
[20]As was noted in Chapter 6, sensory stimulation is an important part of social reinforcers, too.

Naturally, discrimination occurs, too. People often form groups with certain types of people but not others. And in some situations, even people who normally respond to togetherness as a strong generalized reinforcer may find it more reinforcing to be alone.

People can respond to unique generalized reinforcers to which most others do not respond. Some people have learned to find music a generalized reinforcer, and they often hum or play music because these activities are instrumental in producing the generalized reinforcer. Other people have learned to find knowledge a conditioned reinforcer; and they read, collect books, or visit museums because of the knowledge that these activities bring. Some find beauty a generalized reinforcer; and they dedicate an unusual amount of time to painting, sculpting, decorating, or landscaping under the influence of this reinforcer.

When people learn that certain stimuli are predictive of a variety of different kinds of punishment in a broad range of circumstances, these stimuli become generalized punishers. Generalized punishers are aversive in a large number of contexts. Frowns, cold stares, harsh tones of voice, and other social cues tend to be generalized punishers for most people. As a consequence, people usually learn to avoid topics that cause others to respond with these social cues. Fines, traffic tickets, and other legal devices are conditioned punishers of rather broad generality.

The variability of everyday life facilitates the conditioning of many generalized reinforcers and punishers. If smiles were only correlated with food reinforcers—as people sat down to enjoy a meal—they would not serve as generalized reinforcers. When people were not hungry, both food and smiles would have little reinforcement value. However, in everyday life people experience smiles in association with a wide range of reinforcing situations. This generalized conditioning boosts the positive value of the stimulus across much of the generalization gradient.

CHAINS OF OPERANTS

Conditioned reinforcers and punishers play an especially important role in explaining the long sequences of behavior that are typical of everyday life. *A sequence of operants is called an operant behavior chain. Each behavior in the chain is usually joined to the next behavior by conditioned reinforcers, though unconditioned reinforcers may be involved, too.*

Operant → reinforcer → operant → reinforcer → operant → reinforcer → etc.

Each reinforcer links two operants together, serving to reinforce the prior operant and to set the occasion for the next operant. Punishers, if they appear in a chain, decrease the probability of the punished operant and usually function to negatively reinforce other responses.

The most commonly researched type of operant chain consists of a series of operants that terminates in the acquisition of an unconditioned reinforcer.

Operant → conditioned reinforcer → operant → conditioned reinforcer → operant → unconditioned reinforcer

A person might generate a chain of food preparation behavior that terminates with the consumption of food. The last behavior in the chain is followed by an unconditioned reinforcer. All the earlier responses in the chain are followed by conditioned reinforcers that function as reinforcers because they precede and predict the terminal reinforcer of food. Putting a steak on a charcoal grill is a conditioned reinforcer because it precedes and predicts the reinforcing consequences of tasty food. The conditioned reinforcers early in a chain help bridge the time gap between early responses in the chain and the eventual unconditioned reinforcer at the end. A person may spend hours preparing a gourmet meal. Hundreds of separate small steps may be performed in sequence before the dinner is finally served. The unconditioned reinforcer of food is very effective in reinforcing responses such as putting food in the mouth that occur immediately before the unconditioned reinforcer; but it cannot directly reinforce responses that occurred one hour before. It is the conditioned reinforcers that precede and predict good food that bridge the time gap between early elements in the behavioral chain and the final consummatory responses.

Two-Link Operant Chains

In order to see how chains are learned and maintained, let us first examine the simplest of operant chains, the two-link chain composed of two operants that are connected by one conditioned reinforcer and followed by an unconditioned reinforcer. When Julie is bored, she often picks up her guitar and starts playing. The first S^D that controls the response chain is the feeling of boredom. This S^D sets the occasion for the first operant, picking up the guitar. When the guitar is comfortably adjusted and ready to play, this new stimulus pattern functions as the conditioned reinforcer for the first operant. Julie might even smile as she feels the instrument slip into position across her leg, the smile being elicited by the CS's of the conditioned reinforcer. The comfortable positioning of the guitar also functions as the S^D for the second operant in the chain, playing music. The music she creates provides the sensory stimulation which terminates the aversive state of boredom and brings Julie the reinforcers of optimal levels of sensory stimulation.

$S^D \rightarrow$ 1st operant $\rightarrow$	conditioned reinforcer (CS and S^D)	$\rightarrow$ 2nd operant $\rightarrow$	unconditioned reinforcer
Boredom $\rightarrow$ pick up guitar	$\rightarrow$ positioned for playing	$\rightarrow$ playing $\rightarrow$	optimal sensory stimulation

Optimal stimulation is the unconditioned reinforcer that caused Julie to learn this two-link chain. Optimal stimulation directly reinforces the second operant in the chain. Because they predict the reinforcers of optimal sensory stimulation, the stimuli that regularly precede this second operant become conditioned reinforcers. These conditioned reinforcers are responsible for reinforcing the first operant and making boredom an S^D for beginning the response chain.

The conditioned reinforcer in chains is usually a *response produced stimulus:* It is a stimulus that is produced by the prior response. The operant of picking up the guitar leads to the next stimulus pattern of "guitar across the leg," which is the response produced stimulus that both reinforces the prior operant and sets the occasion for the next operant. Response produced stimuli can come from either outside or inside the body. In this case, the response produced stimuli arise from the external stimuli of the guitar lying across the leg and the internal stimuli from the whole body as one settles into a comfortable position for playing. These self-produced stimuli control the timing and coordinate the linking of responses in the chain.

Multiple-Link Operant Chains

Most adult operant behavior consists of chains with more than two links. Long chains are linked in the same manner as short two-link chains. Between each operant is a conditioned reinforcer that reinforces the prior operant and serves as an S^D for the next operant. These conditioned reinforcers usually involve response produced stimuli, though other stimuli may be involved, too.

To illustrate the role of conditioned reinforcers and punishers in multiple-link operant chains, let us analyze the series of operants performed by a skilled pickpocket. As the pickpocket mills through a crowd at a busy airport, he glances quickly but inconspicuously from person to person. After years of practice, he has acquired long chains of skillful behavior, most of which are under the control of conditioned reinforcers. Stimuli that most people never notice are conditioned reinforcers for the pickpocket: a bulge in a gentleman's hip pocket, a wallet peeking out of a lady's purse, a wristwatch carelessly laid beside a briefcase. Although these may be neutral stimuli for most people, the pickpocket finds glimpses of these informative stimuli to be quite rewarding. When his vigilant eye spots the pocket bulge, the stimulus functions as a conditioned reinforcer with properties of a CS and an S^D. As a CS, it reinforces the previous operants of scanning the environment and attending to details in people's appearances (operant 1 in Figure 7–1), and it elicits pleasurable emotional responses. The bulge also functions as an S^D for operant 2: brushing past the unsuspecting victim the next time the victim is closely surrounded by other people. As the victim approaches a group of people, the pickpocket hurries to squeeze between the victim and the group, appearing to be in a rush. As he brushes past the victim, the tactile stimuli serve as conditioned reinforcers for contacting the victim (operant 2). These tactile stimuli are also S^D's for the next response in the chain—lifting the wallet (operant 3). Lifting the wallet leads to new response produced stimuli. The bulge stimulus is now gone, and the pickpocket has his hands on a new stimulus, a brown calfskin wallet. This conditioned reinforcer is a CS that reinforces the operants of skillfully removing wallets from pockets and elicits a subtle smile. It is also an S^D that sets the occasion for such responses as slipping into a nearby restroom and emptying the wallet (operant 4). Money is the next conditioned reinforcer—$280 in 20's and 50's. Having money is an S^D for spending (operant 5). The pickpocket may use the money to obtain terminal reinforcers such as food, drugs, or stimulating entertainment (sensory stimulation). In these cases, the terminal reinforcers are unconditioned reinforcers (the US in Figure 7–1).

If the pickpocket had fumbled during his attempt to lift the wallet, the error would have led to response produced stimuli that function as conditioned punishers that would have interrupted the smooth chain of behavior shown in Figure 7–1. The conditioned

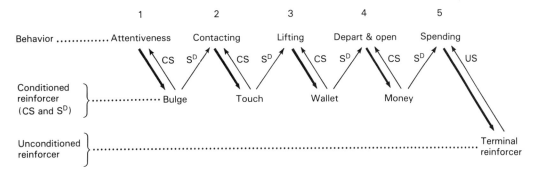

FIGURE 7–1   The chain of behaviors and conditioned reinforcers that produces the terminal reinforcer. Dark arrows show how each behavior leads to a response-produced stimulus. Light arrows show that each conditioned reinforcer is a CS that reinforces the preceding operant and an S^D that sets the occasion for the next operant.

punishers would serve as CS's that punish the clumsy act and elicit aversive emotions. They also would serve as S^Δ's for not emitting the next response and S^D's for actions which in the past allowed the pickpocket to avoid further punishment. If the pickpocket had timed his contact poorly, his hand would not have been correctly located for lifting the wallet. The error would have punished his clumsy approach and served as an S^Δ for not attempting to remove the wallet. After such an error, walking away to avoid the risk of being apprehended would be negatively reinforced.

Although this example breaks the chain of pickpocketing behavior into five links, the analysis could have been done in much finer detail.[21] Closer observation would reveal numerous smaller behavioral units involved in producing each link of the chain. By breaking each response class into finer subdivisions, a chain can be seen as consisting of many small subunits rather than a few broad response classes.

Bridging the Time Gap

We have already discussed three basic functions of conditioned reinforcers and punishers: As CS's, they reinforce or punish prior operants, and they elicit reflexive responses with emotional components. As S^D's, they set the occasion for subsequent operants. In multiple-link behavior chains, conditioned reinforcers and punishers have a fourth function: *They bridge the time gap between early behaviors in a chain and the terminal consequences (which are located at the end of the chain).*

In Chapter 2, we saw that reinforcers and punishers are most effective when they occur *immediately* after a behavior (pp. 32–34). When people generate long chains of behavior before attaining a terminal reinforcer or avoiding a major punisher, the terminal consequences are often too distant from the early behaviors in the chains to have much direct effect on them. The time gap between early links in a chain and terminal consequences may be hours, days, or longer. A student may study very boring material for

---

[21]The degree to which we focus in on details—analyzing the flow of behavior into ever smaller units—depends on the goals of our current study and how useful the information is for illustrative or procedural purposes (Millenson and Leslie, 1979:161).

several days because studying is essential for attaining the terminal reinforcer of a good grade—or avoiding the punisher of a bad grade. Parents may spend weeks toilet training their child before they reach the terminal reinforcer of successful training. In such chains, conditioned reinforcers and punishers bridge the time gap between early operants and final consequences: *The conditioned reinforcers and punishers that occur right after each operant in a chain provide immediate consequences for each behavioral link.* When a student studies several days before a test, the stimuli present at each link of the chain of study behavior are conditioned reinforcers for studying, *if* in the past they have been predictive of earning better scores than are possible without studying. Also, the stimuli present when not studying are conditioned punishers for not studying, *if* they are predictive of poorer grades.

Conditioned reinforcers are "good news" signals that occur when a person successfully completes each behavioral link of a chain and moves closer to the terminal reinforcer at the end of the chain. The first links in the chain for preparing cookies or fudge occur when a person buys the ingredients at the grocery store. These acts are not followed immediately by food reinforcers, but they are followed immediately by conditioned reinforcers, since purchasing food produces stimuli that are predictive that food reinforcement will occur later in the chain. After the person gets home and starts to make some cookies, there are additional conditioned reinforcers, since mixing the ingredients is also predictive of food reinforcement. Although acts that put food in the mouth are immediately reinforced by food, all the preceding operant links are reinforced by the conditioned reinforcers that are predictive of reaching the terminal reinforcer. *Thus the conditioned reinforcers bridge the time gap by providing immediate reinforcement for behaviors that advance a person through a chain toward terminal reinforcers.* Any informative stimuli that occur when a person is "on track"—following a chain—toward a terminal reinforcer can become conditioned reinforcers once the person has rewarding experience with the behavioral chain.

Conditioned punishers are "bad news" signals that can function to bridge the time gap between early links in operant chains and delayed punishers. While performing any long chain—such as interviewing for a job, training for an athletic event, or preparing a dinner—one or two mistakes can endanger the success of the entire chain of behavior. During a job interview, a person may think about making an ethnic joke, then feel a twinge of apprehension. Just thinking about making the joke generates response produced stimuli that are conditioned punishers, because they predict that the whole job interview might be jeopardized by such a joke. The conditioned punishers suppress the thought of making the joke and serve as negative reinforcement for talking about something else. Conditioned punishers function as "warning signals" that bridge the time gap between the current behavior and the eventual aversive consequences.

Slip-ups, goofs, blunders, and other mistakes early in a chain can jeopardize the attainment of a terminal reinforcer and/or lead to aversive events—if no corrective action is taken. *The stimuli produced by mistakes become conditioned punishers that bridge the time gap by providing immediate punishment for actions that could endanger the completion of the behavior chain.* When conditioned punishers appear in operant chains, they tend to (1) suppress the problematic behavior that produced them and (2) provide negative reinforcement for corrective actions that bring the chain of behavior back "on course."

Race car drivers know that each race could involve painful accidents if they do not take precautions. Seeing an unusual leak under a high performance engine is a conditioned punisher that predicts potential danger in the next race—which may be days or weeks away. The conditioned punisher is a CS that elicits emotional responses and punishes whatever negligent acts were responsible for the engine leak; it is an S^D that sets the occasion for repairing the defect. Once the engine is repaired, the conditioned punisher disappears; the disappearance of the punisher provides negative reinforcement for good engine maintenance. Thus, the conditioned punishers bridge the time gap between careful engine maintenance and the next race, helping people avoid serious punishment by taking precautionary actions well in advance. When the surgeon sees that the scalpel has come too close to an artery that must remain intact, the response produced stimuli serve as conditioned punishers that suppress future inaccuracies, as S^Δ's for not cutting further, and as S^D's for corrective action. By escaping the conditioned punishers, the surgeon avoids making mistakes that might cause serious problems at a later time.

Complex Chains

So far, we have discussed two of the most basic forms of operant behavior chains: two-link chains leading to an unconditioned reinforcer and multiple-link chains leading to an unconditioned reinforcer. Other types of operant chains are also seen in everyday life.

First, some chains contain unconditioned reinforcers mixed in with the conditioned reinforcers at various points along the chain. For example, eating dinner is a chain of operants that includes taking another helping of rice, cutting a piece of meat, putting the meat in the mouth, passing the salad, and so forth. Some operants are followed by mouthfuls of food (the unconditioned reinforcer), whereas others are followed by conditioned reinforcers associated with food. In many common behavioral chains, the unconditioned reinforcers of sensory stimulation are superimposed on conditioned reinforcers at various points throughout the chain.[22] Playing music, talking with a friend, exploring a new city, and playing a game all involve chains of behavior in which novel and stimulating sensory experiences appear at various points in the chains and make the behavior more rewarding than it would be if it were only maintained by conditioned reinforcers.

Second, the terminal reinforcers of some chains may not be unconditioned reinforcers. The terminal reinforcer can be one of the more powerful conditioned reinforcers, such as social attention or money. Paychecks are terminal reinforcers that will maintain long chains of work for days at a time. Children who whine or pout may generate behavior chains lasting an hour or more before receiving the terminal reinforcer of social attention.

Third, the terminal reinforcer need not be powerful at all if other reinforcers earlier in the chain are relatively powerful. For example, a telephone conversation ends with ''Good-bye'' and hanging up the phone. The final acts of the phone conversation do not produce terminal reinforcers that are sufficiently rewarding to maintain all the prior social interaction. In most conversations, the terminal reinforcers are of trivial importance

---

[22]In everyday life, it is not uncommon to have sensory stimulation reinforcers appearing at various points along the chain of conditioned reinforcers that precede a terminal reinforcer. Houston (1976:173) notes that even in the laboratory, sensory stimulation may appear at various points along a chain.

compared with the reinforcers of social interaction, meaningful information, and sensory stimulation in making each link in the conversational chain rewarding.

Socially Interlocked Chains

During interaction, two people often interlock their response chains. Figure 7–2 shows such a social chain. Person A asks if B has ever watched a certain TV program. B answers, "Yes." This allows A to tell the latest news about the star of the program. B says, "You're kidding!" A says, "No, I'm not." B makes a joke about the star's social life.

Although conversations sometimes contain lapses and interruptions, smoothly linked chains often appear when people find the topics rewarding and are responding to each other's contributions. When B answers "Yes" to A's question about seeing a TV program, B's answer functions as (1) a conditioned reinforcer with the properties of a CS and S^D. As a CS, it reinforces A's asking questions; and as an S^D, it cues A to tell the latest news. (If B had answered "No," A would have had to either explain more about the program before telling the latest news or switch to another topic. Thus, the word "No" would have been an S^Δ for not continuing the chain in the diagram and an S^D for other verbal responses.) When A tells the latest news, the positive social interaction and novelty of the story reinforce B's saying "yes," and set the occasion for B to say, "You're kidding." Each person's responses serve as conditioned reinforcers for the other person's behavior. Thus, in Figure 7–2, there are two arrows coming from each response: One is the CS that reinforces the other person's last response; and the second is the S^D that sets the occasion for the other person's next response.

Naturally, not all conversations are interlocked as smoothly and completely as the above example. A's comments about the movie star may "fall on deaf ears" if B knows nothing about the topic and is clearly unresponsive to A. This puts discussion of the movie star on extinction and decreases the likelihood that A will mention it or similar topics to B in the future. Something A says may serve as a conditioned punisher for B's last response, and B may become quiet or jump to a totally different topic. The higher the ratio of punishment to reinforcement that there is in a conversation, the less likely the conversation is to flow smoothly and to be enjoyable for the people involved. Conditioned punishers elicit aversive emotional responses and may serve as S^Δ's for not interacting further with the other person.

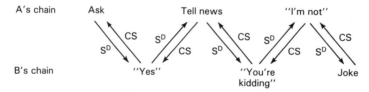

FIGURE 7–2 Conversations consist of socially interlocking chains. Each response is a CS that reinforces the prior behavior and an S^D that sets the occasion for the next behavior.

Learning New Operant Chains

People can learn new operant chains either with or without the help of others. Having help from others and receiving social reinforcers to boost early elements of the chains usually makes learning easier than learning without social assistance.

When people receive no help from others while learning a new chain of operants, they usually have to learn one link of the chain at a time, in reverse order. The last link is learned first, then the second to last link is learned, and so forth. The easiest operant to learn is usually the one that is directly followed by the terminal reinforcer. Thus, when four responses—*d, c, b,* and *a*—lead to a terminal reinforcer, behavior *a* is easiest to learn first

$$d \rightarrow c \rightarrow b \rightarrow a \rightarrow \textbf{terminal reinforcer}$$

because it is followed most closely by the terminal reinforcer. The stimuli that most reliably precede and predict behavior *a* and its consequences—the terminal reinforcer—would become a conditioned reinforcer (S^r). This first conditioned reinforcer (S^r_1) is a CS that can reinforce any behavior (such as *b*) that is instrumental in making it possible to engage in *a*. The S^r_1 is also an S^D that sets the occasion for performing behavior *a*.

$$a \rightarrow \textbf{terminal reinforcer}$$
$$S^r_1 \rightarrow a \rightarrow \textbf{terminal reinforcer}$$
$$b \rightarrow S^r_1 \rightarrow a \rightarrow \textbf{terminal reinforcer}$$

After behavior *b* is added to the chain, the stimuli that precede *b* become a second conditioned reinforcer—S^r_2—that can then reinforce the acquisition of behavior *c*, and cue the performance of behavior *b*.

$$S^r_2 \rightarrow b \rightarrow S^r_1 \rightarrow a \rightarrow \textbf{terminal reinforcer}$$
$$c \rightarrow S^r_2 \rightarrow b \rightarrow S^r_1 \rightarrow a \rightarrow \textbf{terminal reinforcer}$$

After behavior *c* is added to make the chain even longer, the stimuli that precede *c* become a third conditioned reinforcer—S^r_3—that can then reinforce the acquisition of behavior *d*, and cue the performance of behavior *c*.

$$d \rightarrow S^r_3 \rightarrow c \rightarrow S^r_2 \rightarrow b \rightarrow S^r_1 \rightarrow a \rightarrow \textbf{terminal reinforcer}$$

If a hiker had to learn—without help from others—how to stay warm when hiking in the woods, the first behavior the hiker might acquire would be the skill of building a good fire. Building the fire (behavior *a*) is reinforced by warmth (an unconditioned terminal reinforcer). If there are times when dry wood is not handy, there will be reinforcement for any behavior *b* that makes it possible to perform behavior *a* (building a fire). Collecting fallen wood belongs to this response class (*b*) because it allows one to build a fire; hence collecting wood is reinforced. Several hikes later, after this behavior *b* is well learned, the hiker may set up camp in a place where there is no fallen wood. Any behavior *c* that produces fallen wood will be reinforced because it permits the hiker to complete the chain of responses and gain the eventual unconditioned reinforcer of warmth. The hiker may learn the behavior *c* of pulling down dead branches and thus lengthen the chain by another link. Finally, the hiker may learn behavior *d*—of carrying a pocket chain saw to help cut down dead branches that otherwise could not be easily pulled down.

When people have the help of others in learning chains, the social assistance frees them from the constraints of having to learn the chain one link at a time in reverse order (as described above). Models, rules, and prompts may help a person learn responses at any location (early or late) along a lengthy chain; and social reinforcement for performing these responses can facilitate the acquisition of the responses long before the person can perform the entire chain from beginning to end and acquire the terminal reinforcer. Years before the child learns to build a campfire without help from others, the parents may teach the child to collect fallen wood and bring it to camp so the parents can build the fire. In another context, the parents may teach the child how to use saws or knock down dead branches, giving social reinforcers when the child successfully follows rules or imitates the example they model for the child. Years may pass before the child is camping with some friends, needs to build a fire, and uses all the links of the *d–c–b–a* chain described above.

Most people have extensive social learning experience in which they gradually acquire long chains of operants by learning to perform single responses or fragments of chains and then to link these into longer, more sophisticated chains. Generally, people learn the easier sections of a chain first by watching models, hearing rules, or receiving prompts, and by receiving social reinforcers for making progress. The learner may have to practice and learn quite a few responses in a chain before the chain is adequate to produce the terminal reinforcers that will maintain the chain without extra social reinforcers. After a person has learned a certain number of the basic links in a chain, the chain will produce enough terminal reinforcers to maintain the chain without further social reinforcement and the person will be less dependent on social reinforcers for future learning (though the social reinforcers may not hinder further learning).[23]

A novelist must produce long chains of writing behavior for hours at a time over many months to complete a novel. Beginning in childhood, it takes years to acquire the skills for producing such long chains of behavior. At first, social assistance and reinforcement are of crucial importance in helping the child learn how to begin writing; however, social reinforcement gradually becomes less important as the writer gains skills. The child who someday will write novels begins by acquiring the skills of forming letters of the alphabet, then linking these letters together to create one word at a time. Perhaps the child draws a picture of a house and labels it, ''My HouSe.'' Teachers and parents reward these early skills with loving attention, displaying the ''masterpiece'' for all to see and comment on. After the child can write single words, the child is given practice in creating sentences, then paragraphs, and finally short essays. The early essays are not of literary quality, but the child receives social reinforcers for having learned longer chains of writing behavior. After the child has mastered even longer chains of behavior for lengthier

---

[23]Bandura (1977:104f).

essays, a high school teacher may help the budding writer insert extra links in the writing chain to increase creative word use, literary allusion, and character development. Over the years, the student may continue to receive social reinforcers for adding more links into the behavior chains that will be involved in the eventual production of novels.

Whereas the first grader received social reinforcers after completing each word or sentence, the novelist can link together thousands of words without external social reinforcers for each link. This is because each link in the writing chain is followed by response produced conditioned reinforcers that owe their strength to a prior history of being paired with other reinforcers. Others may be impressed by the writer's "internal motivation" for writing five hours a day. They could not do that! But then they have learned other long chains of behavior and not the chains the novelist has received reinforcers for acquiring. The novelist's "internal motivation" results from the conditioned reinforcers the novelist receives at each link of writing a book and from the sensory stimulation reinforcers arising from creative writing (Chapter 6).

It is unlikely that any of us would ever produce great novels, musical compositions, scientific discoveries, or other peaks of human accomplishment if we relied on unguided learning rather than help from others. Those who have learned a skill before us can help us acquire the links needed to produce similar accomplishments. If they use generous reinforcement for teaching us the links, the links will become conditioned reinforcers that will reinforce our practicing and mastering the links of progressively longer chains. If the links lead to novel, creative output, the sensory stimulation of new experience will take over as an unconditioned reinforcer for maintaining our behavior even in the absence of other reinforcement.

CONCLUSION

Neutral stimuli can become conditioned reinforcers or conditioned punishers if they precede and predict other reinforcers or punishers. Each person tends to learn a unique set of conditioned reinforcers and punishers due to his or her unique history of learning experience. Some of the most common conditioned reinforcers and punishers are social cues, tokens, and the response produced stimuli of our own actions as we carry out chains of operants. Conditioned reinforcers reward us for staying "on course" as we move through a long sequence of operants toward some terminal reinforcers. They serve to bridge the time gap between early links in the chain and delayed terminal reinforcers. Conditioned punishers provide early punishment if we begin to drift "off course" during a chain, hence they often suppress sloppy behavior before careless responses can produce unconditioned punishment.

In the next four chapters we turn our attention to the four main ways in which people learn new operant behavior: differential reinforcement and shaping, models and observational learning, prompts, and rules.

8

Differential Reinforcement and Shaping

● *In this chapter you will learn about the ways in which behavior is gradually modified, molded, and shaped into new patterns by its consequences.*

What is the origin of new behavior? How are new responses created in an individual's behavior repertoire? This chapter and the following three describe four different types of learning processes that explain how new behavior is acquired and old behavior is modified. This chapter describes the role of *differential reinforcement* and *shaping* in behavioral change. The next three chapters examine social learning processes: *modeling and observational learning, prompting,* and *rules.* In everyday life, these four processes are often intertwined in various combinations. We discuss each process separately in order to clarify its unique contribution to behavioral change, but pure examples of each process are less common than mixed examples. Although the major emphasis of these chapters is on operant behavior, these operant processes can influence and be influenced by Pavlovian conditioning (as discussed in Chapter 4).

DIFFERENTIAL REINFORCEMENT

Variability is a natural part of human behavior. Each time we greet a friend or say our names, there are usually variations in pitch, loudness, tone of voice, inflections, and other subtleties. We rarely repeat any behavior exactly the same way on two different occasions. *Whenever people's behavior is variable* and *some of these variations lead to reinforcement but others do not, the behavior is under differential reinforcement.* As you would expect, the reinforced variations become more frequent while the nonreinforced or punished variations become less frequent.

When a young child is first given a spoon while eating, the child may stick the spoon into the applesauce in any of a variety of different ways. If the spoon is upside down, it fails to pick up much applesauce and fails to produce much reinforcement. If the spoon is right side up, the child may succeed in loading it with a mouthful of applesauce. The parents wait somewhat nervously for the next event: Will the applesauce reach the child's mouth or end up on the floor, the bib, or them? Sometimes, the spoon flies across the room. Sometimes it moves toward the mouth—for a near-miss on the chin.

The young child who is sitting in the high chair with a spoon in hand is in an S^D context that sets the occasion for several behaviors (B_1 through B_7): pushing, hitting, eating, throwing, dropping, patting, and mashing.

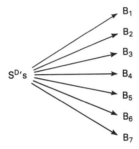

The S^D's of the stimulus collage can lead to any of seven different responses. The child's behavior may show considerable variability, as the child alternates among the seven activities.

As the child skips back and forth among the seven behaviors, the consequences that follow each behavior begin to modify its frequency.

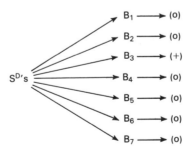

If behavior 1 (B_1) causes food to fall on the floor, the child receives no food reinforcement (indicated by a zero); and the behavior begins to extinguish.[1] If behavior 2 (B_2) causes

---

[1]Although there is no food reinforcement, there is novel sensory stimulation in playing with a spoon and propelling food in many different directions; hence there is some reinforcement for food play at first, until the novelty wears off (pages 105–109).

food to be splattered all over the high chair, again there is no food reinforcement (another zero); and behavior 2 is also on extinction. If behavior 3 (B_3) brings food into the mouth, it is followed by food reinforcement (a positive effect). As a result, behavior 3 begins to become more frequent (while the nonreinforced behaviors become less frequent). If the remaining responses (B_4 through B_7) dump food on the bib, the dog, the parent's clothes, or other places, they also are followed by nonreinforcement (the other zeros). As the child has repeated experiences with the consequences of each behavior, gradually behavior 3 (B_3) becomes the most frequent response to the S^D's of sitting in the high chair with spoon in hand; and the other responses decline in frequency. Eventually the child learns to direct almost all food to the mouth and none onto the floor.

Whenever some responses in a given S^D context leads to reinforcement but others do not, differential reinforcement is in effect. The different levels of reinforcement cause the reinforced behavior to become more frequent while the nonreinforced responses decline in frequency. Eventually the S^D context sets the occasion for only those behaviors that are rewarded (B_3 in the above example). In addition, the context stimuli become S^Δ's for not performing all the other behaviors (B_1, B_2, B_4, B_5, B_6, and B_7) that are not reinforced.

$$S^\Delta\text{'s} - - - - - \text{NO} \quad B_1$$

$$S^\Delta\text{'s} - - - - - \text{NO} \quad B_2$$

$$S^D\text{'s} \longrightarrow B_3 \longrightarrow (+)$$

$$S^\Delta\text{'s} - - - - - \text{NO} \quad B_4$$

$$S^\Delta\text{'s} - - - - - \text{NO} \quad B_5$$

$$S^\Delta\text{'s} - - - - - \text{NO} \quad B_6$$

$$S^\Delta\text{'s} - - - - - \text{NO} \quad B_7$$

Differential reinforcement produces two effects: (1) it causes the frequency of the various behaviors to either increase or decrease, and (2) it brings the reinforced behaviors under S^D control while bringing the other behaviors under S^Δ control.[2] Differential reinforcement is often in effect when there is a "right" way and a "wrong" way to do something. The right way leads to reinforcement and the wrong way results in either no reinforcement (extinction) or punishment. In everyday language, this type of learning is often called "trial and error learning."[3] A more accurate nontechnical label might be "success and failure learning," since appropriate behavior leads to successes and inappropriate behavior leads to failures.

In one sense, differential reinforcement *selects* those responses that are useful, practical, and rewarding for each S^D context, while allowing less well-suited responses to disappear. Of all the things a child can do with a spoon, accurate movement of food to the

---

[2]Skinner (1953); Catania (1971); Nevin (1971a); Rilling (1977).

[3]Behaviorists object to the term "trial and error learning" because (1) a person need not be "trying" to learn something in order to be influenced by differential reinforcement, and (2) the term "error" focuses on failures without stressing the more important successes.

mouth is automatically selected by differential reinforcement because it produces the most rewarding results. This natural reinforcement process has important parallels with natural selection, in which well-adapted members of a species survive while poorly adapted members do not.[4] In both cases, selective processes mold and change things—either *behaviors* or *species*—in ways that are usually suited to environmental conditions.

Since children have so much to learn, numerous examples of differential reinforcement can be found in childhood. When young children attempt to open screw-top bottles, they often pull, twist, push, and pry the lids in a variety of ways. Many of their efforts have no effect on the bottle tops; however, a counterclockwise twist often succeeds in opening a bottle. Opening a bottle is usually more rewarding than manipulating a lid that will not budge—since an open bottle may provide reinforcers such as food or novel objects. Thus, a child's early responses to bottles are influenced by differential reinforcement: Those responses that produce an open bottle are reinforced, and those that fail to open bottles are extinguished. After repeated experiences with bottles, the child learns to open them quickly and efficiently by twisting the lid counterclockwise and not wasting time with other types of manipulations. Bottle tops become S^D's for counterclockwise twists and S^Δ's for not using the other techniques.

Continuous Variations

So far we have described the differential reinforcement of several separate response classes (B_1 through B_7 in the first example). We have seen that early alternations between response classes produce behavioral variability and that differential reinforcement selects the most effective response class. There is a second way to analyze differential reinforcement: Here we focus on the *continuous variability* in behavior, rather than on several separate response classes. To do this, it is useful to graph response variations as is shown in Figure 8–1. All the variations in a given behavior are represented by locations along the horizontal axis in Figure 8–1. For example, if a behavior could be performed at different levels of physical strength, we might graph the weakest performances at the left of the figure, the strongest performances at the right, and all intermediate cases in between these extremes. The frequency of each variation is indicated by the height of the curve. For example, those behavioral variations near the left end of the continuum (in the zone marked A in Figure 8–1) are less frequent than those behaviors in the middle zones (marked B and C).

Continuous variations in behavior can be molded by differential reinforcement if some variations are reinforced and others are not. When children first learn to tie their shoes, they create a variety of different knots: some with more loops than others; some pulled tighter than others. Some of these *succeed* in keeping the shoes on, and others *fail* to stay tied. Due to differential reinforcement, the child eventually learns the effective way to tie shoes; this operant skill comes under such strong S^D control that older children and adults can perform the task without paying attention.

---

[4]The similarities between differential reinforcement and natural selection have stimulated the development of interdisciplinary theories of behavioral change and social evolution; but the important differences between these two processes must be recognized, too (Skinner, 1966; Langton, 1979; Blute, 1981; Baldwin and Baldwin, 1981; Carroll. 1984).

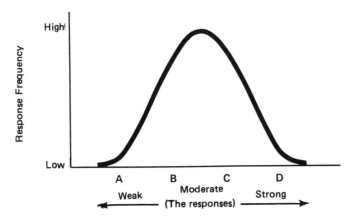

FIGURE 8–1   The responses before differential reinforcement.

For simplicity, let us only focus on the variations in the tightness of knots. The loosest ties are shown at the left end of Figure 8–1, and the tightest ties are at the right end. Ties of intermediate tightness are the most frequent (in zones B and C). What happens as a child ties knots of different strengths and experiences the consequences associated with each different type of knot? Since the weaker ties—response variations in zones A and B—fail to keep the shoes on, they fail to produce reinforcement. As a result, they gradually become less frequent. Since the tighter ties—those response variations in zones C and D—are usually successful in producing reinforcement, they gradually become more frequent. After repeated differential reinforcement, the frequencies of the various responses are modified as shown in Figure 8–2. The responses which are reinforced (indicated by + signs) become more frequent (upward arrows); whereas the responses that are followed by nonreinforcement (indicated by zeros) become less frequent, due to extinction (downward arrows). The original response pattern is thereby shifted to

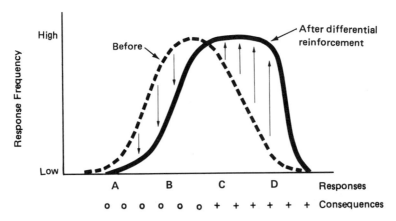

FIGURE 8–2   The responses after differential reinforcement.

the right—such that most knots are tied tightly enough to keep the shoes on and produce reinforcing results. Due to differential reinforcement, the child has learned to attain successful results most of the time.

Response Differentiation

The changes in behavior produced by differential reinforcement are called *response differentiation*. An early, undifferentiated, unspecialized response pattern becomes differentiated into two separate response classes: the reinforced responses (in zones C and D) and the unreinforced responses (in zones A and B). During response differentiation, the reinforced responses become high probability operants under S^D control, whereas the unreinforced responses become low probability operants under S^Δ control.

The process of response differentiation can be seen in many everyday situations. For example, when children are first learning to play baseball, they usually have difficulty throwing the ball from the outfield to home plate. Their long throws reveal a high level of response variability, which is typical of untrained, undifferentiated behavior. Some throws come close to home plate, but others fall far from the mark. The poor throws are not reinforced; they may even be punished by criticisms from the coach or other players. The good throws are reinforced by holding a runner at third base, producing an "out" at home plate, or allowing for a spectacular double play. As the outfielder repeatedly hurls the ball toward home plate, this differential reinforcement conditions improved accuracy. Gradually, the early, undifferentiated behavior is split into two response classes—accurate throws and inaccurate throws. Over time, the frequency of accurate throws continues to increase. Naturally the more often a person practices long throws under differential reinforcement, the sooner the person will gain the skills needed for accuracy. In addition, the more effective the reinforcers and punishers are, the more rapid the learning. (In this and most other examples, it should be realized that models, prompts, and rules can affect the rate of learning, too.)

During the early days after giving birth, new mothers hold their babies in a variety of different positions: high and low, on the right side or the left. Most mothers—both left-handed and right-handed—learn to hold their babies on their left side more than on the right.[5] Differential reinforcement may explain this tendency to hold the babies on the left. Infants are calmed by the sound of the human heart. When a mother holds her baby on the left side, the infant can hear sounds of the heart better and is more likely to be calm than if held on the right side. Since a calm infant provides more reinforcers and fewer punishers for mother than a crying infant, there is differential reinforcement for the mother to hold the infant on her left. The undifferentiated early responses of holding the baby on either side become differentiated into left-holding due to the differential reinforcement.

Response differentiation can be seen in the learning of conformity. Children are not good conformists since they have not yet learned the difference between conformity and nonconformity. However, over the years the undifferentiated behavior of youth comes under at least some degree of differential reinforcement when conformity is reinforced more than nonconformity. Most people will tolerate a small amount of deviance or

[5]Salk (1973).

nonconformity from their peers and associates; but generally they reinforce conformity and punish nonconformity. In a street gang where membership is marked by leather jackets, Levis, and old clothes, the nonconformist who dares to wear "straight" clothes is crying out to be heckled. On Madison Avenue, the executive who comes to work in Levis and a sweatshirt is the nonconformist. The person who deviates feels the "pressure to conform." In behavioral terms, feeling the pressure to conform is merely the subjective sensation resulting from the nonreinforcement or punishment that follows nonconformist behavior. Subjectively, it feels aversive when other people snicker when you walk by, or avoid you, or shake their heads, or cancel their advertising contracts with your agency. Conformity, on the other hand, results in acceptance, integration into one's group and access to the social reinforcers shared by most others. This differential reinforcement for conforming and punishment for deviating tends to bring most people into line with their social group. Learning to conform and to avoid nonconformity represents response differentiation, as two distinctive responses emerge from an earlier undifferentiated set of responses. (Naturally, people will be less likely to conform if they are not well integrated in a group, if they belong to multiple groups which reinforce different patterns of behavior, or if they are not dependent on social contacts for reinforcement.)

In many situations a person's opening lines can make or break a social interaction. A good approach is reinforced; a poor one punished. People who are frequently thrown into these situations will have their behavior modified by differential reinforcement. For example, the door-to-door saleswoman may depend heavily on her introductory few sentences to get her foot in the door. Something catchy, surprising, cheerful, or disarming may succeed better than a dull or straight pitch. The inexperienced saleswoman may employ a variety of lines; but the success of some lines and failure of others will differentially reinforce the use of the more effective openers.

Differential reinforcement from the social environment tends to be less consistent than differential reinforcement from the nonsocial environment. Bottle tops reinforce counterclockwise twists, though extra force may be needed if the lid is on too tight. Patterns of differential reinforcement from the physical environment tend to be stable. Most bottles can be opened with counterclockwise turns. Most shoes can be tied with a simple knot. The social environment tends to be much less consistent. A saleswoman's cheerful opening line may work well with one person and poorly with another. The saleswoman who is learning to be more cheerful and witty—due to several recent successes with this opening performance—may have the door slammed in her face at the next house. These inconsistent patterns of reinforcement generally complicate the acquisition of social behavior and discriminations, making the process of response differentiation considerably slower than it would have been with more consistent feedback. Thus, the learning of many social skills is often more difficult than the learning of skills for coping with the nonsocial environment.

Because differential reinforcement brings operants under S^D or S^Δ control, the complex learning experience may result in subtle discriminations about the appropriate context for each differentiated operant. A saleswoman may learn to use witty opening lines with people who are smiling, friendly lines with people who are not smiling, and sympathetic lines with people who look sad.

When people have failed to learn appropriate social skills, differential reinforcement can be used to help them acquire these skills. For example, George had a very difficult time meeting women and seldom got a date. After years of frustration, he went to a therapist for help. During the initial interview, the therapist noted that George talked too much, rarely asked questions, did not listen well, and frequently digressed to the topic of fixing cars and engines. No wonder George had little success with women. For George to learn better skills for interacting with women, the therapist arranged for George to have a series of "practice dates." Three times a week a woman would go to lunch with George, listen to his conversation, and provide differential reinforcement for the good and bad variations in his social behavior. The woman was instructed to provide differential feedback by (1) making normal conversation when George interacted in any manner that a woman might enjoy, and (2) holding up her hand and saying "Boring" when George began rambling about things of little interest to women.

On the first practice lunch date on Monday, Linda had to give the "Boring" signal over twenty-five times, as George kept talking about his latest engine repair project, the difficulty of getting precision parts, and the problems caused by overheating at high speeds. However, George did come up with several good topics: He wondered if Linda would like to take a ride in his dune buggy. He asked her about her plans for the future. In these cases, it was easy for Linda to respond with genuinely sincere conversation. Nevertheless, when George returned to discussing the new cam shaft he installed in his dune buggy engine and the effects of RPM on horse power, Linda would raise her hand and say "Boring."

Two days later, George had a lunch date with Maria, and he again found that technical details about his vehicles were boring but that a variety of other topics led to mutually rewarding conversations. On Friday, Julie showed more interest in cars and engines than the other two women, but she too let George know when his highly specialized interests were boring. Julie was a law student, and she and George got into a very interesting discussion of women moving into the professions. George was interested to hear Julie's opinion about the career choices available for the modern woman, and his sincere questions helped him learn a lot about the thoughts and feelings of a career-oriented woman.

As George continued with his practice lunch dates the following week, he bored his partners less and received much less negative feedback. As he developed a more serious concern for the issues of interest to women, he asked more meaningful and relevant questions. These questions helped him learn a lot about women his age and ways to interact with them in a mutually rewarding manner. Several weeks later, George told the therapist that he and Julie—the woman he had met on his third date—were getting "serious," and he suggested that he no longer needed the practice lunch dates. Seven months later, George again contacted the therapist with the good news that Julie and he were engaged to be married.

Differential reinforcement had successfully changed George's interaction style. An early response pattern underwent response differentiation as George learned to avoid boring his companions and to focus on topics of mutual interest. Both he and his companions found the new style more rewarding.

INDUCTION[6]

In pure cases of differential reinforcement, new behavior is not being created. Some variations in existing behavior are being made more probable while others are being made less probable. At the end of differential reinforcement, no new variations have been created. As shown in Figure 8–2, all the response variability lay in zones A, B, C, and D both *before* and *after* differential reinforcement. Only the distribution of the responses was changed—by being shifted to the right.

However, there are processes that often accompany differential reinforcement that result in the creation of new behavior. These creative processes are *induction* and *shaping*, both of which allow us to develop new behavior patterns that lie beyond old response classes.

When an operant is reinforced and increases in frequency, similar responses may also appear and increase in frequency, even though they have not been reinforced. This process is called *induction* to indicate that reinforcement has induced changes in behaviors that are similar to those that were reinforced. When behavioral variations in zones C and D are reinforced—but other variations in zones A and B are not reinforced—all the responses in zones C and D increase in frequency. In addition, other changes occur due to induction. First, those variations in zone B that are most similar to the reinforced behavior in zone C become more frequent, because they bear some resemblance to the reinforced behaviors. Second, there is a tendency for new responses to appear (the shaded area above E in Figure 8–3). Thus, the process of reinforcing behaviors of type C and D increases the frequency of those behaviors *and* similar responses, some of which are totally new (namely those in zone E). The new behaviors of type E are natural variations on the reinforced operants of type D.

For example, when a person first learns to high jump, there is usually a broad range of variation in the height of the early jumps. Some may be only 5 feet, the majority may be 5½ feet, and the highest may be 6 feet (the "before" curve in Figure 8–4). When differential reinforcement is initiated, reinforcement may be given for all jumps of 5½ to 6 feet, but not for other heights. The person soon learns to produce more of the higher jumps and fewer short jumps. The high jumper may be learning many skills for approaching the crossbar from the best angle, selecting the correct spot for jumping, tensing the muscles more, thrusting harder with the takeoff leg, turning more smoothly in midair to avoid hitting the bar, and so forth. All these skills are reinforced when they result in higher jumps; and eventually the average jump increases from 5½ to 5¾ feet (the solid curve in Figure 8–4). As these skills are mastered, the person may actually be able to produce jumps higher than the original 6-foot maximum jump. New behavior has been created via induction. This new behavior (shaded area in Figure 8–4) appears as a natural consequence of learning the skills for higher jumping, even if no jumps above 6 feet are ever reinforced.

Typically, newly induced behavior *is* reinforced. A coach who is reinforcing 6-foot jumps is very likely to give even more reinforcement for jumps higher than 6 feet. Since

---

[6]Induction—also called response generalization or transfer—is discussed by Skinner (1938; 1953:93f) and Catania (1971).

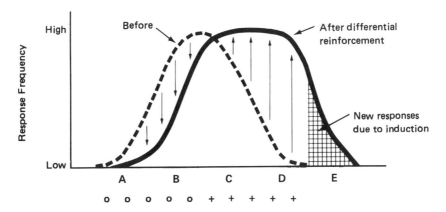

FIGURE 8–3   Induction of new behavior (shaded area).

jumps over 6 feet are also reinforced, the frequency of jumps above 6 feet is even greater than shown in Figure 8–4 (where only jumps between 5½ and 6 feet were reinforced). Thus, induction *plus* extra reinforcement increases the total amount of new behavior created (shaded area in Figure 8–5). This is easily seen by comparing the shaded areas in Figure 8–5 and Figure 8–4.

In everyday life, newly created behavior resulting from induction is often reinforced. If a real estate agent increased the average number of sales from 6 units a month to 6½ per month, the higher level of productivity would be reinforced. If a newspaper journalist increased average output from 6 quality articles per week to 6½ quality articles per week, additional reinforcement would be likely. If a person who enjoyed improvising at the piano gained extra skills for creating new melodies, the extra novelty would provide sensory stimulation reinforcers for the new ability. Listeners might also appreciate the increased novelty created by the pianist and provide a second source of reinforcement—social reinforcement—for the new behavioral ability.

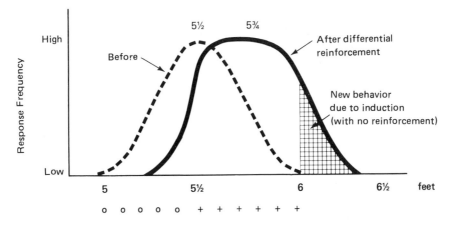

FIGURE 8–4   Induction without reinforcement for new behavior.

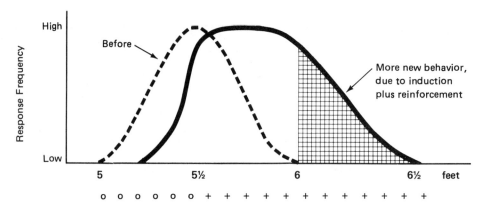

FIGURE 8–5 Induction plus reinforcement for new behavior.

Induction plus reinforcement is often used as a teaching tool. Comedians and stage performers are often given special training to help them be more spontaneous and say more "crazy" things on stage. One method that directors use requires the performer to free associate aloud and rapidly.[7] Once the performer starts spilling out words and phrases, the director gives positive feedback for the funny, silly, weird, or playful statements: "That's it!" "You're hot!" "Keep it up." "Another one like that." All of us can come up with crazy phrases, but reinforcement is needed to get a person to spew them out at a high rate. Differential reinforcement for the funny phrases and extinction for prosaic phrases teaches the performer the skills for selecting funny lines and skipping dull ones. A side effect of this exercise is often the induction of entirely new styles of humorous banter that the performer had never practiced before. Since these new humorous responses are likely to be reinforced, too, the actor's newly induced skills are reinforced along with the old skills that were the original target of differential reinforcement.

SHAPING

Shaping is a process by which operants are changed in a series of steps from an initial performance toward a final performance. Each step results from the application of a new criterion for differential reinforcement. Each step of conditioning produces both response differentiation and induction, and these make possible the next step of behavior change.[8]

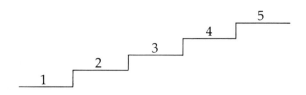

[7]Schulman (1973).
[8]Skinner (1953:63ff, 91ff); Staats (1963:77ff); Catania (1971).

The would-be comedian starts at step 1 with differential reinforcement for making funny free associations out loud. As this skill is reinforced to a high frequency, a variety of novel responses—including humorous little stories—will appear due to induction. After a period of time, the director and comedian decide to move to step 2, and now to reinforce witty stories, but not simpler types of humorous free associations that had been reinforced during step 1. Differential reinforcement at step 1 had produced the response differentiation and induction that made it possible to reach step 2. A new pattern of differential reinforcement at step 2 will produce further changes in behavior making it possible to reach step 3. Differential reinforcement for witty stories (step 3) will improve the comedian's skills for telling funny stories and will cause the induction of even further new responses. Perhaps some of the step 2 stories will involve a dialogue between two fictitious characters, and the comedian may use two different styles of voice to make it clear which character is talking. The director and comedian may decide to use these newly induced responses as the raw material for step 3 of shaping, and require the acting out of different humorous characters as the criterion for reinforcement. Now the director gives reinforcement only when the comedian creates funny stories with impersonations of the characters. As this new pattern of differential reinforcement increases the frequency of good impersonations, induction might make possible even further steps. At step 4 the comedian might learn to act out the various impersonations while ad-libbing with another performer. At step 5 the comedian might devise entire scripts for interweaving multiple impersonations with lines for several other performers. Eventually, the comedian might be ready to create a full length stage performance that incorporated the skills learned during all five steps.

In everyday life, there is a continuum of different types of shaping, from systematic to unsystematic. Systematic shaping is more likely to produce rapid and effective behavioral change—with the minimum of failure and aversive consequences—whereas unsystematic shaping is more likely to be slow and disorganized, with a higher risk of failures and aversive consequences. In order to clarify the mechanisms of shaping, we will first turn to more systematic examples of shaping. Later we will consider less systematic, less efficient forms of shaping.

Systematic Shaping

The type of shaping that has been best studied in the laboratory is systematic and carefully executed. *Systematic shaping involves changing behavior in steps of successive approximation toward a preestablished final performance. At each step, reinforcement is given for behavior that best approximates the final performance.* No new step is taken until the last step is well learned and enough desirable new responses appear (due to induction) to allow an easy transition to the next step of differential reinforcement.

Step 1 always begins with the behavior a person is currently capable of performing well. The steps are typically kept small to make progress easy and highly reinforcing. At each step the portions of a person's behavior which best approximate the final performance are reinforced while other portions of response variation are either extinguished or punished. As induction produces new variations, the variations which best approximate the final performance are also reinforced; and as a result the person learns ever more advanced skills. After mastering enough skills, the person is ready to progress to the next step of successive approximation with more demanding criteria of differential reinforcement. The individual is not rushed up the steps at a rate that would decrease the chances of success and increase the chances of failure. Keeping the level of success and reinforcement high makes learning a positive experience and reduces the chances that the individual will avoid further steps of shaping. Although behavior is modified in a series of small, gradual steps, the steps can add up to a major overall change.

If an initial operant performance contained behavioral variations that fell in zones A, B, C, and D (of Figure 8–6), it would be possible to shape a totally new performance that fell in zones E, F, G, and H (in the same figure). We would start precisely as described in the first part of the chapter with a pattern of differential reinforcement that reinforced responses in zones C and D, but did not reinforce responses in zones A and B. This would cause the behavior to change as is shown in Figure 8–6. There is a shift toward C and D plus the induction of new responses in zone E. Once this change has occurred a second step of differential reinforcement would replace the first, such that only responses in zones D and E would be reinforced (but responses in zones A, B, and C would not be). The result of this second pattern of reinforcement is shown in Figure 8–7. Responses in zones D and E become more frequent and the new responses in zone F appear, due to induction. The overall response pattern has changed considerably from the earliest undifferentiated pattern (marked "before" in Figure 8–7).

If a third and fourth step of successive approximation were to follow after these first two steps, the shaping process would produce even further behavior change. After the fourth step, the overall response pattern (step 4 in Figure 8–8) is *entirely new* compared with the earliest performance. Each step had created some new responses via induction; and the series of steps of differential reinforcement shaped these into a totally new performance.

Everyday life examples of systematic shaping are usually found in situations where a person is being taught a new skill in a well-organized manner. Although rules, models, and prompts may be used as supplemental aids to facilitate learning, many skills can only

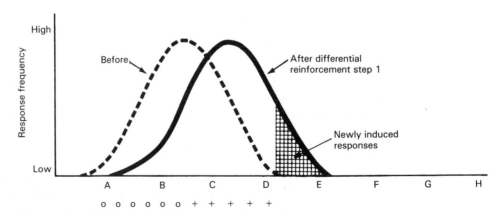

FIGURE 8–6   Shaping: the results of the first step.

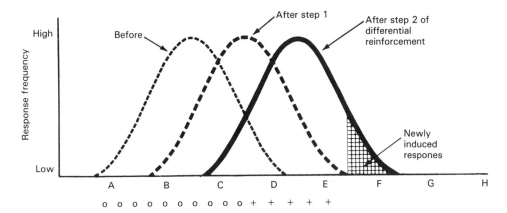

FIGURE 8-7 Shaping: the results of the second step.

be learned through prolonged practice. Repeating a behavior over and over enough times in a series of steps of differential reinforcement will gradually shape advanced skills. You can tell a person how to shoot a bow and arrow or how to play the piano, but it takes years of practice—success and failure learning, along with steps of successive approximation—to condition the advanced skills.

For example, there are many systematic shaping methods a parent could use to teach a child to shoot a rifle well. The parent might have the child learn the basic skills of handling a gun by starting the child with a BB gun. Using a gun that is lightweight and easy to handle facilitates the first learning steps. Because the ammunition is inexpensive, the child can practice repeatedly without much cost. Step one might involve shooting at tin cans or other big targets. Hitting the can provides reinforcement while missing does not. This differential reinforcement will gradually produce response differentiation—accuracy increases and inaccuracy decreases. When it is clear that the child is ready for step two, the parent might introduce a large bull's-eye target. If hitting the bull's-eye is

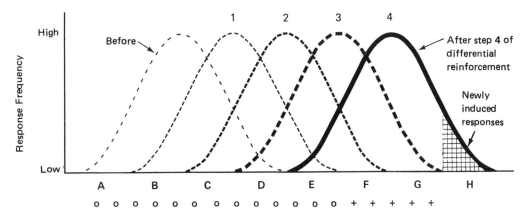

FIGURE 8-8 Shaping: the results of the third and fourth steps.

worth 10 points and each ring further away from the bull's-eye is worth less, the points will provide differential reinforcement for increasingly accurate shooting and help train improved skills. Dozens of skills are involved in learning increasing accuracy: good muscle control, a steady trigger pull, controlled breathing, and so forth. Differential reinforcement hones all these skills, since improved skills lead to increased reinforcement. After the child gains skill at step two, the parent might move the child to step three, by giving the child a 22 rifle. Because a well-built rifle with accurate sights and precision machining allows even greater accuracy, the child can shoot at smaller targets and experience the differential reinforcement needed for learning even more advanced skills. Step three may begin with the child in the prone position, where the gun is easiest to handle. After making progress at step three, the child may advance to step four, shooting from kneeling and standing positions. This fourth step requires even more skills of balance and total body control to retain accuracy. If the steps are carefully designed and generous reinforcement is given at each step, the child will steadily gain skill and will learn to enjoy shooting.

Naturally, some students will advance faster than others. A person who had learned a variety of sports and activities that trained body coordination, muscle control, and balance would already have a head start in learning several of the key skills for shooting; thus this person would have an advantage over someone without prior training in these skills. A person who had been conditioned to fear guns would be at a disadvantage in learning to shoot and would require more positive reinforcement—perhaps supportive feedback from a friend—to have the fear counterconditioned to the point that it did not interfere with learning to shoot. Thus, some people might be able to move through the series of steps quickly, or take larger steps; whereas others might require more practice and reinforcement at each step. Everyone's rate of progress through the steps should be regulated by their own abilities; and no one should be moved ahead to the next step until the last step has been mastered and induction has provided desirable new responses that prepare the student for having success at the next more difficult step.

Naturally Occurring Efficient Shaping

Carefully conducted systematic shaping is not too common in everyday life. Most people do not know how to use behavior principles for shaping behavior. There are, however, some cases that approach systematic shaping; and these are most likely to occur when someone acts as a "teacher" to help another person (the "student") learn a specific behavior. After students have seen how a teacher uses shaping to train increasing skills, the students may learn to apply similar methods to their own behavior, hence learn to be self-shapers.

Teachers.   People who play the teacher role sometimes become effective shapers, whether they are parents, teachers, roommates, or anyone else you might turn to for help in learning a new skill. Clearly, not all teachers are effective, even if they have had long experience in the role; but some teachers demonstrate considerable skill at shaping.

The teacher who is effective at shaping behavior watches the variation in the student's behavior, gives positive feedback for the desirable parts of the variation, and changes the criteria for reinforcement in small steps as behavior shows successive approximations toward the desired final performance. The effective teacher-shaper begins dealing with each student's behavior at precisely the level of skill that the student has already attained. During shaping, reinforcers are given for behavior the student *can do* at present: The better variations are reinforced and the poorer variations are not. An art teacher might comment on the better aspects of a student's latest sketches: ''Your use of shading has improved nicely in the past several days.'' By always focusing on the finer features of the student's work, the teacher provides differential reinforcement that automatically includes newly induced responses. Focusing on the best behavior the student can do at present also helps the teacher adjust the criteria for reinforcement at the same rate that the student's work improves.

Shaping is an ideal way for assuring that developing new skills is an enjoyable experience, since students are rewarded at every step for doing what they do best at that step. Shaping minimizes the problems and aversive experiences that arise when teachers attempt to develop new skills by comparing a student's behavior with that of more advanced students or with impossibly high criteria. Comparing a beginning student with advanced students may be quite aversive for the beginner, because it vividly reveals the inadequacies of the beginner's behavior and suggests that much effort will be needed to reach advanced levels of performance. Teaching a student to strive for perfection or near perfection can also be quite aversive because the final goal looks too distant and unattainable. Shaping is a more positive and rewarding teaching method because each student's behavior is evaluated and rewarded according to that student's own current performance level rather than being compared with other people's behavior; all students receive generous reinforcement for the better variations in their own present behavior, no matter what step of skill development they have reached. Shaping does not demand that a person do better than he or she can already do. That is unnecessary since improved performances will appear naturally and automatically (due to induction) as current good behavior is further reinforced.

Parents are teachers when they help their children learn to walk or talk, to do addition or carpentry, or to master other skills. When the parents first hear babbling that sounds like words—''meh-meh,'' ''deh-deh''—they may shower the child with loving attention, smiles, and other reinforcers that they do not give as abundantly when the child makes sounds like ''ngakagraga.'' This is differential reinforcement, and after a few more steps, the child will be saying ''Mama'' and ''Daddy.'' There is variation in verbal behavior, walking responses, school performance; and parents usually reward the better performances and adjust their criteria for reinforcement each time their child reaches a new level of skill. This sets up natural steps of successive approximation oriented toward the goal of full competence.

A good teacher-shaper is quick to discriminate when a person is making progress or slipping back. In a drawing class a good art teacher might say, ''That's a good facial expression. I think you are learning how to capture eye expressions with a minimum of strokes. But the lips aren't as good as the ones you did in the charcoal drawing yesterday.'' The teacher is noticing variation in drawing and is reinforcing the behavior that shows progress toward desired goals while criticizing the behavior that does not live up to past achievement. This differential reinforcement will tend to increase skillful practices and suppress sloppy performances. Because the teacher reinforces the student's best performances at each point, new responses will appear by induction. As the student learns to draw more skillfully, the teacher-shaper will change the reinforcement criteria in slow steps of successive approximation toward relevant goals.

At one time or another almost everyone serves as a shaper who modifies the behavior of others. This is most clear when people ask for feedback about skills they are trying to learn. For example, a person may ask a tennis partner, "Tell me how my serves are today, O.K.?" If the partner provides feedback (saying which serves are good and bad) and sets higher criteria for "good serving" as serving improves, the feedback will help shape serving toward the desired final performance. It is true that the verbal feedback we receive from others may contain rules—"Don't toss the ball up so high when you're serving"—and thus blend with the type of learning described in Chapter 11. However, much verbal feedback provides differential reinforcement—positive or negative feedback—independent of the verbally encoded rules that may also be present. If this differential reinforcement is combined with steps of successive approximation, it produces the shaping needed for developing higher levels of skills.

Self-Shaping.   Most people learn at least some skills for shaping their own behavior toward desired goals. When parents, teachers, and friends give differential reinforcement and use steps of successive approximation, they serve as models that we can imitate for shaping our own behavior. Some people become quite skillful at shaping at least portions of their own behavior repertoire.

Self-shaping can produce rapid effects. Often the best person to know when a behavior was done well or poorly is the person who did the behavior. A teacher who checks a student's drawings every 15 or 20 minutes sees only the end product of many small units of behavior. The teacher's reinforcers are infrequent and often distant from the actual behavior that produced the desirable effects. However, when a teacher helps shape a student's skills, the teacher is also serving as a model that the student can imitate. If the teacher says, "The eyes are sensitively done in this picture," the student may learn to evaluate and reinforce future art work according to similar criteria.[9] If the teacher keeps raising the criteria for reinforcement as the student improves, the student may also learn to impose higher criteria for self-reinforcement with each step of progress. As the student learns these self-shaping skills by observational learning (Chapter 9), the self-shaping skills become increasingly useful to the student in shaping subsequent improvement in drawing. The student can watch each pen line and give instant self-reinforcement for quality behavior: "Hey, I got it perfect that time. Just right." The reinforcement is both immediate and directly related to the relevant behavior. Likewise, if there is a slip of the pen and part of the sketch is marred by a clumsy line, the student spots the error instantly and gives a punitive evaluation: "Rats! How clumsy!" Each time the student sees new developments in artistic skills (due to induction), the student will probably give especially generous self-reinforcement: "Wow, that's the best face I've ever drawn. I never thought

---

[9]Bandura (1971) and Mahoney (1974) summarize the literature on the observational learning of self-evaluation and self-reinforcement skills. Gewirtz (1971a,b) and some other psychologists are critical of Bandura's use of the concepts of self-reinforcement, claiming that the process of self-reinforcement is more similar to Skinner's model than Bandura suggests.

I'd be so good.'' After several repeated successes at this new level of performance, the student is likely to raise the criterion for giving self-reinforcement; a series of such adjustments in reinforcement criteria create natural steps of successive approximation that shapes continued development of artistic skills.

When a student produces a good drawing, the student receives two kinds of conditioned reinforcers. First, beautiful art is a conditioned reinforcer for many people, especially art students. Thus, the mere act of creating a beautiful drawing automatically provides the student with conditioned reinforcers for skillful drawing. Second, self-evaluation and self-reinforcement consist of thinking positive words, such as ''Mmm. I like that effect.'' These words—whether spoken out loud or not—are also conditioned reinforcers. In addition, artistic behavior is shaped by the unconditioned reinforcers of sensory stimulation (Chapter 6).[10] Finally, the art student may receive social rewards in the form of compliments, admiring comments, prizes, or offers to purchase the work.

There are natural sources of reinforcement which help people learn skills for doing self-shaping. If a student has observed people who are effective shapers and has imitated their methods, the student's self-shaping will be rewarded by: (1) faster learning, since self-reinforcement is immediate and efficient, (2) positive reinforcers from people who appreciate the student's progress, (3) escape from the aversive consequences of errors and criticisms which come from making mistakes, and (4) the positive consequences of having greater independence in guiding one's own development.

Not everyone has equal skills for self-reinforcement and shaping. In addition, a person's skills for shaping one aspect of his or her behavior may not generalize for shaping other aspects of behavior. An artist may be very sensitive in reinforcing and shaping improved artistic skill, but be poor in shaping athletic skills. An athlete who relies on self-reinforcement and shaping to condition new athletic skills may be poor at controlling other skills. Thus, self-control by self-shaping is not a global skill that automatically generalizes for modifying all aspects of a person's behavior.

Although self-shaping is a common behavior, it is often done in private, such that it is not easily seen. People often do not let others know how long they have worked on improving their behavior by systematic practice. The reason is simple: Behavior that clearly resulted from a long period of practice often seems less impressive—hence receives less attention and praise—than does similar behavior that appears to have required no practice or effort. If an artist told you that it took ten to fifteen practice canvases and many failures to refine each artistic idea into a completed work, the artist's painting might seem less impressive than if the artist told you that it only took a few hours to develop an artistic idea into a fully finished canvas. Just before his death at age 88, Michelangelo, the famous Renaissance artist, burned nearly all the drawings he still owned in order that people would not know how hard he had struggled to perfect his art.[11] Unfortunately, because people often hide the fact that considerable self-shaping was involved in developing advanced skills, many young people do not see how important self-shaping is in producing quality behavior; hence they fail to use this powerful technique for improving their own skills.

[10]Platt (1961).
[11]Baker (1979).

Haphazard Shaping

People often shape behavior in a haphazard manner. They reinforce behavior without paying careful attention to which behavior they are reinforcing, without having specific goals, and without using orderly steps of successive approximation. Although haphazard shaping can produce considerable behavior change, the change is often sporadic, chaotic, fraught with failures, and suboptimally rewarding.

A *good* teacher-shaper uses *small* steps of successive approximation in order to make each step easy and minimally aversive (see Figure 8–9). The student is not forced to progress up the steps any faster than is comfortable. The use of small, slow steps reduces the risk that the student will experience failure and avoid further steps of shaping. Haphazard shaping is often not conducted in small, slow steps. Often an inappropriately large step is introduced or a person is rushed to the next step before mastering prior steps. Both rushing and taking big steps can be aversive and increase the risk of failure. For example, when someone with advanced skills at any activity tries to introduce a friend to the activity, the skilled person may be very eager to have the friend progress very rapidly to high levels of skill—in order that both of them can share the activity at the same advanced level. As a result, the skilled person may rush the friend up the steps too quickly or encourage the friend to make a big step before the friend has all the needed skills. The professional dirt track motorcyclist is overjoyed to discover that a close friend wants to learn dirt track skills. The pro may carefully show the friend the ropes, going slowly in small steps for the first five steps (Figure 8–10). The friend shows nice progress on these five easy steps. Encouraged by this flawless progress and excited by the possibility of having the friend enter the big race on the weekend, the pro talks the friend into entering the event—the big step number 6 in Figure 8–10. The novice may be frightened by the race, may experience several failures (by losing control at the unexpected high speeds) and suffer injury (perhaps a broken leg). This type of haphazard shaping may produce such punishing results that the student finds the activity aversive and avoids further shaping. The parents who expect very rapid progress in their child's musical skills—and volunteer the child for a public recital (a big step) before the child is ready—are committing the same errors. The husband who is eager to have his wife share rock climbing or scuba diving—and rushes her to reach his level of proficiency—often creates an aversive learning situation and finds that she no longer wants to learn new activities from him.[12]

During social interaction, people frequently shape each other's behavior quite unintentionally. When people interact with each other, there is usually variation in their performance: Sometimes they carry off their interactions smoothly; at other times they bungle. Because other people respond differently to good and bad performances (e.g., by showing either enthusiasm or boredom, friendliness or hostility), they provide differential reinforcement for interaction skills. As a person moves from Hometown to college and then to Big City, the patterns of differential reinforcement may be changed in a stepwise manner. This usually produces shaping effects, though not in a carefully designed way. In Hometown, a person may receive reinforcers for being innocent and enthusiastic; in

---

[12]Studies show that usually "the woman must make a greater adjustment in marriage than the man" and that this often involves aversive consequences for the wife, since people often do not use effective and positive means for changing each other's behavior (Ahammer, 1973).

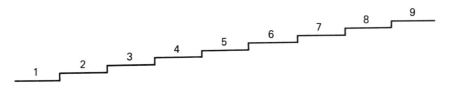

FIGURE 8–9   Small steps of successive approximation.

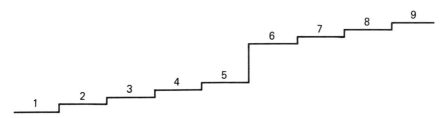

FIGURE 8–10   One big step can create problems.

college for being nonchalant; and in Big City for being worldy wise and a big spender. The other people usually do not have a conscious or planned strategy for shaping the changes in social presentation, but their social responses can have powerful and systematic effects.

When an individual's behavior is being shaped by social feedback from two or more people with dissimilar values and goals, the individual's behavior may be shaped in multiple, and sometimes conflicting, directions. Jenny's parents are shaping her behavior to create a daughter who is demure, tactful, and quiet. At work, however, Jenny's peers may be shaping her skills for asserting herself, speaking up for women's rights, and becoming politically active. Each step Jenny takes in learning to be more assertive and socially active earns her more respect and admiration from her peers. Yet each evening when she comes home from work, her behavior is shaped in another direction. Jenny may learn two repertoires of social behavior under S^D control of different social contexts. She may be assertive at work and demure at home. Having one's behavior shaped in two different directions can be very stressful and aversive for the person if the two repertoires of behavior contain incompatible responses.[13] Jenny may feel torn, confused, pulled in opposite directions.

Even if Jenny decides to move to an apartment of her own, she may not totally escape conflicting shaping effects. Because her friends have different personalities, interests, and goals in life, Jenny's behavior may continue to be shaped in multiple directions. If one of Jenny's roommates is excited about modern dance, Jenny may join her for lessons and practice, and move several steps up the ladder of learning to dance. But when the novelty wears off—and the effort involved in developing good skills becomes more apparent—Jenny may no longer experience enough reinforcement to progress further in

[13]Skinner (1974:149f) explains that the internal conflicts a person feels should be traced to the conflicting contingencies of reinforcement.

improving her dance skills. At this time, however, Jenny's other roommate invites her to go jogging in the evening after work. They start easy at first, then progress in small steps to longer runs. When someone at work invites Jenny to try the 10 kilometer race on Saturday, Jenny takes too big a shaping step and ends up pulling a tendon that prevents her from running. During the following weeks, Jenny's behavior may be shaped through several steps in an evening art class, a business finance class, and in other contexts. Looking back, we see that Jenny's behavior has been shaped a few steps one way, a few steps another way, and so forth in a variety of directions; but there has not been any single, stable goal. As a result, Jenny has made quite a few steps of behavior change, but not attained any single target. This process may be judged as either good or bad: Jenny has explored a variety of activities and may continue to do so until she finds one that suits her well; but after several years of dabbling briefly in a variety of activities, she may regret never having learned any one skill thoroughly.

Indiscriminant Use of Reinforcement and Punishment

There are other situations that result in haphazard shaping. People often give rein-forcers or punishers to others because they (the givers) are happy or sad, and not because the other people have exhibited good or bad behavior. For example, parents may punish a child because they, the parents, are unhappy or in a bad mood, even though the child was not doing anything unusual or bad.[14] Later, the parents may be in a good mood and not punish their child's bad behavior, even though they should. A husband may criticize his wife not because she was unkind, but because he got in a bad mood during the golf game he lost. All through life people often give reinforcers or punishers with little regard for the quality of the behavior that they are reinforcing or punishing. The parents might be inadvertently conditioning their child to discriminate that bad behavior is acceptable when the parents are in a good mood. If the parents pay attention to the child each time the child misbehaves, the parents may be shaping increasingly troublesome behavior by reinforcing misbehavior with their attention. The husband who gets in bad moods after losing at golf may be inadvertently shaping his wife's skills for avoiding him more effectively.

Much of the literature concerning the wise use of behavior principles in everyday life stresses the following:[15] *People should not give reinforcers and punishers in response to their own emotions. Instead reinforcers and punishers should be given for good and bad behavior—whether it be a person's own behavior or the behavior of others.* Parents should resist the tendency to criticize, snap at, or otherwise punish their child simply because they (the parents) are angry. Concern for the behavior of the child should dictate when they give reinforcers or punishers. Lovers should talk about the things they most hope to attain in their relationship and provide each other with generous positive feedback for progress toward those goals. For example, two people may set the goal of rationally and democratically discussing their problems rather than bickering and fighting. If they express a genuine appreciation for improvements in each other's use of rational and democratic problem solving skills, there is a much better chance that they will arrive at the

---

[14]McIntire (1970).

[15]McIntire (1970); Skinner (1971); Bannatyne and Bannatyne (1973); Mahoney (1974).

goal than if they randomly allocate reinforcers. As it is, haphazard shaping often leads to suboptimal results. A more careful use of positive and negative feedback oriented toward carefully chosen goals would help us shape quality behavior and sensitive discriminations better than can be expected on the random plan.

Shaping Without Other People Present

Shaping can occur without anyone playing the role of teacher or shaper. A person's successes and failures when dealing with the physical environment—with either natural or human made objects—often shape behavior in complex and subtle ways without social feedback.

The *natural environment* contains many objects, forces, and living things that can shape behavior without social intervention. Gravity, storms, ice, surf, mountains, thorns, poison ivy, stinging insects, large animals, and the rest of nature have properties that can lead to the differential reinforcement and sometimes shaping of behavior. When walking or driving on icy roads during the winter, people learn skills for caution. Although some children avoid walking and sliding on icy areas after several painful falls, others learn to balance and eventually slide gracefully. These skills are learned in a series of natural steps beginning with short slides (e.g., one foot long), and increasing to ever longer glides. At each step of shaping, differential reinforcement conditions a new level of skills that allow progression to the next step of taking longer slides. The physical environment does not need to be animate in order to shape behavior. Differential reinforcement is operating whenever our behavior for dealing with the physical environment leads to successes and failures; and induction provides the raw material for the next step of shaping more advanced skills. Natural shaping can be more consistent than social shaping. Although no one may be present to shape the child's skill at sliding on ice, each clumsy response is punished by falls and each step of increasing skill is reinforced by success and the sensory stimulation of longer, faster, and more exciting slides. When a person learns to hike and climb in the mountains, each improved skill brings more reinforcers in the form of more proficient climbing and more spectacular views. A careless hand or foot position while climbing on a rocky cliff is punished by slips, scrapes, or falls.

In one sense, much of science and technology has been shaped by successes and failures in dealing with nature. When people started building kites, gliders, and motorized aircraft, some designs were more successful than others. Success and failure provided the differential reinforcement for improving the aircraft; and through induction, even better forms were invented. Whenever a new design of airplane flew longer and carried more weight, there was differential reinforcement for moving to this new step of design. As new scientific principles were discovered that further improved designs, the steps of advancing scientific research were also reinforced. Naturally, other kinds of learning (such as observational learning, prompting, and rule-using) are involved in any complex technological development; but, in the final analysis, success and failure shape the course of technological change.

Note! There is no guiding force toward progress or perfection which guarantees that people's skills, science, or technology for coping with nature must improve. Interaction with the natural environment can lead to a long series of failures, setbacks, and futile explorations. Many a scientist or inventor has received reinforcers for spending years researching and developing some "crazy" innovation that "almost" seemed to work, but eventually failed. Other scientific or technological discoveries *do* work, and do produce immediate reinforcement for a time; but they may produce unforeseen problems that punish later use of the discovery. What looked like progress yesterday begins to look like a bad idea today. The discovery of DDT seemed like progress at first, since it gave us a means of controlling insects; however, as the dangerous side effects of DDT were discovered, the aversive consequences suppressed the use of the chemical. Although the positive value of nuclear energy has reinforced the stepwise shaping of a technology for harnessing nuclear energy for generating electrical power, the aversive nature of cost overrides, safety problems, and nuclear waste disposal have greatly slowed the growth of nuclear power as these drawbacks have become more salient in recent years. At present it is not clear if the long term problems will outweigh the benefits. Obviously, it is much easier to evaluate these issues in retrospect, after both the reinforcers and possible punishers have had their effects on people's behavior.

Not only does the natural environment shape behavior, the *human-made environment* shapes behavior, too. Before a child can effectively use a sharp knife or scissors, he or she must learn many steps of increasing skill. Each time the child learns a new level of skill, the advantages provided by the tool give increased reinforcement for progressing up the steps of successive approximation.

Even though we learn a good deal about human-made things and about nature from models, rules, and prompts, it must be stressed that differential reinforcement and shaping are a fundamental part of the learning process. The best student, after reading the most complete rules for operating a new machine, usually requires extensive "real life experience" (in which early rule-governed behavior can be shaped by success and failure) before all the needed skills are mastered. When people learn to drive a car, they may be given rules and demonstrations to start them driving safely; but the ensuing months or years of practice involve the shaping of improved skills. As the beginning driver struggles to parallel park, errors are punished by scraping against the curb or bumping other cars until, gradually, these responses are suppressed. Each step in the shaping of new skills is negatively reinforced by avoiding errors and positively reinforced by successes. Similar shaping occurs during the process of learning to drive a bicycle, motorcycle, or airplane; to operate a typewriter, calculator, or sewing machine; to play musical instruments, games, or sports; or to master many other skills. Even with an excellent set of rules, models, and prompts, it usually takes practice to become truly efficient at using most objects, and it is the period of practice in which shaping occurs.

CONCLUSION

Differential reinforcement modifies the frequencies of responses that already exist in a person's behavior repertoire. Differential reinforcement can come from the social or nonsocial environment, as an individual has success or failure in dealing with others or with the nonsocial environment. Differential reinforcement often leads to the production of new responses, via the process of induction; and these new responses are the raw material for further behavior change. Once new responses are produced through induction, they may be put under new contingencies of differential reinforcement. Changing patterns of differential reinforcement produce changing patterns of behavior as behavior is shaped into forms that may be quite different from the original pattern. When shaping is done in a series of well-designed steps of successive approximation toward a clearly defined final performance, it can produce efficient behavior change. Unfortunately, in everyday life, steps of behavior change are often not well designed and shaping is not conducted in an efficient manner. As a consequence people's behavior often changes in haphazard ways that involve unnecessary amounts of aversive experience. A knowledge of the principles of differential reinforcement and shaping can help people minimize the problems resulting from haphazard conditioning.

The next three chapters present three types of social learning that are often superimposed on differential reinforcement and shaping. These three types of social experience usually speed the learning process if they assist the person in performing behavior that is compatible with the basic patterns of reinforcement operating in the individual's environment.

9

Modeling and Observational Learning

● *In this chapter you will discover how people learn by observing the behavior of others—why sometimes they imitate others, while at other times they do just the opposite of what they see others do.*

When one person observes the actions of another, the experience may change the observer's future behavior. While leaving a crowded theater, someone may try an unused exit door that had been closed. If the door opens, the person's explorative behavior is reinforced by a rapid exit and escape from slow lines. When people nearby see the first person leave, several follow and eventually this new exit is as crowded as the rest. *People are influenced by observing the behavior of others. The person who first displays a behavior is called a model. Observers who see, hear, or read about a model's behavior (1) gain information about the behavior and (2) may use this information to guide their own behavior.*

Because we are frequently in situations where we can observe other people's behavior, there are many ways for us to be affected by social models. The effects of the social modeling process are often subtle. For instance, during a conversation one person may use a generous number of intellectually sophisticated words. If the second person likes the individual who is talking, the second person may show a slight increase in the use of larger, more erudite words. The effects need not be subtle, however. For example, models can produce powerful effects during mass gatherings when the actions of a few salient individuals influence many people to do the same thing at once. When suddenly several people begin to shout and rush at the police, nearby observers who previously had no intention of participating in violence may find themselves irresistibly attracted to joining those who are modeling aggressive action.[1] Panics, fads, and mob behavior all reflect modeling effects, as observers imitate the behavior of those around them.

Social modeling can influence behavior in many ways. Models can be real (bodily present) or symbolic (presented via books, movies, TV, or verbal descriptions). The observer can be a passive onlooker or an active participant in the model's activity. The observer may show behavior changes immediately after seeing the model's behavior, after a delay, or never. Observers tend to imitate modeled behavior if they like or respect the model, see the model receive reinforcement, see the model give off signs of pleasure, or are in an environment where imitating the model's performance is reinforced. There are times when an observer does the opposite from the model. This inverse imitation is common when an observer does not like the model, sees the model get punished, or is in an environment where conformity is being punished. This chapter will describe the types of modeling effects which are most common in everyday life.

THREE TYPES OF MODELING EFFECTS

There are three main types of modeling effects: (1) observational learning, (2) inhibitory and disinhibitory effects, and (3) response facilitation effects.[2]

1. *Observational learning involves the learning of new behavior*. When an observer sees a model do a behavior that the observer has never done, the observer may learn how to do the behavior merely by watching. A child watches Mother planting the spring garden, then picks up a tool and makes the same motions Mother did. A new member in a teenage street gang sees a few of the older members chugalugging whole cans of beer at once; so the observer picks up a can, snaps it open in the same nonchalant manner that was just modeled, and pours it down in one long gulp. The business school graduate applying for an executive job in a bank watches how the executives dress, walk, talk, and smile. Soon the graduate is acting in a way that closely resembles the models' mannerisms. This does not mean that the child becomes proficient at planting a garden after the first exposure to a model; and the new gang member may half choke while pouring down a can of beer. Nor does the green business school graduate become a polished executive overnight. Much additional modeling, shaping, prompting, or rule use may be involved in polishing the observer's behavior. Nevertheless, people learn a great deal about new activities by observing others.

When the new behavior is only one or two steps ahead of the observer's present level of competence, the observer may satisfactorily replicate the new behavior after the first exposure to the model's behavior. When the athletic young mountain climber sees how the pro prepares the ropes and rappels down a sheer cliff, one observation may suffice to impart the needed skills. The visitor to a foreign culture may only need one

---

[1]Bandura (1973).
[2]Experimental evidence related to the three modeling effects is presented by Bandura and Walters (1963) and Bandura (1969, 1977).

exposure to a new hand gesture to learn the practice. It is only when a model's behavior is several steps ahead of the observer's present skills that the observer is less likely to imitate the behavior successfully without practice.[3]

New behavior can usually be learned much more rapidly and efficiently by observational learning than by shaping alone.[4] Life would be quite short if we had to learn how to deal with the hazards of exposed electrical wiring, guns, poisonous snakes, automobile driving, or machine operation via differential reinforcement alone. The presence of appropriate social models speeds learning and minimizes the dangers of potentially lethal accidents. In addition it is unlikely that complex cultural behavior—such as verbal behavior, cultural practices, or technology—could be learned by shaping alone; yet, these activities are often acquired quickly by observing real or symbolic models. In preliterate societies, observational learning of cultural practices is obtained from real models and from symbolic models presented by word of mouth. Since the advent of writing, books, and electronic media, cultural practices are portrayed in many more numerous and diverse symbolic formats, which only facilitates the dissemination of cultural information through the imitation of symbolic models.

The word *imitation* has negative connotations to some people, because it may suggest that the observer is an unoriginal copycat. However, in everyday life, observational learning does not usually lead to exact imitations of modeled behavior. When an observer replicates a model's performance, the observer usually introduces novel features into the replication, reflecting unique aspects of the observer's behavior repertoire or personality. In addition, observers typically see *multiple models* of any given behavior; and they tend to piece together fragments of each model's performance into a new production that differs from anything they have seen.[5] Exposure to numerous real and symbolic models is in fact a major source of creativity. Art students who study the styles of many famous painters are more likely to arrive at a creative style than art students who never study the works of others, or only study one artist.

2. *Inhibitory and disinhibitory effects occur when observing a model changes the probabilities of already learned operants.* No new behavior is learned. Instead, the probability of an already existing behavior is merely decreased or increased. If a model is punished for a given behavior, not only will the model be less likely to repeat the behavior in the future, the observer will also be less likely to do the behavior. This is the *inhibitory effect*. If a model receives reinforcers for a certain performance, not only will the model be more likely to repeat the behavior in the future, the observer will be more likely to do the behavior, too. This is the *disinhibitory effect*. When the high school graduate arrives at college and sees that all the people she likes wear jeans, it is more likely that she will dress that way, too. If she also sees her new college friends belittle a student who pursues activities she enjoyed in high school, the frequency of these operants will be lowered even though no one had ever criticized her for doing the behavior. She might even laugh at the childishness of the behavior she was doing only two months ago. Numerous conformity effects are mediated by this type of observational learning: Many people are influenced to

---

[3]Practice may involve either overt replications of the behavior or cognitive rehearsal (Mahoney, 1974; Bandura, 1977). Learning is much faster when a person does *both* overt and covert practice (Kazdin, 1982).

[4]Bandura (1969:143f).

[5]Bandura et al. (1963); Bandura (1977:48f).

do what they see modeled for them by people who are liked or who are receiving reinforcers.

   3. *Response facilitation effects occur when the behavior of the model serves as an S^D for a similar response by the observer.* The behavior of one person facilitates the second person's doing the same thing. Facilitative effects do not involve new learning (modeling effect 1) nor do they produce lasting effects that increase or decrease the frequency of future performances of old behavior (modeling effect 2). Facilitation effects are relatively fleeting, occurring shortly after the model's behavior serves as an S^D for a similar response from the observer. For example, the person who has already learned to smoke one and only one pack of cigarettes a day has learned a stable frequency of responding—twenty smokes a day. When this smoker sees a second person pull out a cigarette and light up, the second person's behavior is part of the S^D collage that controls the first person's own smoking behavior; and the first person is likely to light up, too. There is no new learning and no overall change in the number of cigarettes smoked per day. Social facilitation occurs only because a model's behavior has provided S^D's that help set the occasion for the observer's response.

   If you are walking down the street and see several people watching something that is happening in a department store window, the models provide S^D's that increase the likelihood that you too will feel the inclination to stop and have a look. If you are exposed to other S^D's—perhaps a stimulating conversation with a friend—that produce competing responses, the S^D's from the people at the store window may not produce much effect on your behavior. But if there are few S^D's for competing responses and the people seem to be particularly interested in the events in the store window, the social facilitation effect will be noticeable and you may stop to look, too. Social facilitation can be quite strong when an observer sees a crowd of people gathering and staring at some person or object. Perhaps someone is injured. Maybe there was an accident. What's that guy doing on the ground? Seeing the crowd gathering and looking can provide strong S^D control for stopping and looking. Other common examples of social facilitation are seen when observers do altruistic acts, volunteer their services, donate money to a cause, or pick up certain conversational topics after someone else takes the lead.

OBSERVATIONAL LEARNING

In the remainder of the chapter, we will focus primarily on observational learning, the first of the three types of modeling effects discussed above. However, many of the variables that influence observational learning also affect inhibitory or disinhibitory effects and social facilitation.

PAVLOVIAN CONDITIONING

   When a person observes a model, various aspects of the model and the model's behavior may serve as CS's for the observer. First, the ability of social cues to serve as CS's is traced to Pavlovian conditioning. Among the most important responses elicited by

CS's from models are conditioned emotional responses, which are called *vicarious emotional responses*. Second, when new stimuli are paired with the CS's from a model, the new stimuli become CS's, too, through a process known as *vicarious Pavlovian conditioning*. Third, all of the CS's derived from a model can function as conditioned reinforcers and punishers, called *vicarious reinforcers and punishers*.

1. Vicarious Emotional Responses. *Models give off many social cues that may function as CS's for the observer; and these CS's elicit conditioned reflexes—including conditioned emotional responses—in the observer.*[6] When an observer sees someone else smiling, the smiles are likely to serve as CS's that elicit pleasurable emotional responses—perhaps even a smile—in the observer. When an observer sees someone sobbing, the crying may serve as a CS that elicits sadness—perhaps even tears—in the observer. These conditioned emotional responses are called *vicarious emotional responses,* and they are learned through Pavlovian conditioning in situations where the model's behavior is paired with US's or CS's that elicit emotional responses in the observer.

Starting in infancy, a large number of social cues—such as twinkling eyes, laughter, frowns, tears, and words—become CS's; the conditioning continues all through life, maintaining some emotional responses and changing others. For example, the smiles of friendly people usually become CS's for pleasant emotions in the observer. From the early months of life, smiles from the parents are predictive stimuli that frequently precede events that are pleasurable for the infant. The mother smiles when she picks up and plays with the child. The father smiles as he feeds and bathes the child. Since the smiles of friendly people usually precede pleasurable experiences, they become CS's that elicit pleasurable emotions in the infant. Eventually, just seeing the mother or father smile elicits pleasure in the infant—including a smile in return—even if the parents do not play with, feed, or do anything else with the child. The child is learning to respond with pleasure to signs of other people's pleasure.

The Pavlovian conditioning of smiles continues all through life. When a friend greets us with a big smile, the smile is a predictive stimulus that is usually associated with pleasurable interaction, further conditioning smiles as CS's for pleasurable emotions. People often smile when telling jokes or engaging us in friendly banter; and this adds to the conditioning of smiles as CS's for pleasurable emotions. Just seeing a friend smile before starting to tell a joke elicits pleasant feelings that help us enjoy the joke long before we hear the punch line. These feelings are vicarious emotional responses that allow us to enjoy our friend's pleasure even before we learn why the joke is funny.

The conditioning of smiles and other social cues is influenced by numerous cues in the stimulus collage, often allowing us to learn subtle discriminations. Although the smiles of friends usually elicit pleasurable feelings, the smiles of people who deceive or take advantage of us come to elicit quite different feelings through the following type of Pavlovian conditioning. When devious people smile at us just before taking advantage of us, their smiles become associated with aversive situations, and we learn to discriminate between different uses of smiles. Thereafter, smiles used in suspicious manners will elicit

---

[6]Bandura (1969:167f).

uncomfortable feelings—feelings of uneasiness—even though we may not be able to verbalize precisely why we feel uncomfortable about the person who is smiling at us.

After years of experience, most people respond to numerous social cues—such as facial expressions, words, tones of voice, and body postures—of other people as CS's that elicit vicarious emotions. Words become especially important CS's for vicarious emotional responses, since words can vividly describe situations that are associated with emotional experiences. When one person describes how exciting it was to visit a recording studio while a major group was recording their latest album, the verbal descriptions— along with tone of voice and excited gestures—can elicit strong vicarious emotional responses in the listeners.

Empathy for the feelings of others is based largely on vicarious emotional responses. When we see a child wide-eyed with excitement while opening birthday presents, the child's bright eyes, smiles, and laughter are likely to be CS's that elicit pleasant feelings in us. We cannot share exactly the same emotional responses that the child is having, but the vicarious response is pleasurable and somewhat similar. Seeing a friend crying at her mother's funeral may make us feel sad, even though we never met her mother. Naturally, the observer does not feel the *same* emotional responses that the model feels. However, there is often a similarity in emotional responses if the observer has had enough emotional conditioning in situations similar to the one the model is experiencing. For example, a young child who is present at the funeral of your friend's mother may feel sad, in response to social cues such as tears, hushed voices, and somber colors. However, the child's ability to empathize with your friend and her family is quite limited compared with that of adults who have lost someone very close.

The more similar the past social learning experiences of a model and observer, the more likely it is that the observer can empathize with the model (and vice versa). If several women are talking and one tells how she was attacked and raped several months ago, her words, gestures, and trembling tone of voice serve as CS's that elicit vicarious emotional responses in the listeners. The other people in the room will be able to empathize with her feelings to varying degrees, depending on their prior experience with rape. A listener who has been raped herself is more likely to feel strong vicarious emotional responses than is a second listener who has never been raped and never been sensitized to the fear and anguish associated with rape. People who have had similar past experience—hence similar emotional conditioning—are most likely to feel vicarious emotional responses that allow them to empathize sensitively with each other's feelings. Strong empathetic responses are most likely when the similarities of the model and listeners are salient, the model vividly and emotionally describes the shared similar experiences, and the listeners try to imagine themselves in the role of the model.[7]

When observers have strong vicarious emotional responses, they sometimes *feel* as if they can empathize with a model, even though their vicarious feelings may be quite different from the model's feelings. For example, men and women who have been raised with the double standard of sexuality sometimes make mistakes in responding to the feelings of the other sex. When men and women meet in a bar and exchange smiles and pleasant words, these social cues often elicit vicarious emotions of pleasure and sexual

[7]Bandura (1969:167f).

feelings in the men; and the men *feel* as if the women are more sexually interested than most women really are.[8] Women are often surprised that men feel that a smile in a bar means more than friendly attraction. The different socializations of males and females can lead to vicarious feelings that provide misleading cues about the other person's feelings. Such cases of misunderstood feelings can occur whenever two people have had past emotional conditioning that is quite different.

2. Vicarious Pavlovian Conditioning.   *When models provide CS's that elicit vicarious emotional responses in an observer, neutral stimuli that are paired with these CS's can also become CS's due to higher order Pavlovian conditioning. This is the observational learning of new conditioned responses via vicarious Pavlovian conditioning.*[9] For instance, if your best friend is becoming skillful at playing the banjo *and* is visibly enthusiastic about her newest music, there is a strong likelihood that you will find yourself beginning to respond to her music as a CS for pleasurable feelings. Her signs of enthusiasm (which are positive CS's) will elicit positive emotional responses in you while you hear the banjo music. The stronger the signs of enthusiasm, the sooner the banjo music will become a positive CS for you due to vicarious Pavlovian conditioning. Naturally, the background variables must also be correct: If your friend did not have enough skill to create listenable music or if she only played one song—"Turkey in the Straw"—over and over again, these aversive stimuli could outweigh the positive effects of her enthusiasm. However, if the background variables are neutral or positive, your friend's unbridled enthusiasm will produce vicarious Pavlovian conditioning of banjo music. The next time you hear a banjo on the radio, you may smile and feel good. Because banjo music is now a positive CS, it functions as a conditioned reinforcer that will increase the likelihood that you will listen more attentively to the banjo music than you would have before hearing your friend play. Having friends, teachers, or other models who truly enjoy the things they are doing—and show it—brings an abundance of vicarious pleasures into our lives and causes the vicarious conditioning of many new positive CS's. Enthusiasm is contagious: Due to your friend's enthusiasm about the banjo, you have come to enjoy the banjo, too. People who surround themselves with enthusiastic models learn—through vicarious Pavlovian conditioning—to enjoy many of the things their friends enjoy, whether it be art, jogging, political activism, motorcycling, or anything else.

Seeing sad or unhappy models can cause neutral stimuli to become CS's for sad feelings due to vicarious Pavlovian conditioning. Seeing movies that show the human suffering in some of the underdeveloped countries can provide many CS's that elicit aversive emotional responses, perhaps sadness or anger. The stimuli that are paired with these pictures of sad, hungry people also become CS's through vicarious Pavlovian conditioning. Thus, words such as "overpopulation," "unequal food distribution," and "political exploitation" may become CS's for unpleasant emotions if they are paired with these aversive pictures. After seeing several documentaries or reading several articles on the underdeveloped countries, this conditioning may cause you to feel strong emotional responses when you hear someone mention overpopulation or political exploitation.

[8]Abbey (1982).
[9]See Berger (1962), Craig and Weinstein (1965), Bandura and Rosenthal (1966), and Bandura et al. (1969) for data on vicarious Pavlovian conditioning.

3. Vicarious Reinforcement and Punishment.   *The CS's produced by a model can function as conditioned reinforcers and punishers for the observer.* These conditioned stimuli are called *vicarious reinforcers* and *vicarious punishers,* and they can come either directly from the model's social cues (such as smiles) or indirectly from stimuli (such as banjo music) that have been paired with the model's social cues. Vicarious reinforcement and punishment play an important role in the observational learning of operant behavior, as we will see in the next section.

Vicarious reinforcement occurs when a behavior is followed by CS's that are conditioned reinforcers due to vicarious Pavlovian conditioning. Because your friend truly enjoys playing the banjo, you may pick up the instrument and give it a try. If your friend smiles approvingly as you explore the strings, her smile provides vicarious reinforcement for your attempting to play. Even if your friend is not in the room, you will obtain vicarious reinforcement for plucking the strings, since the banjo sounds themselves are now reinforcing, due to earlier vicarious Pavlovian conditioning when you heard your friend play. Vicarious punishment occurs when a behavior is followed by CS's that are conditioned punishers due to vicarious Pavlovian conditioning. Seeing other people's pain, suffering, and sadness both elicits vicarious emotions in the observer and serves as vicarious punishment for relevant operants. For example, if several people are playing a rough game, and one person is badly injured, the signs of pain are likely to serve as CS's that are vicarious punishers for others. Suddenly the game seems less fun; and someone suggests that you stop playing and do something else. Vicarious punishment stopped the game. Some people cannot bring themselves to criticize sensitive people because in the past their criticisms of sensitive people have been followed by signs of sadness from the sensitive people; and this sadness is the CS that provides vicarious punishment for giving further criticism.

OPERANT BEHAVIOR[10]

When operants are being learned or modified by observational learning, the learning has two phases: acquisition and performance.[11] *Acquisition involves perceiving and remembering information about a model's behavior. Performance involves turning that information into actual behavior.* For example, a child may watch father take pennies out of the piggy bank and instantly acquire the knowledge about how the trick is done; but it may be days or weeks before the child performs an imitative response. Because acquisition and performance are affected by different variables and because performance can occur seconds, weeks, or even years after acquisition, these two aspects of observational learning are quite distinct and must be analyzed separately.

[10]Although operant behavior can be acquired and modified by observational learning, there has been considerable debate between those who claim that observational learning does not fit the Skinnerian model of stimulus-response-consequences and those who claim that it does (compare Bandura, 1969:127, and Rosenthal and Zimmerman, 1978, with Skinner, 1953, and Gewirtz, 1971a,b).

[11]The distinction between acquisition and performance is central to modern theories of observational learning (Bandura and Walters, 1963:52–60).

Acquisition

Acquisition is a prerequisite for performance; but many responses are acquired that are never performed. TV provides dozens of models of violence, killing, and crime each day. Most of us have acquired the information for doing these operants; but few of us will ever perform acts of violence learned from TV models.

Several factors increase the likelihood that an observer will acquire information about the behavior of a model:[12]

1. The model's behavior has utilitarian value—i.e., it produces reinforcing consequences.
2. There are similarities between the model and the observer.
3. The model and observer are engaged in similar activities.
4. There are reinforcers for watching the model.
5. The model's behavior is salient and easily visible.
6. The model's behavior is not far beyond the observer's present level of skill.

1. The Model's Behavior Is Reinforced. *If the observer sees that the model's behavior has utilitarian value (that is, produces reinforcing consequences), the observer is likely to acquire information about the behavior.* The rewards associated with the model's behavior may not be consciously evaluated by the observer, but observers do respond to several kinds of cues that enhance the acquisition of rewarding behavior.

1a. Seeing Consequences of a Model's Behavior. *Seeing a model receive reinforcers or escape punishers is obvious evidence of the utilitarian value of a behavior.* When TV ads show how popular, attractive, or sexy people become when they use Product X, the advertising psychologists are capitalizing on the fact that the positive consequences will facilitate the acquisition of the advertised message by the TV observers. When a high school student sees another student escape "detention" by making excuses, the negative reinforcement increases the likelihood that the behavior will be remembered by the observer, even though acquisition alone does not determine whether the observer will ever perform the behavior.

When a model and observer respond to different reinforcers, a model may be doing something that produces reinforcing consequences for the model, and yet not be noticed by observers who do not respond to the consequences as reinforcers. A stamp collector may receive frequent reinforcers for systematically checking through the office's incoming mail for interesting foreign stamps; yet observers who do not respond to foreign stamps as reinforcers are unlikely to notice that the collector's behavior is producing rewarding results. Hence, they are not likely to pay attention to, acquire information about, or remember details of the behavior. Thus, a modeled behavior is likely to be acquired only if it has utility "in the eyes of the beholder," that is, functions as a reinforcer for the observer.

---

[12]This is only a partial list of the factors known to affect the acquisition of information about modeled behavior (Bandura and Walters, 1963:59,81ff; Bandura, 1969:128–143).

1b. Seeing a Model's Emotional Responses. *Even though an observer may not notice any detectable reinforcers associated with a model's behavior, the pleasurable emotional cues that the model gives off can be powerful CS's which indicate that the behavior is reinforcing by eliciting pleasurable feelings in the observer.* These CS's associated with pleasure function as vicarious reinforcers that help the observer acquire information about the behavior. If a model is smiling, chuckling, or showing other signs of happiness while reading a magazine, a passerby may note the name of the magazine as something worth looking into, even though it is not clear what reinforcers had caused the model so much apparent pleasure. Whenever an observer sees someone showing signs of pleasure, the observer tends to remember the model's activities. If an observer sees a group of people clearly enjoying a game of croquet, the observer may feel positive vicarious emotional responses and stand to watch for a while. While watching, the observer acquires information about the nature of the game, its rules, good strategies, and so forth. If the people had been playing the game of croquet without showing signs of enjoying themselves, the observer would have been less likely to stop and watch because there were no signs of pleasure to indicate that playing the game was reinforcing.

Some people smile a lot, even if they are engaged in a boring task, whereas others rarely smile, even if they are engaged in a favorite activity. The people who show signs of pleasure are more likely to attract attention and cause the acquisition of modeled information than their unsmiling counterparts. Unemotional expressions can mislead the observer. Sarah has been thinking about becoming a doctor or a lawyer. She meets a doctor who seems to be constantly cheerful and happy, and a lawyer who has a deadpan facial expression. The positive social cues given off by the doctor will attract Sarah's attention and increase the likelihood that she will acquire information about the doctor's job. The fact that the lawyer does not give off positive cues makes it likely that Sarah will acquire less information from the lawyer. Sarah may be misled by the social cues, however. The doctor might have smiled just as much if she had been a lawyer or an accountant; and her enthusiasm would have caused Sarah to learn about law or accounting rather than medicine. In addition, the deadpan lawyer might love the law as much as the smiling doctor loves medicine; but the absence of visible social cues makes it difficult for others to appreciate this. Tom Sawyer's apparent enjoyment while whitewashing the fence worked quite nicely in attracting other people to watch his work (and eventually take over). The person who enjoys an activity, but frowns, grumbles, and gripes all the time, provides an unattractive model; and observers will show little interest in the activity even though they might have enjoyed learning about it.

1c. Characteristics of a Model. *If an observer respects, admires, or likes a model—because the model is a fine person, has status, or whatever—the observer will often attend to and acquire information from the model's behavior.* Acquisition can occur even though the observer may not see a model receive reinforcers (1a) or show signs of pleasure (1b). Because the model is liked, respected, or of high status, almost everything the model does takes on positive qualities due to association with the model. Merely seeing the model's behavior provides the observer with vicarious reinforcement for paying attention to and acquiring information about the model's actions. Little children usually acquire a great deal of information by observing their parents' behavior, since the parents are associated with many positive and loving experiences.[13] If the mother is a realtor, the children are likely to imitate realtor behavior during play because mother is loved. Father may not enjoy driving a truck for his livelihood, but the children may attend to and acquire all sorts of information related to trucks because they love him. Simply thinking about mother and father—and their behavior—provides vicarious pleasure; hence there is vicarious reinforcement for attending to and acquiring information from them. (For the same reason, there is vicarious reinforcement for performing the behavior modeled by the parents.)

All through life, we tend to acquire information about behavior from models we respect or admire. The 5-year-old child may want to be a fire fighter or law officer because the uniforms and heroic work of these people elicit respect and admiration in children. The ten year old's models may include movie stars, athletes, detectives, doctors, teachers, and so forth. The fifteen year old may be influenced by peers, rock stars, fashion models, or race track drivers. The models who have "status" in our eyes keep changing as we grow up, change social settings, and play different roles.

Behavior performed by models who are loved and respected is often well worth learning. Such people seem to be doing something right, since we feel so good about them. Somehow their behavior is compatible with good things in life, with reinforcement. The observer may attend to and learn about any of a number of the model's overt activities without knowing which of these is really associated with the model's success or happiness. Perhaps a respected model owes his or her happiness to self-discipline, but on the surface appears to be undisciplined and carefree. The observer may learn the hang-loose style of the model and never pick up on the actual behavior that makes the model happy and successful.

2. Similarity of the Observer and the Model.   *If an observer sees two models doing two different things, the observer usually learns more from the model who is more similar to the observer (assuming that all other variables are equal).* At a doctors' convention, surgeons tend to pay attention to and learn from other surgeons, rather than from psychiatrists, gynecologists, or pediatricians.

When people come together for interaction, it often does not take long until they split up in groups having similar interests, similar ages, similar jobs, and the same sex. Having things in common makes it easier to locate mutually interesting and hence mutually reinforcing topics about which to exchange information. At a cocktail party, the golfers may end up in one group, the new mothers in another group, the football fans elsewhere. Even as people switch groups, they tend to stay longer with people with whom they share things. Thus, similarity increases the likelihood that people will acquire modeled information through observational learning.

3. Similarity of Behavior.   *When two people are engaged in similar tasks, they tend to be more observant of the other person's behavior than when they are doing different tasks.* "Follow the leader" comes close to being a pure example of modeling effects due

---

[13]Bandura et al. (1963).

to "similar behavior." The eighth person to climb into the lifeboat is likely to use the same method of climbing in that the seventh person used. If person number seven holds onto the rigging to climb in, the eighth person is likely to do the same without considering the utility of the behavior or the similarities of personalities: It may not be the best way to enter the boat (point 1), and the two people may have little in common (point 2). People standing in line often attend to and copy each other's behavior as if they were playing follow the leader. Crowds, mobs, and mass happenings often demonstrate that people observe and copy each other simply because they are engaged in similar activities.

An interesting variation on "follow the leader" is "the blind leading the blind." No one may know whether or not to clap at a pause in a unique musical presentation, and everyone is influenced by the behavior of others. If enough people begin clapping, the entire audience may break into applause at an inappropriate point. Riots, fads, and rumors sometimes result from the blind leading the blind.

All of the above factors that influence acquisition can operate at the same time. For example, when a novice is learning from an experienced friend how to paddle a canoe, all the factors may be present. The novice can see the utilitarian value of the model's skillful use of the paddle. The utilitarian value is usually even more salient once the novice tries paddling and finds that canoeing skills are not easily acquired: Now the observer looks twice to see how the model holds and uses the paddle. The friendship factor adds to the modeling effect. If the novice likes and respects the model there will be more reinforcement for acquiring information about the model's behavior. The effect of doing similar behavior is also present. After the two canoeists have pushed off from shore, the novice picks up the rhythm and style of the model's paddling motions. As the experienced canoeist changes pace to suit different currents, the novice watches and imitates in a "follow the leader" style.

4. Reinforcement for Vigilance and Attention.   An observer's degree of attentiveness to a model can lie anywhere on a continuum from not paying any attention to focusing very close attention to the model's activities. Clearly, there can be no acquisition when there is no attention. *Increasing vigilance increases the likelihood that the observer will acquire information about the model's behavior.* Attention and vigilance are responses that can be modified by (a) differential reinforcement, (b) observational learning, (c) prompts, and (d) rules.

4a. Differential Reinforcement.   Attentiveness can be increased if the observer receives reinforcers for showing signs of paying attention, that is, looking, describing what the model is doing, or imitating the modeled behavior. Teachers and shapers can consciously set about to reinforce good attention skills. However, the natural patterns of reinforcement are often effective in training people to observe models, at least in areas where it counts. Without teachers, people learn to be attentive to the behavior of others in times of danger or emergency, in uneasy social situations, when new behavior is demanded, and so forth.

4b. Observational Learning.   People also learn when to be vigilant or lax by observing others. Seeing other people pay close attention to a snake, or fire, or a department store window increases the likelihood that the observer will attend and acquire information. On the other hand, when an observer sees that everyone in a group is relaxed and inattentive to details, the observer will also be inclined to relax and monitor other people less closely.

4c. Prompts.   Vigilance and attention can be prompted by turning a person's head or body toward the model who is to be attended. Little children are often bodily picked up and aimed at the model which the adults would like the children to observe. Pointing a finger toward a model is another prompt that can focus a person's attention on a model and increase the likelihood that information is acquired.

4d. Rules.   Rules or verbal commands provide an easy means of modifying attention. Explicit rules, such as "Watch how he does it if you want to learn how to do it right," clearly point to modeled behavior and indicate the utilitarian value of observing. Less explicit rules can also direct attention to models: "Wow, those people are fantastic." "That's worth seeing."

5.   Visibility of the Modeled Behavior.   *The more visible a model's behavior is for an observer, the more the observer can learn from watching.* Acquisition of information from a model is usually facilitated by being close enough to see and hear the model, having good eyes and ears, being on the correct side of the model to see the most important movements, and so forth. Also, some behavior is inherently more visible than others: External responses such as body movements or facial expressions are more visible than internal responses such as using the glottis to roll "r's" in a foreign language. Anyone who has tried to learn complex internal responses—such as yodeling, whistling, ventriloquy, or voice impersonations—knows that the invisibility of the muscle patterns creates major problems for replicating a model's behavior. Thus, modeled behavior can be anywhere on a continuum from total invisibility to total visibility, and the acquisition of information usually improves as visibility improves.

6. The Easiness of the Modeled Behavior.   The easiness of modeled behavior can best be understood by locating the behavior of both the model and the observer on the appropriate steps of increasing skill. *If the modeled behavior is too many steps ahead of the observer's skills, the observer may not be able to acquire much useful information from the model.* For example, the attempt of an experienced guitarist to show a friend how to play advanced classical music (at step 10 in Figure 9–1) may be useless if the friend is at step 1, still learning the first three chords. The observer sees a flurry of rapid finger movements, but the information is too complex to be of much use. The model would help the observer more by coming down to the lower steps and showing the observer the best methods for playing the basic chords. As the novice advances to higher steps of improved skills, the model can demonstrate progressively more complex motor patterns and expect the observer to learn from them.

In everyday life, the fifth and sixth factors—visibility and easiness of modeled behavior—often hinder the acquisition of complex, advanced skills through observational learning. Models frequently do not know that observers are interested in learning from

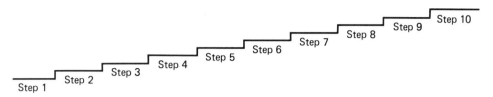

FIGURE 9-1   Modeled behavior may be many steps ahead of an observer's skills.

them, thus they do not make their behavior more visible and easy to imitate. Models may not know how to do an effective job of demonstrating behavior of the appropriate step of complexity even if they are aware of their role.

There are two kinds of models: mastery models and coping models.[14] *Mastery models demonstrate only the final step of mastering a skill (step 10); hence they deprive the observer of the information needed to traverse the intervening steps (1 through 9). Coping models provide information about how to cope with the intervening steps of skill acquisition by letting the observer see something of the coping skills needed to move from one step to the next.* Coping models can model behavior that is suitably simplified for observers with fewer skills. If they are performing advanced skills, they may emphasize or describe the basic aspects of their performance, about which the beginner needs knowledge. They may talk about the "old days" when they were at earlier steps and describe their past behavior. Thus, the coping model provides both real and symbolic modeling that helps the beginner cope with the early stages of skill acquisition.

The mastery model has behavior that is not simple and skills that are not completely visible. Both complexity and poor visibility are impediments to observational learning and create problems when observers see mastery models they would like to emulate. When people see or read about a person they greatly admire—perhaps an athlete, politician, or scientist—they usually see very advanced behavior (step 10) that is the product of years of learning. Many elements of the model's behavior—especially all the years of practice— are likely to be invisible. However excited and eager the observer may be to acquire the modeled behavior, he or she may not even know where to begin.

For instance, after hearing a world-famous novelist discuss the exhilaration of creative writing, a student may become very enthusiastic about writing. The novelist's wrinkled face, sparkling eyes, gentle humor, mysterious tone of voice, and skillful use of words are all CS's that elicit positive responses in the observer and provide vicarious reinforcement for listening to the novelist's advice. However, the novelist's behavior gives no clue about the years of practice, study, rejections from publishers, and rewrites that went before. Thus, the observer does not have access to information about all the steps involved in becoming a master of writing. The enthusiastic observer may resolve to try writing, too, and get a chapter or two onto paper before realizing that the story is simplistic and uninteresting. Because the young writer saw step 10 behavior from the mastery model—rather than steps 1 and 2—the student novelist may not realize that the model went through similar struggles in the beginning.

[14]Meichenbaum (1971); Bandura and Barab (1973).

Most people have had numerous experiences in which seeing a mastery model created great enthusiasm for becoming a doctor, athlete, lawyer, musician, or artist; but the absence of modeled information about the skills needed to progress from step 1 to step 10 left the enthusiastic beginner stranded. Mastery models do not provide all the information that beginners need. Nevertheless, seeing mastery models is beneficial for beginners. A master's spectacular performance provides CS's that elicit positive emotional responses in the observer and add to the Pavlovian conditioning that makes the modeled behavior serve as a conditioned reinforcer for the observer. In addition, mastery models help observers learn to set high standards of performance for themselves.[15] However, if beginners are actually to acquire advanced levels of skill, it is important for them to have access to coping models who provide useful information about the skills that beginners need to learn first.

Performance

After information has been acquired by observation, several factors determine when and how that information will affect operant performance. *The key determinants of performance are the past and present patterns of reinforcement and punishment associated with imitating certain models and behaviors in specific contexts.* Observers are most likely to perform imitative behavior when models have been and still are rewarded for that behavior in situations that are similar to the observer's present situation.

1. Past Reinforcement.   *Past reinforcement for imitating a certain model or a certain type of behavior increases the probability of performing the modeled behavior in S^D contexts similar to those in which reinforcement occurred in the past.* Beginning early in life, people learn to discriminate which kinds of *models* and *behavior* to imitate and which *contexts* are appropriate for imitation. As is true of all discrimination, the discriminations about who, what, and where to perform a modeled behavior are the result of differential reinforcement. Cues about behavior, models, or contexts that precede reinforcement for imitation become S^D's for performing the modeled behavior. Cues that precede nonreinforcement or punishment for imitation become S^Δ's for not performing the modeled behavior.

1a. Behavior.   *Due to differential reinforcement, people learn that certain kinds of behavior should be imitated but that other kinds of behavior should not be imitated.* People often receive reinforcers for imitating the driving speed of others. If everyone else on the road slows down, we tend to slow down. This imitative performance is often reinforced by our avoiding a police trap, not hitting slower cars, or getting to see an accident better. Thus the speed of the general traffic flow becomes an S^D for imitation. In contrast, imitating behavior which may produce an automobile accident is likely to be punished or extinguished. Hence other peoples' accident-prone behavior becomes an S^Δ for not imitating. As we gain experience, many modeled activities become S^D's or S^Δ's that increase or decrease the likelihood of imitation.

[15]Skinner (1980:283).

A child is more likely to receive reinforcers for imitating same-sex behavior than behavior typical of the other sex. This differential reinforcement causes the child to discriminate and perform same-sex behavior more readily than the child would perform responses seen only in the other sex. Boys are more strongly punished than girls for imitating the behavior unique to the other sex, and boys do less of this cross-sex imitation.[16] If a little boy imitates some of his mother's or sister's behavior, the imitation may be punished with a comment such as, "Little boys aren't supposed to do that." The neighbor boys might mock, "Billy is a sissy. Billy is a sissy." These punishments suppress the imitation of behavior seen only in females, and make feminine behavior an S^Δ for not imitating. If the boy imitates the masculine behavior of his father or brother, the imitative behavior is more likely to be reinforced. This makes same-sex behavior an S^D for future imitation. Thus, the boy's imitativeness comes under S^D control for performing male behavior and under S^Δ control for not performing female behavior. Little boys often *acquire* the information about how females apply makeup or put on stockings, but they would not *perform* the behavior! Little girls receive less punishment for cross-sex imitation and are more likely to do cross-sex imitation than boys are.

1b. Models.   After imitating the behavior of various models, we learn that imitating some people is more reinforcing than imitating others. *Imitating competent or well-liked people is usually more reinforcing than imitating incompetent or unpopular people; thus certain models become S^D's for imitation and other models become S^Δ's for not imitating.* We may watch both good and bad skiers and acquire information about their different styles; yet we are more likely to attempt to perform the responses shown by the competent models than those shown by the incompetent ones. Children often learn to imitate people of their own ethnic or religious group rather than those of other groups. The child may be criticized or punished a few times for acting like "they" act. As a result, the other group becomes an S^Δ for not imitating. Movie and TV stars often become S^D's for imitation. People may pick up mannerisms, styles of dress, or idioms from performers they like, and if this produces reinforcing results, the stars become S^D's for further imitative performances. Leaders, popular individuals, and friends may become S^D's for imitation for similar reasons. One of the reasons these people are leaders or stars, popular or liked, is that they have certain desirable social skills; thus imitating these people is likely to add a social skill that brings reinforcers to the person who imitates.

Naturally, people learn to discriminate that a certain subset of the behavior shown by any model can be reinforcing to imitate, while other subsets of behavior are not. An observer may imitate the way an attractive model dresses, but not imitate the way the model treats others. A little girl may imitate her father's use of complex words, but not imitate his repertoire of behavior for handling guns. An athlete may imitate the running style of a champion without imitating any of the rest of the champion's behavior.

1c. Contexts.   *Because a behavior may be reinforced in one context but not in others, context cues become important S^D's or S^Δ's that influence the performance of imitative behavior.* For example, if a child imitates some of father's profanity while at

---

[16]Bandura et al. (1963); Lynn (1969).

home, the child may be punished and thus learn that the home is a context for not imitating father's profanity. Yet the child may receive numerous reinforcers for using profanity in interaction with peers. Thus, interaction with peers becomes an S^D for imitative swearing, while the home is an S^Δ for not imitating. If a deeply respected friend likes to talk about serious philosophic topics—death, religion, truth, the purpose of life—an observer may learn to talk more about these topics, too. Yet imitation will come under stimulus control of context cues. Serious conversation may be very reinforcing in certain situations; but in those situations where it puts a damper on fun or destroys a light mood, serious talk may evoke critical or derogatory comments from others.

2. Present Reinforcement.   *Performance is also influenced by present patterns of reinforcement and punishment.* Cues that correlate with the present patterns of reinforcement and punishment may become S^D's or S^Δ's for imitative performance. These cues can come from the model or from other people who have imitated the model.

An observer's decision of whether or not to imitate a behavior is influenced by seeing others receive reinforcement or punishment for the behavior, or seeing their emotional responses (signs of pleasure or pain) associated with the behavior. Other cues related to the status, success, or popularity of the people who do the behavior also influence whether or not the observer will imitate.

2a. Reinforcers.   If an observer sees someone repeatedly winning big payoffs on the slot machines, the present reinforcers to the model will increase the probability of the observer's trying the slots, too.

2b. Punishers.   Seeing someone get a ticket for speeding decreases our tendency to imitate the speeders who pass us.

2c. Positive Emotional Responses.   Seeing people smiling as they leave the ice cream store increases the probability of our going in for a cone, too.

2d. Negative Emotional Responses.   Seeing people sitting around inside a restaurant looking bored decreases the chances that we will imitate their choice of restaurants.

2e. Status, Success, or Popularity.   Hearing a popular, successful person speak out on a controversial political issue increases the probability that others will speak up for the same issue.

Often an observer can watch what happens to other people when they imitate a given model's behavior. The present consequences to other imitators often indicate the type of consequences the observer can expect. If the first person who jumps into the cold water appears to enjoy rollicking in the waves, you may be somewhat inclined to get in the cold water, too. If several other people imitate the model and all show signs of enjoying themselves, it is even clearer that imitation is reinforcing; and you will be even more inclined to follow suit. But imitation is not always reinforced. The first person in the water may be an excellent swimmer who can handle the strong rip tides and heavy waves. The people who imitate and get into the water next may not fare so well in the rough seas. They may be thrown down or dunked by the waves and come out of the water with facial expressions that communicate the aversiveness of the situation and serve as vicarious punishers. The consequences to these imitators will influence your decision about imitating.

Inverse Imitation

Up to this point we have considered imitation in which the observer performs a response that is *similar* to the model's response. *When an observer performs a response that is the inverse of the model's behavior, the observer is doing inverse imitation.*[17] *People learn to do inverse imitation when there is reinforcement for behavior that complements or differs in other ways from the model's performance.* When a student is learning how to waltz by taking lessons from a good dancer, the student must imitate the teacher but must invert the information. When the teacher puts her left foot forward, the student must put his right foot back. If the teacher steps one step to the right, the student must step one step to the left. The student is acquiring information from the model much as in regular imitation. However, performance is an inverted version of the modeled behavior because only the inverse produces positive reinforcement. Situations in which inverse imitation is reinforced often involve punishment for regular imitation. If the dance student performed precisely the same waltz steps that the model did—stepping forward at the same time the teacher did—the two dancers would collide or step on each other's feet. Thus, regular imitation is punished in this situation. When inverse imitation helps avoid these collisions and aversive consequences, there is negative reinforcement for inverse imitation.

One type of inverse imitation occurs when the observer's behavior must *complement* the model's. The movements of the two waltzers must complement each other to produce reinforcing results. When two people are cutting down a large tree with a lumberman's saw, one must push the saw while the other pulls in order for each behavior to complement the other and produce effective results. Thus, each person watches the other and coordinates with an inverse imitation of the other's behavior. Many tasks with a push-pull or give-take structure involve inverse imitation to synchronize the complementary roles.

Sometimes inverse imitation is only reinforced when the observer does a complementary response. At other times, inverse imitation is reinforced when the observer does anything that clearly differs in any way from the model's behavior. There is reinforcement for *being different,* rather than for complementing the model. For example, members of a tough juvenile gang often hate the police. Any behavior that looks like the "straight" behavior modeled by the cops is likely to be punished by other gang members. Behavior that differs from the straight behavior is negatively reinforced by escape from social criticism from peers, and it may also be positively reinforced by peers who approve of "rebellion"—that is, doing anything different from straight behavior. The gang members

[17]Skinner (1953:121).

see that the police walk with straight posture and maintain a neat appearance, so they learn to avoid similar behavior by slouching, sliding down in chairs, and wearing sloppy clothing.

Inverse imitation for "being different" often occurs when observers dislike the model, see negative consequences follow the model's behavior, or receive strong reinforcers for demonstrating to others (or to themselves) that they are not conformists.

1. Dislike.   People often go out of their way to refrain from doing activities or wearing things that are customarily associated with ethnic, religious, political, or social groups that they dislike. The Catholics and the Protestants in Northern Ireland show inverse imitation of each other. Each group gives reinforcers to its members for being different from the other group, thus exacerbating the differences. Society's dropouts often cultivate standards and lifestyles that clearly differ from the achievement-oriented society. When people interact with a disliked group, they often find that their own mannerisms, vocabulary, and conversation topics are chosen to be opposite from those of the disliked group. Their behavior can become so biased toward oppositeness that they find themselves acting with unusual mannerisms or saying things they do not really believe just so they do not replicate the behavior of the people they do not respect.

2. Negative Consequences to Model.   When a motorcyclist sees a close friend get killed because the friend did not wear a helmet, the negative consequences to the model will increase the likelihood that the observer will use a helmet more. When the market analyst sees investors losing their shirts in electronics, the analyst may sell all stock related to electronics.

3. Nonconformists.   Some people do inverse imitation because they have been rewarded for being different or have been punished for being conformists. When men start wearing long hair and beards, the nonconformist shaves off his. When the skirt length goes up, the nonconformist gives her short skirts to the Salvation Army. When the person who was once a strong supporter of ideology A finds that others are also switching to espouse A, the nonconformist begins to preach the dangers of A.

MASS MEDIA MODELING

The mass media—TV, movies, radio, newspapers, magazines—present models of a wide range of behaviors, some desirable and some undesirable. There has been a great deal of concern that the frequent and vivid presentation of violence and brutal behavior in the media may increase people's use of violence in their daily lives. Every day on TV alone, millions of people see multiple acts of violence in programs showing domestic fighting, assault, rape, murder, war, and terrorism. There has been considerable debate about the possible harmful effects of media violence on observers. Although the debate is not completely resolved,[18] there is increasing evidence that *the violent behavior presented by the media causes some people to commit imitative acts of violence.*

[18]Milavsky et al. (1982); National Institutes of Mental Health (1982).

Much of the research on mass media modeling has been done in psychological laboratories.[19] Under experimental conditions, it has been shown that after people view a series of gory movie murders, they are less horrified by murder than they were beforehand. After seeing aggressive behavior modeled on TV, people are more willing to hurt others, and they imitate the types of aggression they saw modeled on the screen. However, critics have questioned whether these types of modeling effects occur outside the laboratory: Do people imitate media violence in their everyday lives? Although it is not easy to do controlled experiments in the natural environment, several studies indicate that media violence has significant effects outside the laboratory. For example, media modeling effects are conspicuous—and statistically significant—after highly publicized acts of violence such as prize fights, executions, suicides, and murder-suicides.[20]

Prize fights are regularly covered by the mass media. After the average heavyweight prize fight, homicides increase by over 12 percent. The effect is largest when the media coverage is most extensive. Even more impressive is the fact that the modeling effects are quite specific. When a young, white boxer is defeated in the ring, homicides of young, white males increase. When a young, black boxer is defeated in the ring, homicides of young, black males increase. This is called *victim modeling*. People direct their imitative aggression at the same kinds of people that were the victims of the modeled aggression. Such findings raise many questions. For example, do movies and TV shows that contain violent scenes in which a woman is beaten and raped produce victim modeling effects, increasing the likelihood that women will be assaulted and raped?

In prize fights, violence is publicly rewarded. What modeling effects would be expected if violence were punished? Data from England for a 63-year period in which capital punishment was used and given extensive media coverage reveal that there was a decrease in homicides during the 2-week period just after a highly publicized execution. This reflects the effects of vicarious punishment. Since punishment usually produces only temporary suppression of behavior, it is not surprising to find that public executions only reduced homicide rates for a 2-week period.

When people take their own lives and the event receives extensive media attention, the suicide rate in the general population increases significantly. The more media coverage that a suicide receives, the more imitative suicides there are. If a suicide is publicized primarily in one part of the country, most of the imitative suicides occur in the geographic area where the media coverage is most extensive. Some suicides are masked as automobile "accidents." After a well-publicized suicide, the number of single-vehicle accidents increases by 9.12 percent. The drivers of the crashed cars tend to be about the same age as the person in the publicized suicide: When the media report the suicide of an older person, the drivers of the crashed cars tend to be older; when the reported suicide is young, the drivers tend to be young. People tend to imitate models of similar age. Again, the greater the media coverage of the suicide, the greater the increase in single-vehicle fatalities. Also, these single-vehicle accidents are most likely to take place in the geographic area where the suicide received the greatest media coverage.

When the media report a *murder-suicide*—in which a person kills someone else then

[19]Murray and Kippax (1979); National Institutes of Mental Health (1982).

[20]These findings of Phillips (1983, in press) are summarized in the next five paragraphs. Due to methodological problems, it has been difficult to evaluate the impact of most other forms of media violence in the natural environment.

commits suicide—there is an increase in automobile accidents; but these accidents are different from those that take place after suicides that are not associated with murder. After murder-suicides, there is an increase in multiple-vehicle accidents in which several people are killed. The behavior presented by the media is imitated closely: Multiple-death accidents do not increase after suicides, but they increase significantly after murder-suicides. Again, the more media coverage the murder-suicide receives, the more multiple-vehicle accidents there are; and the multiple-death accidents are most common in the area where the murder-suicide receives the greatest media coverage.

Some violent movies produce conspicuous modeling effects. For example, *The Warriors* shows the violent acts of menacing street gangs, and it has triggered brawls and fights in moviehouses in several cities in which it was shown.[21] Many people have been injured in the fights and some have died. Some theaters have stopped showing the movie and others have hired special guards to maintain order.

When airline hijacking first began in the early 1960's, the hijackers often succeeded in commandeering airplanes to chosen destinations without being apprehended and punished.[22] These skyjackings received considerable media coverage, and the rate of skyjacking rose during the subsequent years. Gradually, as airports improved their security systems and police protection, increasing numbers of skyjackers were apprehended. As the mass media began to report failure after failure in skyjacking attempts, vicarious punishment suppressed the rate of skyjacking. Terrorist activity also receives considerable media coverage. After a successful terrorist attack, other terrorist groups are more likely to take similar action. For this reason, most countries have developed tactics for dealing swiftly and harshly with terrorism. Media coverage of terrorist activities that fail helps deter subsequent acts of terrorism via vicarious punishment.

Evidence from the natural environment supports the laboratory findings that media violence causes significant increases in violence in some people. There have been many attempts to limit the amount of violence presented in the media, but none have had much success. Violence is popular. It sells newspapers and magazines. Fast action and violence are part of the formula for success in making movies and TV programs. Most people find media violence exciting. The fast pace, thrills, intense action, and adventure shown in violent TV scenes provide an abundance of rewarding sensory stimulation that keeps people's eyes glued to the screen. Even reading about violence provides sensory stimulation: Stories of kidnappings, murders, suicides, rapes, terrorism, and war contain information that is novel and unusual because it is so different from most people's daily experience. In short, violence provides so much sensory stimulation that most people continue watching even if they are shocked or frightened by what they see. As long as large numbers of people continue to find violence rewarding, the media will probably continue to present it.

People who have learned nonviolent means of dealing with problems and frustrations may be able to resist the modeling effects of media violence. If parents both model nonviolent coping skills and teach their importance, they may reduce the adverse effects of media violence on their children. However, media violence does reach a significant

[21]"Flick" (1979).
[22]Bandura (1973:105f).

number of people who do not have a behavior repertoire that prevents their imitating some of the violence modeled in the media; these are the people who are most likely to show the effects of media violence.

CONCLUSION

Much of the behavior seen in everyday life is learned or modified by observing other people. Observing a model gives the observer a great deal of information about the model's behavior and often provides sufficient information that the observer can imitate the behavior. Exposure to a model can influence an observer in three ways: (1) by allowing the observer to learn a new response, (2) by inhibiting or disinhibiting old responses in the observer's behavior repertoire, or (3) by providing S^D's that set the occasion for a similar response from the observer. Models can serve as sources of CS's that elicit vicarious emotional responses in the observer and cause vicarious Pavlovian conditioning of new patterns of responses. The CS's given off by the model can also function as vicarious reinforcers and vicarious punishers for the observational learning of operant behavior. The operant learning from models occurs in two phases—acquisition of information from the model and performance of imitative responses. Both acquisition and performance are influenced by a variety of factors, including reinforcement and punishment, the competence and likeability of the model, the nature of the modeled behavior, and context cues. Finally, there are certain contingencies of reinforcement that cause inverse imitation, in which the observer's response complements or is opposite from the model's response. The mass media provide models of both desirable and undesirable behavior, and these media models have significant effects on some people's behavior.

The next chapter describes another way in which people learn from others, by receiving prompts that assist them in producing a behavior that otherwise they might not be able to perform.

10

Prompts

● *In this chapter you will learn how prompts can help start the learning process, and how people naturally fade out prompts as learning progresses.*

It is the third rehearsal, with two months still to go before the new play opens. The stage is bare and the set crew is noisily constructing the props in the wings. On stage the performers are practicing the second scene. The lines, gestures, and movements are far from well mastered. As the players work through their lines, they often pause and glance at the director for help. A brief prompt such as giving the first three words of the next line is usually enough to start the performers on the right track again. The prompting is frequent and freely given in order that the players can keep moving through the scene and learn the broad outlines of the entire scene. The director knows that after a few more practice sessions, the performers will speak the lines much more naturally and the prompting can be gradually faded out. If the players are good, there is no doubt that the prompts will be reduced to zero well before opening night.

Prompting is a common part of social learning in childhood, though it is used less and less extensively as people grow up. The process usually consists of two phases. *First, a behavior is prompted or guided then reinforced until it occurs frequently. Second, as learning proceeds, the prompts are gradually faded out until the behavior occurs without prompts.*[1] Prompted behavior is generally learned most

---

[1]Skinner (1953), Moore and Goldiamond (1964), Bandura (1969), Kanfer and Phillips (1970), and Reese (1972) discuss various ways in which prompting and fading are used in conditioning. Although prompting is less important than differential reinforcement, modeling, and rules, it is a distinctive method of learning that occurs often enough in everyday life to deserve separate attention.

rapidly when it is followed by frequent reinforcement. Thus, performers whose careers and reputations depend on learning a complex set of lines will respond quickly to the director's prompts; but another person might not learn the lines even after a thousand prompts if there were no reinforcers for learning. In everyday life, the fading procedure is usually a very natural aftereffect of successful prompting; as the performer learns the lines, the director will phase out the prompts since prompting is no longer needed, hence no longer reinforced. New behavior is acquired most efficiently if fading is done neither too rapidly nor too slowly, but is paced according to the learner's rate of progress. Naturally, someone who is very experienced and skilled at prompting is likely to do both prompting and fading in a more sensitive and efficient manner than a person with less experience.

This chapter describes several of the modalities through which prompting and fading occur.

PHYSICAL GUIDANCE

People frequently use prompts—especially physical guidance—in helping children learn new behavior.[2] Adults often discover that moving a child's arms, legs, or body through the desired behavior sequence may be easier than telling the child what to do. For the preverbal child, prompting is especially effective since verbal rules are not yet of use.

When a child reaches the age for beginning to walk, the parents are likely to support and move the child in ways that promote walking and prevent falling. These physical prompts facilitate the walking response. Shifting the child's weight from foot to foot helps the child take the first steps. Most parents give generous reinforcement in the form of affection, cheerful talk, and attention as the prompted behavior appears—and this speeds the learning process. Next, the fading process is a very natural aftereffect of successful prompting. Because parents find it rewarding to see their child walk unaided, they receive reinforcement for removing their assistance as soon as they can.

An infant may be prompted to play with a new toy when the parents physically guide the child's hands to touch, hold, pull, or shake the toy in a manner that produces noise, lights, or other effects. After the infant has been prompted several times to pull the string, hearing the toy go "Quack-quack" and seeing the colorful wheels go around will provide the sensory stimulation that reinforces pulling. As the child learns to pull the string, the parents can fade their prompts. Older children and adults are often aided in learning various athletic activities, musical instruments, and dances by prompting. A teacher may put a bow and arrow in the student's hands, then move the student's arms into the correct position. The swimming teacher often supports the student in the water and physically moves the student's arms or legs to produce swimming movements. These movements are then reinforced by praise and positive feedback. As the student learns the proper stroking patterns, the teacher can remove the prompts and supports.

Children are often prompted into social interactions by physical guidance. The first time a young child confronts Santa Claus in a department store, the child may be reluctant

[2]Gelfand and Hartmann (1975).

to climb onto Santa's knee. The parent may physically push or lift the child into place to start the interaction. A friendly greeting from Santa and some candy will reinforce the prompted behavior; and future trips to see Santa will require less prompting.[3] When a distant relative comes to visit, the child may be pushed toward Uncle Freddie to encourage interaction. If a child shows reluctance about approaching a new teacher, a doctor, a barber, or the neighbor's dog, prompting may be used to create first approximations of the desired behavior. The ensuing consequences—reinforcement or punishment—determine whether the prompted behavior becomes more or less frequent.

Prompting is often used for teaching people to abstain from certain responses. A parent can prompt a child to be quiet in church by gently touching the wiggling leg and holding it still. A gentle prompt alone would not be expected to produce lasting effects in stopping the wiggling; however, if the child receives reinforcers for the prompted behavior or is punished for resuming the wiggling response, the prompts are more effective.

Prompting by physical guidance is not as common in adulthood as in the early years. Because adults respond to verbal instructions—either written or spoken—better than children do, rules can be used with adults as an alternative to prompts. However, in certain situations physical prompting with the hand is superior to verbal instruction. For example, during sexual interaction, a gentle hand can often communicate and guide the movements of the partner much better than words could ever do. A prompting hand shows exactly what needs to be done. Masters and Johnson recommend hand on hand guidance as a useful step for helping partners learn how to best gratify each other's sexual needs.[4]

Physical prompting also occurs during the learning and rehearsal of theater performances. Dancers may be prompted by the guiding hand of their choreographer or of fellow dancers to move their bodies in certain patterns. Likewise, performers may learn various gestures in this manner. Football players, karate students, and other athletes also find that a guiding hand often communicates the desired information more efficiently than words can.

MECHANICAL PROMPTS

In order to help their child learn to ride a two-wheeler, parents sometimes attach a set of training wheels to the sides of the bike to prevent the bike from falling over. The side wheels serve as mechanical prompts that help teach bike riding and prevent falling. By adjusting the training wheels so that both touch the ground simultaneously, the bike can be kept in the vertical position, and the child can learn the basics of pedaling, turning, and stopping, without having problems with balancing. Once these basic skills are mastered, the training wheels can be adjusted upward a bit such that the bike can tip slightly from side to side. Now the child can begin to learn how to balance. When the child makes mistakes, the bike does not fall over because the training wheels keep it up. As the child's skills for balancing improve, the training wheels can be lifted further off the ground. This

---

[3]The role of social learning, including prompts, in establishing social spacing patterns has been discussed by Hall (1959) and Baldwin and Baldwin (1974).

[4]Masters and Johnson (1970).

gradual removal of mechanical support is the fading of mechanical prompts. During each step in which support is faded out, the child can lean the bike over further and learn from the consequences.

Metronomes are a form of mechanical prompt that provide stimuli which help guide the timing of music. As the student masters the rhythm of a given passage, it is possible to decrease the use of the metronome and thus fade out the prompt.

In TV studios, performers, announcers, and newscasters occasionally fall back on mechanical prompters which provide a large, easily read script. If speakers come to a section they remember, they can let their eyes wander from the machine and talk without prompts until they hit the next rough spot.

Some automobiles are built with buzzers and lights that prompt people to fasten their seat belts, check the emergency brake, keep below certain maximum speeds, and so forth. Computers that are programmed to teach reading, mathematics, or other subjects often use prompting procedures. Easy problems—filled with hints, underlined words, informative diagrams—are used at the beginning of each lesson; and as the student learns to answer questions correctly, the hints are automatically faded.

PICTURES

When children first learn to read, they are often given books that contain many pictures related to the words. The simplest books may have one word per picture. The word *apple* appears in bold print under a picture of an apple. The word *rabbit* appears under a picture of a cottontail. Seeing the word and picture together assists the child in saying the correct word. Later, as the child has more experience with printed words, the pictures can be faded: Smaller or sketchier pictures may be used; increasing numbers of words may appear per picture. As the pictures are faded, the child will rely more and more heavily on the printed words as the S^D's that control the verbal responses. Studies have shown that fading the prompts is crucial for efficient learning. Children who always see the picture of an apple above the word *apple* do not learn to respond to the word alone as rapidly as children who have the picture prompts gradually faded until only the word is visible.[5]

The control knobs on the dashboards of some automobiles have pictures that show a horn, lights, wipers, radio, and other features. When a person first drives the car, the person may rely on the pictures to determine which knob to turn for air or music. After learning the placement of the controls, the driver will not need to look at the pictures to reach the correct knob; hence the driver automatically fades the use of the pictorial prompts.

GESTURES

With a few gestures, a conductor can prompt the musicians to modify the tempo, volume, or tone quality of their music. After several rehearsals, the musicians learn how the conductor expects them to play each piece, and the conductor can fade out the more

[5]Corey and Shamow (1972).

exaggerated gestures. By the time of the concert, much of the conductor's hard work is over and is no longer reflected in the gestures that now keep the players coordinated.

Performers and dancers also learn from gesture prompts. When a performer speaks too quietly, the director may give arm gestures, emphasizing the upward movements, in order to encourage more vigor and volume from the speaker's voice. A turning motion made with the hands can prompt the dancer to face further toward the right or the left. When the director creates new gestures that succeed in prompting the desired behavior, the successful effects reinforce creative prompting.

Teachers and lecturers frequently use prompts to guide the attention of their listeners. A lecturer who points a finger to guide your eyes to one part of a diagram or chart is prompting attention to the correct target. All through life, people rely on pointing to direct other people's eyes and attention.

Since they usually cannot hear each other, pedestrians and automobile drivers often resort to numerous gestures to prompt each other to stop, go, slow down, and so forth. Athletes often use gestures to prompt their teammates to run or wait, turn or move.

WORDS

When a person is learning new patterns of verbal behavior, words are effective prompts. The performer learning a new script is in the same type of position as the child trying to learn a poem or a prayer. When the last words that were spoken do not have enough S^D control to cue the next phrase, it helps to have someone prompt the correct verbal pattern. Parents frequently use verbal prompts to teach their children to say "Hello, Mrs. Lopez," "Thank you," "Good-bye," and other social niceties. When people cannot remember a certain important detail while telling a story, they may look to a friend who knows what they are trying to say, waiting for a prompt. They may even prompt their friend to give the verbal prompt by looking helpless or speechless or by gesturing. Then the friend may respond with the missing words that help the original speaker finish the story. For example, when two people try to tell about the places they went on a trip together they may often turn to each other for help in filling in the names of various cities, shops, museums, or restaurants.

CONCLUSION

Prompts are physical, verbal, or other assists that help a person perform a behavior that would have been unlikely without this assistance. After a behavior has been emitted due to prompting, reinforcement further increases the probability of the behavior. After sufficient reinforcement, the prompts may be removed through the process of fading.

11

Rules

● *In this chapter you will learn how advice, instructions, and other verbal rules influence—or fail to influence—behavior.*

In Chapter 9 on modeling and observational learning, we saw how information can influence behavior: The information that an observer obtains from watching a model's behavior can speed the observer's learning similar responses. The subject of this chapter is how verbal instructions, either spoken or written, can serve as *rules* that influence behavior patterns.[1] Instructions for coping with multitudes of situations can be symbolically encoded—as rules—that can help people learn new behavior patterns rapidly and efficiently. *Rules are verbally encoded guidelines— such as instructions, suggestions, or hints—that indicate ways of coping with certain situations.* After worrying about their child's frequent pouting and sulking, parents may read the following instructions: "Whenever your child pouts, avoid paying attention to the child. By removing the social reinforcement for pouting, you will cause the frequency of the unwanted behavior to decline." Parents who are concerned about stopping the pouting can learn an effective means of coping with the problem within minutes if they have access to good instructions. Without good rules some parents might never discover an effective solution to the problem.

[1]There is a difference between symbolic models and symbolically encoded rules. "Go west, young man" is a rule that directs one to behave in a certain way. "The young men are going west" is a symbolic description of modeled behavior. We must consider numerous variables aside from the symbolic rule or symbolic model before predicting how the rule or model will affect a listener's behavior.

Rules generally describe some aspect of the contingencies of reinforcement: that is, the relationship among S^D's, behavior, and consequences.[2] The guidelines for helping parents cope with their child's pouting specify all three elements of the desirable contingencies of reinforcement: If the S^D's of pouting are present, the *response* of not showing attention will produce the *consequences* of a gradual decline in pouting. All three elements of the contingencies of reinforcement—stimulus, behavior, and consequences— need not always be made explicit, since people's prior learning often allows them to fill in the missing elements. The instructions on a fire alarm—"In case of fire, break glass and pull handle"—describe only the relevant S^D's (the presence of fire) and operants (break glass and pull handle). The instructions on the fire alarm do not need to describe the reinforcer—alarm bells and the arrival of fire trucks—because most people know this, even if they have never used an alarm. "Push button to cross street" describes the operant to be performed and the reinforcement that will follow. The sign does not need to specify that the S^D's for pressing the button are the presence of the DON'T WALK signal or heavy traffic. No one would need to push the button unless the S^D of a DON'T WALK sign or traffic were already present. A big poster on the wall saying, "Smile," only indicates the behavior to be done; but some people find that even this vague, generalized rule will increase the frequency of smiles, which in turn improves their social interactions or boosts their mood. "Smile when you say that, partner," is a hint for the chap who failed to show that he was only kidding when he joked about the other person's odd-looking motorcycle. There are times when the rules need to be spelled out completely in order to minimize misunderstanding or maximize their effectiveness. Stating a complete rule, such as "If you clean up your room before dinner, you can watch TV tonight," is much more likely to generate the desired behavior than is stating a brief rule, such as "Clean up your room."

When you consider the incredibly large number of rules that barrage a person every day, it becomes clear that the majority of rules go unattended. "Buy this product now," "Save at our friendly bank," "Seek and ye shall find," "Fight pollution," "Help stamp out everything that needs stamping out," "Join the millions who. . . ." Clearly there is more to rule use than meets the eye. People do not automatically follow rules. What determines whether a rule will modify a person's behavior? How does a person discriminate among the countless rules and follow a select few while neglecting the rest?

RULE USE IS LEARNED

Rules are meaningless to infants. One obvious prerequisite for rule use is knowledge of the language. When working in a specialized area—such as learning new skills at rock climbing, emergency first aid, or psychological counseling—prior experience with the jargon, equipment, and relevant social skills may be a second prerequisite.

Normally, children can begin learning rule use as soon as they understand the language.[3] When Betsy is beginning to crawl, before she can respond to rules, she learns

[2]Skinner (1969).
[3]Skinner (1957).

to go to Daddy when he is smiling and his arms are open to give her a big hug. The S^D's for approach are the smiles and open arms; the reinforcers are social attention and affection. As Betsy gains an understanding of the language, the parents may say, ''Come here, Betsy,'' while Betsy is toddling toward them; and the rule becomes part of the S^D collage associated with the behavior and reinforcers. After several repetitions, the rule becomes a well-established part of the stimulus collage and may be enough to cause Betsy to approach even if the parents omit the smile or open-arm gesture. If the child follows the rule and the parents show affection, the likelihood of the child's using rules in the future is further increased. Naturally, if the parents do not reinforce rule following, the child would be less likely to follow rules, due to extinction. In addition, parents who say, ''Come here, Betsy,'' so they can *punish* the child, often find that the child *goes* when they say *come*.

A person learns to follow rules when rule use leads to reinforcement.[4] *Rule use is suppressed—and a person may even learn to do the opposite of the rule—when following rules leads to punishment. Nonreinforcement decreases rule use due to extinction.* The more consistently a person receives reinforcers for following a large number of rules, given by many different people in many different contexts, the more likely the person is to follow rules in the future.[5]

Sometimes young children go through a cute period of overgeneralized rule use when they are first learning to use rules. This is most likely to occur if their parents, brothers, and sisters are consistent in giving reasonable rules and then reinforcing rule use. ''Come to Mommy,'' ''Go to Daddy,'' ''Don't touch the hot skillet!'' ''Stay out of the street.'' If the parents and siblings follow through with reinforcement for obeying and punishment for not obeying, the child may become very responsive to rules.

Little Laura is playing with her older brother and sister on the living room floor. While her brother is stacking blocks to make a very complex tower, Laura keeps pushing off the top blocks and watching them fall to the floor. Crash, crash; sensory stimulation; what fun! But Laura's brother is less than happy with his little sister's behavior and says, ''Stop that! You'll knock my tower down.'' Laura obeys and turns to the model ranch her sister has created. In short order, Laura receives sensory stimulation reinforcers from playing with the little plastic horses and tiny people. Soon she has eight people stacked on top of one horse. This clearly perturbs her sister, who is taking her ranchers' lives more seriously. ''Get out of here. Go see Daddy, Laura.''

Off Laura goes to the garage to see Daddy. Daddy is busy potting; and he has little time to pay attention to Laura. After the child squashes a freshly thrown pot by accidently stepping on it, Father orders Laura to go play with Timmy and Debbie. Firmly pushed in the direction of the living room, Laura goes back to her brother and sister. Timmy's tower is taller and tottering now. When he sees Laura about ready to reach for the tower, Timmy interjects, ''Hey, Laura! Don't touch that. Why don't you go play with some of Debbie's things.'' However, as Laura goes through the scene the second time, she begins to learn an important discrimination. She is getting the runaround. People are telling her to go see someone else just to make her go away.

[4]Staats (1968); Skinner (1969); Schutte and Hopkins (1970); Ferster et al. (1975).
[5]Karen (1974:123).

In one sense, it is cute to watch the little child go back and forth, so trustingly, so obediently. There may even be enough sensory stimulation in the game of following the rule of "Go see so-and-so" to reinforce obedience for several repetitions. But as the novelty dies off, nonreinforcement causes the child to learn an important discrimination. Laura begins to ask, "Why should I go see Daddy? He said I should stay here and play with you." The child is learning that rules can be challenged. "Daddy said you should share some of your blocks with me!" The child is learning that one person's rule (Timmy's) can be counteracted with another person's rule (Daddy's). If Timmy begrudgingly gives in and allows Laura to have some blocks, this reinforcer hastens Laura on her way toward developing the discrimination that not all rules must be obeyed. The period of overgeneralized rule use will come to an end as these discriminations and skills for critically evaluating rules are further reinforced. When given a rule or instruction, the child may learn to counter with "Why?" "Why should I go play in my own room?" This might cause some people to resort to the use of authority or the threat of force to get the child to obey. "You'll do it because *I* told you so." They might use reasoning, "You should leave the kitchen because I'm very tired and cannot cook with constant distractions." They might introduce extra incentives—namely the promise of special reinforcers: "If you'll go play in the living room, I'll let you lick the beaters when I'm done."

THE S^D's FOR FOLLOWING RULES

People are bombarded by more rules than they can follow, and many rules do not lead to reinforcement; consequently, people learn to disregard most rules. People are likely to follow rules only when S^D's are present in (1) the *rule* and (2) the *context*, indicating that there has been past reinforcement for using similar rules in similar contexts.

1. *If following a certain rule has been reinforced, the rule becomes an S^D for future rule-governed behavior. If following another rule has resulted in nonreinforcement or punishment, this second rule becomes an S$^\Delta$ for not following the second rule in the future.* People learn to discriminate. They learn to follow those rules that have "paid off" in the past and to disregard rules that have led to nonreinforcement or punishment. *Commands* and *good advice* are the rules that are most likely to be followed.

2. However, things are more complex. Following a given rule may be reinforced in one context but not in another context. As a result, *certain context cues in the stimulus collage can become S^D's or S$^\Delta$'s that help determine whether a person will follow a rule.*[6] When parents state a rule, they often give extra cues that they "really mean it"—that they will reward or punish, depending on the child's performance. The serious tone of voice that accompanies the rule is an S^D that puts the rule in a "serious" context and helps the child discriminate that the rule is important and hence compliance is likely to be followed by reinforcement. Countless stimuli from the rule giver, the audience, and the surrounding environment can become *context cues*—S^D's or S$^\Delta$'s—that determine whether people follow or disregard a given rule.

[6]Ferster et al. (1975).

Commands and Good Advice

A command is a rule that is enforced by reinforcement from the rule giver. Good advice is a rule whose use is reinforced by the natural consequences of following the rule (without enforcement from the rule giver).[7] A command takes the following form: "An authority tells you to do a certain behavior, and the authority will reward compliance and/or punish noncompliance." Advice takes the following form: "Try a certain activity, and you will find that it leads to reinforcement." Commands generally have a stronger effect on behavior than advice, especially if the person who gives the commands actually has the power to reinforce or punish. Advice lacks the extra social enforcement associated with commands. Advice is backed up by reinforcement only to the degree that it is good advice, i.e., that it actually helps the rule user attain more reinforcers.

Because children lack experience with rule use, they often need commands—backed up by extra social sanctions—in order to follow rules well. Merely advising a 2-year-old that it is somewhat risky to play in the street will have less effect than the command, "Do not play in the street or you'll get a spanking." As people grow up and gain experience at rule use, many learn the value of good advice; and this in turn allows them to rely more on advice as they learn to discriminate good advice from poor advice.

There are special areas in which commands are superior to advice—for both children and adults. If a good rule is not obviously true, if the rewards of rule following are in the distant future, or if the rule demands that the follower do something aversive (that is, strange, uncomfortable, unusual, or socially unacceptable), the listener may follow the rule only if commanded to do so. Friends may advise Uncle George to stop drinking so much, yet George may not be able to appreciate the future health benefits or see how he can stand to get along without the pleasures of the bottle. On the other hand, when George's boss commands George to stop drinking or lose his job, the command form of the rule may have a powerful effect.

Often rule givers who want to change someone else's behavior will start out at a hint level—casually giving some advice. Then, if hints fail to change behavior, they will explicitly offer the advice: "George, I've got some important advice for you." Next, they may restate their advice in the format of a command—"George, stop drinking"—even though no sanctions are stated. Finally, the rule givers may escalate to the use of commands, with the attendant promises of reward or threats of punishment needed to give commands full strength.

People are less likely to follow advice than to obey commands. Because advice is cheap, and easy to give, people hear more advice than they can follow. Thus, people learn not to follow most advice. Because it is often difficult to discriminate between good advice and bad advice, people may not even respond to good advice unless clear S^D's are present which indicate that "this advice really works." If it takes special effort to discriminate between good advice and bad advice, the effort serves as a punisher that decreases the likelihood that people will try to find out if the advice is really valuable.

Even when people need advice, they may first try to get along without seeking the verbal information. Because it sometimes takes a certain amount of effort to locate good advice and figure out how to use it—and because effort can function as a punisher—some

---

[7]Skinner (1969:148–149).

people do not seek out advice until they have exhausted easier methods of solving their problems. This means that even good advice and rules may not be sought and used until other easier methods have been tried and failed. A person who cannot make a brand new tape recorder function properly may try turning various control knobs in search of a quick, low-effort solution. But if the low-effort behavior fails, the individual will be motivated to pull out the instruction manual or ask an expert for advice. When faced with a new problem, people frequently try to apply their old skills before turning to the potentially more effortful behavior of locating and applying the appropriate rules. Naturally, people learn to discriminate that some activities are much more likely to require instructions than others. A cook who has had misfortune with French dishes may turn to a cookbook or advice from a friend for help with *Coquilles Saint-Jacques,* though the cook seldom uses rules when cooking other recipes. Once we discriminate that some problems are beyond our skills, we often turn to rules to cope with them if rule use has been reinforced by success in the past.

People often have problems running their own lives; and they may seek out or invent rules to use as self-instruction for solving their problems. After being bothered by obsessive thoughts, a person may formulate a self-instruction such as, "I've got to stop thinking about that." Many repetitions of rule use may be necessary to overcome difficult problems. People often carry on an extensive internal dialogue as they work at mastering the problem.[8] "Quit thinking such stupid thoughts. You'll only drag yourself down to depression." If these little bits of good advice alleviate the person's worries even temporarily, the success of the rule reinforces future rule use.

Context Cues

Rules always appear in a context, and various cues from the rule giver, audience, and surrounding environment serve as S^D's or S^Δ's that can increase or decrease the likelihood of rule use. If a close or respected friend suggests that we do something, we are more likely to respond than if a less close or less respected acquaintance had made the same suggestion. If we have received reinforcers for following rules given by a certain person in the past, we are more likely to follow future rules from this person. A serious tone of voice is often an S^D that increases the likelihood of rule use. If the rule is presented in a logical or sensible manner, the listener is more likely to follow the rule than if it were tossed out in a flip, trivial manner. If the rule sounds reasonable or helpful, its appeal will be enhanced.

Also, the authoritativeness of the source of the rule is important, along with the rule user's past experience with authority. An authoritative book—such as a famous cookbook or well-known manual on engine repair—is much more likely to lead to rule use than an unreliable text, especially for people who have learned to discriminate that accurate advice is valuable (that is, useful in attaining reinforcement). Authoritative advice from a doctor—"Your lung x-ray indicates that you had better stop smoking or else!"—is much more likely to have an effect than similar pleas from a friend or spouse. A given authority

---

[8]When people work on changing their own behavior, it is common for them to carry on internal conversations filled with self-instructions (Meichenbaum and Cameron, 1974; Mahoney and Thoresen, 1974; Watson and Tharp, 1981; Martin and Pear, 1983).

may not be respected by all people, of course. Advice from a law officer may cause one person to obey, but create rebelliousness and rule breaking in another. When a supervisor gives instructions on a production line, many of the workers may obey; but there are enough cases of sabotage by workers to show that some people have learned to respond hostilely to certain types of authority.[9]

Thus, many elements of the context that surrounds a rule can serve as S^D's and S^Δ's that determine how a person will respond to the rule. Because each individual has a unique socialization history, each person will tend to respond to a given rule and its context in a manner consistent with his or her prior learning.

EXPLICIT VERSUS IMPLICIT RULES

There is a continuum from explicit to implicit rules. Children usually need rather explicit rules if they are to succeed in following them. A vague rule, such as "Set the table, Billy," is not likely to produce satisfactory results; but an explicit rule, such as "Put napkins on the left side of each plate and come back and I'll tell you what to do next," is more likely to produce results that are rewarding for the parents.

As people gain experience with rule use, most learn to do rule-governed behavior in response to increasingly vague formulations of rules and statements in which a rule is only implicit. "The table, Joe," may be enough to get an adult to set the table when guests are expected. People even advance to the point where they can extract rules from verbal statements that were not actually rules in the first place. During a conversation, one person may mention that "Investment properties yielded a higher annual income than any other type of investment in Pogwash County last year, and the same is predicted for next year." The listener may respond to the sentence as if it were a rule to invest in property for best payoffs. The rule was *implicit* in the sentence, but extracting and following such unspoken rules require skills that come only with experience. (Naturally, a person may be skilled at locating implicit rules in some areas of life, but be insensitive to implicit rules in other areas, depending on past conditioning in each area.)

ON RULE GIVING

People learn to give rules to others because rules often provide a rapid way of helping— or forcing—another person to do specific responses which are reinforcing to the rule giver. The success of rules in modifying behavior in the desired direction increases the probability that the rule giver will give rules in the future. Parents usually find that telling children a rule, such as "Don't go in the street or you'll have to stay in the house," speeds their learning considerably. It helps children discriminate which behavior is forbidden and helps them do self-instructed, rule-governed behavior the next time they are about to dash into the street. If the children follow the rules, the parents' practice of giving rules will be reinforced.

[9]Björk (1975).

In many situations where shaping, observational learning, or prompting may take a long time to produce the desired behavior, a few seriously given rules can take effect immediately. If your chubby friend is on the way to the kitchen to get some peanuts, you may modify your friend's behavior by a tactfully worded rule such as, "Hey, I thought your new diet didn't allow you to eat peanuts." The rule may be effective in helping your friend realize that he didn't need peanuts after all, whereas shaping and modeling would not have worked nearly so efficiently.

Rules are especially important in facilitating learning and behavior change in the following circumstances:

1. *The reinforcers associated with a given behavior are too distant in the future to allow differential reinforcement to modify behavior.* A college student may receive few immediate reinforcers for diligent studying. By creating a rule, "I've got to study hard so I'll have an interesting career," the student allows future rewards to have more influence over current behavior.

2. *When reinforcers are few and far between, rules can keep a person going.* The door-to-door salesman may sell an encyclopedia only once in a hundred houses; yet the rule, "Keep going and you may sell another one today," helps link the rewards to the needed behavior.

3. *When severe punishment is involved, rules can help people avoid having to learn "the hard way."* Advice from a coworker—"Never mention that you are a Democrat in front of the boss or he'll fire you"—can help a person learn without ever having to be punished.

In some circumstances, rules sum up years of firsthand experience and pass it on to another person. A woman who has owned and run a shop for half her life has learned many skills for treating customers nicely, maintaining all items in stock, keeping the books accurately, and so forth. Much of this learning resulted from firsthand experience in her own shop: Success and failure served as the differential reinforcement that changed her behavior and gradually shaped a repertoire of skills. When the storekeeper hires new assistants, the easiest way to orient the assistants to the routine of the shop is to formulate rules. "Remember, the customer is always right." "When you leave the front room, close the cash register and lock it." What the woman learned the slow, painful way can be formulated in a few words and can prevent the assistants' having to learn the slow way, too. The woman may have learned by losing sales not to criticize or challenge customers; but the assistants learn by hearing the rule and by receiving either praise if they follow it well or reprimands if they fail to use it.

Learning from firsthand experience (the way the shopkeeper did) differs from learning by rules in several ways:[10]

1. When they are used correctly, rules usually produce more rapid learning than shaping during firsthand experience.

2. If the rules are formulated well, they can help the rule user avoid many of the

[10]Skinner (1969:139–171).

mistakes and aversive consequences that are involved in much of natural shaping and observational learning.

3. Rule-governed behavior often has a mechanical quality not found in behavior acquired by firsthand experience. The linear structure of language imposes a linear structure on rules: "Do A, then B, then C and D." The resulting behavior is often performed in more rigid steps than similar behavior learned by firsthand experience.

4. Learning from rules and learning from firsthand experience often involve different reinforcers and punishers. Gain or loss of customers taught the shopkeeper; whereas praise, raises, and reprimands teach the assistants.

5. All of these differences contribute to the fact that the person who was taught by rules knows different things than the person whose behavior was learned by other means. The shopkeeper knows the whole history of her running of the business, and she has a "feel" for the infinite complexities involved. The rule-using apprentices know the rules—a rigid list of dos and don'ts—but lack the shopkeeper's "feel" for whether or not to bend a rule in a given situation.

Thus, the person who creates rules tries to capture the essence of firsthand experience and pass this on to the rule user, but the two people are responding to their environment in different ways. The person who formulates a rule for a complex behavior will almost always be disappointed in the rule users' failure to understand the situation as well as the rule giver does. Even if the rule giver expands on the rule with several auxiliary rules, the less experienced rule user simply will not show all the finesse of the person who learned from firsthand experience. "I told my assistants a dozen times how to deal with grouchy old Mr. Wurtzel, but they never seem to handle him the way I want them to." One solution to the problem is to let the rule user gain some firsthand experience directly from the environment in order to supplement the learning begun with rules alone.

RULES PLUS FIRSTHAND EXPERIENCE

If the rule is simple and the operant is not difficult, a person may perform an operant flawlessly the first time, after hearing the rule only once. However, *when rules are complex and require operant performances that are beyond a person's present level of skills, the person may require extra, firsthand experience (differential reinforcement, shaping, observational learning, or prompts) to learn the behavior.* "Just follow the instructions on the video-display and the computer will do all the work for you," is an easy rule for people to follow if they have successfully operated computers in the past. However, the same instruction may be quite inadequate for the person who has never used a computer. While trying to follow these instructions, a novice might misunderstand several of the computer's prompts, enter several improper commands, and cause the system to malfunction. However, with a little extra instruction and several hours of firsthand experience at the computer keyboard, the novice will gradually gain the skills needed for successfully operating a variety of computer programs.

As a person gains firsthand experience with a new activity, early rule-governed behavior undergoes important changes. When people have had no prior experience with a complex behavior, they are likely to be clumsy and mechanical in their first attempts to follow the rule. *As people repeat rule-governed behavior several times and gain firsthand experience, the clumsy and mechanical early performances usually are smoothed out under the influence of differential reinforcement, shaping, observational learning, and prompting.* As people follow a rule, they gain firsthand experience that conditions more "natural," coordinated, and subtle behavior.

For example, a woman taking tennis lessons hears the rules for how to swing the racket, how to move across the court, how to use backhand, and so on. At first, the rule user's behavior looks much more rigid and mechanical than her teacher's. As the ball comes over the net, the student tries to think quickly, "Start with the left foot forward and prepare for a backhand, but don't cross the legs. Whoops, it's falling short!" Her response is slow. It lacks spontaneity. In a moment of hesitation, you can almost hear her thinking, "What should I do now?"

However, if the tennis student sticks with the game, her ability to apply and follow the rules will speed up with practice and firsthand experience. She will learn to discriminate more subtle S^D's and be able to learn finer variations on the rules. A fortunate twist of the wrist may put a nice spin on the ball and win a volley (positive reinforcement); but a clumsy move may produce the opposite result. Repeated differential reinforcement shapes more advanced skills than those that can be learned from verbal rules alone. Gradually, she begins to win more games. Watching a good model serve the ball provides additional learning experience, as does receiving a physical prompt on how to hold the arms. This extra learning helps smooth out the clumsiness of early rule-governed behavior, decrease some of the mechanicalness of pure rule use, and make the player look more like a "natural." (The "natural" is the person who never had lessons, but went out and learned an entire repertoire of behavior from firsthand experience, that is, from differential reinforcement, shaping, observational learning, and prompts.)

Since most rules are not entirely accurate, firsthand experience helps correct for errors or inadequacies in the rules. Few behavior patterns are so simple that the behavior can be described completely by a set of rules; hence, extra experience after learning the rules is crucial to fill in the gaps. Also, the person who formulates a rule may accidentally include some wrong advice or omit some important steps in explaining the behavior. One tennis coach may think that breathing is crucial and teach students many unnecessary rules about breathing. While focusing on breathing, the coach may have forgotten to mention some important points on footwork. While the coach's advice may mislead students who are struggling to learn the game, firsthand experience on the court will help the students learn the correct responses and compensate for the imperfect rules.

Not everyone gets a chance to have the needed firsthand experience. In some cases, rule givers become impatient when they observe that a rule receiver cannot perform the required behavior; and they may intercede in order to finish the task themselves rather than let the rule user struggle with the problem and gain firsthand experience. If a mother tells her young son how to string some beans for dinner, she may get a bit perturbed as the son fumbles along slowly and delays the casserole. If she takes over the task herself, however, she only prevents the child from learning the needed skills from direct experience with differential reinforcement. The perfectionist father may tell his daughter how to use the saw and drill, but then not let her help in building a bookcase for fear that her work will be less than perfect. The parent may be amazed at how little the child learns from him: "I've taught her all I know about carpentry, but this *thing* she made is an eyesore. This just proves that you can't teach females to do a male's job." After ten years, the daughter has finally built enough things to learn advanced skills via firsthand experience. Now the father says, "I taught her all I knew, and you can see that she turned out to be a darn good craftsman, just like her dad." When his daughter was young, the father failed to see the need for giving his daughter something more than rules; and ten years later, he failed to see that it was the extra firsthand experience that had refined her skills so nicely.

TACIT AND EXPLICIT KNOWLEDGE

When we compare two people who have learned similar behavior—but one learned from rules and the other without rules—we find that they know different things. The "natural" tennis player who never took lessons but learned from firsthand experience knows different things than the equally good player who originally learned from rules.

People who have learned a behavior from rules find it much easier to verbalize and talk about the behavior than if they had learned from firsthand experience only. Rule users learned the behavior by hearing others talk about it, so the behavior and talking about it go hand in hand. Much of the time they may be merely reiterating the rules that were given to them when they learned the activity; but they may be adding their own innovations based on those rules, too. Even when no one is asking them to verbalize about the behavior, they are likely to be thinking relevant words in their internal dialogue while doing the behavior (at least in the early phases before the behavior becomes well learned).

"Naturals" who did not learn by rules are generally less likely to talk or verbally think about how they are performing a given behavior. If someone asks them how they manage such a powerful and accurate backhand, they are likely to give a vague response such as, "You just swing and you know it's right when it feels right." They can describe the conspicuous parts of the behavior, "You just swing"; but the rule users would have added, "keeping your center of gravity in front of your feet so you can fall toward the stroke." "Naturals" are more likely to say, "You just have to get the feel for the right way." They are discriminating among various S^D's and S^Δ's that "feel" right or wrong, but many of these discriminative stimuli may be very hard for them to describe in words. How do you describe precise differences in the feelings of balance, muscle tension, knee bend, or arm stretching? Of course, if "naturals" receive reinforcement for creating rules, they usually learn to formulate verbal descriptions of their behavior. Since these verbal accounts appear *after* the behavior has been learned by firsthand experience, they should not be confused with the rules that guide rule-governed behavior. (Note that people who are "naturals" at one behavior may be rule users when doing another behavior. When we identify people as "naturals" in regard to a specific behavior, we are merely noting that this particular behavior was learned without rules, instructions, or lessons. Thus, being labeled a "natural" for one behavior does not indicate the existence of some universal personality trait that affects all behavior.[11])

[11]Mischel (1968, 1981).

The person who learned a behavior from rules thinks about the behavior in terms of rules and has explicit knowledge about the behavior. The person who learned from firsthand experience, without rules, is less likely to think about the behavior in terms of rules and has unspoken—or tacit—knowledge.[12] Rules provide people with *explicit knowledge* that is easy to verbalize and easy to share with others because the knowledge was verbally encoded from the start, when the person first heard the rules. Explicit knowledge is readily made public knowledge, since it is easy to communicate. Explicit knowledge makes people feel that they are consciously and verbally aware of the reasons for their behavior. "The coach says I should increase my running to 15 miles per day, five times a week, to build up my endurance." On the other hand, the "natural" is playing it by feel, often without verbal awareness of the causes of behavior. A person who is a natural at athletics exercises at a level that "feels" right. Naturals clearly know something about the behavior they do, but it is *tacit knowledge,* unspoken knowledge. It is personal knowledge as opposed to public knowledge, and it has an intuitive[13] quality since it is guided more by nonverbal sensations than by verbal instructions. Tacit knowledge is based on firsthand experience; and when the person dies, all the unique, personal knowledge of a lifetime dies, too. Public knowledge, encoded in rules, can be passed from person to person or through media, hence can outlive the rule formulator.[14] *Even though public knowledge is secondhand and sometimes crude, culturally accumulated rules help people learn more than any single person could learn in a lifetime from firsthand, personal experience alone.* Many people have tried jogging and injured themselves before learning the basic information contained in simple books for the beginning jogger.

Since "naturals" may not be skilled at accurately explaining how they perform their behavior or how they acquired the behavior, their behavior often appears more interesting, more mysterious, or more inexplicable than the behavior of rule users. Because a person who had guitar lessons can tell you the rules for learning to play, there is no mystery to the behavior. On the other hand, when a "natural" guitarist tells you that playing the guitar just came naturally, the causes for the behavior are less apparent, leaving more room for wonder. "She's really good and never had lessons. She must have a special musical talent!" It is not at all uncommon to see people receive more attention, respect, and admiration for a behavior that was not learned via rules. The "natural" athlete or artist tends to enthrall people's imaginations more than the athlete or artist who obviously studied technique and practiced prescribed exercises. Many people have realized this fact and kept quiet about how much they have practiced rule-governed behavior, pretending that they are "naturals" when they are not.[15]

Actually, "natural" behavior is no more mysterious than rule-governed behavior. Both are learned; only the method of learning differs. When we know all the prompting,

---

[12]Skinner (1969); Baldwin and Baldwin (1978a).

[13]Intuitive knowledge is not always correct (McCloskey, 1983). Of course, explicit knowledge is not always correct either, but it is easier to locate and correct errors in explicit knowledge than in intuitive (that is, tacit) knowledge (Skinner, 1969:167).

[14]Polanyi (1960).

[15]Goffman (1959) has observed that people will go to great lengths to cover up the fact that deliberate planning (rules) and extensive practice were involved in polishing a given behavior. Potter's (1948, 1951) advice clearly reflects that people who can hide their prior rule use and practice are likely to be "one up" on the person who cannot.

observational learning, and shaping that go into learning a "natural" behavior, it does not appear any more mysterious or difficult to explain than rule-governed behavior.

PEOPLE KNOW MORE THAN THEY CAN TELL[16]

It is clear that "naturals" know when their behavior feels right or feels wrong. These "feelings" result from S^D's, S^Δ's, and CS's that have been conditioned while the "natural" learned from models, prompts, and differential reinforcement. Tacit knowledge is clearly demonstrated when "naturals" are producing the behavior in question, but this knowledge is hard for them to describe. "Naturals" know more than they can tell.

Even rule users are likely to know more than they can tell, especially as firsthand experience conditions their behavior beyond the early phases of mechanical rule use. The rules they know may be very good for starting a new student in learning the behavior, but the rules do not tell the whole story. As additional firsthand experience adds extra complexity to the rule users' behavior, these people also develop tacit knowledge that goes beyond the original rules. Eventually, they too know more than they can tell.

Because people cannot tell all they know about complex behavior, communication concerning many areas of life tends to be sketchy. In trying to tell what they know, people often punctuate their explanation with phrases like, "You know what I mean?" "You know?" "Sort of like this," "Right?" When they are finished explaining, you may *not* be sure you know exactly what they meant. You know what I mean?

People are not used to locating rules for all their actions. Sketchiness is both common and accepted; being explicit is rarely demanded. People usually get quite irritated if too many "whys" are asked. It is true that many children go through a "why" stage in which they ask their parents a million "whys," but eventually the behavior is suppressed by punishment when adults get too aggravated. People cannot tell all they know and the child learns to live with incomplete information.

People often describe human behavior *as if* it were guided by rules or norms; and some seem to be quite surprised when people cannot describe the rules or norms that were presumed to be controlling their behavior. According to the behavioral analysis, much of everyday behavior is based on tacit knowledge gained without much assistance from rules. Thus, it is no wonder that people have little explicit verbal awareness about the exact procedures they use to negotiate their way through everyday life.[17]

THE PRESSURE TO INVENT RULES

When people are put in a situation where they have to explain their actions, there is a tendency for them to explain their behavior *as if* it were rule governed. If a woman is asked why she was so polite when dealing with a man who was stealing from the firm, her

[16]Polanyi (1960).

[17]Whenever they see regularly patterned behavior, some social scientists attempt to locate "norms" and "rules" for the behavior, as if all patterned behavior were rule-governed. This creates problems when the people they study cannot state any rules for the observed behavior. Scott (1971:72) has redefined the sociological notion of "norms" to include all regular patterns of sanctions, whether they be verbally mediated or not. This helps resolve problems such as those encountered by Caplow (1984).

answer may sound like a rule: "We must always be as considerate as possible in order to minimize unnecessary hostility toward the company." The woman has provided a *verbal account* of her behavior and this account sounds like it might be a rule that guides her behavior. However, in most cases it is difficult to determine whether such verbal accounts are ad hoc descriptions of "natural" behavior or accurate summations of rules that were used to guide rule-governed behavior.

Because behavior is the product of many influences besides rules, it is often unwise to infer that behavior is strictly rule governed even when people allude to rules to explain their activities. All too often verbal explanations do not reflect the real causes of behavior. People are especially handicapped in describing "natural" behavior because, first, it was learned without verbal instruction, and, second, most people are not aware of how differential reinforcement, models, and prompts affect their behavior. Hence, they find it hard to explain the real causes of behavior.

Even when people do not know why they did a certain behavior, they may create any of a large number of feasible verbal accounts for it. Creating a credible account—especially an intelligent sounding one—usually leads to more reinforcement than not saying anything, thus appearing ignorant about one's own actions. When asked why he double-parked, the driver might answer, "I don't know—I just did it." Or he might say, "I was in a hurry and I figured that I would be in the shop for such a short time that I'd never get a ticket." The second explanation sounds like the person rationally planned the behavior; and because it sounds a little more intelligent than the first answer, it is more likely to be instrumental in avoiding criticism. An answer such as "I don't know—I just did it" is virtually asking for a critical rejoinder, "The next time you ought to think before you do something stupid like that." By making behavior *sound* like it was rational and rule guided, people avoid some of this criticism. As a result, *most of us learn to talk as if our behavior were rational, planned out, and rule governed, even if this is not the case.* The more skilled people become in inventing reasonable and intelligent sounding accounts, the more likely they are to escape aversive consequences and to be admired for their intelligence.

In much of everyday life, it is not possible to know if one account is more accurate than another; hence, listeners cannot easily differentially reinforce accurate accounts while punishing or extinguishing inaccurate ones. As a result, there can be considerable differences between people's verbal explanations of their behavior and the actual causes of behavior. When "natural" behavior is described in terms of rational planning, rules, or norms, "natural" behavior may appear to be rule governed when it is not.

So much of everyday behavior is influenced by complex mixtures of differential reinforcement, models, and prompts that verbal accounts in terms of rules often mask the actual determinants of behavior with a simplistic cover story. Even if rules were used in the initial acquisition of a behavior, all the extra firsthand experience that polishes rule-governed behavior into a more natural performance is rarely captured by restating the rules in simple verbal accounts. A thorough analysis of behavior can be hindered by assuming that verbal accounts of behavior always reflect the rules that guide behavior. Anyone who tries to explain behavior by referring to rules or norms should be wary of this problem. The mere fact that people say they did something because of such-and-such a rule or norm does not necessarily justify the assumption that the rule or norm was among the key controlling factors of the behavior. Behavioral science can help us see through the biases in people's accounts of their own actions and focus on the broader range of behavioral determinants—differential reinforcement, shaping, models, prompts, and rules. This broader view of behavior helps us gain a better understanding of ourselves and others, which is useful in coping effectively with the complexities of everyday life.

CONCLUSION

The capacity for language allows humans to symbolically encode information as rules that can guide behavior. These verbal rules appear in many formats, from strong commands to gentle advice. Some rules are very explicit statements of the contingencies of reinforcement: In the presence of a given set of S^D's do a specific behavior and certain reinforcing consequences will follow. In contrast, many rules are only vaguely stated; and some verbal statements are not presented as rules even though a skillful rule user may be able to extract information from the statement and respond to the information with rule-governed behavior. Rules have the ability to guide behavior only because following rules in the past has been reinforced. Depending on each individual's unique history of prior reinforcement, various rules and context cues become S^D's and S^Δ's for following or not following any given rule in a given context. People also learn to create and give rules to others because these practices often produce reinforcing results. However, rules alone are seldom adequate to produce the desired behavioral output unless the rule user has other learning experience gained from differential reinforcement, models, and prompts. Thus, rule-governed behavior usually merges into the other types of behavior learned without rules. Even when people describe their behavior *as if* it were completely directed by rules, it is likely that other types of learning were involved, although these other types of learning are more difficult to describe because they are less likely to be mediated by words.

Superimposed on all the considerations described in this and the previous chapters are several remaining behavioral variables of importance in everyday life. The next three chapters describe schedules of reinforcement, the influences of positive and negative control, and thinking. These three important determinants influence behavior, no matter whether the behavior is learned by differential reinforcement, observation, prompts, or rules.

12

Schedules

● *In this chapter you will learn how different patterns of reinforcement—different timing and spacing of consequences—affect behavior.*

Behavior is not always followed by reinforcement or punishment. On one day a salesman may give his pitch to ten customers with the result of a reinforcing sale each time. However, the next day may be a "slow" day, and every one of the ten potential customers may decide not to buy the product. *The patterns of reinforcement that are associated with a given operant are called schedules of reinforcement.* There are schedules of punishment, too. In some towns speeders are picked up each and every time they exceed the speed limits; but in other locations, arrests are made less frequently, and individual speeders may be punished only one time in twenty that they break the law. *The patterns of punishment that are associated with a given operant are called schedules of punishment.*[1]

There are many possible schedules of reinforcement and punishment, and these can be combined to produce compound schedules. Each type of schedule has specific effects on behavior, and these effects are superimposed on the effects created by differential reinforcement, models, prompts, and rules. This chapter describes the major types of schedules that have been systematically studied and their characteristic effects on behavior.

[1]There has been considerably less research on the schedules of punishment than on the schedules of reinforcement (Walters and Grusec, 1977).

THE UBIQUITOUS EFFECTS OF SCHEDULES

Schedules are among the most powerful determinants of behavior.[2] All reinforcers and punishers are embedded in one schedule or another, and each type of schedule has its own characteristic effects on behavior. Hence schedule effects are ubiquitous. In addition, they interact with and influence other variables—such as satiation or deprivation, generalization or discrimination—to produce the complexity and variety of behavior seen in everyday life. Since any response may be under the control of several schedules, the effects of these schedules can interact and influence each other.

Past schedules of reinforcement or punishment often have a powerful influence on current behavior, making it important to know the past schedules in order to understand present responses. Two examples will illustrate this.

Some parents use monetary rewards to encourage their children to work hard at school. If one set of parents gave their ten year old a dollar for every "A" and another set of parents rewarded their child with the same total amount of money but on a more irregular basis, how would the different schedules of reinforcement affect the children's behavior? When a behavior is reinforced each and every time it occurs, the pattern is called a *continuous reinforcement* (CRF) schedule. When reinforcement occurs only a portion of the time, the pattern is called a *partial reinforcement* (PR) schedule.

After two people have learned a given operant—one under CRF and the other under PR schedules—they respond differently when reinforcement for the operant is withdrawn. In times of nonreinforcement (i.e., extinction), people who had learned on CRF schedules generally stop responding much faster than people who had learned on PR schedules. During extinction, the ten year old who had always been given a dollar for every A would stop working for A's before a second student who had received reinforcers less regularly. Once the parents stop giving dollars for grades, the student who had been on PR would continue working harder for A's than the student who had been on CRF. The reason for this partial reinforcement effect is explained later in the chapter.

When there is a slow, gradual change from reinforcement to punishment schedules, often a person will continue to emit a response long after the punishment outweighs the reinforcement.[3] This is less likely if the shift is not gradual. For example, when a person first plays a slot machine, the behavior may be followed by a few lucky wins, along with novelty and social reinforcement. However, the novelty of the game slowly wears off after repeated play. Social attention for stories of tonight's adventures with the slots also drops off as others cease to find the stories novel and no longer reward the slot player with attentive listening for telling them. When there is a *slow removal of reinforcement* for a given operant, people often continue responding even when they are losing (that is, being punished). Some slot players continue playing even though they are losing $20 a night at an activity that has lost most of its novelty and brings social punishment in the form of criticism from others.

If another person had experienced a rapid removal of reinforcement and rapid onset

[2]Ferster and Skinner (1957); Dews (1963:148); Morse and Kelleher (1970, 1977); Zeiler (1977); Foltin and Schuster (1982).

[3]Weiner (1965, 1969).

of social criticism for playing the slots, this person would be less likely to continue playing when losing $20 a night. If the first big win were followed by 100 straight losses in which not a single cent was won, it would be easier to give up the game than if an occasional small win reinforced the expectation that another big win could come at any moment.

In both the above examples, past schedules play a decisive role in determining how people respond to the same set of present schedules of reinforcement and punishment. Behavior is controlled by both past and present reinforcers and punishers.

ACQUISITION AND MAINTENANCE

Reinforcement is needed for both the acquisition of new behavior and the maintenance of old behavior. *When an operant is first being learned (the acquisition phase), it is often under different schedules of reinforcement than it will be at later times (the maintenance phase).* Generally, a higher frequency of reinforcement is required to produce the acquisition of new responses than to maintain old responses. Thus, reinforcement may be more conspicuous during acquisition than maintenance. As a result, it sometimes appears that well-learned old responses do not even need reinforcement.

The fact that reinforcement is often less frequent and conspicuous during maintenance misleads some to believe that the maintenance of old behavior is automatic, and not dependent on reinforcement. It is common to hear people say that so-and-so "learned his lesson" or "internalized the values of the group." This implies that getting the lesson or the values into the person (the acquisition phase) is the only process needed to modify and produce behavior. However, behavior does not remain in a person's active behavior repertoire unless there continue to be reinforcers which maintain the frequency of the response.

For instance, personal hygiene—behavior we acquire early in life—requires reinforcement to be maintained. During toilet training we all learn (or "internalize") hygienic practices. The praise and punishment that parents use in toilet training make it quite obvious that acquisition depends on reinforcement and punishment. Once the responses are acquired, however, they *appear* to be rather automatic. But are they? Is their maintenance independent of reinforcement?

A study on people working as fish wardens demonstrates what can happen to hygienic behavior when maintenance schedules are changed.[4] College students who served as fish wardens spent the summer camping along the rivers of Alaska to watch for illegal fishing. Each warden was dropped at an inlet to live and work alone for the summer. When the wardens first made camp, they usually set up a latrine at a respectable distance from camp, such that the latrine was out of sight and "private." For the first several days or weeks, the wardens went to the latrine to relieve themselves, much as one would expect from a person who had learned good hygienic practices. However, walking to the latrine took effort, and no one was around to provide social reinforcement for maintaining hygienic practices. By the end of the summer, the wardens no longer left

[4]Scott (1971:180).

camp to relieve themselves, even though the buildup of excrement near the tent resulted in strong odors and poor hygiene. One of the first "civilized" habits to be acquired in childhood can be lost if social reinforcement is removed. Upon returning to civilization, the wardens resumed good hygienic practices due to the reestablishment of the maintenance schedules of social reinforcement.

People in mental hospitals and homes for the aged sometimes begin to urinate and defecate in their clothing.[5] In some cases they clearly get more attention and reinforcement for this behavior than they receive for hygienic practices. Again, when the maintenance schedules that operate in normal social life are disrupted, well-learned behavior extinguishes.

Clearly, maintenance schedules are as important as the more obvious schedules of reinforcement seen in the acquisition of new behavior.

FIXED RATIO SCHEDULES[6]

If a response is reinforced after a fixed number of repetitions, the schedule is called a fixed ratio schedule, or FR schedule. If every single response is reinforced, the behavior is on an FR 1 schedule, indicating that the fixed ratio is one response per reinforcer. (This is also called a continuous reinforcement or CRF schedule.) When there must be two responses before reinforcement, the behavior is on an FR 2 schedule. FR 10 indicates that ten responses must occur before reinforcement. The ratio number can be any number, but different ratios have different effects on behavior.

FR 1 schedules of reinforcement are the most efficient in producing rapid acquisition of behavior. People learn quickly when each correct response is reinforced. If parents want their child to learn to be polite, they will model politeness then reward the child every time the child is polite. Young children who receive loving words, caring smiles, or tender touches each time they are polite or considerate acquire these skills much faster than children who are rewarded less frequently or less consistently. Parents who value seeing their children make rapid progress often learn to use the continuous reinforcement of FR 1 schedules because they—the parents—are rewarded by seeing the rapid progress their child makes with continuous reinforcement.

Skillful teachers also learn the importance of giving continuous reinforcement during the early phases of acquisition. The continuous use of positive words and enthusiastic smiles makes learning maximally reinforcing. When the flying instructor watches the new student use the controls in the cockpit, the use of continuous reinforcement—"That's right," "Good," "Well done"—for every correct response is the best schedule for the rapid acquisition of flying skill. The tennis coach who gives positive feedback to the novice for each and every good play is also providing the best schedule of reinforcement for producing rapid learning.

Also, FR 1 schedules continue to produce high rates of responding even after a

---

[5]Schwartz and Stanton (1950:404–416); Walen et al. (1977:65–105).

[6]For more information on specific schedules, see Ferster and Skinner (1957); Nevin (1971b), Williams (1973:43f).

behavior is established. Some factories use an FR 1 schedule called piecework, in which the employee is paid for each piece of work that is finished. Thus, an employee might earn $50 on the day that he or she finished fifty pieces, but earn only $35 on a day in which thirty-five pieces were finished. Most people respond by working very fast on this type of FR 1 schedule:[7] after all they can double their salary by doubling their speed. Speeding up the pace of activity sometimes makes the work more stimulating, challenging, and exciting,[8] but it can also create considerable strain. Unions and labor groups usually oppose the use of FR 1 schedules because they fear that once workers increase their output, management will cut the amount paid per piece, which would leave the employees working harder for less.[9]

FR 1 schedules of punishment produce rapid response suppression and maintain low rates of responding. Parents who punish their child every time the child runs into the street are more likely to suppress the behavior quickly than if they punished the response every fifth time (FR 5) or every tenth time (FR 10). The flight instructor who criticizes the student for each error is more likely to suppress these undesired responses quickly than if punishment were less frequent.

Many nonsocial reinforcers and punishers also appear on FR 1 schedules. Every time a child picks up a crayon correctly, the child is rewarded by being able to make colorful lines, and the child's clumsy early responses are quickly replaced by effective ones. Every time people get their fingers too close to the fire, they get burned. Learning proceeds rapidly! Many skills learned from nonsocial FR 1 schedules are acquired quickly and maintained all through life due to the strong control of these schedules.

Although FR 1 schedules are the most common fixed ratio schedule in everyday life, there are higher ratio FR schedules, too. Turning the handle of a crank that pulls a water bucket out of a well requires a fixed number of turns to bring the bucket to the top. If thirty-five turns were needed, cranking would be on an FR 35 schedule. Whenever a precise number of responses is needed to complete an activity, behavior is on an FR schedule. "Mix five eggs and three cups of flour," involves an FR 5 schedule and an FR 3 schedule. "Remove the six transmission bolts" is an FR 6 schedule. Work on assembly lines often involves repeating the same number of responses over and over: soldering nine leads in a stereo tuner (FR 9), sewing six belt loops onto pants (FR 6), welding four seams in a casing (FR 4).

FR schedules tend to produce high rates of responding, often with a pause after each reinforcer. For example, a drill press operator may have to drill twenty-five precision holes in an engine block to complete a piece of work worth $1. The operator is on an FR 25 schedule where every twenty-fifth drilling response is reinforced by the dollar earned. On this FR 25 schedule, workers will usually drill all twenty-five holes at a steady pace, then take a short pause at the completion of the twenty-fifth. Generally, the higher the ratio, the longer the pause. If a worker had to drill forty holes to finish one piece, the FR 40 schedule would tend to produce a steady rate of responding while drilling all forty holes, then a long pause at the end, before beginning the next piece. Figure 12–1 shows

[7]Lincoln (1946).
[8]Roy (1953).
[9]Homans (1974:99).

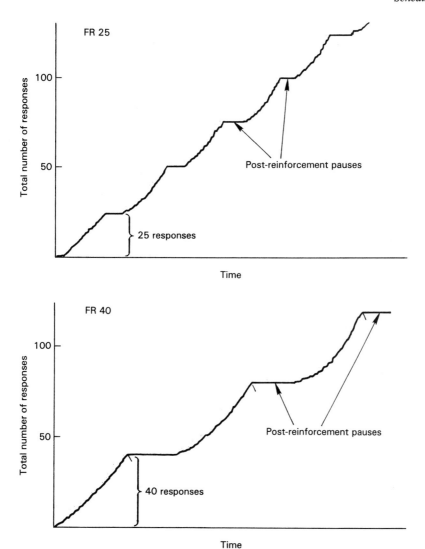

FIGURE 12–1   The cumulative record of responses on FR 25 and FR 40 schedules. Each reinforcement is marked by a slash. Note the longer post-reinforcement pauses on the thinner schedule.

that the *post-reinforcement pause* after the fortieth response on an FR 40 schedule is longer than the post-reinforcement pause after the twenty-fifth response on an FR 25 schedule.

As the ratio number on FR schedules increases, the person has to work longer for the same amount of reinforcement. Increasing the ratio number is called *stretching* or *thinning* the schedule of reinforcement. Typically, the thinner a ratio becomes, the less a person works at it and the longer the post-reinforcement pauses. The pause is actually the result of extinction. After a drill press operator finishes forty holes and experiences the reinforcement of thinking of the dollar earned, the next thirty-nine responses will not be reinforced. Thus, finishing the last piece is an S^Δ correlated with nonreinforcement for the next responses, and S^Δ's control nonresponding. As a result, the first few responses after the post-reinforcement pause tend to be slow, with short pauses between them. However, after the first few responses are emitted, the person responds at a rapid, steady pace because rapidity leads to earlier reinforcement. *Hence, FR schedules tend to produce rapid responding, interspersed with post-reinforcement pauses; and the higher the ratio of the schedule, the longer the pauses.* This produces cumulative records with characteristic "scallop" shaped curves. After each post-reinforcement pause, there is a slow start-up, then increasingly rapid responding as the end of the schedule—and reinforcement—draws near.

If ratios become *too high,* extinction can outweigh reinforcement and the person stops responding. You can ask a child to count to 20 and expect twenty responses as the child completes the entire FR 20 schedule; but what if you ask the child to count to 200, or 2000? At FR 2000, the schedule has been stretched too far to produce much behavior.

Punishment can also occur on FR schedules other than FR 1. One person may get a "second chance" (FR 2) before receiving punishment. Another person may get three chances (FR 3). In general, punishment becomes less effective in suppressing behavior as the ratio number increases.[10]

VARIABLE RATIO SCHEDULES

It may take an average of three twists to unscrew bottle lids. Some come off with one twist and others take five. Bottle lid twisting is on a VR 3 schedule, averaging three turns per bottle, but varying from bottle to bottle. Variability is a common feature of everyday life, thus variable ratio schedules are more common than fixed ratio schedules. It may take twenty swings with an ax to fell one tree and sixty swings to fell the next. Twenty sentences may convince one listener to sign your petition for stricter pollution control, but sixty sentences may be needed to persuade the next person. *Whenever reinforcement comes after a variable number of responses, the schedule is called a variable ratio (VR) schedule.*

When one person is teaching a second person a new skill, it is common to see the teacher begin with FR 1 schedules of reinforcement to produce fast early learning, then switch to variable ratio (VR) schedules as the student gains competence. The flight instructor may give continuous reinforcement (FR 1) as the beginning pilot learns the early skills. However, when the new pilot begins to master flying skills, the instructor is likely to stop using FR 1 schedules and reinforce every fourth correct response (on the average), then later, every tenth correct response (on the average). The instructor is "stretching the schedule," thinning out the number of reinforcers given for correct responses, and thus shifting the trainee from an FR 1 to a VR 4, then a VR 10 schedule. On a VR 10 schedule, the number of responses needed to produce reinforcement might vary from five to fifteen—or any other numbers—as long as it averaged ten. The flight

---

[10]Walters and Grusec (1977:71f).

instructor is stretching the schedule because it takes less effort to give intermittent reinforcement than to give continuous reinforcement. Hence, thinning the schedule is negatively reinforced because the teacher is avoiding the effort of giving continuous reinforcement, once it is clear that the student is successfully acquiring the responses.

VR schedules are quite adequate for reinforcing behavior as a person moves from the acquisition phase to the maintenance phase. (In fact, as we will see, VR schedules are better than FR 1 for producing resistance to extinction and enhancing maintenance in a broad range of settings.) However, performance is likely to be interrupted if a schedule is thinned too fast; thus the teacher will be punished if he or she stretches the schedule faster than the student can tolerate.

Parents usually do not reinforce each and every desired response that their child emits (FR 1); nor do they count responses and reinforce precisely every fifth or tenth response (FR 5 or FR 10). Instead, their patterns of reinforcement may vary considerably, perhaps averaging one reinforcer for every five desired responses (VR 5). In social interaction, we do not always tell other people when they have chosen their words well; but every once in awhile someone says, "That was a colorful choice of words." This intermittent use of reinforcement may not provide enough reinforcers to produce rapid acquisition of colorful word use; but it is adequate to maintain the response in the behavior repertoire of the person who already has the skill. Friendly compliments on any of a person's skills—how they sew, dress, dance, treat others—help maintain the skills, even if the reinforcers are few and far between.

VR schedules usually produce more variable response patterns than FR schedules do. An FR 10 schedule tends to produce ten rapid responses followed by a post-reinforcement pause. A VR 10 schedule also produces behavior patterns that contain pauses; but the pauses are briefer and more randomly interspersed among the responses. A writer may work for 5, 10, or 15 days without having a story accepted for publication or without even hearing a compliment on his or her work. The next reinforcer is quite unpredictable— maybe tomorrow, maybe next week. During a period in which several articles were completed, the writer may pound out six pages a night for weeks in a row, then after a low period with no positive feedback, the writer may have a period in which little gets written.

As is shown in Figure 12–2, response rate is usually quite high and there are few post-reinforcement pauses when the variable reinforcers come frequently (e.g., VR 10); but the response rate can drop off to a sporadic low rate when the variable schedule becomes too stretched out, too thin (e.g., VR 75). If a writer hears encouraging feedback on a VR 75 schedule—in which positive feedback comes only after writing perhaps seventy or eighty pages—the rate of writing may become irregular, and the writer may produce only a few pages at a time on a very unpredictable basis. The writer's low productivity results from the high ratio of extinction to reinforcement.

Numerous other activities are on VR schedules of reinforcement: for example, hunting, fishing, sales, begging, horse betting, card games, scientific research. There is no fixed relationship between the number of responses and reinforcement. A salesperson may have to talk to two, four, ten, or twenty customers before making the next sale. A gambler may have to make three, five, or nine bets before getting a winner. In all VR schedules, people with the skills to keep the ratio numbers low will experience more reinforcement and show higher rates of responding. People with the skills needed to pick winning horses are usually much more devoted to betting on the horses than people who

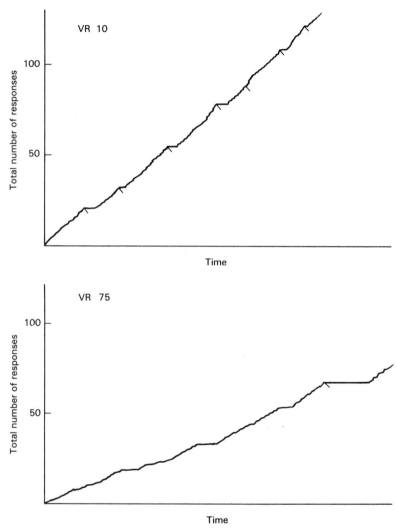

FIGURE 12–2 The cumulative record of responses on VR 10 and VR 75 schedules. Each reinforcement is marked by a slash. Note the long post-reinforcement pause and slow rate of responding on the thinner schedule.

lose almost all the time (unless the losers are getting other rewards for betting—such as being with friends or avoiding work).[11]

Punishment often appears on VR schedules. VR punishment is less effective than FR 1 punishment of the same intensity, but it can still suppress behavior. A study on preschool children showed that VR 4 punishment was almost as effective as FR 1 punishment; and it had the advantages of first, requiring less effort by the teachers and, second, being less aversive for the students (who were punished for only one misdeed in four).[12]

[11]Rosecrance (1984).
[12]Clark et al. (1973).

Speeders do not get arrested every time they exceed the speed limit; but a series of traffic tickets on a VR schedule may eventually suppress their speeding. At a cocktail party, the hostess offers a guest another drink. The guest says, "This must be about my fourth drink." The hostess replies in a sarcastic tone, "This is your sixth. But who counts?" Someone counts! And punishment for overdrinking may come on a VR 4 or VR 6 schedule, depending on who is counting.

FIXED INTERVAL SCHEDULES

There are many circumstances in which behavior cannot be reinforced or punished until a fixed interval of time has elapsed. After that fixed interval, the first response is reinforced. These are fixed interval, or FI, schedules. If the interval is one minute, the schedule is designated as FI 1 minute. If the interval is one day, the schedule is designated as FI 1 day. The interval can be any length. The person who finds the evening news on TV to be very stimulating and reinforcing is on an FI 1 day schedule. Every twenty-four hours, turning on the TV after the fixed interval has elapsed is reinforced by seeing the news. Not unexpectedly, the news lover learns to turn on the TV at about the same time each night. Fixed interval schedules tend to produce patterns of responding in which responses are timed to occur near the point where reinforcement first becomes available. When two lovers live in different cities and one phones the other each night at 9:00, the other may notice that as 9:00 rolls around, there is a tendency to hang around the phone, to pick it up after the first ring, and to make sure roommates are not on the phone. When important reinforcers are timed precisely, our behavior becomes timed. Obviously, clocks and watches help people time responses closer to the crucial fixed interval than would be possible without these mechanical aids.

On FI schedules, the first appropriate response after a fixed time interval has elapsed is reinforced.[13] Increasing the interval length usually increases the time gap between clusters of responses and lowers the total number of responses.

Fixed interval schedules are often coupled with a *limited hold*. The first appropriate response after the interval has elapsed is reinforced; but if the appropriate response does not occur during the limited hold period, reinforcement ceases to be available. If the news comes on at 7:00 and ends at 7:30, there is a 30-minute limited hold. After the limited hold has ended, turning on the TV is no longer reinforced by seeing the news. The limited hold schedule usually conditions people to respond during the hold period, because only responses emitted during the hold period are reinforced.

VARIABLE INTERVAL SCHEDULES

In everyday life, most interval schedules are not as perfectly fixed as the schedules of TV programs, election days, the return of Halley's comet, or other rigorously timed events. Life is more variable. The mail carrier usually comes around 10:00 A.M., but the timing

---

[13]In the laboratory, the next interval does not begin until the behavior is emitted. In everyday life, intervals often begin at a fixed length of time from the start of the previous interval, independent of the occurrence or timing of the behavior involved.

may vary from 9:00 A.M. to noon. The schedule is a variable interval—VI 24-hour schedule—with intervals averaging 24 hours, though variations of an hour or more are common. *On VI schedules, the first appropriate response after a variable time interval has elapsed is reinforced.*

Variable interval schedules produce more variable behavior and higher rates of responding than FI schedules do. If the mail came *precisely* at 10:00 each day (FI 24-hour

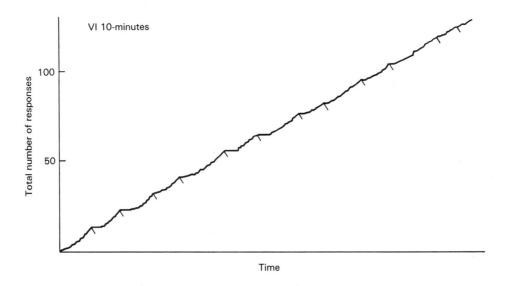

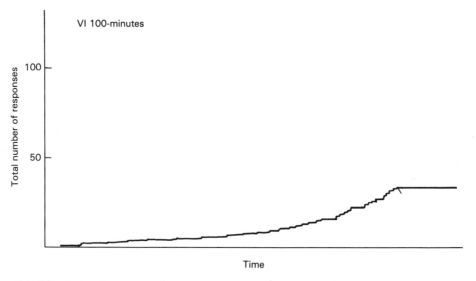

FIGURE 12–3   The cumulative record of responses on VI 10-minute and VI 100-minute schedules. Note the slow initial rate of responding on the long interval schedule.

schedule), people would never go to the box before 10:00, and would make only one trip after 10:00. The VI schedule is different. People start looking out the window for signs of the mail carrier by 9:00. Some go to the mailbox two or three times before the mail carrier comes. Their behavior is less predictable than if the mail came precisely at 10:00, because *any* time might be mail time. In the past, they may have received reinforcers for checking the mail at 9:15, 9:45, 10:30, 10:45, 11:30, and various other times; hence variable responding has been reinforced. VI schedules can produce very unpredictable behavior since different people may have received reinforcers at any of a variety of time intervals. Some parents reward and punish their children on VI schedules, timed according to the changing whims and emotions of the parents, rather than contingent on the child's misbehavior. Not surprisingly, this method of child rearing produces variable results.

When the average intervals are short, VI schedules can produce high rates of responding, hence they can be effective maintenance schedules. If the busses run at frequent but variable intervals (VI 10-min), people may look several times a minute to see if a bus is coming. However, if the busses only run every 1 or 2 hours (VI 100-min), few people will look for the bus during the half hour after the last bus, and looking will only gradually increase in frequency as the time passes (Figure 12–3).

A variable interval schedule may be linked with a *limited hold*. Old folks may like to chat with the neighbor children when the children are outside. The children may come out on variable schedules and be around for only a few minutes before heading down the street. If the old folks peek out the window frequently, they may see when the children are around and be able to initiate a rewarding interaction. Because the children usually leave after being outside for a few minutes, the old folks have to check more often and respond quickly when the children are present than if the children stayed in their yard. Thus *both* variable interval and limited hold increase the rate of responding compared with fixed interval and no hold.

Variable interval schedules are operating whenever we see people waiting for unpredictable events. When refugees are escaping a war-torn city or disaster area, it is hard to know when the next boat or plane will leave. Each boat or plane is on limited hold since it fills up rapidly and leaves no room for additional passengers. The refugees learn quickly to check frequently to see if a new boat or plane has arrived and to respond rapidly when it does.

SCHEDULE EFFECTS

Figure 12–4 shows the typical cumulative records produced on the four types of schedules discussed in the preceding sections (if the schedules have not been stretched too far). It is clear that variable schedules tend to produce more uninterrupted and faster responding than do fixed schedules. Fixed schedules are interrupted with longer post-reinforcement pauses that reduce overall rates of responding. On variable schedules that are not too thin, there are numerous occasions in which a few fast responses produce several reinforcers in rapid succession, and these periods of frequent reinforcement for fast responding cause people to learn to respond at high rates. After several wins in a row on the slot machines, people learn that fast responding can be very rewarding, and they continue rapid responding, even if the last fifteen plays have not produced a single win.

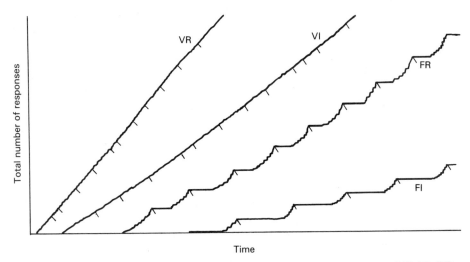

FIGURE 12–4   Cumulative records showing typical response patterns on VR, VI, FR, and FI schedules (if they have not been stretched too far). Each reinforcement is marked by a slash.

In addition, ratio schedules usually produce more rapid responding than interval schedules, as can be seen from their steeper slopes. On all ratio schedules, the faster you respond, the more the rewards you obtain. This is not true of interval schedules, where time intervals determine when reinforcement next becomes possible. Turning on the TV set six times a day does not make the 7:00 P.M. news come any faster, so fast responding is extinguished on interval schedules.

Behavioral Contrast

Switching from one type of schedule to a very different type can have significant behavioral effects, called *behavioral contrast*. When people switch from a thin schedule to a highly reinforcing one, they often respond quite differently from people who have always been on the highly reinforcing schedule. For example, when poor refugees first arrive in the United States—where their labors earn much greater wealth than was possible in the "old country"—they often work much harder than Americans who have lived here for a long time. For any given job, the work and pay schedules are identical for both the refugees and the Americans, but the refugees tend to work harder because the rewards are so much greater than in the old country, where the refugees had been on a thin schedule. (After enough time the immigrants slow down to work at the same speed as the Americans.)

When people are suddenly shifted from a very generous schedule to a very thin one, they act differently from people who have been on a thin schedule for a long time. When well-paid workers are forced to take a big cut in salary or forced to switch to unrewarding jobs, they often become angry and stop working. This again is behavioral contrast. (If they cannot negotiate pay increases or find better jobs, they may finally accommodate to working on thin schedules of reinforcement.)

Partial Reinforcement Effects

If reinforcement follows an operant only part of the time, the operant is on a schedule of partial reinforcement, also called intermittent reinforcement. VR and FR schedules (except for FR 1) produce partial reinforcement. VI schedules—and, to a lesser extent, FI schedules—usually involve partial reinforcement because people frequently produce several responses for each single reinforcer received. Partial reinforcement (PR) is often very effective in maintaining behavior.

Shifting people to progressively thinner ratio schedules is especially effective in maintaining behavior, because it produces persistence, or "stick-to-it-iveness." When children are first given jig-saw puzzles, they frequently begin with such simple puzzles that it is easy to put each piece in the correct location after one, two, or three attempts: This is a VR 2 schedule that provides rather high levels of reinforcement for early learning. Over time, the parents may bring the child puzzles of gradually increasing difficulty. As the puzzles become more complex, the child may have to make ten or twenty attempts at placing a piece before finding the correct position (VR 15). As the child gradually accommodates to these schedules of partial reinforcement, the child learns to keep working at a puzzle even when the last fifteen, twenty, or twenty-five attempts at placing a piece have failed. After being on a VR 15 schedule for some time, the child learns that eventually each piece will fit in somewhere. Sticking to the task inevitably leads to reinforcement, "if you just keep trying." Sometimes it only takes one or two tries; sometimes it takes twenty-five or thirty tries. But in the end, there is always success: Persistence pays off. After children have accommodated to the thin PR schedules of difficult puzzles, they often show an amazing persistence in working puzzles, trying dozens of pieces in every possible location even though most of their moves result in failure. They have learned to be persistent, to persevere in the face of failure. They have learned "stick-to-it-iveness."

In contrast, children who are shifted to difficult puzzles too rapidly experience high rates of failure. The rapid shift to thin schedules may cause these children to become frustrated and quit doing puzzles before they learn persistence. It usually takes a series of gradual shifts to progressively thinner PR schedules to produce behavioral persistence.

Sometimes the persistence created by the gradual thinning of PR schedules is admirable; sometimes it is a nuisance. It depends on whether the behavior in question is desirable or undesirable. We usually consider it admirable when a person is persistent at desirable behavior. The child who does not give up on difficult homework problems may eventually solve the problems, thereby learning more than the child who gave up before finding the solution. The minority group leader who keeps fighting for the rights of his or her people in spite of frequent failure and only limited success is admired for dedication and determination. The diplomat who keeps trying to work out a peaceful settlement between hostile nations—and does not give up in spite of countless failures—may eventually negotiate a treaty that averts war and saves thousands of lives. In all areas of life, there are many admirable people who have the stick-to-it-iveness to withstand long periods of failure and eventually accomplish important tasks when others would have quit trying long before.

However, when people show persistence at undesirable behavior, they are often thought of as nuisances. A little boy who whines and whimpers for hours at a time may be on a thin PR schedule, if the parents give in every so often and let him have his way. One reinforcement every couple of hours can maintain the whining quite effectively. The child has learned that if he whines long enough, the parents will give in. Military governments often think of guerillas in the hinterlands as nuisances: Even though the guerillas may only have rare successes in fighting the government, they are persistent in their efforts because occasionally their efforts are successful. Note that behavior that is judged as undesirable to one group may be judged as desirable to another: The government sees the persistent guerillas as a nuisance, and the people who hate the government see the persistent guerillas as being courageous freedom fighters.

One of the most important effects of partial reinforcement is seen when behavior is shifted to extinction: A history of prior PR helps maintain behavior even after all reinforcement is withdrawn, that is, during extinction. *Behavior that has been on schedules of partial reinforcement is more resistant to extinction than behavior that has been on continuous reinforcement.* Let us contrast the behavior of two children, both of whom throw tantrums (Figure 12–5). Connie has received continuous reinforcement for tantrums, and Patti, partial reinforcement. That is, every time Connie throws a tantrum, her parents give in and let her have her way. Patti's parents have two other children and have stopped responding to most tantrums. Without knowing it, Patti's parents have put her on a VR 6 schedule (which is a partial reinforcement schedule). When Connie and Patti enter kindergarten, the teacher finds the tantrums disruptive and suggests to their parents that they use behavior modification to eliminate the tantrums. The teacher and both sets of parents decide to extinguish the behavior. Both at school and at home, they will remove all reinforcement for tantrums by not paying any attention when the child has a tantrum.

How do the children respond during extinction? On the first day of extinction after continuous reinforcement, Connie has *more* tantrums than she had been having before. However, the frequency of her tantrums declines rapidly over the next few days of nonreinforcement. Due to a history of partial reinforcement, Patti's tantrums show a much less rapid change. On the first day of extinction, there is no noticeable difference in the frequency of tantrums. In the first week, there is little change. Only after two or three weeks does the frequency of Patti's tantrums decline. Long after Connie had virtually ceased having tantrums, Patti is still having them, in spite of the lack of reinforcement.

Why do prior histories of continuous and partial reinforcement produce such different patterns of behavior during extinction? The answer involves discrimination. Before extinction, Connie was receiving reinforcers for each tantrum. After extinction tantrums were no longer followed by reinforcement. This is an easy black and white discrimination: all versus none. It is easy to discriminate that "now things are different." On Connie's first day of extinction she had 20 percent more tantrums; but the frequency of tantrums soon dropped rapidly to zero. The temporary increase on day one is common. Tantrums had *always* helped Connie get her way; thus they were under strong S^D control in situations where Connie did not get what she wanted. When Connie gave tantrums but did not get her way on the first day of extinction, "not getting her way" had strong S^D control for throwing another tantrum. Because Connie's parents and teacher were consistent in not reinforcing these tantrums, Connie quickly learned to discriminate that tantrums no longer brought attention and stopped throwing tantrums.

Patti had a much harder time discriminating that extinction had begun. Patti's prior

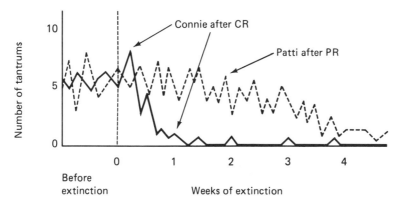

FIGURE 12–5 This hypothetical graph shows the general patterns of behavior seen in extinction after continuous reinforcement and after partial reinforcement.

experience on a VR 6 schedule had made her very used to nonreinforcement. After all, on the average, five out of six of her tantrums had not been reinforced. In addition, Patti's VR 6 schedule had included several occasions on which she had had ten or twelve tantrums before receiving reinforcers. The first few days that her behavior was on extinction were similar to those past experiences in which Patti had thrown ten or twelve tantrums without reinforcement. It took Patti weeks to discriminate the differences between the two situations: (1) the old VR 6 schedule (in which five out of six responses were not reinforced), and (2) the new extinction situation (in which six out of six responses are not reinforced).

Partial reinforcement effects are commonly visible as children grow up and childish responses—whining, pouting, crying, being a nuisance—are shifted to partial reinforcement schedules and finally to extinction. People who go through a period of partial reinforcement before extinction retain childish habits later into life than people who have attention for their childish behaviors cut off more abruptly. Often the death of one parent leaves the remaining parent with less time to pay attention to childish behavior; and in the weeks after the death, the children learn to ''grow up'' fast and help with household chores without whining or pouting.

The effects of partial reinforcement can be seen elsewhere, too. The mediocre artist or writer was given some encouragement (partial reinforcement) in high school by teachers who hoped for improvement. In college, the PR schedule was thinned further as fewer people praised the person's mediocre work. Since PR schedules can maintain behavior for a long period of time, the artist kept on turning out pictures even though reinforcers were few and far between. Finally, after college, the artist may find no one who praises the mediocre work and no one who buys it. This is extinction. Due to prior PR schedules, the artist may struggle for months before beginning to discriminate that there are no longer any rewards for painting. (An artist who had gone from continuous reinforcement to extinction overnight would have discriminated very quickly that there were no longer any rewards in painting and would have quit sooner!)

Because most adult behavior is maintained on PR schedules, it is common for people to go through long transition periods of not knowing whether to continue when their work, athletics, art, or hobbies cease to bring external rewards. A person may question whether this is merely a "bad streak of luck" when the last twenty canvases do not sell. Maybe the next one will sell for a handsome price. Should the person give up art, or work harder in hopes of a breakthrough? These thoughts are common side effects of being on a very stretched out schedule or being on extinction after partial reinforcement. Only after a long period of nonreinforcement does it become clear—an easy discrimination—that art is a dead end, for which the person can expect few future external rewards.

DIFFERENTIAL REINFORCEMENT OF HIGH RATES OF RESPONDING

When a behavior must be done rapidly to produce reinforcement, the behavior is on a schedule of differential reinforcement for high rates of responding (DRH). Racing bicyclists and sprinters are on DRH schedules to pedal or run as fast as they can, if they are to be rewarded by a victory. The lawyer who races against the clock to document a case before court convenes is on a DRH schedule. Typists and stenographers may be required to pass a speed test to qualify for their jobs. Police, fire, and other emergency workers often must work fast in order to be rewarded by the successful accomplishment of their tasks.

All DRH schedules modify response rates by reinforcing high rates of responding while either punishing or extinguishing low rates. For example, there are various fast drying paints, cements, and glues that impose DRH schedules on their users. When people first work with a fast drying cement, their original response rates may show considerable variability (broken line in Figure 12–6). Response rates slower than rate X are punished since the cement sets before it has been worked into the correct shape. Therefore, these slow rates are suppressed (downward arrows in Figure 12–6). High

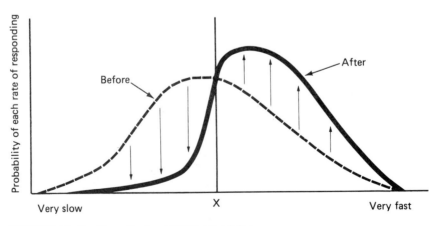

FIGURE 12–6 The effects of DRH schedules.

response rates, on the other hand, are reinforced since they allow the user to shape the cement into a suitable form before the material becomes unworkable. These rapid rates are reinforced (upward arrows in Figure 12–6). Thus, after differential reinforcement, the response rate is shifted to high levels (the solid curve in Figure 12–6).

DIFFERENTIAL REINFORCEMENT OF LOW RATES OF RESPONDING

When a behavior must be performed slowly to produce reinforcement, the behavior is on a schedule of differential reinforcement for low rates of responding (DRL). Careful, detailed printing and fine art work usually require slow performance rates in order to avoid errors and meet exacting standards. People who drink alcohol too fast at parties often come under DRL schedules. If they drink too fast (the broken line in Figure 12–7), they get drunk and sometimes do things they later regret. If drinking faster than rate X is frequently punished, high rates of drinking become suppressed (downward arrows in Figure 12–7). Slow rates of drinking allow the person to enjoy the alcohol without getting into trouble. Hence these slow rates are reinforced and become more frequent (upward arrows). If the differential reinforcement of low rates is strong enough, the person who used to drink too fast learns to drink more slowly (solid line in Figure 12–7).

A helpful strategy for weight watchers is to impose a DRL schedule on eating activities. Instead of shoveling the food in at a high rate, the weight watcher learns to slow down and pause between each bite of food. A sip of water between bites also helps decrease eating rates and fill the stomach. Some people need the help of others to enforce the DRL schedule and prevent a return to rapid eating. By slowing down, an overweight person avoids cleaning the plate too soon, and thus avoids the S^D's for taking seconds or thirds.

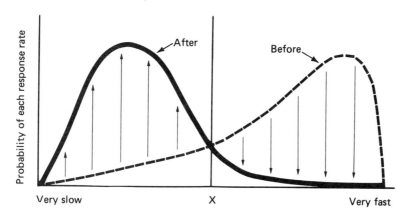

FIGURE 12–7 The effects of DRL schedules.

PACING SCHEDULES

Pacing schedules are related to DRH and DRL schedules. *On pacing schedules, responses must be neither too fast nor too slow; they must be paced at a certain rhythm in order to be reinforced.* The child who plays jump rope must pace each jump with the rhythm of the rope in order to continue the game. Musicians must pace their playing with the conductor—or with each other—in order to produce beautiful music. Whatever the pace, responding at the specified rate is necessary for reinforcement. Other rates are either punished or not reinforced. The beginning music student may often play passages too rapidly or too slowly. At first, a teacher rewards correct pacing and criticizes wrong pacing. Later the sounds of good music reinforce correct pacing and bad sounds punish incorrect pacing. Eventually, the musician learns skills for precise pacing. Punishment suppresses poor pacing (downward arrows in Figure 12–8), and reinforcement increases the probability of correct pacing (upward arrows).

Typewriters impose a pacing schedule on the rate of typing. If two keys are struck too close together in time, the keys jam and either nothing is typed on the page or a misprint appears. Thus, after one key is struck, there is a brief interval in which striking the next key will be punished or at least not reinforced. Typists learn to avoid pacing their strokes too close together to avoid these nonreinforcing events. Yet they also learn to avoid pacing too slowly, because they never get their work done at extremely slow rates. Typing paced at intermediate rates produces maximal reinforcement.

Some pacing schedules are very demanding, such that responses occurring a millisecond too soon or too late are punished. Others leave much more room for variation. The video-game player may lose the game if responses are only a few milliseconds out of synch with the pace of the game; but a typist at a word processor can stop the normal pace of typing at any time without penalty. Two figure skaters may get out of pace with each other for several seconds: If they are in Olympic competition, they may lose their chance for a gold medal; but if they are merely skating for fun, getting out of pace is not a problem.

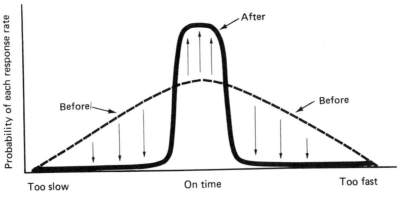

FIGURE 12–8   The effects of pacing schedules.

DIFFERENTIAL REINFORCEMENT OF OTHER BEHAVIOR

Whenever a person must abstain from a specified response for a certain time interval, the schedule is called differential reinforcement of other behavior (DRO). Doing *anything* other than the specified behavior—even doing nothing—will bring reinforcement. Parents can help their teenager overcome childish behavior—such as whining and pouting—by rewarding any other response class besides childish behavior. As long as the teen abstains from childish behavior, the parents are friendly and cheerful. This is a DRO schedule.

People sometimes impose DRO schedules on themselves to reward *not* doing a problematic behavior. If frequent trips to the kitchen result in snacking and gaining unwanted weight, doing any other behavior besides visiting the kitchen will be rewarded by avoiding food, hence avoiding weight problems. When a person feels hungry, making a phone call or getting a glass of water from the bathroom may distract the person, and be rewarded by the successful avoidance of food. People who hate gaining weight often learn a repertoire of these competing responses that are rewarded on DRO schedules. Because the competing responses prevent people from doing the unwanted behavior, the competing responses are reinforced.

Alcoholics Anonymous uses DRO to help ex-alcoholics stay off the bottle. During AA meetings, ex-drinkers reward each other for learning any new activities or skills that help them avoid drinking. Various drug rehabilitation centers, smoking clinics, and weight watching groups reward the acquisition and maintenance of competing activities that help people stay away from their problem behavior. For example, the Delancey Street drug rehabilitation center rewards its members for doing volunteer work in the community, teaching the police how to deal with drug addicts, learning new job skills, and so forth. These DRO schedules give each person freedom to select whatever competing responses he or she finds most rewarding.

In general, DRO schedules are better than punishment for reducing the frequency of unwanted behavior because DRO gives people alternative new activities to enjoy instead of merely suppressing undesirable old activities.

Sometimes desirable activities are suppressed by DRO. After college, reading serious books is often on a DRO schedule. There is so much reinforcement for doing other things besides reading—raising children, socializing, working, watching TV, traveling—that many people do not have the time to read serious books after college. Whenever you hear someone say, "I never have time to do . . . (some behavior) . . . any more," there is a good chance that the activity has been suppressed by DRO, because there are too many reinforcers for competing responses.

COMPOUND SCHEDULES

When different schedules are linked together or intermixed, they are called compound schedules. Everyday life contains complex and frequently changing patterns of compound schedules, especially *chained, multiple,* and *concurrent* schedules.

Cooking often involves all three of these types of compound schedules. A recipe may state: Add three egg whites (FR 3), five tablespoons of sugar (FR 5), and beat at high speed (DRH) until they form stiff white peaks. This is actually a chain of several smaller schedules. *Chained schedules consist of a linear series of component schedules, each cued by a distinctive S^D, that leads up to some final reinforcer.* The completion of each step of the recipe is the S^D to move to the next step, with its unique schedule of activities. All the steps lead to the final reinforcer—such as something delicious to eat.

Multiple schedules cause people to cycle back and forth between two or more activities. *Multiple schedules consist of two or more component schedules that appear in a cycle or a randomized alternation, each cued by a distinctive S^D.* When the 10-minute timer on the oven rings, it is time to remove the cookie sheet (FI 10-min) and move each of the twenty-four cookies to the cooling rack (FR 24). Then it is time to load the cookie sheet with twenty-four balls of raw cookie dough (FR 24) and set the timer. Ten minutes later, the cycle of component schedules will be repeated.

Concurrent schedules allow a person to alternate between two or more schedules at will—on an ad lib basis. The person chooses when to alternate activities, rather than having the sequence of activities imposed by the nature of the task. *Concurrent schedules consist of two or more separate schedules that operate at the same time, allowing the person to switch back and forth on an ad lib basis.* While working on preparing the main course (with its unique schedule of activities), a cook may occasionally switch over to other activities—fixing the salad, making a dressing, preparing a dessert—whenever one of these activities (with its separate schedules of reinforcement) happens to fit in well.

Concurrent Schedules and Choice

Concurrent schedules—which allow people to switch back and forth between different activities—are extremely common in everyday life. Concurrent schedules operate whenever people can choose how much time they wish to devote to different activities and their distinctive schedules of reinforcement.

An amusement park provides a large number of concurrent schedules of reinforcement: There are all sorts of rides and activities you can choose from, and all are available at the same time. Each activity has its own schedule of reinforcement that is separate and independent from the others. For example, the shooting gallery provides a VR 3 schedule if you hit the target about every third time you shoot. The haunted house provides a VR 12 schedule if there is a new surprising experience about every twelve steps. The roller coaster provides almost continuous reinforcement (CRF) once it starts moving. You can alternate back and forth among the activities in any order you want, going first to the shooting gallery, then the haunted house, then the roller coaster. The choice is yours.

When people come home from work in the evening, they can choose between numerous alternative activities, each choice providing different schedules of reinforcement. There is the choice of making dinner from scratch (which involves a long chain of small FR and FI schedules) or putting a frozen dinner in the oven (which is a much less demanding, but often less rewarding, schedule). In addition, there are the choices among pacing schedules: pacing the evening's activities to synchronize with the best TV shows, or pacing with the bar and disco schedules. There are countless other choices, such as settling down with a good book, calling some friends, or going out for a drive. Different people respond to these concurrent schedules with different choices, selecting some options and neglecting others.

The first thing to notice about choice is that *choice is relative*. The choice of any activity A depends on all the alternatives—B, C, and D. If activity A becomes more attractive, it affects people's choices of all activities—A, B, C, and D—even though only A has changed: As people choose A more, they devote less time to B, C, or D. If Disco D is always exciting and a couple has always chosen to go there on Saturday night, their choice may be changed if one of their alternative activities (A, B, or C) becomes more or less attractive, even though the disco itself remains unchanged. If several great movies come to town for the weekend, the couple may choose to go to the movies on both Friday and Saturday evenings and skip the disco. The attractiveness of the disco is *relative* to the alternatives. *On concurrent schedules, changes in the attractiveness of one schedule can affect a person's choices of both this and the other schedules.*

A world class long distance runner may use pacing schedules when training for major competitions. The runner chooses among three fellow athletes who set three different running paces. If one of these three athletes is injured and has to run at a slower pace, the long distance runner may decide to spend less time running with the injured athlete and more with the other two athletes, even though these two have not changed their pace in the least.

Since choice is influenced by the alternatives, we cannot understand a person's choices without knowing the alternatives that are available. Just knowing that a person loves music and has a new record by a favorite artist does not tell us enough to predict that the person will stay home and listen to music. The choice depends on the alternatives: Is there an exiting new movie in town? Was the person called to the hospital because of an emergency in the family?

Considerable research has been done on concurrent schedules in order to identify the variables that influence choice.[14] *Three of the most important variables that influence a person's choice among different concurrent schedules are: the frequency (F), magnitude (M), and delay (D) of reinforcement provided by each schedule.* The following simple equation shows the general attractiveness of any given choice:

Attractiveness is proportional to $\dfrac{F \times M}{D}$ (also written F × M ÷ D)

Increasing the frequency or magnitude of reinforcers increases the attractiveness of a schedule. Delay has the opposite effect: Increasing the delay between the moment of choice and the time of reinforcement decreases a schedule's attractiveness. *Generally, schedules of reinforcement that provide frequent reinforcers of high magnitude and minimal delay are very attractive.*

If we wanted to evaluate the attractiveness of video games that simulate spaceship battles, we would look at all three aspects of their reinforcement schedules: F, M, and D. A game that scheduled *frequent* opportunities to shoot enemy spaceships should be more

[14]Herrnstein (1961, 1970); de Villiers (1977).

attractive than a game that scheduled only rare opportunities to blast enemy targets. The *magnitude* of the video display and sound effects is also important: The attractiveness of space war games usually increases as the magnitude of the reinforcing stimuli increase. Seeing an enemy spaceship explode in a brilliant starburst of colorful fragments provides a greater magnitude of sensory stimulation than merely seeing the ship disappear from the screen; and games with high magnitude displays are usually a more attractive choice. Finally, time *delays* that are scheduled between the player's action and the events on the screen have an inverse effect on attractiveness: Increasing the delay between action and reinforcement causes a decrease in the attractiveness of the game. Short delays keep the total attractiveness high. It is no wonder that video-game designers program their games to have nearly instant responsiveness. It is much more exciting to shoot a laser beam and score an instant hit on the enemy spaceship than to fire a "slow ball" weapon that may not reach the target for two minutes. Increasing the delay of reinforcement reduces the attractiveness of an activity.

The three part equation—F $\times$ M $\div$ D—tells us something about the attractiveness of any given schedule of reinforcement, but it alone does not predict choice. *Choice always involves a comparison of the relative attractiveness of two or more alternatives.* The values of F, M, and D for each schedule of reinforcement help predict which choice is more attractive. If we wanted to know which of two space war games would be more popular, we could compare the F $\times$ M $\div$ D equations for the two games. We might find that Game A allowed a player to score 20 hits per minute on enemy targets (F = 20 per min), that hits caused an explosion of light 2 inches in diameter on the video screen (M = 2 in.), and the delay between shooting and seeing the explosion was 10 milliseconds (D = 10 msec.). Game B might allow 50 hits per minute (F = 50), with smaller explosions that were 1 inch in diameter (M = 1), and longer delays of 50 milliseconds (D = 50).

Game A	**Game B**
F = 20, M = 2	**F = 50, M = 1**
D = 10	**D = 50**

$$\frac{F \times M}{D} = \frac{20 \times 2}{10} = 4 \qquad\qquad \frac{F \times M}{D} = \frac{50 \times 1}{50} = 1$$

The numbers 4 and 1 indicate the relative attractiveness of each game, revealing that the schedules of reinforcement in game A are 4 times more attractive than those in Game B.

The matching law describes how the attractiveness of different concurrent schedules affects choice: *Individuals tend to match the frequency of their behavior to the relative attractiveness of the available concurrent schedules.*[15] If two schedules are equally attractive, people usually spend equal amounts of time on each, alternating between the two. If one schedule is twice as attractive as a second, people usually spend twice as much time on the more attractive alternative. A couple that enjoys a night at the disco twice as much

---

[15]de Villiers (1977); Logue (1983). Choice behavior has been analyzed in terms of both matching and maximizing; and the relative merits of the two theories are still being debated (Rachlin et al., 1981; and commentaries thereon). For simplicity, only matching is presented here.

as a night at the movies would go to the disco about twice as often as to the movies. If video game A is four times more attractive than game B, most people would play game A four times more often than game B. The frequency of different choices matches their attractiveness.

The matching law cannot predict all choices, because there are other variables besides F, M, and D that influence choice; but this simple law is surprisingly successful in explaining patterns of choice.[16] (Reasoning and rule-governed choice are explained in Chapter 14.)

If we want to know how much time a person will spend on any given schedule, we must compare it to all the available alternative schedules. In the simplest case of two activities—A and B—the amount of time devoted to schedule A is proportional to the attractiveness of A divided by the total attractiveness of A and B.

$$\textbf{Choice of A} = \frac{\textbf{attractiveness of A}}{\textbf{(attractiveness of A)} + \textbf{(attractiveness of B)}}$$

This equation merely means that the portion of time a person chooses to devote to A is based on the attractiveness of A compared with the total attractiveness of A and B. If two schedules A and B are equally attractive, with each scored as +1, then the equation would read as follows:

$$\textbf{Choice of A} = \frac{\textbf{attractiveness of A}}{\textbf{(attractiveness of A)} + \textbf{(attractiveness of B)}} = \frac{1}{1+1} = \frac{1}{2}$$

which means that half the time people will do activity A (and half the time they will do B). If someone liked chocolate and vanilla ice cream just the same (and couldn't buy any other flavor), the person would choose chocolate about half the time and vanilla about half the time.

If video game A has an attractiveness of +4 and game B an attractiveness of +1, the equation reads as follows:

$$\textbf{Choice of A} = \frac{\textbf{attractiveness of A}}{\textbf{(attractiveness of A)} + \textbf{(attractiveness of B)}} = \frac{4}{4+1} = \frac{4}{5}$$

which means that four times out of five, people will play game A (and the remaining one time out of five they will play game B).

Since we know that attractiveness is proportional to F × M÷D, we can write the equation for *the matching law* of choice as follows:

$$\textbf{Choice of A} = \frac{\textbf{F} \times \textbf{M} \div \textbf{D} \textit{ for A}}{\textbf{(F} \times \textbf{M} \div \textbf{D} \textit{ for A)} + \textbf{(F} \times \textbf{M} \div \textbf{D} \textit{ for B)}}$$

This is the same as writing the equation as follows:

[16]de Villiers (1977); Baum (1979); Zeiler and Blakely (1983); Todorov et al. (1983); Wearden (1983).

$$\text{Choice of A} = \frac{\dfrac{F_A \times M_A}{D_A}}{\dfrac{F_A \times M_A}{D_A} + \dfrac{F_B \times M_B}{D_B}}$$

These equations merely state that the amount of the time that a person chooses schedule X equals the attractiveness of X divided by the total attractiveness of X + Y (where attractiveness is determined by the frequency, magnitude, and delay of reinforcement).

Let us examine some everyday examples of the matching law of choice. If a person has to choose between writing letters to a friend who lives in a distant city or interacting with an equally good friend who lives nearby, the matching law predicts that the person will prefer to communicate most often with the nearby friend. Why? Since the strength (or magnitude) of both friendships is the same, M is the same in both equations.

Letter writing	Face-to-face interaction
$\dfrac{F \times M}{D}$	$\dfrac{F \times M}{D}$

Therefore, the choice depends on F and D: the frequency and delay of reinforcement associated with letter writing and face-to-face interaction. Because writing letters is slow and laborious, most people exchange fewer ideas per letter than they would in a face-to-face interaction. Thus, the frequency (F) of rewarding ideas is lower for letter writing than in face-to-face interactions. Since it takes days to exchange ideas by letter, the delay (D) in friendly exchanges is longer among distant friends. Even if we do not put exact numbers into the equations, we can see that the schedule of reinforcement for interacting with nearby friends is more reinforcing and attractive: F is larger and D is smaller. Although we often promise to write old friends when we split up and move to different cities, those promises usually are hard to keep if we have nearby friends with whom we can enjoy frequent reinforcement with little delay.

Naturally, things change considerably if the distant friend is a very special person. Lovers who live in different cities sometimes write every day, taking time away from nearby friends to exchange lengthy letters. Love makes the magnitude (M) of gratification so high that it can override the long delay (D) and limited frequency (F) of ideas exchanged in letters. Nevertheless, exchanging letters is not as attractive as actually being with the special person. In addition, if a couple has enough money to make phone bills tolerable, they usually prefer phoning to letter writing. Phone calls decrease the delay and increase the frequency of information exchanged, making this choice more attractive than letter writing, when the budget allows.

When choosing careers, people are also influenced by the relationship of F, M, and D. The frequency, magnitude, and delay of reinforcement differ from career to career, and careers that offer frequent rewards of generous magnitude and minimal delay tend to be the most appealing. Teenagers sometimes dream of hitchhiking to Hollywood, walking into a studio and being swamped with numerous big contracts. The ideal career offers high values of F and M, with minimal D.

Someone who is good at sales might be torn between going into real estate or appliance sales. In real estate, the frequency of sales is low (perhaps only one sale every month or two), but each sale may involve a commission of several thousand dollars. This high magnitude of reward is much more attractive than the relatively small commission for selling appliances; however, the frequency of sales is much lower in real estate than appliances. In addition, there is a longer delay involved in becoming a real estate agent. A person who estimated that it might take a year or two to obtain a real estate license and become established in a good brokerage might find the delay unacceptably long and snap up a job in appliance sales if it was available without delay.

In choosing between schedules that provide immediate rewards and those that involve delayed rewards, *immediate rewards are often quite tempting, unless the frequency and/or magnitude of the delayed rewards make delayed gratification worth the wait.* College students often have to struggle with the choice of (1) working hard for many years to enter law, medicine, clinical psychology, or other professions (hoping that the future rewards will make up for the delay), or (2) having fun now, without delaying gratification (hoping that something nice will come their way after college). If a hard working student receives a few bad grades that endanger the plans for a professional career, immediate gratification becomes especially tempting.

People often become aware that the temptations of immediate gratification can lead them to unwise decisions. The brief delay (low value of D) associated with one choice may seduce them away from a much superior option (with high F and M of reinforcement) which involves a longer delay (high value of D). Overweight people may be perfectly aware that losing 30 pounds is much more important than the brief pleasures of enjoying a piece of fudge, but the immediate rewards of eating seduce them away from their long term goal of losing weight.

The concurrent schedules of reinforcement make it hard for some people to avoid overeating. If they choose to eat, they are on a FR 1 schedule that produces immediate gratification for each bite of food. If they choose to diet, they can expect to lose weight, but there may be a two-day delay before they even begin to notice a rewarding change on the bathroom scales. Many fat people would like to diet; but the delayed reinforcement of weight loss is often less attractive than the immediate pleasures of eating another piece of fudge.

How can a person escape the seductive power of immediate reinforcement when it endangers a long term goal? One solution is to proact: Make crucial choices *before* tempting situations arise—while the time delay until the next reinforcer is still long. People who are overweight often cannot resist eating when they have fudge, ice cream, cake, and other rich food in the house. When the food is nearby, the decision to eat something is very attractive and hard to resist: It may take only 30 seconds to walk to the kitchen and find something fattening to eat. It would be much easier to decide to diet if there were no fattening foods in the house to make immediate gratification so tempting.

By planning ahead at the grocery store, people can arrange to minimize the temptations caused by having fattening food in the house. If they decide to buy fruit, vegetables, lean meat, and no sweets while at the grocery, then their proactive behavior reduces later temptations to eat fattening foods. Once they get home and stock the kitchen with healthy, low-calorie food instead of sweets, they have less difficulty staying on the diet than if they had bought fudge mix, ice cream, and cake.

Fat people find it easier to make wise diet decisions in the grocery than in the fudge kitchen because there is a longer time delay between diet decisions and eating. The longer delay reduces temptations for immediate gratification. The following table of delay times shows why proacting is useful. If the decision to eat or to diet is made at home, the delay until reinforcement is 30 seconds for eating (since food is nearby) and 2 days for dieting (since it takes 2 days before the scales show progress).

	EAT	DIET
HOME	30-sec delay	2-day delay
GROCERY	30-min delay	2-day delay

When they are in the grocery store, the choice involves a 30-minute delay for eating (since it takes time to check out, get home, and eat) and a 2-day delay for dieting (since it takes 2 days to see improvement on the scales). People have a much better chance of choosing the diet while in the grocery than in the kitchen. Because the delay until eating is sixty times longer (30 minutes is sixty times longer than 30 seconds), the attractiveness of fattening foods is *much* lower in the grocery than in their own home. That does not mean that all people can decide to resist fattening foods while in the grocery; but the chances are much better when there is less temptation for immediate gratification. After making wise decisions in the grocery and purchasing low-calorie food, they help insure that they will have minimal temptations to eat fattening foods when they get home.

A man and woman might find that they cannot resist the temptation to fight and say ugly things to each other when they get angry. However, if they can proact and set up some firm rules long before they get angry the next time, they may avert some bad fights. Useful rules might include: "Walk around the block—separately—and calm down before talking about your problems. Do not use harsh, cruel, or ugly words when you talk. Since you can create a better future but you cannot change the past, focus less on past problems than on future solutions." If the couple agrees to follow these rules the next time they get angry with each other, they will avoid some of the temptation to say ugly things to each other.

NONCONTINGENT (RESPONSE-INDEPENDENT) SCHEDULES

Ever since introducing FR 1 schedules, we have been discussing contingent (that is, response-dependent) schedules. *In schedules of contingent reinforcement, reinforcement is dependent upon the occurrence of a response.* On an FR 10 schedule, the tenth response is reinforced. On an FI 10-minute schedule, the first response after a 10 minute period is reinforced. Reinforcement is contingent upon the response occurring: no response, no reinforcement.

What if reinforcement appears independent of behavior? *When reinforcers occur irrespective of the response preceding them, the reinforcers are noncontingent or re-*

sponse-independent. These reinforcers are sometimes called "free" reinforcers or "windfall" rewards to show that no particular response was needed to earn them. As was explained at the end of the chapter on operant conditioning (pp. 32–34), noncontingent reinforcement is usually much less effective than contingent reinforcement in modifying operant behavior; but sometimes accidental reinforcers produce unusual and dramatic effects. A variety of different effects have been observed, depending on the frequency and magnitude of the noncontingent events, whether reinforcement or punishment is involved, and other variables.

Superstitious Behavior

When noncontingent reinforcement accidentally follows a certain operant, it may cause the operant to occur more frequently. *Behavior produced by this random, noncontingent reinforcement is called superstitious behavior.*[17]

Athletes often develop superstitious behavior based on the reinforcers of scoring and winning. If a baseball pitcher accidentally fingers the ball in a certain way before throwing three strikes in a row, this irrelevant behavior may become a learned superstitious response. If a quarterback mumbles the name of the pass receiver before throwing the ball, and if this is followed by several good passes, the reinforcement may create a verbal superstition.

Since noncontingent reinforcement has less effect on behavior than does contingent reinforcement, superstitious behavior usually develops when the costs of doing the behavior are low (for example, mumbling a name) and the rewards are high (for example, winning an important game).[18] The more that there *appears* to be a possible connection between a behavior and reinforcement, the more likely that a superstition will develop. The appearance of a contingent relationship can mask the accidental, noncontingent sequence of events. For example, what happens if a swimmer chances to sample some of her roommate's fad diet supplement at breakfast then breaks her own personal record to win a swim meet that afternoon? The chance association between the unusual breakfast and the big win could lead to the learning of the superstitious habit of eating the fad diet supplement whenever the swimmer was preparing for her event.[19] Even if the roommate gave up the fad diet, the swimmer might continue using it, in part because she feared that she might lose her next competition if she did not use the diet.

Whenever people have highly rewarding experiences, just about any preceding activity that stands out as unusual, novel, different, or out of the ordinary may be reinforced and become a superstitious practice. The history student who happened to study in the physics library before earning the highest grade on a history final might learn the superstitious practice of studying history in the physics library. The unusualness of

---

[17]Superstitious learning was the first effect of noncontingent reinforcement to be studied (Skinner, 1948, 1957); but recent work shows that it is much more complex than was originally thought (Staddon, 1977; Killeen, 1978; Hammond, 1980; Schwartz, 1984:154–173).

[18]Gmelch and Felson (1980).

[19]The long time lag between behavior and consequences in some cases of superstitious learning suggests that conditioning results during cognitive rehearsal (Bandura, 1977; Klatzky, 1980), as the people ruminate over the unusual and rewarding events of the past several hours or days (Klinger, 1977, 1978).

both the behavior and the reward creates conditions conducive to the development of superstition, especially if the behavior is not costly to perform and the rewards are high.

Valued rewards that are not completely under our own control—not completely assured by skill alone—often cause the learning of superstitions. Athletes learn more superstitions for their sport than for driving cars: The car is much more under their own personal control than is the outcome of the next game. The anthropologist Malinowski found that the Trobriand Islanders have quite different practices for fishing on the open sea and in the lagoon. Fishing in the lagoon is relatively safe; but fishing at sea is dangerous and the catches are less predictable. Which type of fishing involves more magic, rituals, and superstitions? The risk and uncertainties of fishing at sea are more conducive to the use of magic and superstitions—as if magic might help ward off danger and insure better catches. When people's skills are adequate for dealing with a situation, success is clearly contingent upon their skills; and irrelevant behavior is not likely to be reinforced. However, in situations where skill alone does not always produce success— because there are too many uncontrollable factors—success is much more capricious, and any unusual activity associated with success can be reinforced and become a superstitious behavior.

After a superstition has been acquired via noncontingent reinforcement, the behavior may be maintained by contingent reinforcement. Sometimes the friendly social attention that a person gets for unusual and colorful superstitions can reinforce their use. "Hey, Wendy, do you still think that green powder you put in your cereal really helps you swim any better?" Of course, social criticism can have the opposite effect, punishing and suppressing the frequency of a superstition—in public at least. Second, superstitious behavior can create an illusion of control and the feeling that one has a special edge in dealing with difficult situations. These positive thoughts can reduce anxiety in the face of uncertainty and reinforce the continued use of superstitions.

Superstitious responses add spice and color to human activity. There are so many noncontingent reinforcers in everyday life that many people learn unique patterns of superstitious operants. Superstitions can be passed on to others by observational learning or rules. Thus, superstitions can spread through a culture once one individual acquires the response. There are many culturally transmitted superstitions: dropping coins in wishing wells, knocking on wood, praying to rain gods, not walking under ladders, and so forth. Americans are so superstitious about not accepting $2 bills that the government is stuck with four million $2 bills that people will not use.

Passivity

Noncontingent consequences that occur at high frequency can condition passivity. This has been best demonstrated with noncontingent punishment; but it appears to occur with noncontingent reinforcement, too.

Frequent experience with noncontingent punishment can induce *learned helplessness,* involving passivity, apathy, and depression.[20] When people are first exposed to noncontingent punishment, they try to avoid it or stop it. However, if the punishment is

[20]Seligman (1975); Garber and Seligman (1980).

truly noncontingent, then there is no relationship between it and the person's behavior; hence there is nothing that the person can do to stop it. Gradually, attempts to avoid punishment extinguish (since they all fail), and the victim learns to passively accept the pain. Victims of noncontingent punishment often feel helpless, hopeless, and depressed.

Children raised in highly abusive homes sometimes develop learned helplessness. When parents take out *their* anger on the children—independent of the children's behavior—the children are punished noncontingently. Since children are weaker than and dependent on the adults, there is not much the children can do to avoid the physical and verbal abuse. Unavoidable punishment can induce passivity, depression, and feelings of helplessness.

Once people develop learned helplessness, often they do not attempt to escape later contingent punishment—even when they *could* avoid it by merely taking a more active role. Women who were raised in abusive homes are often quite fatalistic if they get married to men who beat them: They tolerate abuses that other women would resist. Once people become passive due to learned helplessness, the passivity interferes with their learning to actively resist punishment in later situations—unless a friend or therapist helps them learn to be more active and assertive.

One study on street prostitutes found that many of these women had come from violent homes, been victims of incest at home, been abused and beaten up by their pimps and customers, and been robbed and raped while on the streets.[21] After a long history of victimization, many were "psychologically paralyzed." They believed that there was little or nothing they could do to avoid further abuse. They felt powerless to change their lives, and their habits of passivity biased them not to explore active means for avoiding aversive experiences.

Slaves were often punished at the whim of their masters. Those slaves with cruel masters were victims of the noncontingent punishment that produced learned helplessness. After years of repeated beatings, slaves often became passive, dispirited, helpless, and defeated.

Whereas frequent noncontingent punishment can produce learned helplessness, generous and frequent noncontingent reinforcement can produce *learned laziness*.[22] Large amounts of free rewards can create apathy, passivity, and lack of motivation. It is not surprising that free reinforcers promote passivity. If you could do absolutely nothing and still receive free reinforcers, why do anything? There is no incentive—no motivation—to exert the effort to do much other than lounge around, goof off, waste time.

Children who are showered with attention, toys, and treats by doting parents often become "spoiled."[23] They may refuse to do anything that takes effort—such as doing homework, chores, yard work, or cleaning their room—and still they receive free reinforcers. Some spoiled children—though not all—become rather lazy. Very attractive people sometimes become spoiled, too. They receive all sorts of attention because they are beautiful, even if they do nothing. If they become increasingly unmotivated and passive,

[21]Pines and Silbert (1981).
[22]Seligman (1975).
[23]Skinner (1980:100).

they still receive attention and flattery. Reinforcement is not contingent upon behavior: It merely comes for being beautiful.

LOOSELY DEFINED CONTINGENCIES OF REINFORCEMENT

Loosely defined contingencies of reinforcement allow reinforcement for any of a variety of responses within a large, loosely defined response class. Loosely defined contingencies of reinforcement lie between the two extremes of the continuum between (1) the random, noncontingent reinforcement which produces superstitious or passive behavior, and (2) the strictly defined contingencies which produce precisely specified behavior. Loosely defined contingencies increase the variability of behavior by only loosely specifying which behavior may be reinforced. Within these broad limits, each person can learn unique patterns of responses that contribute to their individuality. Two important products of loosely defined contingencies are personal style and behavior drift.

Personal style usually arises in instrumental tasks that can be performed in a variety of ways. Any response in the response class will produce reinforcement. It does not matter *which* subset of the response class is emitted. One person may learn to perform one subset of the response class; and a second person another subset of the class. Each does the operant, but with different *style*. For instance, legible handwriting is a broad response class that contains millions of different styles, all of which communicate and hence are reinforced. One person writes backhand, another with flourishes, and yet another with italic strokes. There are countless variations that are readable. As long as a style works— that is, brings reinforcement because it communicates—it does not matter which style is used. After years of writing and countless reinforcers, each of us develops a unique style.

The difference between style and superstitious behavior is traced to the size of the response class that is reinforced. Superstitious behavior arises when *any* possible response can be reinforced: The response class is infinitely large and contains all possible responses. Reinforcers come no matter what. Style arises when any variation *within* a specific but broad response class can be reinforced. Handwriting consists of making marks on the page. There is nothing superstitious about making the letters; some kind of style is necessary. A quarterback can throw a pass without mumbling the name of the pass receiver; but a person cannot do handwriting without using some style of writing. Because the response class of readable writing is very broad, there are countless different writing patterns possible; and each person can learn his or her own unique style.

There is some looseness in the definition of most response classes, hence some room for style to appear. The broader the definition of the response class, the more room for style. As a result, each of us learns personal styles of dress, speech, posture, hand gestures, eye contact, walking, greetings, and so forth.

Behavior drift appears when behavior that is under loosely defined contingencies of reinforcement changes over time.[24] A person's handwriting style can drift over the years, perhaps tilting more to the right or the left, perhaps becoming larger or smaller, some-

---

[24]Behavior drift is analyzed along with superstitious learning by Skinner (1948, 1957).

times becoming more sloppy or illegible. Drift refers to random changes that are traced to haphazard reinforcement rather than to models, prompts, rules, or nonrandom differential reinforcement. Thus, drift usually involves unpredictable changes. Since random changes in behavior rarely improve the quality of performance, drift is more likely to undermine quality behavior than to improve it.

It is common to find that the behavior of young people is under strictly defined contingencies of reinforcement, but that ever larger and more loosely defined response classes are accepted and reinforced as people grow older. Hence behavior drift often becomes more visible in older people. For example, young people are often expected to say things clearly, simply, and efficiently. Adults may become irritated when their time is wasted by a youngster who cannot express an idea succinctly. Under such contingencies most young people learn to get to the point and minimize redundancy. However, as the years go by and people gain seniority, status, or merely age, there are fewer people who criticize irrelevant or redundant ramblings. When seventy year olds are expounding on their past, younger people may abstain from criticizing out of kindness or respect. This means that succinct speech is under loosely defined contingencies, and it is common to find older people talking and thinking less clearly. Long before senility or physical impairment hampers their abilities, the verbal behavior of older people—both their speech and verbal thoughts—may begin to drift. Eventually some older people become absent-minded, repetitive, confused about simple points, and inattentive to detail. The senior citizens who show least behavior drift are often those who continue to demand quality performance by applying high standards to their own behavior or having honest friends to catch their errors.

Behavior drift is not a result of biological aging. It can occur in young people, too. Verbal behavior seems especially prone to drift, which can lead to large discrepancies between what people say and what they actually do. When a person first begins to slip out of the habit of punctuality or living up to promises, it may be laughed off or forgotten because "everyone slips up once in awhile." But when a person's behavior drifts further, there may be an increasing frequency of promising one thing—"I'll be there at 8:00 for sure"—and doing something else. This drift may be prevented if the person is criticized: "You caused twelve people to sit around and waste 45 minutes waiting for you this morning." But without critical feedback, the drift can continue. In subcultures where it is considered right for people to do what they want to do, when they want to do it, there may be an explicit code for not criticizing others. Whatever the reason, the less critical feedback a person gets, the easier it is for verbal and actual behavior to drift apart. People with job security sometimes become sloppy and drift into poor work habits. Before people get job security, there are often strict definitions concerning the quantity and quality of the work that is expected of them, coupled with the threat of dismissal if they fail to live up to the standards. Once a person gains seniority and job security, the definition of the job usually becomes broader, since the person must show gross incompetence to be fired after attaining job security. Anything short of gross incompetence is tolerated. This broader definition of the job permits behavioral drift in just about any direction, including downhill.

Behavior drift is one source of behavior variability that contributes to the colorfulness of everyday life. Behavior drift, along with superstitious behavior and style, produces unpredictable variations which may strike others as interesting, funny, imaginative, or creative. However, if behavior drifts beyond certain limits, it may appear inconsiderate, pathetic, deviant, or even pathological.[25]

CONCLUSION

There are many different kinds of schedules of reinforcement and punishment. This chapter presents the major types of schedules and a description of their basic effects on behavior. Schedule effects are superimposed on all the other types of conditioning effects described in the previous chapters. Schedules have ubiquitous effects on behavior because *some* type of schedule is always in operation and each type of schedule has its own kinds of effects on behavior.

In everyday life, partial (or intermittent) reinforcement is more common than continuous reinforcement; and partial reinforcement produces behavior that is both more variable and more resistant to extinction. Variable schedules are more common than fixed schedules in everyday life, and these variable schedules also increase the amount of behavior variability seen in natural settings. When under interval, DRH, DRL, and pacing schedules, people learn to time their responses to synchronize with the cycles and rhythms of daily events. In everyday life, numerous schedules operate simultaneously—as concurrent schedules—and people have to choose among them. The matching law describes how choices are related to the attractiveness of the alternative schedules. Noncontingent reinforcement and punishment can produce passivity or superstitious behavior. Loosely defined contingencies of reinforcement foster the idiosyncratic response variations seen in style and behavior drift. A certain amount of variability is accepted as normal, and even welcomed because variety is the spice of life. However, when behavior drifts beyond certain limits, people usually begin to define variations as inappropriate, deviant, or pathological.

The next chapter describes another major aspect of conditioning closely related to schedules: positive and negative control. Almost any operant can be learned and maintained under either positive or negative control, but there are important differences in the ways people respond to these two forms of control.

---

[25]Much of the behavior that is labeled as psychopathological consists of behavior that was once rather normal but that has drifted outside the limits most people define as normal. From the behavioral viewpoint, therapy consists largely of reintroducing more strictly defined contingencies of reinforcement that will return the behavior to the realm of normalcy. Models, rules, and prompts may be used in conjunction with more strictly defined contingencies of reinforcement. The various methods used in behavior therapy are described by Ullman and Krasner (1965); O'Leary and Wilson (1975); Bellack and Hersen (1977); Walen et al. (1977); Redd et al. (1979); Daitzman (1980, 1981); Schwartz (1982); Hersen (1983).

13

Positive and Negative Control

● *In this chapter you will learn the various problems associated with negative control— punishment and negative reinforcement—along with techniques for replacing negative control with more positive alternatives.*

People love positive control. They hate negative control. People go back for more positive control, and this gives them the chance for continued learning under positive control. In contrast, people devise all kinds of methods for avoiding negative control.

Positive control consists of all conditioning and stimulus control that is based on positive reinforcement. Positive reinforcement increases the frequency of operants, and it causes predictive stimuli to become CS's that elicit pleasurable emotions. Under positive control, learning new skills is enjoyable; hence people are eager to continue developing more skill. *Negative control consists of all conditioning and stimulus control that is based on punishment and negative reinforcement.* Punishment suppresses the frequency of operants and causes predictive stimuli to become CS's that elicit fear, anxiety, and other aversive emotions. Negative control also motivates escape and avoidance, since these responses often lead to negative reinforcement.

People respond quite differently to positive and negative control. People seek out and enjoy positive stimuli. They dislike and avoid negative stimuli. Almost any activity can be learned under either positive or negative control; but there are important differences in the behavior produced by the two methods. Pamela is learning to play the piano under positive control. Because her parents play the piano and show their love of music, Pamela experiences vicarious reinforcement when she sees how much her parents enjoy music. Pamela is given generous encouragement and positive feedback for her playing, since her parents are happy to see her showing an interest in music. She obtains the reinforcers of optimal sensory stimulation from the music she is learning to create for herself. As a result of all this positive conditioning, Pamela comes to love the piano, squeezes in extra time here and there to play, and looks forward to learning more difficult music in the future. Nancy, on the other hand, is learning to play the piano under negative control. Her family and friends do not play, and some of her peers make fun of her for having to practice. Nancy's parents give sharp reprimands for errors but seldom comment on correct passages. Any failure to advance as rapidly as possible is criticized. The teacher often compares Nancy with other students who are excelling, and tells her that her playing is dull and uninspired. Nancy's parents tell her how disappointed they are. Everyone nags her to practice harder. As a result of this negative control Nancy learns to hate the instrument, to hate the nagging about practice, to avoid playing, and to fear whatever future learning may be demanded of her.

HUMANISTIC APPLICATIONS

Much of human technology and culture functions to increase our contact with positive stimuli and decrease our exposure to aversive stimuli. Technologies for coping with the physical environment provide clear examples. Medicine has given us much happier lives by protecting us from disease and helping us to be more healthy. Mechanical and electronic inventions are usually designed to make work easier and play more fun. Architecture and technology have made our living space more pleasant, commodious, and free of aversive climatic extremes. Many cultural practices have also been shaped over the millennia to help us avoid aversive stimuli and attain positive experiences. The arts and humanities have fostered creativity and collected the beautiful works of each era. Rules of etiquette and courtesy instruct people to behave in ways that can avoid aversive incidents and help interaction flow smoothly.

However, our current technology and culture are far from perfect. Aversive stimuli are still with us, generating a great deal of unhappiness and misery in many people's lives. There is room for much improvement in making the world a more positive place in which to live. Behavior science may well be one of the most important scientific and humanistic breakthroughs for making life more positive. Behavior science is the first science to analyze positive and negative control, develop better methods of positive control, devise alternatives to aversive control, and give people the information they need to switch from negative to positive methods of interacting with others.

These discoveries are new. Most people have never learned how to make use of behavior principles for this end. Yet the positive approach of behavior science has already been successfully implemented in many realms of behavior modification—interpersonal relations, marital counseling, sexual therapies, child-rearing practices, educational programs, self-control strategies, self-actualization programs, correctional programs for juvenile delinquents, and so forth.[1] Considering how young behavior science is, it is reasonable to assume that many more behavior situations will be analyzed and converted to positive control as the science progresses.

A major goal of behavior science is to help people learn behavior that increases their ability to bring positive reinforcers into their own lives and the lives of others.[2] Almost all behavior can be brought under positive control. As people acquire the skills for using positive control, we will have created a much happier society, free of guilt, fear, anxiety, hatred, and numerous other ugly side effects of aversive control.

How does one increase the use of positive control and decrease negative control? The answer depends somewhat on the situation. If other people are engaging in *desirable* behavior, it is easier to use positive control than if they are engaging in *undesirable* activities. The remainder of the chapter will explain the positive way of responding to desirable and undesirable behavior.

DESIRABLE BEHAVIOR

When a person is learning any desirable behavior—kindness, honesty, musical skill—the advantages of positive control are obvious. Positive control will increase the frequency of the behavior and make the person seek to learn more. Positive control also conditions the behavior itself into a conditioned reinforcer, such that doing the behavior becomes intrinsically rewarding and elicits positive emotional responses.

The disadvantages of using negative control with desirable behavior are also clear. Negative control conditions the behavior into a conditioned punisher. Desirable activities that could have been enjoyable become aversive. Under most circumstances, people try to escape from or avoid aversive control and the behavior conditioned by it. When parents, teachers, friends, spouse or others rely on aversive control while attempting to teach valuable skills, the avoidance responses generated by the aversive control may interfere with or prevent the acquisition of the desirable behavior.

The obvious advantages of positive control for desirable behavior help many people avoid putting such behavior under negative control. But many lack skill in being as positive as they could be; and if their positive approaches fail, they often fall back on negative control. Linda suggests to George that it would be great fun to go water skiing this weekend, and he mumbles, "I'm busy." Then she gives another positive line, "You remember how much fun we used to have skiing at the lake. I know you'll love it once you get there." Showing irritation, George repeats, "I'm biizzy!" This time Linda turns to the aversive mode and snaps, "George, you never want to do anything anymore except watch those stupid games on TV. If you won't get up, I'll just go with José and Harry." Now Linda may get some action; but she had to use negative control to get it. Even if

[1]Bandura (1969); Mahoney and Thoresen (1974); Gottman et al. (1976); Bellack and Hersen (1977); Redd et al. (1979); Kazdin (1980); Watson and Tharp (1981); Martin and Pear (1983).
[2]Skinner (1953, 1971); Bandura (1969, 1973); Mahoney (1974, 1975). However, there are times when punishment is desirable (Newsom et al., 1983).

George agrees to go, the aversive control may make the weekend trip less pleasant than it could have been if both Linda and George were more skillful at and appreciative of positive interaction styles.

The research on behavior acquisition and maintenance indicates that virtually all behavior can be learned and maintained under positive control. Merely teaching Linda a few more positive phrases cannot resolve all the problems between George and Linda. However, real progress can be expected if *both* people learn a large repertoire of positive skills that make him more rewarding to talk with, her more rewarding to ski with, and both of them more positive about designing and learning mutually rewarding patterns of interaction. When people succeed in coupling their shared activities with high levels of positive stimuli, it does not take a lot of coaxing by one to convince the other to try again. Activities that have been under positive control in the past become high probability responses that people are eager to repeat.

Becoming more positive involves learning the skills for generating behavior that brings positive reinforcers to oneself and others while avoiding behavior that brings punishers or negative reinforcers. There are four general methods that allow people to increase their use of positive control and decrease their use of negative control in situations involving desirable behavior.

1. Increasing Positive Control by Learning Practices that Bring More Positive Reinforcers for Desirable Behavior.   People benefit enormously by learning how to increase the use of positive reinforcement for their own behavior and the behavior of others. The unconditioned reinforcers are similar for most people, but it takes somewhat more skill to determine whether a particular stimulus serves as a conditioned positive reinforcer or conditioned punisher for an individual.

1a. Unconditioned Reinforcers.   Parents of small children are the main sources of unconditioned positive reinforcers in their children's lives. The parents provide the food, fluids, warmth, clothes, bed, and optimal sensory stimulation that children cannot yet provide for themselves. The parents feed, clothe, rock, play with, and provide toys for their children. Some parents scratch, rub, and tickle their children, providing reinforcers via the tactile senses. With this tremendous supply of unconditioned positive reinforcers coming from the parents, it is not surprising that most young children love their parents immensely.

Two lovers can also provide a generous supply of unconditioned positive reinforcers for each other. Conversations and shared activities provide optimal sensory stimulation. Intimacy provides reinforcing tactile and sexual stimulation. By sharing life, two people can enjoy food together, sleeping together, keeping each other warm on cold winter nights, and so forth. People who realize that love and positive relationships benefit from frequent exchanges of positive reinforcers can learn the skills for increasing the quality and quantity of reinforcers they bring to the relationship.

In other relationships optimal sensory stimulation is the most common unconditioned positive reinforcer that is exchanged. When people talk together, play together, watch or participate in sports, make cheerful banter, engage in horseplay at a dull job, or share activities together, they are creating sensory stimulation for each other. Most people, but not all, learn to keep the stimulation in the optimal—positive reinforcement—zone. However, some people are more skilled than others at creating the novel, meaningful sensory stimulation that is most rewarding. And who do we like most? When we see Boris, the bore, at a party, we avoid getting trapped in a conversation with him. But people who are stimulating are enjoyable to interact with and popular. We also like people who are creative, who are often starting novel projects, or who see special meaningfulness in life around them. It takes skill to generate behavior that brings sensory stimulation to oneself and others. Luckily, a large variety of responses produce sensory stimulation, and each of us can develop the skills that best suit our own personality. Some people might increase their general expressiveness, by gesticulating more, moving more, and expressing emotional responses in more overt behavior. Others might develop new interests in order to have more to talk about. Do sensory stimulation reinforcers make a difference? If boring Boris tried to talk you into playing bridge with him, you would be less likely to try the game than if someone more stimulating had invited you to play. Most people prefer to be with individuals who bring reinforcers into their lives, and optimal sensory stimulation is a major reinforcer in most social exchanges.

1b. Conditioned Reinforcers.   It is possible to introduce large numbers of conditioned reinforcers into social interactions. Almost everyone responds to kindness and consideration as conditioned reinforcers; and once people learn the skills, it seems almost effortless to use kindness and consideration with everyone. Another way to bring conditioned positive reinforcers to others is to show an interest in the things that they are doing. This involves a willingness to listen to people and respond supportively to the desirable aspects of their activities. Showing enthusiasm about other people's goals, interests, and behavior also produces positive reinforcement. Smiles, laughter, positive words, and signs of happiness are other conditioned positive reinforcers for most people.

Helping people to enjoy their favorite activities is another way to increase conditioned positive reinforcers. If you know that your best friend loves art posters or poetry books, it might be easy to bring a poster back the next time you visit a bookstore. You can be confident that they are conditioned reinforcers for your friend. If Janet's favorite sport is golf, your suggesting a game of golf may be a positive thing to do. Naturally, the more similar your values and skills are to those of someone else, the more likely you will be able to create conditioned reinforcers. If you hate golf, you may not be able to enjoy playing with Janet; and she may soon learn that playing with you is not as rewarding as playing with someone who really likes golf. In general, people with similar values and behavior repertoires bring more reinforcers into each other's lives than do people with dissimilar values and behavior repertoires.[3] Note that their values and behavior repertoires do not have to be identical! A certain number of differences adds interest; too many differences can, however, prevent people from *mutually* enjoying their shared activities. If he hates golf—which she loves—the major differences reduce the chances for a mutually positive experience.

Vicarious positive reinforcement provides another source of conditioned reinforcers. If you want to learn to enjoy jazz, will you learn more positive associations from

[3]Homans (1974).

watching and listening to jazz artists who smile, tap their feet, and show enjoyment of the music, or from musicians who are somber, unexpressive, and withdrawn? The emotional responses people give off while engaging in any activity elicit emotional responses in others. By learning to show our love for the desirable things in life—art, kindness, sports, or whatever—we are creating the positive vicarious reinforcers that will help others learn to love those things, too.

2. Decreasing Negative Control by Learning Practices that Reduce the Aversive Stimuli Associated with Desirable Behavior.   Once again, the behavior of parents toward small children provides a classic example. Parents remove diaper pins, sharp objects, soiled diapers, and splinters. They often medicate and soothe colds, cuts, wounds, and bee stings. Their caresses and reassuring words dispel the fears elicited by ghost stories, nightmares, thunderstorms, and sirens. The ability of parents to reduce the aversive stimuli experienced by their children is a second major reason why children love their parents.

All through life, a true friend or loving companion often helps reduce aversive experiences. By providing security and emotional support in times of distress, a friend can help a person escape anguish or suffering. A friend can help by listening carefully, solving problems, and assisting in times of need.

Even in more casual relationships, people can decrease negative stimuli by easing each other's load. When one person has *skills* or *strengths* that a second person does not, the first person can often help the second with little effort. Thus the first person reduces the aversive experiences of the second person without noticeably increasing his or her own effort. The accomplished tennis player can give a few tips to the novice and help the beginner avoid many mistakes. The skillful mechanic can quickly identify the carburetor problem and save the novice hours of frustration in fixing it. Experts, in general, can make life easier for others by sharing their skills and knowledge. The person who has physical or emotional strength can make the lot of others easier by taking on the tasks they find difficult. By volunteering to carry the heavier backpack, the strong person helps ensure that the weaker one will not find the hike so effortful and aversive. The person who has learned to cope with death may be able to take some of the burden off other family members by arranging for the funeral, the legal concerns, and other details.

When helping a person learn a new task that requires practice and effort, the use of models, rules, and prompts can reduce the effort of learning and hence facilitate the process. Whenever any of these strategies are used, the people who receive help will find that the desirable behavior they are doing is less effortful and aversive, hence easier to learn or maintain. (In addition, they are likely to feel warm, friendly feelings for the person who has helped lighten their load.)

3. Decreasing the Use of Negative Control by Abstaining from Practices that Increase Aversive Stimuli Associated with Desirable Behavior.   People who nag, nag, nag are creating aversive stimuli for others. These negative stimuli may be used as punishers—"Don't do this," "Stop doing that"—to suppress behavior. Or they may be used as negative reinforcers—"Take out the trash," "Hang up your clothes"—which cause people to do the behavior to avoid additional nagging. Either type of negative control makes social interaction less positive and generates bad feelings about the nagger.

Nagging, criticizing, and fighting are unfortunately all too common in many people's lives. Because these operants are often successful in controlling the behavior of others, they are reinforced. However, any truly desirable behavior should not be subjected to these types of negative control because the behavior will become a CS that elicits aversive feelings. This, in turn, makes people dislike a desirable behavior, and causes people to do the behavior less frequently. Many of the positive practices in the prior two sections can be substituted for these methods of negative control. Instead of nagging, a person can try polite requests before the desired behavior, coupled with positive reinforcement during and after the behavior. Naturally, anyone who has used negative control for a long time cannot expect prior victims to respond instantly to positive control the same as they would if they had usually received positive reinforcement from this person. The reformed nagger may require some practice to polish the new positive skills; and the prior victims will need time for all the stimuli associated with both the ex-nagger and the previously nagged behavior to be counterconditioned into CS's that elicit positive feelings.

Other types of negative control that can usually be avoided are sarcasm, snide remarks, one-upmanship, insults, irritability, rudeness, hostility, domination, dogmatism, pulling rank, and using guilt trips. These all bring aversive stimuli to others, hence are worth avoiding.

4. Decreasing the Use of Negative Control by Abstaining from Practices that Remove Positive Stimuli Normally Associated with Desirable Behavior.   People often punish each other by removing positive stimuli. When he does not get his way, George pouts. He becomes silent and will not talk to Linda for hours, and sometimes for days. By terminating interaction, George has removed the reinforcers he and Linda enjoy together. The loss of reinforcers is aversive for both George and Linda. But George can hold out longer, and Linda usually comes around. ''George, I'm sorry we couldn't go to the football game last weekend. How about going next weekend?'' This reinforces pouting, the behavior that removes positive stimuli from the relationship.

Pouting, sulking, withdrawal, and withholding love are all common ways of controlling others by removing positive stimuli. People often learn such behavior in childhood. The sullen child who will not talk because her parents refused to let her watch TV may be allowed to watch TV after the parents find the sulking aversive enough. Often people do not ''outgrow'' these childhood responses, especially if they have not learned more successful positive social skills. Whether or not people ''outgrow'' pouting often depends on extinction. After people grow up and leave home, their pouting often ceases to produce much reinforcement. If adults act aloof, unsociable, or standoffish after not getting their way, other people may leave them alone as long as they want to be alone. Pouting is no longer followed by the high levels of reinforcement that were common in childhood. As a result of this extinction, people usually learn not to exhibit childish behavior in public. However, a person's spouse, family, and coworkers who have to share the same house or office may ''give in'' to stop the pouting, thereby reinforcing the childish response. Due to this differential reinforcement, pouting is more likely to be maintained in close relationships than in the presence of strangers or casual acquaintances.

UNDESIRABLE BEHAVIOR

It may seem obvious that desirable behavior should be under positive control, with the minimum of negative control. What about undesirable behavior? If a child lies or steals, is positive control possible? Would negative control be better suited than positive control for undesirable behavior? How should one respond to selfishness, rudeness, or inconsiderateness? Can juvenile delinquency, adult crime, and legal problems be dealt with under positive control? If a person is killing himself or herself with alcohol, smoking or dangerous drugs, how can one suppress the undesirable behavior except with aversive control?

Undesirable behavior is behavior that people would like to stop; and most people rely on punishment for suppressing such behavior. However, there are problems with the use of punishment. In the next section, we will review the disadvantages of using aversive control to suppress undesirable behavior. In the final section, we will examine the alternatives that allow us to minimize negative control even in the area of undesirable behavior.

The Problems with Punishment

There are six main problems with using punishment. Because alternatives are available that work in many situations, it is possible to minimize the use of punishment. It is probably unrealistic, however, to think that punishment can be totally avoided. Many believe that punishment will have to be used in certain cases, though it should be used as sparingly as possible.[4]

1. Punishment Often Teaches Aggression.   When parents, teachers, the military, penal systems, or other socializing agents use punishment, they may inadvertently provide models for aggression, violence, or the use of force in dealing with others. The recipient of the punishment—and any onlookers—may easily learn that aggression is an effective means of coping with others. Thus, punishment often teaches aggression via modeling. The observers may not perform aggressive acts in the presence of the punitive model, but they may use the modeled aggression at a later time.

Studies on boys raised by punitive parents in middle-class homes show the principles clearly.[5] When Tommy misbehaves, his parents try to suppress the undesirable behavior with verbal and physical punishment. They raise their voices and shout harsh words. "You idiot! Why did you do such a dumb thing?" They may push Tommy around roughly, then spank or hit him. Most children learn not to fight back, since punitive parents usually apply more punishment if the child returns the violence. Many children

---

[4]Walters and Grusec (1977); Axelrod and Apsche (1983).

[5]Bandura and Walters (1959); Hoffman (1960). Girls usually receive so much more conditioning against the use of violence that they do not readily imitate aggressive parents (Bandura, 1973; J. I. Baldwin, 1983).

who experience verbal and physical punishment at home do not imitate the violent behavior at home. However, boys from such homes tend to use verbal and physical aggression when interacting with their peers. On the playground, Tommy uses harsh words and hits other children more than other boys do.

Violence begets violence, via observational learning. People who use verbal and physical punishment are teaching observers that verbal and physical aggression are effective means of coping with other people. While one person is punishing another, the immediate success of punishment is visible, but the various problems with punishment are not as visible. Thus, the observer may be inclined to use aggressive behavior on others in the future. If the person does not have a repertoire of more positive skills for coping successfully with others, aggressive behavior may be one of the more reinforcing means of dealing with others and may become a high probability response. Aggressive behavior can be under the S^D control of various stimuli. For example, as Tommy grows up, he learns to be polite and friendly as long as everyone else is friendly. But any type of disagreement or conflict provides the S^D's for raising his voice, using strong language, yelling and making aggressive gestures. If others do not give in, the S^D's for physical violence are present.

2. Punishment Causes More Vigorous Responding.　When a person receives intense aversive stimuli—a verbal dressing down, a tirade, sharp criticism, or physical blows—the person is likely to show a general increase in muscle tension and increase in vigor of responding.[6] Whatever responses the person emits next—crying, talking, hitting back—are likely to be more intense than they would otherwise have been. The increased vigor and intensity can turn talking into shouting and threatening gestures into physical blows. In these cases, the increased vigor has the effect of increasing the aggressiveness of the person who received aversive stimulation.

It is true that some people have learned not to shout at or threaten people who punish them. They may have learned to plead for forgiveness, to count to 20, to turn the other cheek, or to seek a more rational solution to the problems at hand. However, individuals who have learned to talk back or threaten may find that punishment from others only increases the violence of their own responses. Tommy may not have been aggressive to his parents when they punished him; but on the playground, Tommy frequently uses aggression, and punishment from others only increases Tommy's own violence. Later, in marriage, when Tom threatens his wife and she shouts back at him, her shouting is an aversive stimulus that causes Tom's responses to become increasingly vigorous until he actually hits her and knocks her to the floor.

3. Punishment Produces Only Temporary Response Suppression.　If an undesired behavior is punished, the rate of responding will be suppressed; but the suppression tends to be only temporary.[7] Thus, punishment is only a temporary solution to the problem of undesirable behavior, unless the person wielding punishment is willing and able to contin-

---

[6]Bandura (1973:53f); Walters and Grusec (1977:142f).

[7]The effects of reinforcement are temporary, too; but intermittent reinforcement can maintain high rates of responding more effectively than intermittent punishment can suppress behavior (Walters and Grusec, 1977).

uously monitor and frequently punish the unwanted responses. One of the reasons we learn relatively well-suppressed responses from the nonsocial environment is that the physical environment imposes strict contingencies of punishment. When we are clumsy with the butcher knife and cut a finger, the punishment is both immediate and on an FR 1 schedule. This is the most efficient mode of punishment, and it suppresses the clumsy use of knives to a low level. Social punishment is rarely as immediate as a painful cut, and is rarely on an FR 1 schedule; thus social punishment tends to be less effective. A child may get caught on the average of every eighth lie (VR 8 schedule) and the punishment may follow the lie by several hours or days. Delayed and intermittent punishment is not as effective as immediate FR 1 punishment in suppressing behavior, hence people who rely on social punishment as the *primary* method of socialization often fail to achieve the desired results.

4. The Recipient of Punishment Learns to Avoid Both Punishment and the People Who Punish.   Whenever people use punishment, they set up conditions that negatively reinforce any responses that are successful in avoiding punishment. Socializing agents must realize that if they use punishment in order to suppress an individual's undesirable responses, they will negatively reinforce any skills the punished person might have for avoiding detection and/or avoiding the socializing agent.[8] First, the child who is punished for lying may learn how to tell better lies—lies that are harder to detect—rather than learning not to lie. The juvenile delinquent who is punished for stealing cars may learn to be more skillful in avoiding detection rather than learning not to steal. Second, if the socializing agent relies too heavily on punishment, the child or the juvenile delinquent eventually learns to avoid the person who punishes. Once this happens, the socializing agent has less opportunity to exert either positive or negative control. This is a double loss. The punitive agent can no longer control undesirable behavior and can no longer teach desirable alternatives. Since avoidance responses are often resistant to extinction, there is a chance that the socializing agent may suffer a permanent loss of influence. Once their child runs away from home, the parents can no longer guide the child's development.

The punished person can avoid punishment either physically or psychologically. Runaways physically distance themselves from excessively aversive households. The juvenile delinquent or criminal goes "underground" and learns to live in a world not easily monitored by the police. If physical escape is not possible, some people may learn to withdraw psychologically, spending increasing time in a fantasy world, or becoming preoccupied with reading, hobbies, or individual sports. After the Communist insurgents established an extremely brutal, death-dealing police state in Cambodia in 1975, many people risked their lives crossing minefields and deadly booby traps to flee the country.[9] Others retreated into total silence or suffered emotional breakdowns. Some committed suicide—the ultimate means for avoiding aversive experience.

5. Punishment Produces Negative Emotional Conditioning.   Negative control is aversive. Through Pavlovian conditioning, the aversive stimuli cause many other stimuli

[8]Staats (1963:51f); Cressey (1978:45).
[9]"Dirge" (1978).

in the punished person's world to become CS's that elicit unpleasant emotions. Some of these aversive emotions may be adaptive, but others are often maladaptive. Parents who punish their child for running into the street may condition the child to fear playing near traffic (which is adaptive); but they may also condition the child to fear the parents (which is not adaptive). The music student who is frequently criticized for sloppy performances may have sloppy playing conditioned into an aversive CS (which is adaptive), but too much criticism can cause music *in general* to be conditioned into an aversive CS (which is not adaptive).

People who have received relatively frequent punishment often learn to respond to a large number of stimuli as CS's for aversive emotional responses such as anxiety, shame, guilt, or bad feelings about themselves. In most societies, females receive more aversive control than males. As a result, females often learn more negative emotional responses than males. Females have more nightmares, depression, insomnia, nervousness, and irrational fears than men.[10] Naturally, not all females have these negative emotional responses and not all males are free of them. The point is that people of either sex are likely to have negative emotional responses if exposed to high levels of negative control, and females tend to receive more negative control than males.

6. Punishment Can Lead to Generalized Response Suppression.   When behavior X is punished, not only behavior X but other similar responses are suppressed, too. This is known as generalized response suppression. If a person is punished for a large number of different responses, generalization increases the number even further so that the person may show a generalized response suppression across much of the entire behavior reper-toire. This produces the "inhibited" person, the person who is afraid to speak up, the person who never takes the lead, the person who fears aversive consequences at every turn. Heavy doses of negative control often give the inhibited person excessively negative emotional responses (item 5 above) and a repertoire of physical or psychological avoid-ance responses (item 4 above). Extreme cases of generalized response suppression are not too common, but milder forms such as shyness are common. A study of high school and college students showed that about forty percent of the students reported feeling shy.[11]

ALTERNATIVES TO PUNISHMENT

Punishment can be brutal and dehumanizing. It can produce many undesirable side effects. There are four major positive alternatives to punishment that have the effect of suppressing undesirable behavior without the undesirable side effects of punishment. Each of these can be used in conjunction with the others. It is frequently possible to use two or more of these methods at once—to minimize the need for punishment.

1. Differential Reinforcement of Other Behavior.   A very effective nonpunitive method for decreasing the frequency of a behavior is the use of differential reinforcement

10Chesler (1971); Tavris and Offir (1977:221).
11Zimbardo et al. (1975); Zimbardo and Radl (1981).

of other behavior (DRO). If Mark is hooked on the TV and Nancy wants to help him kick the habit, she can use DRO. By rewarding Mark for other responses but not rewarding him for TV watching, she may get Mark into bowling, dining out, discos, movies, or visiting with friends in the evening. The more positive reinforcement Nancy can bring to the other activities, the better. If both she and Mark enjoy some common friends, the extra social reinforcement may help lure Mark away from the tube and into more gratifying alternatives.

Differential reinforcement of other behavior works best when the *other* behavior is *incompatible* with the undesired behavior. If a child is aggressing on playmates, DRO will work better if incompatible behavior is reinforced than if *any* nonaggressive behavior is reinforced. Reinforcement for incompatible responses—such as helping, consideration, or concern for others—not only draws the child away from aggression, it gives the child a new style of interpersonal relations which makes aggression much less likely to occur. If your best friend worries a lot, DRO for any other behavior besides worry would be less efficient than DRO for competing responses that interfere with or distract the person from worry. Differential reinforcement for *any* behavior other than worry might include reinforcement for reading the newspaper or watching the news on TV; however, the media might expose the person to news about disasters, epidemics, crime, or other things that trigger worry. On the other hand, DRO for competing responses should distract the person from worry by reinforcing attention to positive alternatives, such as gratifying social relations, activities with friends, or stimulating new pastimes. As the person gets wrapped up in rewarding activities, there will be less time for worry.

Differential reinforcement for other behavior can have long-lasting effects. Once a person taps into a new source of reinforcers, the person may never go back to the earlier problematic behavior. After a person learns to be kind, thoughtful, and concerned about others, the rewards of this new style of social relations may be so great that the person could not go back to previous inconsiderate, selfish, or hostile ways. Once a person gets excited about participating in team athletics or charity groups, there may be little time or reinforcement for worrying; and after a couple of years, the ex-worrier may find it hard to believe that there once was a time in which worry used to fill the day.

When it is imperative that the problematic behavior never be emitted again, DRO can be combined with brief punishment or threats of punishment. The ex-alcoholic may receive reinforcers for holding down a stimulating new job that occupies many hours of the day and keeps the person out of the bars (DRO); but the threat of losing the job if caught drunk adds an extra motivation to stay dry. The person need never experience the punisher—that is, never be fired—for the threat of punishment to motivate avoidance of the bottle and keep the person oriented to the healthier and more reinforcing alternative.

2. Extinction.   The frequency of operants can be decreased by removing the reinforcers that maintain the behavior. Although punishment can produce instant results, extinction may require days or weeks to produce equal results (p. 26). Extinction is even slower if the undesirable behavior had previously been on a schedule of partial reinforcement (p. 228). Because extinction does not produce as immediate and rapid a decline in response rate as does punishment, it is harder for people to learn to use. There are advantages, however, for using extinction rather than punishment. Because extinction does not involve the application of aversive stimuli, it does not condition aversive emotional responses and avoidance. Also, it does not provide models for the verbal or physical mistreatment of others.

As we saw in Chapter 7, children may learn a variety of "attention getting" behaviors. Some forms of attention getting are undesirable: shouting, throwing tantrums, starting fights, being insolent, and so forth. If attention from adults is the main source of reinforcement for the behavior, adults can successfully terminate the behavior by ceasing to pay attention. To make extinction work, it is important to know what reinforcers are maintaining the undesirable response and to be able to remove a large portion of these. If it is not possible to remove a large percentage of the reinforcers, then some other method besides extinction will have to be used. For example, if a child's peer group is the key source of reinforcement for attention getting, adults will not be able to stop the behavior by cutting off adult attention alone. Reasoning and DRO might work well in this case.

There are, however, many undesirable responses in everyday life for which extinction is well suited. Because parents provide the major source of reinforcers for their children, they can often terminate unwanted behavior by extinction. The child who wakes the parents and demands a glass of water in the middle of the night will cease demanding after the parents cease giving reinforcement. The child who keeps pestering Mother and Father to help solve homework problems or write an essay will stop pestering after help is no longer forthcoming. Extinction can be combined effectively with any of the other methods in this section. For example, while inconsiderate behavior is being extinguished, the parents could make special efforts to model thoughtful and considerate behavior.

People in intimate relationships often control many of the reinforcers that condition or maintain each other's behavior. She may yell at him because yelling is the only way she can make him listen. That is, yelling is reinforced by his response of listening to her complaints and complying with her demands. On the other hand, he pouts when he does not get his way. Pouting is reinforced when she eventually comes over to him, says nice things, and tries to make up. These and many other behavior problems that blemish intimate relations can often be removed from people's behavior repertoires by extinction. He stops reinforcing her yelling by *not* paying attention to her when she yells. This works especially well in conjunction with DRO: He pays attention to her when she is not yelling. She stops reinforcing his pouting by *not* paying attention when he sulks. She may combine extinction with DRO by being especially friendly and considerate when he is not pouting.

People need not be parents or lovers to be major sources of reinforcers for each other. Friends, coworkers, and acquaintances often exchange many reinforcers. Whenever people are dependent on one another for mutual support, fun and games, sympathy, team effort, etc., they are dependent on each other's reinforcers; hence the removal of reinforcers can decrease the frequency of undesirable behavior via extinction. For example, if several factory workers all depend on each other's joking and horseplay to combat the boredom of a tedious job, stopping the fun and games after one person offends another will help stop the offensive behavior.[12]

3. Observational Learning. Models can provide information and vicarious reinforcement that decreases undesirable behavior and increases desirable alternatives. When an

[12]Roy (1959–1960).

observer sees a model abstain from undesirable behavior and engage in desirable alternative behavior, the observer can learn desirable patterns without having to be punished.

When a positive model is in an S^D context where many people might do an undesirable behavior, the model may abstain from the undesirable behavior and respond in ways that help observers resist the "temptation" (S^D control) to do the behavior. Observers may learn to abstain and to adopt some of the resistance practices used by the model. Some children see their parents get into heated arguments, then see one or both parents resist the tendency to escalate the argument further. "Hey, we can't fight about this. We're both mature adults; we've got to calm down and figure out a reasonable solution." This behavior provides an excellent model of practices for avoiding undesirable behavior and switching to a more positive alternative. If the alternative succeeds and both people show signs of being happy with the new solution, the avoidance of an aversive scene and the vicarious reinforcement from solving the problem will help the children learn skills for coping with heated arguments in a civilized manner.

Coping models provide more information than mastery models and should help the observers gain positive skills faster (p. 185). The mastery model demonstrates perfect mastery without revealing many of the steps needed to attain mastery of positive control. Coping models reveal the methods they apply to any given problem as they struggle to cope with it.[13] Parents who have completely mastered the problem of resolving disagreements may resolve their infrequent conflicts with only a few words. The onlooking child has little opportunity to learn the dozens of skills that the parents may have mastered. Another set of parents may reveal much more of their repertoire of coping skills. After seeing the parents show anger, the child may hear a dialogue of self-instruction for coping with anger. "I don't want to say harsh words; I want to let you see I love you." "I feel the same. Let's try to work out a compromise." "Fine, but first let me be sure I understand your complaint." As the dialogue continues, the child will observe many of the specific skills the parents use to cope with problems. Because the coping models give the child more information, they increase the chances that the child will be able to successfully imitate their interpersonal skills. Note that the coping models may be just as effective in solving their problems as the mastery models. The crucial difference is that the coping models display more of the skills they use to avoid aversive control and to utilize positive control; and they verbalize about those skills in ways that help explain their behavior. The child raised by coping-model parents will be more likely to learn positive interpersonal skills than a child raised by mastery-model parents with equal skills.

Most people are exposed to a multitude of models, some of whom use aversive control, and others, positive control. Any attempt to increase the ratio of positive to negative models may help pass on positive control skills. Many parents attempt to do this by refusing to fight in front of the children (thus decreasing the children's exposure to negative models). However, parents who are unable to resolve their problems in a positive way in front of the children still leave the children deficient in positive skills. In some cases, if the parents are not good positive coping models, the children may learn these positive skills from other models as they grow up—from kind neighbors, good teachers, considerate friends or roommates, a positive spouse, and so forth.

---

[13]Meichenbaum (1971:298–307); Bandura and Barab (1973).

4. Reasoning and Rules.   One of the most effective ways of decreasing the frequency of undesirable behavior is the use of reasoning. Instead of punishing a person for undesirable behavior, it is often possible to have a serious conversation about the pros and cons of both the undesirable behavior and its alternatives. This type of serious conversation teaches people to rationally evaluate the problems or dangers of undesirable behavior, along with positive advantages of more acceptable alternatives. All undesirable behavior is ''undesirable'' because it causes damage to people, places, or things. As people learn to use reasoning to identify the objectionable consequences of problematic behavior, they learn to avoid both undesirable behavior and its aversive consequences.

Of all the ways that reasoning can be done, *humanistic reasoning* is one of the most effective. Humanistic reasoning emphasizes the human happiness or suffering produced by any type of behavior, helping people to understand how their actions affect both themselves and others. Humanistic reasoning has been shown to be far superior to physical punishment in child rearing.[14] What if a 5-year-old child is playing with a ball in the house and knocks over a fine figurine, breaking it? Rather than spank the child, the parent can calmly sit down with the child and explain why the item and other similar ones in the house are valuable.

> *Your great-grandmother gave these figurines to me years ago before she died. Grandma used to have these in a special case in her house in Iowa. They cannot be replaced and they are priceless to me. I hope to give them to you when you grow up. Feel how thin the porcelain is. Here, you can see the light through it when you hold it up to the window. Now you must be careful not to hurt them because they are the only things I have left from Grandma Nelly. I loved Grandma Nelly like you love your Grandma, and it hurts me to see her things destroyed.*

When done gently and lovingly, humanistic reasoning may involve a long conversation about people, their behavior and their feelings. The parent may tell stories about Nelly's concern for other people and her love for beautiful things, responding sensitively to the child's comments and questions. Humanistic reasoning lets the child see why other people suffer when undesirable behavior is done, and it gives the child rules for avoiding both the undesirable behavior and the unhappiness it causes. ''So please, don't throw things around in here where you might break any more of these delicate things.''

A parent who uses reasoning provides a model of self-control and humanistic concern rather than a model of verbal or physical aggression. The parent who uses reasoning is teaching the child a valuable verbal skill for talking and thinking about the positive and negative consequences of behavior. In addition, the parent gives the child useful information and rules that the child can use later. The pros and cons the parent describes serve as verbal CS's that elicit conditioned emotional responses so that the child feels positive about considerate behavior and feels sad about destructive behavior.[15] Also, reasoning provides general principles—broad, humanistic rules of considerate conduct—which aid in producing generalized prosocial behavior. Rather than getting spanked for breaking a specific little figurine, the child has received a broad lesson in appreciation and

---

[14]Hoffman and Saltzstein (1967); Hoffman (1970); Parke (1972); La Voie (1974).
[15]Walters and Parke (1967); Cheyne and Walters (1970).

consideration. Later, if the child brings a frisbee, ball, or butterfly net into the house, the generalized rules for considerate conduct will help the child be much more careful not to damage things than if the child had merely been spanked for breaking a specific figurine.

Reasoning can be useful at any age, but people who have been raised with reasoning ever since childhood are most likely to use it and respond quickly when others use it with them in adulthood. A man and woman who need to resolve a marital conflict are more likely to succeed with reasoning if they both were raised with reasoning rather than physical punishment. As each spouse talks with the other about their problem and its possible solutions, they may use reasoning to create a long list of all the advantages and disadvantages associated with each possible solution to their problem. Eventually, certain solutions will begin to stand out as having more mutually acceptable advantages than the others, and both husband and wife will understand the reasons why they should work toward attaining the most promising solutions to their problem.[16] Reasoning can be used in many other contexts. The board of directors may use reasoning when trying to resolve differences of opinion and to decide how to steer the future of their corporation. The supervisor may use reasoning when explaining to the workers the need for following factory procedures. If the supervisor can present enough positive reasons for adopting the new procedures, the workers will switch to the new activity for positive reasons. If the workers cannot be convinced of the positive value of the new practices, they may convince the supervisor of the need to renegotiate the guidelines with the factory policy makers. Reasoning tends to facilitate democratic decision making and allow more positive solutions to be selected from the available alternatives.

CONCLUSION

There is a continuum from total negative control to total positive control. People usually use combinations of positive and negative control in their interactions with others. Most people are in the positive half of the continuum most of the time; but almost everyone could become more positive. Under positive control, life is much more pleasant. Guilt, anxiety, and worry become things of the past.[17] Under positive control, each person can learn constructive, creative behavior and feel good about his or her contributions.

Although punishment may never be totally abolished, it can be minimized. It is needed only as a backup, a stopgap for those situations in which more positive practices do not work quickly enough.[18] When punishment is combined with positive control, it is usually possible to keep the use of negative control to a minimum. If applied early in the development of undesirable behavior, a few brief, mild punishments—coupled with positive reinforcement for desirable alternative behavior—may suffice to eliminate undesirable behavior.

[16]Marital partners can avoid inflicting unnecessary pain on each other by reasoning with each other on an equal basis rather than fighting (Gottman, 1979).

[17]Kaufmann (1973).

[18]Baer (1974); Walters and Grusec (1977); Newsom et al. (1983).

14

Thinking, the Self, and Self-Control

● *In this chapter you will learn that thinking is a behavior; you will discover the origins of optimistic thinking, pessimistic thinking, rational thought, the self-concept, identity, identity crises, and self-control.*

Early behaviorists focused their attention on *overt* behavior because overt behavior was easy to see, hear, and record on laboratory instruments. As behavior theory and methodology have advanced, increasing attention has been given to *covert* behavior: thinking, feeling, consciousness, awareness of self, self-control, and so forth.[1] The research indicates that covert behavior can be explained by the same principles that explain overt behavior. Thinking is behavior. The things we think about are learned from models, rules, prompts, and reinforcement. Our self-concept appears when people teach us to describe our own behavior as we would describe the behavior of others. Self-control results from a repertoire of skills we learn for modifying our own behavior. Not everyone learns these covert skills equally well; but the same is true of overt·skills—not everyone sings or runs equally well.

First we will examine thinking, the most general form of covert behavior; then we will consider the nature of the self-concept and self-control.

[1]This analysis can be done "without abandoning the basic position of behaviorism" (Skinner, 1969:228) because it treats thinking and other covert processes as behavior rather than spiritual or otherwise dualistically conceived processes (Skinner, 1957:449). For further development of the behavioral position see Mead (1934:38, 40, 47, 105, 260); Skinner (1957, 1969, 1974); Staats (1968, 1975); Bandura (1969, 1971, 1977); Mahoney (1970, 1974); Meichenbaum (1977); Rosenthal and Zimmerman (1978); Rachlin (1980); Mischel (1981); Baldwin (1982, 1985); Last (1984); and the journal *Behaviorism*.

THINKING IS BEHAVIOR[2]

Thinking is the behavior of the brain. Most brain activity is not conscious.[3] We will focus on the fraction of thought processes of which we are aware. Our awareness is mostly occupied with sense perceptions of the current environment along with an *internal dialogue*—or internal conversation—we carry on with ourselves inside our heads. The sense perceptions are given to us through the five external senses and the internal sense receptors. Perception is not passive. People often learn behavior patterns of selective perception that bias their perceptions by directing attention to certain stimuli and away from other stimuli. The internal dialogue that accompanies these perceptions consists of an ongoing conversation we "hear" inside our heads after we begin to learn language in childhood. Thinking is sometimes called *subvocal speech,* because the stream of words we "hear" during thought is similar to spoken words except that it is below the spoken level—hence "subvocal."

The internal dialogue of our thoughts is a gift to us from society, from the verbal community that talks to us, asks us to describe our behavior, and reinforces self-descriptive verbal responses. As George Herbert Mead emphasized, the mind and awareness of "self" have their origins in symbolic social interaction.[4] This is most obvious when you realize that you think in English rather than in Russian or Chinese. During your socialization, the verbal community provided *models* of the English language. You heard the *rules* of English: "Don't use double negatives." Differential reinforcement was given for correct use of English phrases and idioms, and for verbal output that was comprehensible to other speakers of English. Through this process, you not only learned to speak English but also to think—carry out subvocal speech—in English.

The *contents* of a person's thoughts are also a gift of the society in which the person lives. We do not worry about witch-hunts, as they did in Salem, Massachusetts, in 1692. Our thoughts are filled with the issues of the current historical moment, whether they be the questions of nuclear power, the kind of car to buy, tonight's TV program, or current job opportunities. Much of our thought content depends on the subculture in which we live. The motorcycle enthusiast has learned how to talk about cycle engines, the performance of different bikes, and the advantages of various equipment. The artist may speak a very different language, expressing interests in the latest exhibit at the museum, trends in modern art, and the galleries where one's work will get good exposure. The motorcyclist

---

[2]"The simplest and most satisfactory view is that thought is simply *behavior*—verbal or nonverbal, covert or overt" (Skinner, 1957:449).

[3]Skinner (1969:246) stresses that "all behavior is basically unconscious," unless "well-established practices of self-description generate consciousness." To the behaviorist, the unconscious is quite benevolent compared with the Freudian model of the unconscious. The behaviorist does not assume that the unconscious is filled with selfish wishes or lustful drives, as Freud did (Maddi, 1980).

[4]Mead was the originator of social behaviorism. Mead (1934:8, 10, 101, 416) rejected Watson's view that behaviorism should not deal with thoughts and set up a program for tracing thoughts (and self) back to their social origins. "What I want particularly to emphasize is the temporal and logical pre-existence of the social process to the self-conscious individual that arises in it" (Mead, 1934:186). "The content put into the mind is only a development and product of social interaction" (Mead, 1934:191). "We must regard mind, then, as arising and developing within the social process, within the empirical matrix of social interactions" (Mead, 1934:133).

and the artist live in different subcultures, hear different verbal inputs, and learn to think about different things.

Karl Mannheim, a founder of the sociology of knowledge, stated that the individual "speaks the language of his group; he thinks in the manner in which his group thinks. He finds at his disposal only certain words and their meanings. He participates in thinking further what other men have thought before him."[5] If your closest friends frequently talk about politics, overpopulation, alternative energy sources, and rent control, you are likely to talk—and think—about these topics, too. If you hear a news item relevant to the topics, you are likely to both think about and communicate the information to your friends, since these behaviors are often reinforced. Because your history of learning experience is unique, your thoughts will never be the same as anyone else's; hence your rethinking of any topic will usually introduce novel variations into the topic. Since variety is a source of sensory stimulation reinforcement, it makes interaction more reinforcing than if we all thought the same thoughts and said the same things.

We learn the ability to think conscious verbal thoughts from symbolic social interaction. Our thoughts tend to be closely related to verbal patterns common in our historical period and subculture. But each individual's unique history of learning experience introduces unique style and personality into that individual's thoughts and words.

OPERANT CONDITIONING OF THOUGHTS

Speaking and thinking are both verbal behavior. One is overt, the other is covert. Homme labeled thoughts *coverants* to designate their status as covert operants.[6] *The research on coverants indicates that these "operants of the mind" are acquired and maintained in much the same manner as overt operants are.*[7] *Models, rules,* and *verbal prompts* provide exposure to spoken and written words that may become acquired as coverants by the listener-reader. However, the frequency of these coverants in a person's internal dialogue of thoughts depends on the patterns of *reinforcement* and *punishment* that follow each coverant.[8]

Models. An admired friend who talks at length about working in the Peace Corps serves as a positive model for your learning similar thoughts. Later, you may find yourself thinking that perhaps you should join the Peace Corps, too. Because you like the person and the person gave positive emotional cues—smiles and enthusiastic gestures—while describing the humanistic things the Peace Corps worker can do, you will experience vicarious reinforcement as you rethink the thoughts your friend gave you. The novelty of

---

[5]Mannheim (1936:3). Thinking should not be conceived of as the action of a self-sufficient individual but as the action of a person enmeshed in an ongoing social-historical process (Mannheim, 1936:27ff).

[6]Homme (1965).

[7]See Staats (1968, 1975), Mahoney (1974), Bandura (1977), Rosenthal and Zimmerman (1978), and Mischel (1981) for summaries of the research on covert operants.

[8]Verbal conditioning need not involve awareness. Our thoughts and speech can be modified without conscious awareness (Rosenfeld and Baer, 1969). However, rules that make a person aware of patterns of reinforcement and punishment facilitate verbal conditioning (Mahoney, 1974:41f).

thinking about yourself in a Peace Corps job will provide sensory stimulation reinforcers, too. If you have no urgent competing responses to distract you, thoughts about the Peace Corps may become more frequent. Later you may share your new ideas with someone else who spent a year in the Peace Corps in central Africa. What if this person had suffered unbelievable hardships, contracted a serious disease, and felt the work was futile? Each enthusiastic thought you voice is likely to be followed by a pessimistic rebuttal based on this person's negative experiences. The pessimist is simultaneously punishing your thinking of idealistic thoughts and modeling a new set of bleaker thoughts about Peace Corps work. If you like the person, this new description of Peace Corps work will be more strongly reinforced by vicarious reinforcement than if you dislike the person.

Rules.   Rules also affect the acquisition and maintenance of coverants. If you have often heard people say, ''Never trust politicians; always be critical of what they say,'' the rules may influence your internal dialogue. After hearing a political speech full of campaign promises, you may recall the rule and begin to criticize the politician's promises. The campaign promises serve as S^D's for recalling the rule; and the rule serves as an S^D for applying your critical skills. While at a formal party, you may recall a rule of etiquette stating that one should graciously thank the host and hostess before leaving. The rule then serves as an S^D for rehearsing privately—as subvocal speech—several things you might say. Rehearsal gives you practice in wording your comments tactfully and allows you to identify the phrasing that sounds most positive.[9] After you approach the host and hostess and thank them, the good effect of the carefully chosen words will reinforce both the rule use and your subvocal rehearsal skills.

Verbal Prompts.   Thoughts are sometimes influenced by verbal prompts. Verbal prompts are most often used when one person cannot think of the right word or phrase and a second person ''fills in'' or suggests the word or phrase that is needed.

Reinforcement and Punishment.   Thoughts can be modified by any type of reinforcement or punishment, involving either unconditioned or conditioned stimuli. A thought can be modified by *unconditioned reinforcers or punishers* when the thought leads to actions that produce reinforcement or punishment. The thought of popping some popcorn may begin a chain of responses that ends in a delicious snack and the unconditioned reinforcer of food. Thinking of a way to stop the house from losing its heat on windy winter nights is negatively reinforced by the avoidance of being too cold. On the other hand, thoughts that lead to external punishers can be suppressed by unconditioned punishers. The child who thinks that honeybees are pretty little creatures and reaches out to pick one up usually gets stung. Because it leads to external punishers, the thought of touching bees will become less frequent. Likewise, thoughts about various untried activities become less common if the activities turn out to be aversive. Erotic literature may suggest that certain esoteric sexual practices would be fun, and a person may fantasize about trying them. However, after actually doing them, the person discovers that *some* are painful, and the person is likely to stop fantasizing about doing these aversive activities.

[9]Rosenthal and Zimmerman (1978:260f).

Although all reinforcers and punishers can affect the frequency of coverants, sensory stimulation reinforcement plays a special role (Chapter 6). Sensory stimulation produces the only unconditioned reinforcers and punishers that can influence the frequency of thoughts without their having to lead to overt behavior first. (Of course, sensory stimulation can reinforce or punish overt operants, too.) Thinking produces sensory stimulation. If a person is not overstimulated, novel and meaningful thoughts are usually more reinforcing than familiar and meaningless thoughts. When a young person first imagines being a movie star, a doctor, or a professional athlete, much of the reinforcement for the thought comes from imagining oneself in a new, exciting, and meaningful role. Children can spend hours at a time in fantasy role play, as they think about the careers and roles they have seen modeled by adults, TV performers, and their peers. This mental play is reinforced by the sensory stimulation it brings, and it gives the child practice for playing a variety of social roles. The combination of practice and reinforcement helps the child learn various ideas, lines, scripts, and roles used in social interaction. This learning process is called *anticipatory socialization,* and it can occur at any time in life, whenever new, meaningful roles or tasks are modeled by real or symbolic models. Problem solving, playing with new ideas, drug trips, and daydreaming are other examples of thought patterns which are reinforced by the novel or meaningful sensory stimulation that they produce.

Thoughts can be modified by *conditioned reinforcers and punishers* from either inside or outside the body. A clever thought about how to earn more money may be reinforced by the internal conditioned reinforcers of *thinking* about spending all the money. It may also be reinforced by the external conditioned reinforcers of actually earning a sizeable sum of money. The thought of driving to the country may be reinforced by pleasurable thoughts about the beauty of the countryside. The decision to take the drive is reinforced by seeing the pleasant views. For people who find the thought of going to jail aversive enough, thoughts of robbing a bank are usually punished and suppressed by the unpleasant thoughts of being caught and imprisoned.

People can learn to use positive and negative thoughts to produce self-reinforcement and self-punishment, thereby changing the frequency of their own behavior. After making an attractive flower arrangement, thoughts such as "That's a lovely piece of work" serve as self-reinforcement for quality behavior. This type of cognitive self-reward can even be used to reinforce desirable patterns of thought.[10] If a person has a creative thought and then thinks, "That's beautiful!" this subvocal self-reward helps reinforce the skills for creative thinking, even if the thought is not expressed in overt action. Self-punishment after thinking undesirable thoughts can help decrease the frequency of these thoughts.

PAVLOVIAN CONDITIONING OF THOUGHTS

Although thinking is a behavior, thoughts also function as stimuli. Through Pavlovian conditioning, thoughts can become conditioned stimuli (CS's) that can, in turn, elicit conditioned responses, including emotional responses. Merely thinking about someone

---

[10]Bandura (1977).

you find sexually attractive can elicit sexual responses such as vaginal lubrication or penile erection and erotic feelings.[11] Thinking about a recent embarrassing experience can elicit blushing and nervous sweating, along with aversive sensations.

Positive Thoughts

Thoughts that are associated with reinforcing events can become CS's that function as conditioned positive reinforcers and *elicit pleasurable emotional responses.* As young children learn that birthdays are associated with parties and presents, the mere thought that a birthday is coming soon becomes a CS that elicits pleasurable feelings and reinforces frequent thoughts of the party. The closer the big day comes, the more the child thinks about all the ice cream, cake, and presents, since merely thinking these thoughts generates the pleasurable cognitive CS's that reinforce continued thinking about the birthday. Teenagers who love to think about distant places may find that their daydreams about travel are longer and more frequent than daydreams about other, less rewarding activities. Adults often find their thoughts turning to the new furniture or car they plan to buy, to memories of the big bowling tournament they won, or other positive events. Thinking optimistic thoughts and daydreaming about wonderful future possibilities are reinforced by the positive stimuli they produce. A person may also receive social reinforcement for positive thinking, since others usually find interaction with the cheerful, optimistic individual to be rewarding.

If optimistic thoughts are so rewarding, why is it that people do not think positive thoughts all the time? If a person has often experienced disappointment, failure, or other punishments after optimistically planning for future events, the punishment can suppress optimistic thinking. Also, worry can serve as a competing response that decreases optimism (see below).

Negative Thoughts

Thoughts that are associated with punishment can become CS's that function as conditioned punishers and *elicit aversive emotional responses.*[12] Aversive thoughts often suppress the frequency of chains of thoughts that lead to them. Many people find the thought of their own death to be aversive, and after a while they stop thinking about it. Some students hate taking exams. They hate thinking about finals and all the work they have to do. Even though they know that exams are coming up in a few weeks, they avoid thinking about them because the thoughts are aversive. Some students cannot bring themselves to think seriously about studying until fears of failing the course negatively reinforce their thinking about preparing for finals.

Worry and Self-Torment.   If thoughts and worries about aversive things are CS's that function as conditioned punishers, why do some people end up worrying all the time? Why is it that they cannot stop thinking about the problems, heartaches, torments, regrets, uncertainties, and fears that all function as aversive CS's? There are numerous patterns of

---

[11]Kinsey et al. (1953); Masters and Johnson (1966, 1979); Annon (1973); Wagner (1973).
[12]Miller (1951); Barber and Hahn (1964).

conditioning that reinforce worrying more strongly than the CS's of the negative thoughts can punish and suppress the worrying.[13] First, people who worry often receive sympathy from others; and this social reinforcement can condition worry into a high frequency response. People who criticize and belittle themselves in their thoughts and words often find that other people respond by enumerating all their good points. If a person has not learned many other responses that bring social reinforcement, the attention given to worrying and self-criticism can condition these coverants into high frequency responses, even though these thoughts are CS's that elicit aversive emotions.

Second, worry is often negatively reinforced by the escape from or avoidance of major problems. The person who worries about passing a course may plan ahead, study hard, and eventually be rewarded by a good grade. The person who worries about the vacation plans for months ahead may succeed in getting everything arranged so that the vacation goes well. Thus, worry can be a type of problem-solving behavior and can be negatively reinforced because it allows people to avoid various problems. However, *while* people are thinking about possible future problems, they may be exposing themselves to numerous worrisome issues that are cognitive CS's for aversive feelings.

Third, beginning in the early years of life, a child may learn to be self-critical and self-punitive because this behavior often reduces the likelihood that other people will punish the child. For example, parents are less likely to punish their son's transgression if little Freddie is blaming himself for breaking the vase, criticizing his own clumsiness, and saying how bad he feels than if Freddie had shown no self-punishment. Thus, the child learns to escape social punishment by engaging in self-punishment. Because escape and avoidance behavior can be very persistent, the person may engage in self-punishing thoughts long after there is a chance for social punishment.

Fourth, once any of the above three patterns of reinforcement causes a person to begin worrying, the worries may be further reinforced by sensory stimulation. If a person begins to worry about being shy or unattractive, dozens of new worries can follow: "Will I ever meet someone who loves me?" "Will I ever get married?" "Will I be lonely all my life?" The more novel problems a person discovers to worry about, the more sensory stimulation reinforcement there is for worrying. Some people who worry a great deal are especially skilled at locating problems to worry about; and the more things they can find to worry about, the more sensory stimulation reinforcement they receive for their problem-finding skills. Even when things are going right, they focus on everything that could go wrong and discover—or invent—numerous problems that would have never occurred to other people.

Thoughts Condition Thoughts

Through Pavlovian conditioning, the CS's of one train of thoughts can condition other thoughts. *If one set of thoughts functions as a CS for pleasurable feelings, other thoughts that are paired with the positive set of thoughts will also become CS's for pleasurable feelings.*[14] When you fall in love with someone, you often find that the things

[13]Bandura (1971, 1977).
[14]Osgood and Tannenbaum (1955); Staats (1968, 1975); Mahoney (1974); Bandura (1977); Schwartz (1984).

that person likes also become more appealing to you. If the person you love is an avid sailor, you may find yourself—for the first time in your life—fantasizing about sailing in the Caribbean. Each time the fantasies of sailing are paired with the positive thoughts of sharing the experience with your lover, the thoughts of sailing become more strongly conditioned into CS's that elicit pleasure.

Eventually, sailing may become such a strong CS for pleasurable feelings that you notice yourself lingering over magazine pictures of sailboats (indicating that the CS's of the boat pictures reinforce your prolonged attention), and smiling as you picture yourself on the boat (indicating that the CS's of boats have elicited positive emotional responses). The person who loves money may find that thoughts which were once neutral become positive if they become associated with money. The entrepreneur may have never cared much for Florida vacations. But when the entrepreneur gets a good buy on a resort hotel on the beach near Miami, thinking about Florida vacations becomes more positive. The entrepreneur thinks about people flying to Miami for the sun and surf, for the night life, for a leisurely stay in a resort hotel on the beach; and intermixed with these thoughts are positive thoughts of the monetary success of the new investment. Soon, thoughts of the Florida beaches become positive CS's that reinforce the acquisition of Florida posters for the office walls and elicit smiles as the investor imagines the palm-lined shores.

If one set of thoughts functions as a CS for aversive feelings, other thoughts that are paired with those negative thoughts will become increasingly negative. Some people who live in cities near a nuclear power plant have relatively neutral opinions about nuclear power. However, if the plant malfunctions and releases radioactive wastes into the environment, they may find their thoughts and feelings about nuclear power changing, as the thoughts become CS's for aversive feelings. The more the people think about meltdowns, radiation poisoning, and radiation-induced cancers, the more frightened they become, and the more the thought of nuclear power becomes a fear-eliciting CS. (The people who live near Three Mile Island experienced prolonged aversive mental conditioning after the nuclear accident there, and many developed a chronic form of stress that lasted for years.[15])

People who worry a great deal may inadvertently condition a large number of once neutral thoughts into fear-eliciting CS's. After a person has learned to be afraid of dying in an airplane accident, the person may pair other thoughts with the first fear and thereby condition new fears. While worrying about flying home for the vacation, the person may imagine being in an airplane crash, being helplessly trapped in the burning plane, and dying a horrible death. While worrying about these gory details, the person may happen to think about driving to the airport and suddenly imagine that there could be an automobile accident: The car could crash, trap the passengers, then catch on fire. In a panic, the person thinks: "Is there anything that's safe? Even walking is dangerous. A car could go out of control, come careening across the sidewalk and kill you at any moment." What began with worrying about dying in an air accident has become worry about other kinds of travel; and the person has conditioned several new fears by pairing thoughts of driving and walking with thoughts of the feared consequences. Continuing these types of fear-producing worries can condition fear of any kind of travel, and eventually make the person afraid to leave the house.

[15]Herbert (1982).

S^D's AND THOUGHTS

Because thoughts are operants, they come under S^D control. Because thoughts can also function as stimuli, they can become S^D's for other operants. Stimuli that regularly precede a reinforced thought become S^D's that set the occasion for the thought in the future. Each of the following S^D's has strong stimulus control over people's coverants. "What is your name? Where were you born? What is your birthday? What is two times two?" Other S^D's have less predictable S^D control. "Name a color. Name a foreign country." These S^D's allow more room for "free association" since a large range of responses are correct, and hence may be reinforced. At any moment, the stimulus collage exposes us to multitudes of S^D's—some with strong control for specific responses and others with less specific control—that set the occasion for our thoughts.

Those thoughts called "memories" provide a clear example of S^D control. When a child grows up in Hometown, the people, places, and activities unique to Hometown provide the child with firsthand learning experiences that will eventually become memories only. Years later, the person may try to recall memories of childhood in Hometown and be surprised how little comes back. But note what happens when the adult gets out an old photo album, high school yearbooks, or newspaper clippings. The photos of Mom and Dad at the Fourth of July picnic suddenly bring back memories of things that happened on that occasion. A picture of the person's best friend in high school triggers off a long chain of thoughts that the person may not have had in years. Each picture contains many S^D's that set the occasion for dozens of thoughts that may not have been emitted in years. Thus S^D's serve as *keys to memory*. When the S^D's are not present, old memories are unlikely to come back. The more vividly the S^D's are presented, the more memories are called up. When the person goes back to Hometown after 20 years of being away, the experiences of walking down the old familiar streets and looking at the grade school playground expose the person to multitudes of S^D's—in three dimensions and living color—that can bring back old memories that photo albums never did. The more numerous and vivid the S^D's, the more likely that the old coverants are to appear.

The S^D's that call back memories do not need to be visual. A person may use thoughts or conversations with an old friend from Hometown as the S^D's that unlock the memories. Your verbal description of your memories of Hometown will serve as S^D's that set the occasion for other memories. People who set aside time to think about their memories can allow each new memory to serve as an S^D for yet other memories and eventually recall much more of the past than if they focus only on the S^D's of the present environment.

Because S^D's do have stimulus control over thoughts, people often learn to bring up desired memories by setting up the correct S^D's. They may hang pictures of the family on the wall. Mementos from the vacations in Hawaii are placed around the room. These S^D's bring back memories that are in turn CS's that elicit pleasurable emotional responses. Writing a note (a memorandum) to yourself and placing it on the kitchen table where you will see it before leaving the house consists of putting an S^D in a spot where it can "remind" you to do a certain errand while you are out. When you learn a person's name, there are many stimuli in the stimulus collage that might become associated with the name—for example, the person's facial expressions, hair color, clothing, the topic of the conversation, the room where you met. Later when you try to think of the name, you may have to reconstruct several elements of the stimulus collage before enough S^D's are present to bring back the name. People often "search their memories" by presenting a variety of S^D's that might bring up the desired thought. When trying to recall someone's name, you might ask yourself a series of questions: "Who introduced me to her?" "Where did we meet?" "What was she interested in?" Maybe one of these general questions will serve as an S^D that brings back enough thoughts about the person and setting to serve as S^D's for the person's name. Another strategy is to slowly say the letters of the alphabet—"A . . . B . . . C . . . D . . ."—trying to begin several names with each letter: "Carol, Cathy, Diane, Doris. . . ." This systematic review of relevant S^D's is often useful in bringing up the right name: "Donna." Mnemonics help us remember words by providing the first letters or phrases of the correct words. Roy G. Biv is not a person, but a mnemonic that can help you remember the colors of the spectrum, in the correct order: red, orange, yellow, green, blue, indigo, violet.

THE STREAM OF CONSCIOUSNESS

Thinking has been described as a stream of consciousness—a constant flow of images, ideas, flashbacks, fantasies, and other thoughts. The stream of ideas does not necessarily follow a rational order or pattern, though it can. Many of the novels and movies that are done with a "stream of consciousness" style allow scenes to be spliced together as if they were appearing as free associations. Bits and pieces of the main character's past and present life are joined together as if the person were living a complex present and frequently flashing back to past memories. Human thought often follows this pattern, in response to the constant flux and flow of S^D's in the external and internal stimulus collage. Sometimes the stream of consciousness is highly organized and rational; but often it is not. Most thought patterns contain both rational sequences and jumps to irrelevant or only partially relevant ideas. Although some people compare human thought with the logical operations of computers, the computer analogy—which emphasizes rationally programmed data processing and information storage—suggests that human mental activity is more rational and machine-like than it actually is.[16] It is more accurate to portray human thought in terms of a stream of consciousness, with its mixture of both logical and haphazard connections.

The stream of consciousness is actually a long chain of perceptions and thoughts. Perceptions of incoming stimuli from all external and internal sense organs serve as S^D's for thoughts. These thoughts, in turn, can function as S^D's for more thoughts or for overt behavior.

Sometimes the stream of thoughts flows in a systematic and highly rational pattern; but it does not have to do so. Humans are not innately rational. Rational chains of thought usually occur when either of two conditions prevail: (1) when the S^D's from sense perceptions appear in a rational order—for example, while listening to someone develop a clear, logical argument—the stream of consciousness is rational; (2) when a person has learned skills for organizing complex and confusing material in a rational manner, the

[16]Skinner (1974:110).

stream of consciousness will be rational, even when the perceived S^D's are not in logical order. Since our environments often contain a jumble of multiple S^D's that do not fit into simple, logical patterns, and since it is almost impossible to learn enough rational skills to make sense of all the complexities of life, few people have a stream of consciousness that is completely rational.

Everyone learns some skills for reasoning and rational thinking; but it takes special conditions for people to learn to use reasoning frequently and systematically in a wide variety of circumstances. People who have had ample contact with models, rules, and prompts for rational thinking have a good chance of *acquiring* these cognitive skills. However, the frequency of their *utilizing* rational skills depends on reinforcement. Social reinforcement from parents, teachers, friends, and coworkers can help a person learn to use logical, well-reasoned thought and speech. Vicarious reinforcement from seeing respected models demonstrate the power and elegance of rational thought and speech also increases the chances that the observer will utilize similar behavior. Once the person applies reason to daily problems, rational thinking comes under automatic differential reinforcement: Skillful reasoning is reinforced (because it solves problems), but sloppy reasoning is not reinforced. Once the natural reinforcement of effective problem solving becomes frequent enough, social reinforcement from parents, teachers, and other sources can be faded out and the person will continue to use the skills for rational thinking.

Rationality is not a personality trait or global skill that automatically generalizes to apply to all facets of life.[17] Quite often, people who seem highly rational and logical when dealing with some things may not apply logic and reason when dealing with other areas of their lives. For example, a surgeon must think clearly and rationally to perform the long series of precise steps needed in a complex operation. Sloppy thoughts and actions could lead to fatal consequences. To master the precise and rationally ordered steps for performing surgery, it takes years of learning from models, rules, prompts, and differential reinforcement. Even after a surgeon has acquired the needed skills, the continued demands of the task provide differential reinforcement to maintain precise patterns of thought and action. However, rational cognitive skills may not generalize to all S^D contexts. Some surgeons seem absent-minded, scatter-brained, and less than rational when they are in the office—where a staff of several people handles all the appointments, records, billing, and day-to-day problems. Because a surgeon's behavior may not be under strict contingencies of reinforcement in the office—where other people are responsible—cognitive behavior can drift and become quite sloppy in that context. Even people who are world famous for intelligent and rational contributions in art, literature, politics, or science sometimes have quite irrational thoughts about topics outside their area of expertise.

Although some tasks require logical, rational thought and action for success, not all do. There are many circumstances in which reason may not be needed. Hence, thought patterns that are not rational are not necessarily wrong or invaluable. As we saw in Chapter 11 on rules, people who learn a behavior without the use of rules may perform quite well but be unable to verbalize rationally about their behavior (pp. 209–211). They have a "feel" for how to do the behavior, but do not have rational verbal rules for

[17]Mischel (1968, 1981).

explaining the steps for performing it. Although they have tacit and "intuitive" knowledge, they may not be able to think or verbalize about the behavior in a rational manner. Thus, rational thoughts and words are not essential for the performance of many skillful and useful behaviors.

When a person with tacit knowledge gets an idea or thinks of a solution to a problem without the help of a rational series of mental steps, the thought may be described as an "intuition." Since the person cannot identify where the thought came from or what S^D's triggered it, the intuitive thought may seem more mysterious than a rational thought that was developed at a conscious, verbal level through a highly ordered series of logical steps. If the problems of child rearing or machine repair cause a person to "check twice" even when—or especially when—everything *seems* to have worked out nicely on the first try, a person may learn an intuitive thought that does not seem rationally defensible. "Things have been going without a hitch. I'd better check twice because something is bound to be wrong." The S^D's of everything-going-right bring up the thought of checking twice. If the person cannot remember the prior occasions on which he or she learned to have this thought, the intuitive thought may seem especially mysterious, perhaps suggesting ESP or a premonition. If checking twice *does* reveal a problem, the person's belief in ESP or premonitions may be reinforced. Intuitive thoughts sometimes appear to be irrational, and they may be hard to defend when challenged by someone who demands to see the logic behind them. However, they may pay off often enough to reinforce their continued use, even if they are criticized as being irrational.

Naturally, not all nonrational, intuitive thinking is correct, but neither is all rational thinking. *Both intuitive and rational thinking can be either right or wrong. However, intuitive thinking has several limitations not found in rational thinking.*[18] First, although it is possible to determine *if* intuitive thinking is correct or useful, it is difficult to evaluate *why,* since the causes for intuitive thoughts cannot be easily identified and evaluated. Therefore, even if an intuitive thought seems to be true in one situation, it is hard to assess whether or not it will hold true in other situations. Second, if one individual frequently has very good intuitive thoughts, it is difficult for others to learn how to think in a similar manner, since the intuitive thinker cannot easily verbalize any of the mental steps needed for others to arrive at equally accurate intuitive thoughts. Rational thought does not suffer these limitations. First, because the logic behind rational thought is easily put into words, it is possible for others to check the logic, test crucial assumptions against the facts, and correct any errors or prejudices that exist. This type of critical evaluation not only allows rational thoughts to be improved but also helps assess the range of situations in which the ideas are useful. Second, the skills for accurate rational thinking can be passed on to others, so that many people can learn to benefit from this form of thinking. Since steps of rational thinking are easily verbalized and made public, they are easily shared with others via modeling, rules, and verbal prompts. In addition, rational skills can be improved by differential reinforcement and shaping, since positive and negative feedback can be given for accurate versus inaccurate reasoning as a person practices rational thinking and speaking.

[18]This argument parallels Skinner's (1969:167) analysis of the advantages of explicit knowledge over tacit knowledge.

Rational Choice

In Chapter 12 on the schedules of reinforcement, we saw that choice is often well explained by the matching law (pp. 234–240). In many situations, people tend to match the ratio of their choices of different alternatives to the relative amount of reinforcement associated with each choice. A person who likes chocolate and vanilla ice cream equally will choose each flavor about equally; but someone who likes chocolate five times more than vanilla will tend to choose chocolate five times more often than vanilla. Since the goal of rational choice need not be to match the frequency of choices to the relative reinforcement of each alternative, the matching law does not always predict or explain rational choice.

Rational choice involves (1) listing all the alternatives available from which to choose, (2) assembling accurate information on the immediate and delayed consequences (reinforcers and punishers) associated with each of these alternatives, then (3) carefully evaluating all the pros and cons of each alternative, without bias.[19] At any given choice point, a person considers all the possible alternatives along with both the short term and the long term consequences that are associated with each alternative. This process allows the person to compare the pros and cons of each alternative and evaluate which alternatives are more attractive than others.

When a college student is faced with difficult decisions about choosing a major, deciding what kind of summer job to take, or selecting a future job or career, reasoning is a valuable decision-making tool. A student may think of all the summer jobs that are available both near campus and in Hometown. While imagining all the alternatives, the student begins to think of the pros and cons of each job. One job pays more than the others. Another job is more interesting and provides important work experience that could build toward an exciting career. The jobs at Hometown allow the student to renew close contacts with old high school friends; but there are several new college friends who plan to work near campus during the summer, and it would be fun to spend the summer getting to know them better. At times the student may systematically think through all the pros and cons of each job, but free associations may help the student add relevant information to the lists of pros and cons. Hence free associations are not antithetical to the reasoning process: They can promote it by broadening and diversifying the number of topics being considered.[20] What is most important for a well-reasoned choice is that the student (1) consider as many alternatives as feasible, (2) seek as accurate information as possible on the short term and long term consequences of each choice, and (3) honestly evaluate all the pros and cons of each choice without bias.

As people think about all the short term and long term consequences of all their behavioral alternatives, they are allowing their choice to be influenced by the numerous reinforcers and punishers that are cognitively associated with each alternative. For example, if a person has six alternatives to choose from (behaviors 1 through 6 in the figure), a rational decision would be based on an analysis of all the pros and cons of each behavior.

---

[19]Mead (1934); Skinner (1953); Kaufmann (1973); Staats (1975).

[20]Free associations are an important component of problem solving and creative thought (Adams, 1974).

THE ALTERNATIVES	THE CONSEQUENCES										
	short term										long term
behavior 1	(+)	(+)	(−)		(+)	(−)	(+)		(−)		(−)
behavior 2	(−)	(+)		(−)	(+)			(+)	(+)	(+)	(+)
behavior 3	(+)	(−)	(−)	(+)		(+)	(+)	(+)	(−)		
behavior 4	(−)		(+)	(+)	(+)	(−)		(+)	(−)	(−)	(−)
behavior 5	(+)	(−)			(+)	(+)	(−)		(+)		(−)
behavior 6		(+)	(−)	(+)		(−)	(+)			(+)	(−)

As the person reviewed the positive and negative aspects of each choice (the + and − signs in the figure), the positive and negative thoughts would serve as conditioned reinforcers and punishers that would modify and shape the person's preferences for each behavior until a stable preference was reached. After careful evaluation, the person would realize that behavior 2 was the best choice (with behavior 3 being next best), since it was associated with the best outcomes.

The more accurately people identify all the important short term and long term consequences of each alternative, the more likely they are to select the alternative that will have the most rewarding outcomes. When people do not use rational decision processes, they often focus on the immediate consequences of the most conspicuous alternatives: This not only narrows their range of choice to include only obvious options but also biases their selection in favor of immediate gratification rather than long term planning that includes delayed reinforcement. Rational choice avoids these two problems by considering all reasonable alternatives and focusing on both the short term and long term consequences. When asked to quickly select which summer job would be first choice, a student might choose the job that was most fun. However, after using rational procedures, the student might decide that it would actually be wiser to take a summer job that offered valuable firsthand career experience.

When people evaluate the pros and cons of all their alternatives, they are actually learning the *reasons* why they need to select or reject each option. *Knowing the reasons why each alternative is good or bad is useful when carrying out choices that involve sacrificing immediate gratification in the pursuit of a better but more distant reward.* If a pre-law student decided to take a summer job doing library work in a law firm rather than taking a fun job, there might be times when the library work seemed tedious or boring. Instead of feeling bad about researching some dry legal books, the student could mentally review the reasons for making the job choice: The long term rewards of gaining law experience are worth certain sacrifices in immediate rewards. These rational thoughts not only help combat the aversive experience of doing a difficult task, they also orient the student toward doing a good job now in order to attain the distant goal.

When making very complex or momentous decisions, people may spend days, weeks, or months mulling over the pros and cons of all the possible alternatives, imagining what it would be like to carry out each one. In complex or important decisions, it may take self-discipline to work through a careful and unbiased evaluation of all the alternatives. Some people find this self-discipline so effortful and unpleasant that they skip through the rational evaluation process too quickly and fail to reach a well-reasoned decision based on a careful appraisal of all the data.[21] However, some people learn to enjoy the mental process of working through a complex decision and seeing a carefully reasoned choice emerge—if rational thinking has led to rewarding results in the past.

Rational decision methods do not guarantee that people will always make the best choices. The method is based on a careful assessment of the *known* consequences of the *known* alternatives. When little is known about all the alternatives, rational methods may not lead to the best possible choice (although no other method can guarantee better decisions). When people have limited knowledge about the alternatives that they have at any point in time, they need to seek information from other people, newspapers, magazines, or books—or obtain it via personal experience. Naturally, the more complete and accurate the information, the more likely a person is to arrive at a good choice. A student who bases job or career choices on limited information about two or three jobs is less likely to make a wise decision than a student who tries several different jobs, talks with numerous people about the pros and cons of their career choices, and stays abreast of current news about the future prospects for different fields of work.

Rational Therapy.   When people do not have adequate reasoning skills, they sometimes fail at coping with daily problems that could be solved by reasoning. Lacking a rational view of their situation, they may plague themselves with irrational thoughts and fears that amplify rather than resolve their problems. For example, some people are preoccupied with irrational fears about dirt, germs, and disease while their marriage and family relations are falling apart due to their not taking a more responsible role in resolving family problems.

Behavior therapists have developed techniques for helping people cope with their problems more rationally by teaching them to engage in logical, systematic internal dialogues when confronting difficult situations.[22] First, the therapist provides a model for rational thinking and talking: "When things don't seem to be going right, I say to myself: OK. What's my problem? What are all the possible solutions? What are the consequences of each possible solution? Which is the best solution? What steps should I plan to follow? Who can I ask to help me with my plans?" The therapist may spend hours talking with a person, customizing these general rational steps to the person's specific needs, and helping the person learn to devise rational rebuttals to any irrational thoughts he or she might have. The therapist also shares good information—useful rules—for effective problem solving: "Break large problems into small pieces. Attack one piece at a time. Tell yourself encouraging words about your progress and future goals." Many people who used to give up when they faced problems learn to cope better after learning rational problem solving skills from good models and rules. People are most likely to practice and develop these rational skills if their use of reasoning is reinforced. To start the learning

---

[21]Kaufmann (1973) argues from a philosophical perspective that although the most important decisions in life tend to be so complex that many people are afraid to grapple with them, reasoning is the best tool we have for arriving at wise decisions.

[22]Ellis (1962); Mahoney (1974); Goldfried et al. (1974); Meichenbaum (1976, 1977); Rosenthal and Zimmerman (1978); Kendall and Hollon (1979); Watson and Tharp (1981); Martin and Pear (1983).

process, the therapist provides generous positive feedback for all the early steps of acquiring and using reasoning techniques. Gradually, as an individual gains skill at applying reasoning to daily problems, the natural reinforcement that comes from solving problems via rational thinking will replace the therapist's social reinforcement and the therapist's reinforcement can gradually be faded out.

ATTACHING MEANING

While discussing sensory stimulation in Chapter 6, we described meaningfulness as an important component of stimuli. How do stimuli become meaningful? How does a person learn to attach meaning to certain stimuli, and not to others? *Various events, places, people, behavior, symbols, internal feelings, or other stimuli (called referents) become S^D's or CS's for meaningful responses via operant or Pavlovian conditioning.*[23] The meaningful responses include (1) verbal operants, (2) nonverbal operants, and (3) conditioned emotional responses.

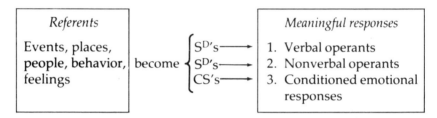

As a child learns the meaning of "a house being on fire," a burning house becomes a referent for meaningful responses. When seeing a burning house, the child may respond (1) by shouting "Fire," (2) by pointing to the house, and (3) with a pounding heart and other emotional responses. The burning house is the referent which functions as an S^D for the verbal operant of shouting "Fire" and the nonverbal operant of pointing. It also functions as a CS for the emotional responses.

In order to see how a stimulus becomes a meaningful referent for a person, it is necessary to examine the past learning experience that made the referent function as an S^D or CS.

Consider some of the ways a child can learn to use the word *love* in a meaningful way. When Janie is very small, the parents may say, "Who do you love, Janie?" Janie may look back in silence. The child has not yet learned the referent for the word *love*. The parents may prompt, "Do you love Mommy, Janie?" After hearing this verbal prompt, Janie may echo the word "Mommy" from her mother's last sentence (since saying *Mommy* is a high probability behavior in the child's verbal repertoire). Mother may hug the child (reinforcing the child's response) and again ask the first question, "Who do you love?" The chances are that the child will again say, "Mommy." Both mother and father may play this verbal game with little Janie in a variety of contexts until the child has

[23]Skinner (1957, 1974:90f).

learned to answer either "Mommy" or "Daddy." It is true that the child does not have a very deep understanding of the concept of *love;* but the learning process has begun. Later, as the father snuggles the child into his arms, he may say, "I love you, Janie." If the child imitates, "I love you, Daddy," the child is likely to receive reinforcers. If the child says "I love you" while being angry or selfish, the parents may give a more critical, punitive answer, such as, "That's not the way to behave when you love someone." Thus, through imitation and differential reinforcement, the child learns how to use the word *love* in S^D contexts associated with correct usage, but not in S^Δ contexts associated with incorrect usage. When the child is happy and the parents are being affectionate, the S^D's are present for the child to say "I love you." When the child is angry or the parents have been punitive, there are S^Δ's for not saying, "I love you." The parents may use rules, too, to help the child learn the meaning of love. They may say, "You should tell your grand-mother that you love her." This helps the child learn to attach the word to new referents, in this case, Grandmother. Even though a two-year-old child cannot give a good definition of the word *love,* an onlooker would see that the child knows *something* about the meaning of the word, once the child has learned to use it in response to the correct S^D's.[24]

As people learn to respond to the referents of a concept with appropriate responses of all three types—verbal, nonverbal, and emotional—observers will be increasingly likely to conclude that the person has learned the "true" meaning of the concept. If a child only makes the verbal response, "I love you," but does not show loving behavior and loving emotional responses, the observer will judge that the child has not yet learned the "deeper" meaning of the word, even though the child uses the word only in the correct S^D context. As a person learns appropriate responses of all three types—verbal, nonverbal, and emotional—the observer is likely to infer a deeper or richer level of meaning. As the years go by, we are exposed to countless learning experiences in which we can acquire all three types of meaningful responses.[25] We hear *models* defining love and see them showing consideration for the people they love. We hear *rules* stating that if you truly love someone, you treat them in special ways. A person we love may physically *prompt* us to touch in a certain way when we are expressing our love. There is *differential reinforcement* for the verbal and nonverbal components of the response class called loving behavior. Via Pavlovian conditioning, the referents of *love* become CS's that elicit emotional responses. Naturally, some people are exposed to more opportunities to learn a refined repertoire of loving responses than others. With good models, rules, prompts, differential reinforcement, and Pavlovian conditioning, a person will acquire a refined repertoire of verbal, nonverbal, and emotional responses. The person will be able to say loving things to his or her partner, treat the partner in a gentle, considerate manner, and feel positive emotional responses. The observer will conclude that this person has learned to attach a great deal of meaning to love and knows the deeper significance of the concept.

Note that it is not merely the *quantity* of learning experience that leads a person to

[24]The behavioral analysis of meaning concurs with Wittgenstein's (1953) position that "the meaning of a word is its use in the language." See Day (1970).

[25]The behavioral analysis is thoroughly sociological because it traces the causes of attached meaning back to the social environment in which the person learned to attach and use meaning. Learning theory provides an ideal tool for sociologists who seek to link social behavior to social causes (Burgess and Bushell, 1969; Scott, 1971; Kunkle, 1975; Baldwin and Baldwin, 1978a; Baldwin, 1982, 1985).

attach meaningful responses to appropriate referents. Certain experiences cause people to learn inappropriate responses to a given referent. A man who verbally claims to attach a great deal of meaning to love—but whose cruel, selfish behavior indicates a lack of respect, affection, and concern—would not be considered to know the true meaning of love. *Because the verbal and nonverbal components of behavior are relatively independent and can be conditioned by very different sets of models, rules, prompts, and differential reinforcement, it is possible for people to learn incongruous, even hypocritical response patterns.*[26] For example, when there are rewards for saying one thing and doing another—professing enduring love, then cashing in on one-night stands—discrepancies can appear between the verbal and nonverbal meanings a person attaches to a given referent. If a man has received reinforcers for saying "I'll love you forever" at night, and received reinforcers for moving on the next morning, he may learn behavior that seems hypocritical. In addition, the emotions attached to the referents in the hypocritical lover's life can be quite different from those of less hypocritical men. If the man has received reinforcers for both his verbal and nonverbal behavior, both aspects of his performance will be CS's that elicit positive emotions for him. He may feel warm, romantic feelings as he speaks of enduring love one night and may also enjoy the feelings of freedom as he hits the road the next morning.

Because we all have unique histories of learning experience, we learn to attach somewhat different meanings to the referents in our lives. Yet each of us attaches meanings that overlap somewhat with those of the people we are close to because (1) we have been raised in the same culture, (2) we learn from each other, and (3) the rewards of social interaction depend on sharing sufficiently similar meanings that we can communicate and coordinate efficiently.

In our analysis of sensory stimulation (Chapter 6), we saw that meaningfulness contributes to sensory stimulation. It should be clear that the greater the meaning a person has learned to attach to a given stimulus (referent), the more sensory stimulation the person is likely to obtain from that stimulus. If you say "What is friendship?" to someone who has never learned to attach much meaning to the word, the stimulus is merely a word that brings up few responses. To someone who has learned a large number of verbal, nonverbal, and emotional responses relevant to friendship, the question "What is friendship?" may trigger a multitude of responses that, in turn, provide a great deal of sensory stimulation for the person and may reinforce long trains of thought about the topic.

THE SELF

Although many people think of the "self" as something that originates from inside a person and guides the rest of the person's behavior, both sociologists and psychologists agree that the self has its origins in society.[27] The baby does not have a sense of self. But parents, brothers, sisters, and others begin early to teach the child to describe his or her

[26]Bryan (1969); Scott (1971).

[27]Mead (1934); Skinner (1969:244f; 1974:149f, 167f); Staats (1963, 1975); Bem (1967); Mischel (1968, 1981).

own body and behavior as the child would describe the body and behavior of another person. It is easy for the child to learn to describe the behavior of others. After hearing Father say, "Your brother drew this in school today," it is easy for Judy to transpose one word and imitate, "My brother drew this in school today." Then Father turns to Judy and asks, "What did Judy draw today?" The child learns to respond, "I drew this today." When others approve of the picture, they are giving Judy reinforcers for both the picture and for describing her own behavior. The child is learning the skills for observing her own actions and describing her own behavior—her "self"—much the same as she describes her brother or mother.

When a person learns to do self-description—describing his or her own body and behavior the same as if describing others—the person comes to have a self-concept. These self-descriptive skills are learned from models, rules, prompts, and differential reinforcement during symbolic social interaction. Parents provide simple models for the young child: "Judy drew a tree and a house." The child quickly learns to substitute "I" for "Judy" and thus produce a self-descriptive response that is likely to be reinforced, "I drew a tree and a house." If the child says, "I glozed the furz," this response probably will not be reinforced. Since older children and adults frequently emit self-descriptive sentences using "I" and "me" to describe their own behavior, the child has thousands of models for more complex self-descriptive statements. Other people's comments—"Daddy's getting angry; he's losing his temper"—can be translated to a self-description, "I'm losing my temper." Rules are often used to encourage self-observation and self-description. "Judy, watch that you don't spill your milk." "Judy, watch that you don't break your brother's toys." These rules focus the child's attention on her own behavior, and often the child receives reinforcers for responding: "I'm watching. I won't break anything."

Toward a Sense of Identity

Our description of "self"—our self-concept—becomes more complex with age and experience. The little child begins learning to describe his or her own actions as "mine," done by "me," or something "I" created. Many of the self-descriptions are provided by the family: "Judy is a nice little girl. Judy draws really pretty trees and houses." As the years go by Judy will learn more subtle skills of self-description that allow her to watch for patterns in her own behavior. "I often promise to do things but then forget." As she gains these self-descriptive skills, she will be able to make increasingly precise observations about her "self" and to label her self as "forgetful" or "busy" or "unreliable" (depending on the models, rules, prompts, and reinforcers associated with the use of each label).

Naturally, not everyone learns advanced self-descriptive skills or learns them equally rapidly. A person surrounded with many models and rules for advanced, sensitive, and subtle self-description skills will have a good chance for learning these skills. The more reinforcers a person receives for using the skills, the more polished and practiced they become. A person with a simple life and consistent behavior patterns can learn accurate self-description more easily than a person with a complex life and highly variable behavior. The first person merely has an easier task because simpler behavior patterns are easier to learn to describe.

When a person learns self-descriptions that (1) cover a broad range of experiences and (2) reveal a consistent pattern of interests and directions, the person acquires a sense of "identity." By the time Judy is in college, her life is much more complex than it was at age four, and she has learned to describe her behavior in a more detailed manner. Thus, her self-concept tends to be much more complex at that age. If her self-concept fits one relatively consistent pattern, she may be described as having an "identity." If Judy's past socialization has pointed her toward one goal—becoming a lawyer—and her thoughts of entering law have received much more reinforcement than any other career plans, she may have a strong sense of identity as a future lawyer. If several family members or close family friends are lawyers, she will have seen enough of the profession to easily describe the things that happen in law school and during the practice of law. This allows her to have a clear picture of her identity as a future lawyer. "I'll be married to a man in one of the professions and we will enjoy sharing the excitement of two stimulating careers. We'll probably postpone having children until I'm thirty, or perhaps decide not to have them."

The person who has come from a complex socialization that has not provided a single pattern of life objectives may not have such an easy time in finding an "identity." Jill has toyed with dozens of different interests including law, dance, art, being a good homemaker and mother. She has received a little support and encouragement for each interest, but no strong and consistent reinforcement for any single one. She has been popular in some circles but unpopular in others. Some days she feels happy about life; other days, very sad. Her self-descriptions are inconsistent. There is no simple, unifying pattern. When other people ask her what she plans to be doing in two years, she does not know. She lacks a sense of identity because her self-descriptions do not reveal a consistent pattern. Her self-descriptions suggest a fragmented person who lacks a unified sense of direction.[28] If no one criticizes Jill about her lack of direction, the lack of identity may not be aversive for her. On the other hand, if people criticize her for not knowing what to do with her life, the lack of identity can become aversive. "Why don't you be like Judy and *do* something with your life?" "You'll never amount to anything." This negative conditioning can make the lack of an identity so aversive that one feels an "identity crisis." Thinking about the lack of identity has become a CS that elicits aversive emotions. Identity crises can come at any time in life. If Judy fails in law school and has to drop out, she will lose the single theme that once gave her a sense of identity. In addition, all her old self-descriptions about being a successful lawyer will cease to bring reinforcers. Her failure at law will make those self-descriptions aversive; and she may have as painful an identity crisis as Jill had earlier.

A person's self-concept or identity will be positive if many of the person's self-descriptions are CS's for pleasant emotions, due to a history of positive experiences. People who have succeeded at many things and received generous social reinforcement will find that many elements of their self-descriptions are CS's that elicit good feelings about themselves. People who have failed, been criticized for many aspects of behavior, or have received reinforcers for frequent self-criticism will have a more negative self-concept, since many elements of their self-descriptions are CS's associated with unpleasant feelings.

How do people change from a negative self-concept to a positive self-concept? One

[28]Skinner (1974:149).

strategy is for them to learn skills that increase their chances of coping successfully with the world and decrease their failures. As the people observe themselves *succeeding* at more things and receiving more reinforcers, the positive experiences will condition their self-descriptions into CS's that elicit positive emotions. Second, if the people can find new friends who use positive feedback rather than criticism—or ask old friends to rely more on positive control and less on negative control—increased social reinforcement and positive descriptions from others will help condition those descriptions into CS's for good feelings. Third, people can learn rational self-instructions that decrease the frequency of self-critical thoughts. A self-instruction—such as, "Stop punishing yourself with those dumb self-critical thoughts; think about the positive things you have accomplished"—is a rule that can reorient one's thoughts in a positive direction. Rational self-instructions are most effective if people reward themselves for following these rules ("That's the way to go. You're learning how to be more positive!").

Having a positive self-concept certainly makes life more pleasant. It allows people to feel good when they think about themselves, their lives, their plans, their futures. It may also help people be more enthusiastic about *doing* things in life, rather than being passive. The people who think of themselves as good athletes, good musicians, or good whatevers have this positive conditioning due to past reinforcement; and they can enjoy looking forward to running harder or playing more complex music tomorrow, because these thoughts elicit good feelings. They look forward to life with pleasure whereas the person who has received more aversive conditioning fears what life may bring next. Because these people have been criticized for not being good enough in the past, their self-descriptive thoughts are CS's that bring up bad feelings when they think of future tasks and obligations where they run the risk of failing and being criticized yet again.

SELF-CONTROL

Self-control consists of behavior—either overt or covert—that we do at one time to control our later behavior. At 4:00 P.M. a person may remember, "I've got to phone Linda tonight," then write a big note saying PHONE LINDA AT EIGHT and tape it on the refrigerator door. This self-control behavior at 4:00 P.M. will help increase the likelihood of phoning at 8:00 P.M. Self-control skills are merely a subset of our total behavior repertoire. As we learn an increasing number of effective self-control skills, we gain more ability to direct our own behavior and to accomplish the things that otherwise we might have failed to do.

Self-control involves chains of operants that often begin with self-observation, self-descriptions, and thoughts about the things one "ought" to do. These chains may lead to subvocal, spoken, or written rules—such as PHONE LINDA AT EIGHT—that finally serve as S^D's for the desired behavior. Thus, *self-control consists of behavioral chains with a minimum of three basic components: self-observation, self-description, and self-instruction.*[29] For example, a person's self-observation may lead to the covert self-

[29]Many other elements and variations on these elements may be present, too, such as rehearsal, practice, keeping written records, making contracts, and self-reinforcement. Several excellent books are now available that provide detailed information on behavioral self-control: Goldfried and Merbaum (1973); Mahoney and Thoresen (1974); Watson and Tharp (1977, 1981); Stuart (1977); Williams and Long (1979); Rudestam (1980).

description, "I'm not spending enough time with my children." If a person has learned a repertoire of self-instruction skills, this self-observation is likely to serve as an S^D for constructing appropriate rules. "I'll promise to spend an hour each evening with the kids." Finally, if the person has received enough reinforcement in the past for doing rule-governed behavior in response to this type of covert rule, the "good intentions" may actually lead to changes in overt behavior—such as setting aside more time for being with the children.

Self-control skills are learned from models, rules, prompts, and reinforcement. This learning begins early in life and additional skill can be added at any age. Why do people seek to teach self-control skills to the young child? Child rearing and social interaction are much less effortful for the socializing agents when children learn to regulate and manage their own behavior. If you have ever seen severely retarded people who—at the age of 10 or 20 years—cannot take care of themselves, you can appreciate how difficult it is for other people to watch over and control someone who has little or no self-control. Early in childhood, socializing agents reward the child for making steps toward learning self-control, and they punish the lack of self-control. Models, rules, and prompts for self-control, in conjunction with both reinforcement and punishment, help people acquire the self-control that will eventually allow them to become more independent of their parents and to guide their own lives. Naturally, not all people learn equal amounts of self-control.

There are times when most of us wish that we had more self-control—so we could change our moods, eating patterns, propensity to argue with people we love, and so forth. Behavior principles make it possible for people to learn advanced levels of self-control and independence skills. The more you learn about the principles of behavior, the more you can use those principles to control your own life. People who do not know the principles by which behavior is acquired, maintained, and modified usually find it more difficult to control their own behavior than those who know the principles and have been rewarded for applying those principles to their own lives.

The following paragraphs briefly demonstrate how the principles stated in earlier chapters can be used to increase self-control.

Chapter 1: Science and Human Behavior.   The scientific approach to the study of behavior is based on careful observation. Self-control begins with careful *self*-observation. It is usually best to keep written records, using diaries or graphs. It is wise to keep records on both desirable and undesirable behavior, along with information on the events that occur before and after each behavior. This provides data on the *A–B–C's* of behavior—the antecedents, behaviors, and consequences. The more careful, objective, and scientific you can be in your self-observation, the better your chances of dovetailing your observations with the following behavior principles.

Chapter 2: Operant Conditioning.   The consequences that follow a behavior are crucial determinants of its frequency. If you want to *increase* the frequency of operants such as creative writing, exercising, thinking rationally, being considerate or whatever, either positive or negative reinforcement will work. Positive reinforcement is usually more pleasant than negative reinforcement: It is fun to treat yourself to a new record album each time you jog one-half mile further than in the past (positive reinforcement). It is aversive to have to give up a favorite activity each time you fail to increase your jogging distance (negative reinforcement). If you want to *decrease* the frequency of operants such as overeating, wasting time, or having temper outbursts, punishment, extinction, or DRO may be useful. If a boy tells his girlfriend that she should simply walk out and go home whenever he loses his temper, he is attempting to suppress his temper outbursts by extinction and punishment: Her leaving removes social reinforcement (extinction), and being left alone may be aversive enough to be a punisher.

People can use either *external* or *internal* reinforcers and punishers. If you ask a friend to give you an encouraging word every time you do something that shows sensitivity to others, the social reinforcement will help you acquire greater sensitivity. After you have observed which features of your behavior your friend is reinforcing, you will learn how to identify when you are being sensitive and learn to give self-reinforcement for those behaviors.[30] Whenever you say positive or negative things to yourself because of an operant you performed, the positive or negative words will provide internal reinforcement or punishment for the operant. Thus, the following type of internal dialogue can be quite useful in modifying behavior: "I'm glad I remembered to thank Sherri for her help. But it was inconsiderate of me not to talk with her roommate."

Chapter 3: Pavlovian Conditioning. People can create new CS's through Pavlovian conditioning. If you would like to increase the number of things you enjoy in life, you can set up pleasurable learning experiences that will create new pleasure-eliciting CS's for you. For example, if you see that other people really enjoy jazz or opera, it is likely that these types of music are CS's that elicit pleasurable emotions for them. If you wanted to learn to enjoy jazz—respond to jazz as a CS for pleasure—you would pair jazz with pleasurable events. You might arrange your next special date to include a jazz concert or drinks at a jazz bar. You could ask a friend who loves jazz to play some favorite records and give you pointers. The jazz lover's smiles and enthusiasm for the music would cause you to experience vicarious positive emotional responses. The "pointers" would be rules to focus your attention on the musical details that others enjoy: "Wow, dig that wild sax!" After a period of positive conditioning, jazz will become a pleasure-eliciting CS for you; and you will feel good when you tune into a radio station that is playing jazz. Pavlovian conditioning can also be used to countercondition CS's that elicit aversive emotions. If thinking about going to graduate school makes you anxious and fearful, you could talk with friends who are excited about taking the next educational step and their positive responses will help countercondition some of your fears and apprehensions.

Chapter 4: Operant and Pavlovian Conditioning Together. Since Pavlovian conditioning often occurs as a natural byproduct of operant conditioning, you might decide to overcome certain fears by learning the relevant operant skills, knowing that the emotional conditioning will occur as a byproduct. For example, you could overcome fear of heights by taking a mountain climbing course from an expert. Choose a skillful and cheerful teacher: Acquiring good skills will minimize the fear of risk or danger while climbing; and

---

[30]See Bandura (1971, 1977) for further information on self-reinforcement and self-punishment.

the teacher's cheerful behavior will guarantee that climbing will be paired with positive social stimuli—which will make climbing a CS for pleasurable emotions. While you are learning the operant skills in a reinforcing social context, the positive experiences will automatically countercondition your old fears. As people receive positive reinforcers for learning any skills—public speaking, debating, swimming, self-defense—old fears about these activities disappear.

Chapter 5: Stimulus Control.   As you keep diaries and records about the stimuli that precede and predict your behavior, you will learn about both your S^D's and CS's. Using this information, you can arrange these antecedent stimuli to produce the behavior you want. If you want to stop thinking about the lover who broke your heart, remove all the person's pictures and belongings (because they are S^D's that bring up thoughts of the person) and immerse yourself in other friendships and activities. If you want to remember to write your parents more often, put their picture on your desk—on top of a box of paper, envelopes, and stamps—to serve as an S^D for the desired response.

Self-observation will help you discover which CS's elicit desirable and undesirable emotions. For example, some record albums may cause you to become sad or blue, whereas others elicit cheerful moods and make you smile. Still other records elicit romantic moods. As you learn the power of music to serve as CS's for various emotions, you can select your musical CS's more wisely and gain increasing control over your moods.

Chapters 6 and 7: Reinforcers and Punishers.   Since reinforcers and punishers are the prime movers of both operant and Pavlovian conditioning, learn how to use these stimuli effectively. First, know your reinforcers and punishers. Use self-observation to find out which reinforcers and punishers are most effective in modifying and maintaining your behavior so you can use these effectively in your own self-control. Second, plan to use reinforcers more than punishers: It makes self-control more rewarding, and it increases the chances that you will continue your efforts to guide your own life—rather than letting your life be controlled by external factors. Some people keep a long list of all the things they most enjoy doing and all the rewards they enjoy receiving in order to have lots of reinforcers to choose from when designing self-reinforcement. You can use your reinforcers to increase or decrease the frequency of many parts of your behavior repertoire. If you want to *increase* the frequency of exercising regularly, you could reward yourself for each step of progress with reinforcers such as a movie, a new record album, some new clothes, or anything else you like. If you can find a friend with whom to jog, the social reinforcers you obtain while exercising will help increase the likelihood of future running and condition jogging as a CS that elicits pleasurable feelings (rather than aversive ones). You can *decrease* unwanted behaviors by reinforcing incompatible, competing responses (DRO). Negative thoughts will gradually disappear if you reinforce positive and optimistic thoughts. The frequency of temper outbursts will decrease automatically if you reinforce gentle and considerate behavior. You may have to punish yourself from time to time for having temper flare-ups with a good friend, but the generous use of reinforcement for consideration will cause slip-ups and punishment to be kept minimal. The more skillful you become at applying your reinforcers and punishers, the more effective you can be at operant conditioning and at gaining the desirable Pavlovian effects that occur as a natural byproduct of operant conditioning (see Chapter 4).

Chapter 8: Differential Reinforcement and Shaping. Differential reinforcement allows you to increase or decrease the frequency of responses you already have in your behavior repertoire. If your singing is sometimes good and sometimes not so good, you can use differential reinforcement to improve it by singing along with your favorite records. When you sing well, your voice will sound good with the record (providing reinforcement for musical skills); but poor singing will not sound good (providing punishment for poor singing). These differential consequences will gradually increase your ability to sing well.

Shaping allows you to reach entirely new levels of performance. Shaping generally proceeds most rapidly and smoothly if it is done in small steps of successive approximation. If you want to be a writer, you cannot expect to write a novel the first time you pick up a pen. Practice on vignettes and short stories. As you gain the skills for creative writing and the self-control to sit for longer periods of time at the writing desk, you will find it easier to produce better and longer works. Trying to advance too rapidly increases the likelihood that you will experience setbacks and other aversive consequences that punish the desired responses and make you stop working toward your goal.

Chapter 9: Modeling and Observational Learning. A rapid way to learn new behavior is to expose yourself to models who already do and enjoy the behavior. Coping models usually provide more useful information than mastery models because the mastery models often do not let you see the actual behavior you must be learning next. You may learn more about playing guitar by watching a friend who is only a few steps better than you than by attending a concert and watching someone with highly advanced skills. If the models you select clearly enjoy their activities and are people you like, you can benefit by the vicarious reinforcement they generate for you. If you want to learn to surf, find a friendly, competent surfer. If you want to help yourself move toward a law career, seek out friends who are enthusiastic about their law studies or volunteer in a busy legal aid center where you can be close to the excitement of constant legal action.

Chapter 10: Prompting. The acquisition of many physical skills can be hastened by prompts. In learning how to hold and comfort a baby, you could ask someone with years of experience to adjust your arms and hands into the best positions. A good archer can help you learn to hold the bow correctly by standing behind you and moving your arms into the proper geometry. You can ask anyone with good skills to guide your performances: Other people are usually happy to share their skills.

Chapter 11: Rules. Clear and accurate rules can facilitate the production of many responses. ''Rock the baby gently in your arms and hum or sing quietly to stop the crying.'' You can often obtain useful rules from other people or books. Experts are better sources of rules than novices—if they can communicate their knowledge effectively. Once you have heard several skilled painters, hunters, or social workers share the rules they have found most valuable, you will be able to give yourself instructions that will steer your behavior in the right direction. You can carry these rules inside your head and use them over and over whenever you need to. People with good coping skills typically carry on a rational internal dialogue as they confront new challenges—asking themselves questions, considering alternative solutions, trying to predict the consequences of each alternative, and using this information to verbally direct each new step of activity.

Chapter 12: Schedules.   Behavior acquisition is most rapid when it is on a schedule of continuous reinforcement (CRF). Be generous with yourself when you are first learning a new activity, and give yourself abundant reinforcement. Every 10-K (10-kilometer) race you finish in your first year of running is worth a big celebration. However, it is sometimes wise to gradually thin the schedule to variable ratio (VR) or variable interval (VI) schedules, since this partial reinforcement (PR) usually makes behavior more durable and resistant to extinction. As you learn to run longer races, it will only seem natural to make less of a "big deal" out of running 10 K, and the frequency of celebrating those races will decline. Strictly defined contingencies of reinforcement produce more efficient and directed change than do loosely defined contingencies. That is why it is better to set precise goals (such as "Four times a week I will run 2½ miles"), rather than loose goals (such as "I'll run some each week.")

Chapter 13: Positive and Negative Control.   The more you can rely on positive control, the more you will enjoy learning new activities, and the longer you are likely to continue your self-control activities. A person who tries to control his temper by punishing each outburst may not continue trying to do self-control as long as people who reward themselves every time they can stay calm in an emotional situation (DRO). People enjoy themselves—and their self-control skills—much more when they reward their progress more than punish their failings. Although some punishment is appropriate for serious errors, it can be minimized by using differential reinforcement for quality alternative activities (DRO).

Chapter 14: Thinking, the Self, and Self-Control.   Because thoughts are influenced by social learning experience, it is wise to insure that your thoughts about improving self-control receive ample social support. As you talk with others about attaining your goals in life, their feedback—if it is positive and supportive—will help reinforce your commitment to achieving those goals. Naturally, if you interact with people who do not value the goals you do, you run the risk of having your goals undermined and thoughts confused—unless you have already had a strong prior socialization for pursuing your goals in the face of adversity. By thinking encouraging thoughts and giving yourself generous positive feedback for self-guidance, you can retain strong self-direction even when other people are nonsupportive. Having a well-learned internal dialogue that allows you to defend your values to yourself gives you someone positive to talk with—your "self"—even when those around you are being negative.

CONCLUSION

Thinking is behavior—sometimes described as subvocal speech or an internal dialogue. It is learned much as any other behavior is learned. We tend to think about things that we see or hear modeled by others, especially if there is positive or negative reinforcement for those thoughts. Rules and advice can also affect the direction of our thoughts. Through Pavlovian conditioning, thoughts can become CS's that elicit positive or negative emotions, and these thoughts can condition other stimuli (including other thoughts) to become CS's that elicit emotions. As we learn to observe and describe ourselves, we gain a self-concept and eventually a sense of identity. The combination of self-observation, self-description, and self-instruction allows a person to gain control over his or her own behavior. The internal dialogue provides rules that can direct the course of a person's own actions. Knowledge of the behavior principles can greatly increase people's skills at guiding their own behavior.

Behavior science has come a long way since Pavlov's early experiments with salivation in dogs. At present, there is a growing interest in the study of learning in natural environments. As we gain increasing knowledge about our own behavior in everyday life, we will come closer to achieving the goal set by the ancient Greeks: "Know then thyself."

References

Abbey, A. (1982). Sex differences in attributions for friendly behavior: Do males misperceive females' friendliness? *Journal of Personality and Social Psychology, 42*, 830–838.

Adams, J. L. (1974). *Conceptual blockbusting: A guide to better ideas*. San Francisco: Freeman.

Ahammer, I. M. (1973). Social-learning theory as a framework for the study of adult personality development. In P. B. Baltes and K. W. Schaie, eds., *Life-span developmental psychology* (253–284). New York: Academic Press.

Ainsworth, M. D. S., Blehar, M. C., Waters, E., and Wall, S. (1978). *Patterns of attachment: A psychological study of the strange situation*. Hillsdale, NJ: Lawrence Erlbaum.

Akers, R. L. (1973). *Deviant behavior: A social learning approach*. Belmont, CA: Wadsworth.

Annon, J. S. (1973). The therapeutic use of masturbation in the treatment of sexual disorders. In R. D. Rubin, J. P. Brady, and J. D. Henderson, eds., *Advances in behavior therapy* (Vol. 4, 199–298). New York: Academic Press.

Annon, J. S. (1975). *The behavioral treatment of sexual problems: Intensive therapy*. Honolulu: Enabling Systems.

Appel, J. B. (1961). Punishment in the squirrel monkey *Saimiri sciurea*. *Science, 133*, 36–37.

Axelrod, S. (1977). *Behavior modification for the classroom teacher*. New York: McGraw-Hill.

Axelrod, S. and Apsche, J., eds. (1983). *The effects of punishment on human behavior*. New York: Academic Press.

Baer, D. M. (1971, October). Let's take another look at punishment. *Psychology Today*, 32–34, 36–37, 111.

Baker, A. T. (1979, July 2). 41 survivors. *Time*, 68.

Baldwin, J. D. (1981). George Herbert Mead and modern behaviorism. *Pacific Sociological Review, 24*, 411–440.

Baldwin, J. D. (1984). A balanced emphasis on environmental influences. *The Behavioral and Brain Sciences, 7,* 434–435.

Baldwin, J. D. (1985). Social behaviorism on emotions: Mead and modern behaviorism compared. *Symbolic Interaction* (in press).

Baldwin, J. D. (in press). *George Herbert Mead: A unifying theory.* Beverly Hills, CA: Sage.

Baldwin, J. I. (1983). The effects of women's liberation and socialization on delinquency and crime. *Humboldt Journal of Social Relations, 10,* 90–111.

Baldwin, J. D. and Baldwin, J. I. (1974). The dynamics of interpersonal spacing in monkeys and man. *American Journal of Orthopsychiatry, 44,* 790–806.

Baldwin, J. D. and Baldwin, J. I. (1977). The role of learning phenomena in the ontogeny of exploration and play. In S. Chevalier-Skolnikoff and F. E. Poirier, eds., *Primate bio-social development* (343–406). New York: Garland Publishing.

Baldwin, J. D. and Baldwin, J. I. (1978a). Behaviorism on *verstehen* and *erklären. American Sociological Review, 43,* 335–347.

Baldwin, J. D. and Baldwin, J. I. (1978b). The primate contribution to the study of play. In M. A. Salter, ed., *Play: Anthropological perspectives* (53–68). West Point, NY: Leisure Press.

Baldwin, J. D. and Baldwin, J. I. (1981). *Beyond sociobiology.* New York: Elsevier.

Bandura, A. (1969). *Principles of behavior modification.* New York: Holt, Rinehart and Winston.

Bandura, A. (1971). Vicarious and self-reinforcement processes. In R. Glaser, ed., *The nature of reinforcement* (228–278). New York: Academic Press.

Bandura, A. (1973). *Aggression: A social learning analysis.* Englewood Cliffs, NJ: Prentice-Hall.

Bandura, A. (1977). *Social learning theory.* Englewood Cliffs, NJ: Prentice-Hall.

Bandura, A. and Barab, P. (1973). Processes governing disinhibitory effects through symbolic modeling. *Journal of Abnormal Psychology, 82,* 1–9.

Bandura, A., Blanchard, E. B., and Ritter, B. (1969). The relative efficacy of desensitization and modeling approaches for inducing behavioral, affective, and attitudinal changes. *Journal of Personality and Social Psychology, 13,* 173–199.

Bandura, A., Grusec, J. E., and Menlove, F. L. (1967). Vicarious extinction of avoidance behavior. *Journal of Personality and Social Psychology, 5,* 16–23.

Bandura, A. and Rosenthal, T. L. (1966). Vicarious classical conditioning as a function of arousal level. *Journal of Personality and Social Psychology, 3,* 54–62.

Bandura, A., Ross, D., and Ross, S. A. (1963). A comparative test of the status envy, social power, and secondary reinforcement theories of identificatory learning. *Journal of Abnormal and Social Psychology, 67,* 527–534.

Bandura, A. and Walters, R. H. (1959). *Adolescent aggression.* New York: Ronald.

Bandura, A. and Walters, R. H. (1963). *Social learning and personality development.* New York: Holt, Rinehart and Winston.

Bannatyne, A. and Bannatyne, M. (1973). *How your children can learn to live a rewarding life.* Springfield, IL: Charles C Thomas.

Barber, T. X. and Hahn, K. W., Jr. (1964). Experimental studies in "hypnotic" behavior: Physiological and subjective effects of imagined pain. *Journal of Nervous and Mental Disease, 139,* 416–425.

Barker, J. C. and Miller, M. (1966). Aversion therapy for compulsive gambling. *Lancet, 1,* 491–492.

Barlow, D. H., Agras, W. S., Leitenberg, H., Callahan, E. J., and Moore, R. C. (1972). The contribution of therapeutic instructions to covert sensitization. *Behavior Research and Therapy, 10,* 411–415.

Barrett, J. E. and Glowa, J. R. (1977). Reinforcement and punishment of behavior by the same consequent event. *Psychological Reports, 40,* 1015–1021.

Baum, W. M. (1979). Matching, undermatching, and overmatching in studies of choice. *Journal of the Experimental Analysis of Behavior, 32,* 269–281.

Becker, H. S. (1963). *Outsiders: Studies in the sociology of deviance.* New York: Free Press.

Becker, H. S. (1964). *The other side.* New York: Free Press.

Bellack, A. S. and Hersen, M. (1977). *Behavior modification: An introductory textbook.* Baltimore: Williams and Wilkins.

Bem, D. J. (1967). Self-perception: An alternative interpretation of cognitive dissonance phenomena. *Psychological Review, 74,* 183–200.

Bem, D. J. (1970). *Beliefs, attitudes, and human affairs.* Monterey, CA: Brooks/Cole.

Berger, S. M. (1962). Conditioning through vicarious instigation. *Psychological Review, 69,* 450–466.

Bernstein, I. L., Webster, M. M., and Bernstein, I. D. (1982). Food aversions in children receiving chemotherapy for cancer. *Cancer, 50,* 2961–2963.

Bijou, S. W. and Baer, D. M. (1965). *Child development: Vol. 2. The universal stage of infancy.* New York: Appleton-Century-Crofts.

Birchler, G., Weiss, R., and Vincent, J. (1975). Multimethod analysis of social reinforcement exchange between maritally distressed and nondistressed spouse and stranger dyads. *Journal of Personality and Social Psychology, 31,* 349–360.

Birnbrauer, J. S. (1976). Mental retardation. In H. Leitenberg, ed., *Handbook of behavior modification and behavior therapy* (361–404). Englewood Cliffs, NJ: Prentice-Hall.

Bitterman, M. E. and Woodard, W. T. (1976). Vertebrate learning: Common processes. In R. B. Masterton, C. B. G. Campbell, M. E. Bitterman, and N. Hotton, eds., *Evolution of brain and behavior in vertebrates* (169–189). Hillsdale, NJ: Lawrence Erlbaum.

Björk, L. E. (1975). An experiment in work satisfaction. *Scientific American, 232*(3), 17–23.

Blum, G. S., Geiwitz, J., and Stewart, C. W. (1967). Cognitive arousal: The evolution of a model. *Journal of Personality and Social Psychology, 5,* 138–151.

Blute, M. (1981). Learning, social learning, and sociocultural evolution: A comment on Langton. *American Journal of Sociology, 86,* 1401–1406.

Brackbill, Y. (1960). Experimental research with children in the Soviet Union: A report of a visit. *American Psychologist, 15,* 226–233.

Breland, K. and Breland M. (1966). *Animal behavior.* New York: Macmillan.

Broad, W. J. (1980). Use of killer weed grows in third world. *Science, 208,* 474–475.

Bronowski, J. (1965). *Science and human values* (rev. ed.). New York: Harper & Row.

Bronowski, J. (1977). *A sense of the future: Essays in natural philosophy.* Cambridge, MA: MIT Press.

Bryan, J. H. (1969, December). How adults teach hypocrisy. *Psychology Today,* 50–65.

Buehler, R. E., Patterson, G. R., and Furniss, J. M. (1966). The reinforcement of behaviour in institutional settings. *Behaviour Research and Therapy, 4,* 157–167.

Burgess, R. L. and Akers, R. L. (1966). Are operant principles tautological? *Psychological Record, 16,* 305–312.

Burgess, R. L. and Bushell, D. (1969). *Behavioral sociology.* New York: Columbia University Press.

Butler, R. A. (1958). The differential effect of visual and auditory incentives on the performance of monkeys. *American Journal of Psychology, 71,* 591–593.

Butler, R. A. (1965). Investigative behavior. In A. M. Schrier, H. F. Harlow, and F. Stollnitz, eds., *Behavior of nonhuman primates* (Vol. 2, 463–493). New York: Academic Press.

Campbell, H. J. (1972). Peripheral self-stimulation as a reward in fish, reptile and mammal. *Physiology and Behavior, 8,* 637–640.

Cantor, J., Ziemke, D., and Sparks, G. (1984). Effect of forewarning on emotional responses to a horror film. *Journal of Broadcasting, 28*(1), 21–31.

Caplow, T. (1984). Rule enforcement without visible means: Christmas gift giving in Middletown. *American Journal of Sociology, 89,* 1306–1323.

Carroll, G. R. (1984). Organizational ecology. *Annual Review of Sociology, 10,* 71–93.

Catania, A. C. (1971). The nature of learning. In J. A. Nevin and G. S. Reynolds, eds., *The study of behavior* (31–68). Glenview, IL: Scott, Foresman.

Cautela, J. R. (1967). Covert sensitization. *Psychological Reports, 20,* 459–468.

Centers, R. (1963). A laboratory adaptation of the conversational procedure for the conditioning of verbal operants. *Journal of Abnormal and Social Psychology, 67,* 334–339.

Chapman, C. (1976). *America's runaways.* New York: William Morrow.

Chesler, P. (1971). Women as psychiatric and psychotherapeutic patients. *Journal of Marriage and the Family, 33,* 746–759.

Cheyne, J. A. and Walters, R. H. (1970). Punishment and prohibition: Some origins of self-control. In T. M. Newcomb, ed., *New directions in psychology.* New York: Holt, Rinehart and Winston.

Clark, H. B., Rowbury, T., Baer, A. M., and Baer, D. M. (1973). Timeout as a punishing stimulus in continuous and intermittent schedules. *Journal of Applied Behavior Analysis, 6,* 443–453.

Cobb, S. and Rose, R. M. (1973). Hypertension, peptic ulcer, and diabetes in air traffic controllers. *Journal of the American Medical Association, 224,* 489–492.

Comfort, A. (1976). *The good age.* New York: Crown.

Condry, J. (1977). Enemies of exploration: Self-initiated versus other-initiated learning. *Journal of Personality and Social Psychology, 35,* 459–477.

Corey, J. R. and Shamow, J. (1972). The effects of fading on the acquisition and retention of oral reading. *Journal of Applied Behavior Analysis, 5,* 311–315.

Costello, J. M. (1983). Generalization across settings: Language intervention with children. In J. Miller, D. E. Yoder, and R. L. Schiefelbusch, eds., *Contemporary issues in language intervention* (275–297). Rockville, MD: ASHA.

Craig, K. D. and Weinstein, M. S. (1965). Conditioning vicarious affective arousal. *Psychological Reports, 17,* 955–963.

Cressey, D. R. (1978). White collar subversives. *The Center Magazine, 11*(6) 44–49.

Csikszentmihalyi, M. (1975). *Beyond boredom and anxiety.* San Francisco: Jossey-Bass.

Curtiss, S. (1977). *Genie: A psycholinguistic study of a modern day "wild child."* New York: Academic Press.

Daitzman, R. J. (1980). *Clinical behavior therapy and behavior modification* (Vol. 1). New York: Garland STPM Press.

Daitzman, R. J. (1981). *Clinical behavior therapy and behavior modification* (Vol. 2). New York: Garland STPM Press.

Danaher, B. G. (1974). Theoretical foundations and clinical applications of the Premack Principle: Review and critique. *Behavior Therapy, 5,* 307–324.

Davis, K. (1940). Extreme social isolation of a child. *American Journal of Sociology, 45,* 554–565.

Davis, K. (1947). Final note on a case of extreme isolation. *American Journal of Sociology, 52,* 432–437.

Day, W. F. (1970). On certain similarities between the philosophical investigations of Ludwig Wittgenstein and the operationism of B. F. Skinner. In P. B. Dews, ed., *Festschrift for B. F. Skinner* (359–376). New York: Appleton-Century-Crofts.

Dekker, E. and Groen, J. (1956). Reproducible psychogenic attacks of asthma: A laboratory study. *Journal of Psychosomatic Research, 1,* 58–67.

de Villiers, P. (1977). Choice in concurrent schedules and a quantitative formulation of the law of effect. In W. K. Honig and J. E. R. Staddon, eds., *Handbook of operant behavior* (233–287). Englewood Cliffs, NJ: Prentice-Hall.

Dews, P. B. (1963). Behavioral effects of drugs. In S. M. Farber and R. H. L. Wilson, eds., *Conflict and creativity* (699–798). New York: McGraw-Hill.

DiCara, L. V. (1970). Learning in the autonomic nervous system. *Scientific American, 222*(1), 30–39.

Dirge of the Kampucheans. (1978, October 2). *Time,* 45.

Dukas, H. and Hoffmann, B. (1979). *Albert Einstein: The human side.* Princeton, NJ: Princeton University Press.

Dunham, P. (1977). The nature of reinforcing stimuli. In W. K. Honig and J. E. R. Staddon, eds., *Handbook of operant behavior* (98–124). Englewood Cliffs, NJ: Prentice-Hall.

Dysinger, W. S. and Ruckmick, C. A. (1933). *The emotional responses of children to the motion-picture situation.* New York: Macmillan.

Egger, M. D. and Miller, N. E. (1962). Secondary reinforcement in rats as a function of information value and reliability of the stimulus. *Journal of Experimental Psychology, 64,* 97–104.

Egger, M. D. and Miller, N. E. (1963). When is a reward reinforcing? An experimental study of the information hypothesis. *Journal of Comparative and Physiological Psychology, 56,* 132–137.

Eisenberger, R., Karpman, M., and Trattner, J. (1967). What is the necessary and sufficient condition for reinforcement in the contingency situation? *Journal of Experimental Psychology, 74,* 342–350.

Ekman, P. (1972). Universal and cultural differences in facial expressions of emotions. In J. K. Cold, ed., *Nebraska symposium on motivation* (207–283). Lincoln: University of Nebraska Press.

Ekman, P. (1980). *The face of man: Expressions of universal emotions in a New Guinea village.* New York: Garland STPM Press.

Ekman, P. (1981). Mistakes when deceiving. *Annals of the New York Academy of Science, 364,* 269–278.

Ekman, P., Roper, G., and Hager, J. C. (1980). Deliberate facial movement. *Child Development, 51,* 886–891.

Ellis, A. (1962). *Reason and emotion in psychotherapy.* New York: Stuart.

Ellis, M. J. (1973). *Why people play.* Englewood Cliffs, NJ: Prentice-Hall.

Elwes, R. H. M. (1955). *Benedict de Spinoza.* New York: Dover.

Fantino, E. (1977). Conditioned reinforcement: Choice and information. In W. K. Honig and J. E. R. Staddon, eds., *Handbook of operant behavior* (313–339). Englewood Cliffs, NJ: Prentice-Hall.

Fantino, E. and Logan, C. A. (1979). *The experimental analysis of behavior: A biological perspective.* San Francisco: W. H. Freeman.

Fantino, E. and Moore, J. (1980). Uncertainty reduction, conditioned reinforcement, and observing. *Journal of the Experimental Analysis of Behavior, 33,* 3–13.

Favell, J. E. (1977). *The power of positive reinforcement: A handbook of behavior modification.* Springfield, IL: Charles C Thomas.

Ferster, C. B., Culbertson, S., and Boren, M. C. P. (1975). *Behavior principles* (2nd ed.). Englewood Cliffs, NJ: Prentice-Hall.

Ferster, C. B. and Skinner, B. F. (1957). *Schedules of reinforcement.* Englewood Cliffs, NJ: Prentice-Hall.

Fischer, C. S. (1981a). *To dwell among friends: Personal networks in town and city.* Chicago: University of Chicago Press.

Fischer, C. S. (1981b). The public and private worlds of city life. *American Sociological Review, 46,* 306–316.

Fiske, D. W. and Maddi, S. R. (1961). *Functions of varied experience.* Homewood, IL: Dorsey Press.

The flick of violence. (1979, March 19). *Time,* 39.

Foltin, R. W. and Schuster, C. R. (1982). Effects of extinction on responding maintained under a second-order schedule of food presentation in rhesus monkeys. *Psychological Record, 32,* 519–528.

Garber, J. and Seligman, M. E. P. (1980). *Human helplessness: Theory and applications.* New York: Academic Press.

Gelfand, D. M. and Hartmann, D. P. (1975). *Child behavior analysis and therapy.* New York: Pergamon.

Gewirtz, J. L. (1971a). Conditional responding as a paradigm for observational, imitative learning and vicarious reinforcement. In H. W. Reese, ed., *Advances in child development and behavior* (Vol. 6, 273–304). New York: Academic Press.

Gewirtz, J. L. (1971b). The roles of overt responding and extrinsic reinforcement in "self" and "vicarious-reinforcement" phenomena and in "observational learning" and imitation. In R. Glaser, ed., *The nature of reinforcement* (279–309). New York: Academic Press.

Gil, D. G. (1974). A conceptual model of child abuse and its implications for social policy. In S. K. Steinmetz and M. A. Straus, eds., *Violence in the family* (205–211). New York: Dodd, Mead & Company.

Gmelch, G. and Felson, R. (1980, December). Can a lucky charm get you through organic chemistry? *Psychology Today*, 75–78.

Goetz, E. M. and Baer, D. M. (1973). Social control of form diversity and the emergence of new forms in children's block building. *Journal of Applied Behavior Analysis*, 6, 209–217.

Goetz, E. M. and Salmonson, M. M. (1972). The effect of general and descriptive reinforcement on "creativity" in easel painting. In G. Semb, ed., *Behavior analysis and education* (53–61). Lawrence, KS: University of Kansas Press.

Goetz, L., Schuler, A., and Sailor, W. (1979). Teaching functional speech to the severely handicapped: Current issues. *Journal of Autisism and Development Disorders*, 9 325–343.

Goetz, L., Schuler, A. L., and Sailor, W. (1981). Functional competence as a factor in communication instruction. *Exceptional Education Quarterly*, 2, 51–60.

Goffman, E. (1959). *The presentation of self in everyday life*. Garden City, NY: Doubleday Anchor.

Goldfried, M. R., Decentecer, E. T., and Weinberg, L. (1974). Systematic rational restructuring as a self-control technique. *Behavior Therapy*, 5, 247–254.

Goldfried, M. R. and Merbaum, M. (1973). *Behavior change through self-control*. New York: Holt, Rinehart and Winston.

Goldstein, A. P. and Kanfer, F. H. (1979). *Maximizing treatment gains*. New York: Academic Press.

Gollub, L. (1977). Conditioned reinforcement: Schedule effects. In W. K. Honig and J. E. R. Staddon, eds., *Handbook of operant behavior* (288–312). Englewood Cliffs, NJ: Prentice-Hall.

Goorney, A. B. (1968). Treatment of a compulsive horse race gambler by aversion therapy. *British Journal of Psychiatry*, 114, 329–333.

Götestam, B., Götestam, K. G., and Melin, L. (1983). Anxiety and coping behavior during an emergency landing. *Behavior Modification*, 7, 569–575.

Gottman, J. M. (1979). *Marital interaction: Experimental investigations*. New York: Academic Press.

Gottman, J. M., Notarius, C., Gonso, J., and Markman, H. (1976). *A couple's guide to communication*. Champaign, IL: Research Press.

Green, L., and Rachlin, H. (1977). Pigeon's preferences for stimulus information: Effects of amount of information. *Journal of the Experimental Analysis of Behavior*, 27, 255–263.

Green, P. C. (1972). Masochism in the laboratory rat: An experimental demonstration. *Psychonomic Science*, 27, 41–44.

Grice, G. R. (1948a). An experimental test of the expectation theory of learning. *Journal of Comparative and Physiological Psychology*, 41, 137–143.

Grice, G. R. (1948b). The relation of secondary reinforcement to delayed reward in visual discrimination learning. *Journal of Experimental Psychology*, 38, 1–16.

Guess, D., Keogh, W., and Sailor, W. (1978). Generalization of speech and language behavior: Measurement and training tactics. In R. L. Schiefelbusch, ed., *Bases of language intervention* (373–395). Baltimore: University Park Press.

Hall, E. (1959). *The silent language*. New York: Fawcett.

Hall, R. V., Axelrod, S., Tyler, L., Grief, E., Jones, F. C., and Robertson, R. (1972). Modification of behavior problems in the home with a parent as observer and experimenter. *Journal of Applied Behavior Analysis, 5,* 53–64.

Hammond, L. J. (1980). The effect of contingency upon the appetitive conditioning of free operant behavior. *Journal of the Experimental Analysis of Behavior, 34,* 297–304.

Hawthorne, N. (1850). *The scarlet letter.*

Hebb, D. O. (1972). *Textbook of psychology* (3rd ed.). Philadelphia: W. B. Saunders.

Hendry, D. P. (1969). Reinforcing value of information: Fixed-ratio schedules. In D. P. Hendry, ed., *Conditioned reinforcement* (300–341). Homewood, IL: Dorsey Press.

Herbert, W. (1982). TMI: Uncertainty is causing chronic stress. *Science News, 121,* 308.

Hermann, J. A., de Montes, A. I., Dominguez, B., Montes, F., and Hopkins, B. L. (1973). Effects of bonuses for punctuality on the tardiness of industrial workers. *Journal of Applied Behavior Analysis, 6,* 563–570.

Herrnstein, R. J. (1961). Relative and absolute strength of response as a function of frequency of reinforcement. *Journal of the Experimental Analysis of Behavior, 4,* 267–272.

Herrnstein, R. J. (1970). On the law of effect. *Journal of the Experimental Analysis of Behavior, 13,* 243–266.

Hersen, M. (1983). *Outpatient behavior therapy: A clinical guide.* New York: Grune & Stratton.

Hilberg, R. (1961). *The destruction of the European Jews.* Chicago: Quadrangle Books.

Hineline, P. N. (1977). Negative reinforcement and avoidance. In W. K. Honig and J. E. R. Staddon, eds., *Handbook of operant behavior* (364–414). Englewood Cliffs, NJ: Prentice-Hall.

Hoffman, M. L. (1960). Power assertion by the parent and its impact on the child. *Child Development, 31,* 129–143.

Hoffman, M. L. (1970). Moral development. In P. H. Mussen, ed., *Manual of child psychology.* New York: Wiley.

Hoffman, M. L. and Saltzstein, H. D. (1967). Parent discipline and the child's moral development. *Journal of Personality and Social Psychology, 5,* 45–57.

Holland, P. C. (1977). Conditioned stimulus as a determinant of the form of the Pavlovian conditioned response. *Journal of Psychology: Animal Behavior Processes, 3,* 77–104.

Homans, G. C. (1974). *Social behavior: Its elementary forms.* New York: Harcourt Brace Jovanovich.

Homme, L. E. (1965). Perspectives in psychology: XXIV. Control of coverants, the operants of the mind. *Psychological Record, 15,* 501–511.

Honig, W. K. and Staddon, J. E. R. (1977). *Handbook of operant behavior.* Englewood Cliffs, NJ: Prentice-Hall.

Honig, W. K. and Urcuioli, P. J. (1981). The legacy of Guttman and Kalish (1956): Twenty-five years of research on stimulus generalization. *Journal of the Experimental Analysis of Behavior, 36,* 405–445.

Houston, J. P. (1976). *Fundamentals of learning.* New York: Academic Press.

Hunt, M. (1974). *Sexual behavior in the 1970's.* Chicago: Playboy Press.

Hursh, S. R. (1977). The conditioned reinforcement of repeated acquisition. *Journal of the Experimental Analysis of Behavior, 27,* 315–326.

Kalish, H. (1981). *From behavioral science to behavior modification.* New York: McGraw-Hill.

Kamin, L. J. (1969). Predictability, surprise, attention, and conditioning. In B. A. Campbell and R. M. Church, eds., *Punishment and aversive behavior.* New York: Appleton-Century-Crofts.

Kanfer, F. H. and Phillips, J. S. (1970). *Learning foundations of behavior therapy.* New York: Wiley.

Kaplan, A. (1964). *The conduct of inquiry.* San Francisco: Chandler.

Karen, R. L. (1974). *An introduction to behavior theory and its applications.* New York: Harper & Row.

Katchadourian, H. A. and Lunde, D. L. (1980). *Fundamentals of human sexuality* (3rd ed.). New York: Holt, Rinehart and Winston.

Kaufmann, W. (1973). *Without guilt and justice.* New York: Peter H. Wyden.

Kazdin, A. E. (1980). *Behavior modification in applied settings* (rev. ed.). Homewood, IL: Dorsey Press.

Kazdin, A. E. (1982). The separate and combined effects of covert and overt rehearsal in developing assertive behavior. *Journal of Behavior Research and Therapy, 20,* 17–25.

Kendall, P. C. and Hollon, S. D. (1979). *Cognitive-behavioral interventions.* New York: Academic Press.

Killeen, P. (1978). Superstition: A matter of bias, not detectability. *Science, 199,* 88–90.

Kimble, G. A. (1961). *Hilgard and Marquis' conditioning and learning.* New York: Appleton-Century-Crofts.

Kinsey, A. C., Pomeroy, W. B., and Martin, C. E. (1948). *Sexual behavior in the human male.* Philadelphia: W. B. Saunders.

Kinsey, A. C., Pomeroy, W. B., Martin, C. E., and Gebhard, P. H. (1953). *Sexual behavior in the human female.* Philadelphia: W. B. Saunders.

Kish, G. B. (1966). Studies of sensory reinforcement. In W. K. Honig, ed., *Operant behavior: Areas of research and application* (109–159). New York: Appleton.

Klatzky, R. (1980). *Human memory: Structures and processes* (2nd ed.). San Francisco: Freeman.

Kleitman, N. (1949). Biological rhythms and cycles. *Physiological Review, 29,* 1–30.

Klinger, E. (1977). *Meaning and void: Inner experience and the incentives in people's lives.* Minneapolis: University of Minnesota Press.

Klinger, E. (1978). Modes of normal conscious flow. In K. S. Pope and J. L. Singer, eds., *The stream of consciousness* (226–258). New York: Plenum.

Knight, M. F. and McKenzie, H. S. (1974). Elimination of bedtime thumbsucking in home settings through contingent reading. *Journal of Applied Behavior Analysis, 7,* 33–38.

Korner, A. (1974). The effect of the infant's state, level of arousal, sex, and ontogenetic stage on the caregiver. In M. Lewis and L. A. Rosenblum, eds., *The effect of the infant on its caregiver* (105–121). New York: Wiley.

Kunkel, J. H. (1975). *Behavior, social problems, and change: A social learning approach.* Englewood Cliffs, NJ: Prentice-Hall.

Langton, J. (1979). Darwinism and the behavioral theory of sociocultural evolution: An analysis. *American Journal of Sociology, 85,* 288–309.

Last, C. G. (1984). Cognitive treatment of phobia. In M. Hersen, R. M. Eisler, and P. M. Miller, eds., *Progress in behavior modification* (Vol. 16, 65–82). New York: Academic Press.

La Voie, J. C. (1974). Aversive, cognitive, and parental determinants of punishment generalization in adolescent males. *Journal of Genetic Psychology, 124,* 29–39.

Lepper, M. R. and Greene, D. (1975). Turning play into work: Effects of adult surveillance and extrinsic rewards on children's intrinsic motivation. *Journal of Personality and Social Psychology, 31,* 479–486.

Leventhal, H. (1970). Findings and theory in the study of fear communications. In L. Berkowitz, ed., *Advances in experimental social psychology* (399–498). New York: Academic Press.

Lewontin, R. C. (1978). Adaptation. *Scientific American, 239*(3), 213–230.

Lincoln, J. F. (1946). *Lincoln's incentive system.* New York: McGraw-Hill.

Little, J. C. and James, B. (1964). Abreaction of conditioned fear reaction after eighteen years. *Behaviour Research and Therapy, 2,* 59–63.

Logue, A. W. (1983). Signal detection and matching: Analyzing choice on concurrent variable-interval schedules. *Journal of the Experimental Analysis of Behavior, 39,* 107–127.

Logue, A. W., Ophir, I., and Strauss, K. E. (1981). *Behaviour Research and Therapy, 19,* 319–333.

Lovaas, O. I. and Simmons, J. Q. (1969). Manipulation of self-destruction in three retarded children. *Journal of Applied Behavior Analysis, 2,* 143–157.

Lynn, D. B. (1969). *Parental and sex role identification: A theoretical formulation.* Berkeley, CA: McCutchan.

Mackintosh, N. J. (1975). A theory of attention. *Psychological Review, 82,* 276–298.

Mackintosh, N. J. (1977). Stimulus control: Attentional factors. In W. K. Honig and J. E. R. Staddon, eds., *Handbook of operant behavior* (481–513). Englewood Cliffs, NJ: Prentice-Hall.

Maddi, S. R. (1980). *Personality theories: A comparative analysis* (4th ed.). Homewood, IL: Dorsey Press.

Mahoney, M. J. (1970). Toward an experimental analysis of coverant control. *Behavior Therapy, 1,* 510–521.

Mahoney, M. J. (1974). *Cognition and behavior modification.* Cambridge, MA: Ballinger.

Mahoney, M. J. (1975). The sensitive scientist and empirical humanism. *American Psychologist, 30,* 864–867.

Mahoney, M. J. (1977). Reflections on the cognitive-learning trend in psychotherapy. *American Psychologist, 32,* 5–13.

Mahoney, M. J. and Thoresen, C. E., eds. (1974). *Self-control: Power to the person.* Monterey, CA: Brooks/Cole.

Maloney, K. B. and Hopkins, B. L. (1973). The modification of sentence structure and its relationship to subjective judgements of creative writing. *Journal of Applied Behavior Analysis, 6,* 425–433.

Mannheim, K. (1936). *Ideology and utopia.* New York: Harvest Book (Harcourt, Brace and World).

Marks, I. M. and Gelder, M. G. (1967). Transvestism and fetishism: Clinical and psychological changes during faradic aversion. *British Journal of Psychiatry, 113,* 711–729.

Marks, I. M., Rachman, S., and Gelder, M. G. (1965). Methods for assessment of aversion treatment in fetishism with masturbation. *Behaviour Research and Therapy, 3,* 253–258.

Martin, D. (1976). *Battered wives.* San Francisco: Glide.

Martin, G. and Pear, J. (1983). *Behavior modification: What it is and how to do it* (2nd ed.). Englewood Cliffs, NJ: Prentice-Hall.

Martindale, D. (1977, February). Sweaty palms in the control tower. *Psychology Today,* 70–75.

Mason, W. A. (1965). Determinants of social behavior in young chimpanzees. In A. M. Schrier, H. F. Harlow, and F. Stollnitz, eds., *Behavior of nonhuman primates* (Vol. 2, 335–364). New York: Academic Press.

Mason, W. A. (1968). Naturalistic and experimental investigations of the social behavior of monkeys and apes. In P. C. Jay, ed., *Primates: Studies in adaptation and variability* (398–419). New York: Holt, Rinehart and Winston.

Masters, W. H. and Johnson, V. E. (1966). *Human sexual response.* Boston: Little, Brown.

Masters, W. H. and Johnson, V. E. (1970). *Human sexual inadequacy.* Boston: Little, Brown.

Masters, W. H. and Johnson, V. E. (1979). *Homosexuality in perspective.* Boston: Little, Brown.

Mayr, E. (1978). Evolution. *Scientific American, 239*(3), 47–55.

McCloskey, M. (1983). Intuitive physics. *Scientific American, 248*(4), 122–130.

McEwan, K. L. and Devins, G. A. (1983). Is increased arousal in social anxiety noticed by others? *Journal of Abnormal Psychology, 92,* 417–421.

McIntire, R. W. (1970). *For love of children.* Del Mar, CA: CRM Books.

Mead, G. H. (1934). *Mind, self and society.* Chicago: University of Chicago Press.

Meehl, P. E. (1950). On the circularity of the law of effect. *Psychological Bulletin, 47,* 52–75.

Mees, H. L. (1966). Sadistic fantasies modified by aversive conditioning and substitution: A case study. *Behaviour Research and Therapy, 4,* 317–320.

Meichenbaum, D. (1971). Examination of model characteristics in reducing avoidance behavior. *Journal of Personality and Social Psychology, 17,* 298–307.

Meichenbaum, D. (1976). A cognitive-behavior modification approach to assessment. In M. Hersen and A. S. Bellack, eds., *Behavior assessment: A practical handbook* (299–398). New York: Pergamon Press.

Meichenbaum, D. (1977). *Cognitive behavior modification.* New York: Plenum Press.

Meichenbaum, D. and Cameron, R. (1974). The clinical potential of modifying what clients say to themselves. In M. J. Mahoney and C. E. Thoresen, eds., *Self-control: Power to the person* (263–290). Monterey, CA: Brooks/Cole.

Milavsky, J. R., Kessler, R. C., Stipp, H. H., and Rubens, W. S. (1982). *Television and aggression: A panel study.* New York: Academic Press.

Millenson, J. R. and Leslie, J. C. (1979). *Principles of behavioral analysis* (2nd ed.). New York: Macmillan.

Miller, L. and Ackley, R. (1970). Summation of responding maintained by fixed-interval schedules. *Journal of the Experimental Analysis of Behavior, 13,* 199–203.

Miller, N. E. (1951). Learnable drives and rewards. In S. S. Stevens, ed., *Handbook of experimental psychology* (435–472). New York: Wiley.

Miller, N. E. (1969). Learning of visceral and glandular responses. *Science, 163,* 434–445.

Miller, N. E. (1978). Biofeedback and visceral learning. *Annual Review of Psychology, 29,* 373–404.

Mischel, W. (1968). *Personality and assessment.* New York: Wiley.

Mischel, W. (1981). *Introduction to personality* (3rd ed.). New York: Holt, Rinehart and Winston.

Montagu, A. (1981). *Growing young*. New York: McGraw-Hill.

Moore, R. and Goldiamond, I. (1964). Errorless establishment of visual discrimination using fading procedures. *Journal of the Experimental Analysis of Behavior, 7,* 269–272.

Morrow, G. R. and Morrell, C. (1982). Behavioral treatment for the anticipatory nausea and vomiting induced by cancer chemotherapy. *The New England Journal of Medicine, 307,* 1476–1480.

Morse, W. H. and Kelleher, R. T. (1970). Schedules as fundamental determinants of behavior. In W. N. Schoenfeld, ed., *The theory of reinforcement schedules* (139–185). Englewood Cliffs, NJ: Prentice-Hall.

Morse, W. H. and Kelleher, R. T. (1977). Determinants of reinforcement and punishment. In W. K. Honig and J. E. R. Staddon, eds., *Handbook of operant behavior* (174–200). Englewood Cliffs, NJ: Prentice-Hall.

Murray, J. and Kippax, S. (1979). From the early window to the late night show: International trends in the study of television's impact on children and adults. *Advances in Experimental Social Psychology, 12,* 253–320.

National Institutes of Mental Health (1982). *Television and behavior: Ten years of scientific evidence and implications for the eighties: Vol. 1. Summary report*. Washington, DC: Government Printing Office.

Nevin, J. A. (1971a). Stimulus control. In J. A. Nevin and G. S. Reynolds, eds., *The study of behavior* (115–149). Glenview, IL: Scott, Foresman.

Nevin, J. A. (1971b). Conditioned reinforcement. In J. A. Nevin and G. S. Reynolds, eds., *The study of behavior* (155–198). Glenview, IL: Scott, Foresman.

Nevin, J. A. and Reynolds, G. S. (1971). *The study of behavior*. Glenview, IL: Scott, Foresman.

Newsom, C., Favell, J. E., and Rincover, A. (1983). The side effects of punishment. In S. Axelrod and J. Apsche, eds., *The effects of punishment on human behavior* (285–316). New York: Academic Press.

O'Leary, K. D., Kaufman, K. F., Kass, R. E., and Drabman, R. (1970). The effects of loud and soft reprimands on the behavior of disruptive students. *Exceptional Children, 37,* 145–155.

O'Leary, K. D. and Wilson, G. T. (1975). *Behavior therapy: Application and outcome*. Englewood Cliffs, NJ: Prentice-Hall.

O'Reilly, J. (1983, September 5). Wife beating: The silent crime. *Time,* 23–26.

Osgood, C. E. and Tannenbaum, P. H. (1955). The principle of congruity in the prediction of attitude change. *Psychological Review, 62,* 42–55.

Oswald, I. (1962). Induction of illusory and mental voices with considerations of behavior therapy. *Journal of Mental Science, 108,* 196–212.

Parke, R. D. (1972). Some effects of punishment on children's behavior. In W. W. Hartup, ed., *The young child* (Vol. 2, 264–283). Washington, DC: National Association for Education of Young Children.

Pavlov, I. P. (1927). *Conditioned reflexes*. Oxford: Oxford University Press.

Phillips, D. P. (1983). The impact of mass media violence on U.S. homicides. *American Sociological Review, 48,* 560–568.

Phillips, D. P. (in press). The found experiment: A new technique for assessing the impact of mass media violence on real-world aggressive behavior. In G. Comstock, ed., *Public communication and behavior*.

Pines, A. M. and Silbert, M. H. (1981). The endless cycle of victimization of street prostitutes. Paper presented at the meeting of the American Psychological Association, Los Angeles, CA.

Platt, J. R. (1961). Beauty: Pattern and change. In D. W. Fiske and S. R. Maddi, eds., *Functions of varied experience* (402–430). Homewood, IL: Dorsey.

Polanyi, M. (1960). *Personal knowledge.* Chicago: University of Chicago Press.

Polanyi, M. (1966). *The tacit dimension.* Garden City, NY: Doubleday.

Potter, S. (1948). *The theory and practice of gamesmanship.* New York: Holt, Rinehart and Winston.

Potter, S. (1951). *One-upmanship.* New York: Holt, Rinehart and Winston.

Premack, D. (1965). Reinforcement theory. In D. Levine, ed., *Nebraska symposium on motivation* (123–180). Lincoln: University of Nebraska Press.

Premack, D. (1971). Catching up with common sense, or two sides of a generalization: reinforcement and punishment. In R. Glaser, ed., *The nature of reinforcement* (121–150). New York: Academic Press.

Pritchett, W. (1978). *World population estimates.* Washington, DC: The Environmental Fund.

Rachlin, H. (1980). *Behaviorism in everyday life.* Englewood Cliffs, NJ: Prentice-Hall.

Rachlin, H., Battalio, R. C., Kagel, J. H., and Green, L. (1981). Maximization theory in behavioral psychology. *The Behavioral and Brain Sciences, 4,* 371–388.

Read, P. P. (1974). *Alive: The story of the Andes survivors.* New York: Lippincott.

Redd, W. H., Porterfield, A. L., and Anderson, B. L. (1979). *Behavior modification: Behavioral approaches to human problems.* New York: Random House.

Reese, E. (1972). *The analysis of human operant behavior.* Dubuque, IA: Wm. C. Brown.

Rescorla, R. A. (1967). Pavlovian conditioning and its proper control procedures. *Psychological Review, 74,* 1–80.

Rescorla, R. A. (1969). Pavlovian conditioned inhibition. *Psychological Bulletin, 72,* 77–94.

Rescorla, R. A. (1980). *Pavlovian second-order conditioning: Studies in associative learning.* Hillsdale, NJ: Lawrence Erlbaum.

Rescorla, R. A. and Wagner, A. R. (1972). A theory of Pavlovian conditioning: Variations in the effectiveness of reinforcement and non-reinforcement. In A. H. Black and W. F. Prokasy, eds., *Classical conditioning II: Current theory and research* (64–99). New York: Appleton-Century-Crofts.

Rhodes, R. (1973). *The ungodly.* New York: McKay.

Rilling, M. (1977). Stimulus control and inhibitory processes. In W. K. Honig and J. E. R. Staddon, eds., *Handbook of operant behavior* (432–480). Englewood Cliffs, NJ: Prentice-Hall.

Rodewald, H. K. (1979). *Stimulus control of behavior.* Baltimore: University Park Press.

Rosecrance, J. (1984). The degenerates of Lake Tahoe: A study of persistence and the social world of horse race gambling. Unpublished doctoral dissertation, University of California, Santa Barbara.

Rosenfeld, H. M. and Baer, D. M. (1969). Unnoticed verbal conditioning of an aware experimenter by a more aware subject: The double-agent effect. *Psychological Review, 76,* 425–432.

Rosenhan, D. L. (1973). On being sane in insane places. *Science, 179,* 250–258.

Rosenthal, T. L. and Zimmerman, B. J. (1978). *Social learning and cognition*. New York: Academic Press.

Roy, D. F. (1953). Work satisfaction and social reward in quota achievement: An analysis of piecework incentive. *American Sociological Review, 18,* 507–514.

Roy, D. F. (1959-60). "Banana time"—job satisfaction and informal interaction. *Human Organization, 18,* 158–168.

Rudestam, K. E. (1980). *Methods of self-change*. Monterey, CA: Brooks/Cole.

Rutter, D. R. and Stephenson, G. M. (1979). The functions of looking: Effects of friendship on gaze. *British Journal of Social and Clinical Psychology, 18,* 203–205.

Ryder, R. G. (1968). Husband-wife dyads versus married strangers. *Family Process, 7,* 233–238.

Salk, L. (1973). The role of the heartbeat in the relations between mother and infant. *Scientific American, 228*(5), 24–29.

Schachter, S. (1967). Cognitive effects on bodily functioning: Studies on obesity and eating. In D. G. Glass, ed., *Neurophysiology and emotion* (117–144). New York: Rockefeller University Press.

Schulman, M. (1973, June). Backstage behaviorism. *Psychology Today,* 51–88.

Schultz, D. D. (1965). *Sensory restriction: Effects on behavior*. New York: Academic Press.

Schur, E. M. (1965). *Crimes without victims*. Englewood Cliffs, NJ: Prentice-Hall.

Schutte, R. C. and Hopkins, B. L. (1970). The effects of teacher attention on following instructions in a kindergarten class. *Journal of Applied Behavior Analysis, 3,* 117–122.

Schwartz, A. (1982). *The behavior therapies: Theories and applications*. New York: Free Press.

Schwartz, B. (1980). Development of complex, stereotyped behavior in pigeons. *Journal of the Experimental Analysis of Behavior, 33,* 153–166.

Schwartz, B. (1984). *Psychology of learning and behavior*. New York: Norton.

Schwartz, B. and Gamzu, E. (1977). Pavlovian control of operant behavior. In W. K. Honig and J. E. R. Staddon, eds., *Handbook of operant behavior* (53–97). Englewood Cliffs, NJ: Prentice-Hall.

Schwartz, M. and Stanton, A. H. (1950). A social psychological study of incontinence. *Psychiatry, 13,* 399–416.

Scott, J. F. (1971). *Internalization of norms: A sociological theory of moral commitment*. Englewood Cliffs, NJ: Prentice-Hall.

Seligman, M. E. P. (1966). CS redundancy and secondary punishment. *Journal of Experimental Psychology, 72,* 546–550.

Seligman, M. E. P. (1975). *Helplessness*. San Francisco: Freeman.

Seligman, M. and Hager, J. (1972). *The biological boundaries of learning*. New York: Appleton-Century-Crofts.

Selye, H. (1956). *The stress of life*. New York: McGraw-Hill.

Serbin, L. A. and O'Leary, K. D. (1975, December). How nursery schools teach girls to shut up. *Psychology Today,* 57–58.

Silbert, M. H. and Pines, A. M. (1981). Occupational hazards of street prostitutes. *Criminal Justice and Behavior, 8,* 395–399.

Silver, L. B., Dublin, C. C., and Lourie, R. S. (1969). Does violence breed violence? Contributions from a study of the child abuse syndrome. *American Journal of Psychiatry, 126,* 404–407.

Skinner, B. F. (1938). *The behavior of organisms: An experimental analysis.* New York: Appleton-Century.

Skinner, B. F. (1948). Superstition in the pigeon. *Journal of Experimental Psychology, 38,* 168–172.

Skinner, B. F. (1953). *Science and human behavior.* New York: Macmillan.

Skinner, B. F. (1957). *Verbal behavior.* New York: Appleton-Century-Crofts.

Skinner, B. F. (1966). The phylogeny and ontogeny of behavior. *Science, 153,* 1205–1213.

Skinner, B. F. (1969). *Contingencies of reinforcement.* New York: Appleton-Century-Crofts.

Skinner, B. F. (1971). *Beyond freedom and dignity.* New York: Knopf.

Skinner, B. F. (1974). *About behaviorism.* New York: Knopf.

Skinner, B. F. (1980). *Notebooks.* Englewood Cliffs, NJ: Prentice-Hall.

Spinetta, J. J. and Rigler, D. (1972). The child-abusing parent: A psychological review. *Psychological Bulletin, 77,* 296–304.

Staats, A. W. (1963). *Complex human behavior.* New York: Holt, Rinehart and Winston.

Staats, A. W. (1968). *Learning, language, and cognition.* New York: Holt, Rinehart and Winston.

Staats, A. W. (1975). *Social behaviorism.* Homewood, IL: Dorsey.

Staddon, J. E. R. (1977). Schedule-induced behavior. In W. K. Honig and J. E. R. Staddon, eds., *Handbook of operant behavior* (125–152). Englewood Cliffs, NJ: Prentice-Hall.

Stein, L. (1958). Secondary reinforcement established with subcortical stimulation. *Science, 127,* 466–467.

Stern, D. (1977). *The first relationship: Mother and infant.* Cambridge, MA: Harvard University Press.

Storms, L. H., Boroczi, G., and Broen, W. E., Jr. (1962). Punishment inhibits an instrumental response in hooded rats. *Science, 135,* 1133–1134.

Strauss, M. A., Gelles, R. J., and Steinmetz, S. K. (1980). *Behind closed doors: Violence in the American family.* Garden City, NY: Doubleday.

Stuart, R. B. (1977). *Behavioral self-management: Strategies, techniques, and outcome.* New York: Brunner/Mazel.

Sulzer, B. and Mayer, G. R. (1972). *Behavior modification procedures for school personnel.* Hinsdale, IL: Dryden Press.

Tavris, C. and Offir, C. (1977). *The longest war: Sex differences in perspective.* New York: Harcourt Brace Jovanovich.

Teitelbaum, P. (1977). Levels of integration of the operant. In W. K. Honig and J. E. R. Staddon, eds., *Handbook of operant behavior* (7–27). Englewood Cliffs, NJ: Prentice-Hall.

Terrace, H. S. (1971). Classical conditioning. In J. A. Nevin and G. S. Reynolds, eds., *The study of behavior.* Glenview, IL: Scott, Foresman.

Thibaut, J. W. and Kelley, H. H. (1959). *The social psychology of groups.* New York: Wiley.

Todorov, J. C., Mendes de Oliveira Castro, J., Hanna, E. S., Neves Bittencourt de Sa, M. C., and de Queiroz Barreta, M. (1983). Choice, experience, and the generalized matching law. *Journal of the Experimental Analysis of Behavior, 40,* 99–111.

Tollison, C. D. and Adams, H. E. (1979). *Sexual disorders: Treatment, theory and research*. New York: Gardner Press.

Ullman, L. P. and Krasner, L. (1965). *Case studies in behavior modification*. New York: Holt, Rinehart and Winston.

Valins, S. and Ray, A. A. (1967). Effects of cognitive desensitization on avoidance behavior. *Journal of Personality and Social Psychology, 7,* 345–350.

Wagner, G. (1973). Physiological responses of the sexually stimulated male in the laboratory. Institute of Medical Physiology: University of Copenhagen. Focus International Films.

Walen, S. R., Hauserman, N. M., and Lavin, P. J. (1977). *Clinical guide to behavior therapy*. Baltimore: Williams and Wilkins.

Walters, G. C. and Grusec, J. F. (1977). *Punishment*. San Francisco: W. H. Freeman.

Walters, R. H. and Parke, R. D. (1967). The influence of punishment and related disciplinary techniques on the social behavior of children: Theory and empirical findings. In B. A. Maher, ed., *Progress in experimental personality research* (Vol. 4). New York: Academic Press.

Watson, D. L. and Tharp, R. G. (1977). *Self-directed behavior: Self-modification for personal adjustment* (3rd ed.). Monterey, CA: Brooks/Cole.

Wearden, J. H. (1983). Undermatching and overmatching as deviations from the matching law. *Journal of the Experimental Analysis of Behavior, 40,* 332–340.

Weiner, H. (1965). Conditioning history and maladaptive human operant behavior. *Psychological Reports, 17,* 935–942.

Weiner, H. (1969). Controlling human fixed-interval performance. *Journal of the Experimental Analysis of Behavior, 12,* 349–373.

Weiss, S. J. (1972). Stimulus compounding in free-operant and classical conditioning: A review and analysis. *Psychological Bulletin, 78,* 189–208.

Welker, W. I. (1961). An analysis of exploratory and play behavior in animals. In D. W. Fiske and S. R. Maddi, eds., *Functions of varied experience* (175–226). Homewood, IL: Dorsey Press.

Welker, W. I. (1971). Ontogeny of play and exploratory behaviors: A definition of problems and a search for new conceptual solutions. In H. Moltz, ed., *The ontogeny of vertebrate behavior* (171–228). New York: Academic Press.

White, C. T. and Schlosberg, H. (1952). Degree of conditioning of the GSR as a function of the period of delay. *Journal of Experimental Psychology, 43,* 357–362.

White, G. L., Fishbein, S., and Rutstein, J. (1981). Passionate love and the misattribution of arousal. *Journal of Personality and Social Psychology, 41,* 56–62.

White, T. H. (1978). *In search of history: A personal adventure*. New York: Harper & Row.

Wienpahl, P. (1979). *The radical Spinoza*. New York: New York University Press.

Williams, J. L. (1973). *Operant learning: Procedures for changing behavior*. Monterey, CA: Brooks/Cole.

Williams, R. L. and Long, J. D. (1979). *Toward a self-managed life-style* (2nd ed.). Boston: Houghton Mifflin.

Winter, F., Ferreira, A., and Bowers, N. (1973). Decision-making in married and unrelated couples. *Family Process, 12,* 83–94.

Wittgenstein, L. (1953). *Philosophical investigations*. New York: Macmillan.

Wyckoff, L. B. (1969). The role of observing response in discrimination learning. In D. P. Hendry, ed., *Conditioned reinforcement* (237–260). Homewood, IL: Dorsey Press.

Zeiler, M. (1977). Schedules of reinforcement: The controlling variables. In W. K. Honig and J. E. R. Staddon, eds., *Handbook of operant behavior* (201–232). Englewood Cliffs, NJ: Prentice-Hall.

Zeiler, M. D. and Blakely, T. F. (1983). Choice between response units: The rate constancy model. *Journal of the Experimental Analysis of Behavior, 39,* 275–291.

Zeiler, M. D. and Harzem, P. (1979). *Reinforcement and the organization of behavior.* New York: Wiley.

Zimbardo, P. G., Pilkonis, P. A., and Norwood, R. M. (1975, May). The social disease called shyness. *Psychology Today,* 69–72.

Zimbardo, P. G. and Radl, S. (1981). *The shy child.* New York: McGraw-Hill.

Zimmerman, D. W. (1957). Durable secondary reinforcement. *Psychological Review, 64,* 373–383.

Zimmerman, D. W. (1959). Sustained performance in rats based on secondary reinforcement. *Journal of Comparative and Physiological Psychology, 52,* 353–358.

Zuckerman, M. (1974). The sensation seeking motive. In B. A. Maher, ed., *Progress in experimental personality research* (Vol. 7, 79–148). New York: Academic Press.

Zuckerman, M. (1984). Sensation seeking: A comparative approach to a human trait. *The Behavioral and Brain Sciences, 7,* 413–434.

Author
Index

Subject Index

and shaping, 148, 158–171
of thoughts, 265–267
Operants (operant behavior):
  defined, 7–8
  external orientation, 60
  observational learning, 179–93
Optimal sensory input, 105–22, 250,
  280
Overgeneralization, 76
  of rule use, 201–2
Overstimulation, 105–6, 109, 113–18
Overt behavior, compared with covert
  behavior, 263–65, 283–84

Pacing schedules, 232
Partial reinforcement (PR) (*See also*
    Schedules):
  defined, 215, 227
  and extinction, 132, 215, 228–30,
    258, 288
Passivity, 242–44
Pasteur, L., 3
Pavlov, I.P., 35, 43, 50, 99, 289
Pavlovian conditioning, 35–58, 59–67,
    99–103, 124–27, 175–79, 256–
    57, 268–70, 285
  backward conditioning, 42
  common conditioned responses, 43–48
  and conditioned reinforcers, 124–25
  conditioned responses (CR), 37–58,
    60
  conditioned stimulus (CS), 37–58, 60
  counterconditioning, 41, 55–58, 99–
    103, 162, 253, 285–86
  delays in conditioning, 42–43
  different from operant conditioning,
    59–61
  and emotions, 45–58, 62, 176–79,
    181, 188, 256–57, 285–86
  extinction, 48–52, 53, 285
  higher order conditioning, 52–54, 178
  intermittent conditioning, 41
  modification of unconditioned rein-
      forcers and punishers, 99–103
  multiple order conditioning, 54
  multiple pairings needed, 39
  and observational learning, 175–79,
    181, 185–86
  and operant together, 59–67, 285
  partial list of unconditioned reflexes,
    44
  rapid conditioning, 35–37, 43
  reflexes, 35–58, 59–60, 66–67
  seven determinants of, 41–43
  sexual responses, 37, 39–41, 60–61,
    73, 101–3, 268
  as side effect of operant conditioning,
    62
  stimulus pairing, 35, 36, 41, 61, 269–
    270
  of thoughts, 268–270, 278–280
  timing of conditioning, 42–43
  unconditioned response (UR), 37–58,
    61
  unconditioned stimulus (US), 37–58,
    61, 94–99
Perception, 264, 272
  selective, 17–18
Performance, determinants of after obser-
    vational learning, 174, 186–89
Persistence, 227–28
Personality, 209, 265, 273
Physical guidance, 195–96
Physical punishment, 42, 53, 98–99,
    254–57, 261–62
Picasso, P., 81, 121
Pickpocket, 140–41
Piecework, 218
Play:
  models, 267

prompted, 195
reinforced by sensory stimulation,
    119–20, 135, 149, 195, 202,
    250, 267
schedule effects, 232
suppressed by punishment, 135, 261
Pointing, under stimulus control, 74–75,
    79
Positive control, 247–62, 288
Post-reinforcement pause, 218–22
Pouting, 143, 199, 253, 259
Predictive stimuli:
  defined, 125–33
  in operant conditioning, 11, 12, 75
  in Pavlovian conditioning, 38–39, 40,
    42, 43, 46, 53
Premack principle, 103–4
Proacting, 18–19, 116–17, 240
Prompts, 48, 194–98, 287
  contrasted with rules, 195–96, 206
  facilitate learning of behavior chains,
    146
  gestures, 197–98
  and observational learning, 173, 184
  physical prompts, 195–96
  pictures, 197
  supplement operant conditioning, 148,
    160, 169–70
  and thinking, 263
  two phases, 194
  words, 198
Prostitutes, 243
Proximity (social spacing), 196
Psychologists, 280
Psychosomatic illnesses, 45
Public speaking:
  fear of, 51, 286
  systematic desensitization, 56
Punctuality, 16–17
Punishers, 92–123, 285
  conditioned, 62–65, 99–100, 124–47,
    178
  defined, 7, 25, 92–95, 97–99, 124
  as eliciting stimuli, 94, 126–27
  functions of, 94, 126–27
  generalized, 137–38
  Pavlovian hypothesis, 93
  Premack principle, 103–4
  primary, 92, 94
  relativity of, 93–94, 99–103
  unconditioned, 92–123, 124–25
  vicarious, 179
Punishment (*See also* Schedules of
    punishment), 25–31
  abused, 93–99
  alternatives to, 257–62
  avoiding overuse of, 222, 247–62
  compared with extinction, 20–21, 26,
    258–59
  cost/benefit ratio, 28
  defined, 8, 25
  discontinuation of, 31–32
  negative, 28–31
  negative control, 247–62
  noncontingent, 242–43
  positive, 28–29
  problems with, 254–57
  self-, 267, 285–86
  temporary effects of, 31, 255
  vicarious, 179, 191

Rape, 93, 177
Rational behavior (*See also* Reasoning):
  other behavior explained as if rational,
    211–12
  subset of thinking, 272–78
  valuable skill, 261–62, 277, 283
Rational choice, 275–78
  advantage of, 276
  defined, 275

Rational therapy, 277–78
Reacting, 18–19, 116–17
Reasoning, 259
  democratic decision making, 262
  as humanistic skill, 261–62, 273, 283
  and rational choice, 275–77
Recovery:
  after extinction, 50
  of novelty effects, 109–10
  after punishment, 31–32
Referents, 278–80
Reflexes, 35–58, 59–60, 66–67
  independent of reinforcement, 60–61
  and internal bodily function, 61
  modifiable by reinforcement, 66–67
Rehearsal, 29, 174, 197, 266
Reinforcement, 8–20
  cost/benefit ratio, 28
  defined, 9
  differential, 79
  negative, 14–15, 18–20, 24–25
  noncontingent, 242–44
  positive, 8–11, 14–18, 22–23, 28–29
  positive control, 249–62
  and thinking, 263
  self-, 164–66, 267, 285
  vicarious, 179, 248, 251–52
Reinforcers, 92–147, 250–52, 285
  conditioned, 62–65, 100, 124–47,
    179, 251–52
  defined, 7, 9, 92–97, 126
  as eliciting stimuli, 94, 126
  functions of, 94, 126
  generalized, 137–38
  Pavlovian hypothesis, 93
  positive, 16, 28
  Premack principle, 103–4
  relativity of, 93–94, 99–102, 103
  unconditioned, 92–123, 124–25, 250–
    51
  vicarious, 179, 181
Reinforcing stimulus, defined, 9
Relativity of reinforcers and punishers,
    93–94, 99–103, 107–13, 235
Relaxation:
  as emotional response, 73
  in natural desensitization, 84, 87
  in systematic desensitization, 56
Resistance to temptation, 260
Respondent conditioning (*See also* Pavlo-
    vian conditioning), 35
Response chains (*See* Chains of
    behavior)
Response class, 8–9, 128, 133, 151,
    153, 244–45, 253
Response dependent conditioning, 240
Response differentiation due to differen-
    tial reinforcement (*See also* Dif-
    ferential reinforcement), 153–
    55, 158, 161
Response disruption, 65
Response generalization (*See* Induction)
Response independent conditioning,
    240–41
Response independent schedules, 240–44
Response produced stimuli:
  conditioned reinforcers and SD's, 139–
    42, 147
  self-generated sensory stimulation, 114
Response variability, 149, 151–53, 156,
    159, 160, 162–63
Reward (*See* Reinforcement,
    Reinforcers)
Role play, 267
Roosevelt, E., 121
Rules, 199–213, 287
  affect observational learning, 173, 184
  commands and advice, 203–204
  contrasted with modeling, 199, 206,
    212